ROGUE REGIME

ROGUE REGIME

Kim Jong Il and the Looming Threat of North Korea

JASPER BECKER

OXFORD
UNIVERSITY PRESS
2005

OXFORD
UNIVERSITY PRESS

Oxford University Press, Inc., publishes works that
further Oxford University's objective of excellence
in research, scholarship, and education.

Oxford   New York
Auckland   Cape Town   Dar es Salaam   Hong Kong   Karachi
Kuala Lumpur   Madrid   Melbourne   Mexico City   Nairobi
New Delhi   Shanghai   Taipei   Toronto

With offices in
Argentina   Austria   Brazil   Chile   Czech Republic   France   Greece
Guatemala   Hungary   Italy   Japan   Poland   Portugal   Singapore
South Korea   Switzerland   Thailand   Turkey   Ukraine   Vietnam

Published by Oxford University Press, Inc.
198 Madison Avenue, New York, New York 10016

www.oup.com

Oxford is a registered trademark of Oxford University Press

Library of Congress Cataloging-in-Publication Data
Becker, Jasper.
Rogue regime : Kim Jong Il and the looming threat of North Korea by Jasper Becker.
p. cm.
ISBN-13: 978-0-19-517044-3
ISBN-10: 0-19-517044-X
1. Korea (North)—History.
2. Korea (North)—Politics and government.
3. Kim, Chæong-il, 1942- I. Title.
DS935.B43 2004
951.9304'3—dc22
2004012967

1 3 5 7 9 8 6 4 2
Printed in the United States of America
on acid-free paper

To the children of North Korea

Contents

Preface: Rogue State

North Korea is the quintessential rogue regime, and its end may only come after a terrifying war. The term "rogue state" is reserved only for the most incorrigible in the international system. Rogue states engage in rash behavior, subjugate their populations, are hostile to the ideologies and interests of the free world, and, most troublingly, breach established international rules in many areas: diplomacy, trade, terrorism, human rights, dangerous weapons, narcotics, and so on. In particular these states' active pursuit of weapons of mass destruction qualifies them for the label "rogue," a certificate of dangerous insanity in the diplomatic world. If, like North Korea, there is also a record of sponsoring terrorism around the world, they are bound to attract concern.

North Korea answers to this description but it is also a failed state: the ruling family, founded by Kim Il Sung, has brutalized its own population for half a century, murdering or starving to death some four million people. The Kims have squandered precious resources on a religious cult devoted to their own worship while they have built palaces, swilled imported French cognac, and gifted their concubines with Swiss watches. Any such regime must be rated as highly unstable and combustible.

In recent years, foreign troops have arrived on humanitarian peacekeeping missions in Haiti, Cambodia, Rwanda, Somalia, Sierra Leone, Liberia, Bosnia, Kosovo, Macedonia, and Congo, all states which tend to be described as failed rather than rogue states. It is conceivable that North Korea may become another case that justifies outside intervention on humanitarian grounds. However, it is North Korea's record as the worst violator of the Nuclear Non-Proliferation Treaty, the world's most important instrument for controlling the spread of nuclear weapons that may trigger intervention.

In the 15 years that have passed since the collapse of the Soviet Union and the end of the Cold War, North Korea is one of the very few regimes that has not adjusted to a changed world. Even though its economy started to collapse from the mid-1980s onward, North Korea's determination to acquire weapons of mass destruction (WMD) has only increased. North Korea now possesses a huge arsenal of chemical, biological, nuclear, and conventional weapons, which makes its political instability a danger to the entire global community.

In 1979, the U.S. State Department drew up a list of all nations deemed to be providing a "safe haven" for those engaged in the "active, immediate support of acts of international terrorism or the indirect support of terrorist organizations." This list of designated states supporting terrorism was compiled annually and published in the Code of Federal Regulations. Libya and Syria were listed in 1979, and North Korea was added in 1988 after the bombing of KAL Flight 858 by two North Korean agents. Others on the list are Cuba (1982), Iran (1984), Iraq (1990), and Sudan (1993). The nations on this list later came to be known as "rogue states."

The term "rogue state" entered into common use during the Clinton administration. It was first used by the President in 1994 to refer to the "clear and present danger" that Iran and Libya posed to Europe. An article in *Foreign Affairs* by National Security Adviser Anthony Lake identified "rogues" as those nations that "exhibit a chronic inability to engage constructively with the outside world." Once coined, the term came to be used frequently in presidential speeches. Later Defense Secretary William S. Cohen used it when explaining the reasons for the deployment of a limited missile defense system: "Traditional deterrence rests on our ability to launch a devastating counter-strike against any country that uses weapons of mass destruction against America, its allies or deployed forces. Such measures worked against the Soviet Union, whose leaders were rational and risk-averse, but they may not deter rogue states whose leaders are indifferent to their people's welfare. Iraq, Iran, and North Korea do not need long-range missiles to intimidate their neighbors; they want long-range missiles to

coerce and threaten more distant countries in North America and Europe."[1]
Soon the term entered the common lexicon where it was used more loosely
to refer to states that openly reject basic human values and undermine the
norms of international behavior.

Secretary of State Madeleine Albright later tried to use the more neutral
term "states of concern." After the Bush administration took office, however,
"rogue state" was again used to mean "states supporting international terrorism." The State Department's "list of countries supporting international
terrorism" however, is not one that is recognized by either the United Nations or international law. It has put the United States at odds with the
United Nations and created a major rift in international relations which has
come to a head over Iraq, another country labelled as a rogue state. Washington decided to invade Iraq in 2003 for several reasons: It came to believe that
the United Nations' system had proved incapable of controlling Saddam
Hussein's weapons programs with weapons inspections, of solving the humanitarian crisis through sanctions and the oil-for-food program, and their
suspected support of the terrorist organization Al Queda. A rogue state, in
this case, Iraq, has come to mean a country that poses problems which
confound the resources of existing machinery of international diplomacy.

After 9/11, the list was essentially reduced to three states—North Korea,
Iraq, and Iran, which were dubbed the "axis of evil" in President Bush's State
of the Union Address in January 2002. The three states were lumped together because they were accused of colluding in a trade of WMD technology
thus undermining the international efforts to control proliferation, and making it possible for terrorists to get their hands on WMD. "States like these
and their terrorist allies constitute an axis of evil, arming to threaten the
peace of the world. By seeking weapons of mass destruction, these regimes
pose a grave and growing danger," Bush said. "They could provide these
arms to terrorists, giving them the means to match their hatred. They could
attack our allies or attempt to blackmail the United States. In any of these
cases, the price of indifference would be catastrophic," he added.

After that speech, the United States and its allies carried out the invasion in Iraq and toppled Saddam Hussein. Libya has come forward and
revealed the full extent of its hidden weapons program and placed itself
under the supervision of the International Atomic Energy Agency (IAEA).
At the time of writing, Libya is close to being removed from the list. Iran

[handwritten margin notes:]
If told to find to link a
these countries would never collude with each other. They were for 8 years
⇒
No WMD found and the country is now in civil war. What a great intervention

has opened its doors further to IAEA inspections and revealed hitherto unknown research programs. Pakistan has admitted much more about its role in the international market for nuclear technology and vowed to stop the activities of key figures, including Abdul Qadeer Khan, the top Pakistani nuclear scientist. Others on the list of terrorist states, such as Cuba and Sudan, are not currently engaged in trafficking in dangerous missile or nuclear technology, and furthermore their activities linked to terrorism have diminished.

That leaves North Korea. Far from being cowed, as Libya was, by the example of the "shock and awe" campaign that quickly defeated Iraq, North Korea has been openly defiant, throwing out the IAEA inspectors and withdrawing from the Non-Proliferation Treaty. Under severe pressure from China, North Korea grudgingly agreed to take part in two rounds of six party talks held in Beijing, which were followed by a working group meeting in May 2004. In this case, Washington is using diplomatic means in coordination with neighboring countries to pressure North Korea but the United Nations is not involved. If these meetings continue to prove ineffectual, the United State may decide to pursue other means to deal with North Korea's looming threat.

Any rogue state by definition is one whose problems have long defied an obvious solution, but one could argue that the situation now is even more dangerous than before 9/11. After the United States produced evidence in 2002 of North Korea's secret program to develop a bomb by enriching uranium, the North walked away from the 1994 Agreed Framework in which they had consented to freeze their plutonium program and not to remove spent fuel rods from supervision. Further, the North said it was going to begin reprocessing these rods. The CIA detected telltale signs of krypton being released, a sign that the fuel rods were indeed being reprocessed to make bomb material.

North Korea is a case apart because it has proved uniquely impervious to both sticks and carrots. The engagement policy of the Clinton presidency failed to change North Korea's basic policies. Even the 1994 Agreed Framework failed to freeze the North's nuclear program. The Bush administration that followed set itself even more ambitious goals by pressing for "complete, verifiable, and irreversible dismantlement of North Korea's nuclear programs" so far without any success.

We know now that sometime around 1989, North Korea obtained the material to make one or two nuclear bombs. This was the first time a small Third World power managed to do so. Without oil or any other vital resources, North Korea managed to pull off of a technological feat that 45 years earlier was only just within the reach of a superpower. North Korea shows how easy it has become to acquire on the black market everything necessary to build a nuclear arsenal. It did this without a functional domestic economy or any real exports, and indeed without powerful allies. North Korea is not like Iraq or Iran where a huge flow of oil revenues can finance a nuclear weapons program. Pyongyang, the North Korean capitol, has shown it can achieve this by earning relatively small sums trafficking in drugs, trading in conventional weapons, and bartering missile technology. The price of WMD technology, just as with so many technologies from computers to cars, is falling rapidly and is becoming affordable not only to the most bankrupt state but to terrorist groups like Al-Qaeda.

To paraphrase Tolstoy, all rogue states are rogue states in their own way, but North Korea is the only one to present multiple dangers and on a massive scale. Uniquely, it is simultaneously a major humanitarian crisis and the greatest challenge to the global effort to control WMD. As President Bush has observed, North Korea is "arming with missiles and weapons of mass destruction, while starving its citizens."

This book describes how North Korea came to be the way it is, particularly highlighting Kim Jong Il's role as the architect of its worst policies. It has been written because in one way or another, North Korea seems destined to survive and be a "state of concern" for a long time to come. It outlines both the cruelties of North Korea's rulers and the ineffectual efforts by actors inside and outside the country to bring about change.

The danger that Kim Jong Il poses to his own people and to the world is palpable. In the pages that follow I attempt to clarify the nature of both the internal and external threats, and to provide some insight into the usually veiled Hermit Kingdom. I describe the full extent of the internal devastation that Kim has wrought, a devastation that is akin to genocide. Interviews with refugees reveal a country collapsing under the strain of its own inefficiency and the grandiosity of the mad dictator at its helm. Rampant famine turns prisons into death camps. Ordinary people ransack factories for parts that can be sold for food. Party members face detention or death for questioning the beautiful lies of the Great Leader. The economy deteriorates as white elephants rise to glorify Kim. And all the while, the construction of tunnels designed to hide weapons of mass destruction proceeds apace as Kim holds fast to his plan to manufacture and test a nuclear bomb.

This book can be read simply as an account of how absolute power leads to evil and madness. Yet, it also highlights the impossible moral choices that any rogue state, especially North Korea, poses. How do you help the North Koreans without furthering the power of an evil regime? Is it right to attempt "regime change" when it is ordinary North Koreans who might suffer the brunt of sanctions or war? No it is not right

The most frightening connection between WMD and rogue regimes is just this: The more rotten and evil a ruler, the more he will crave a weapon that can shield him from outside pressure. Would Saddam Hussein or Slobodan Milosevic or the perpetrators of the Rwandan massacres ever have been brought to trial if they had possessed nuclear weapons? The possession of WMD could free a despot from all restraints. Convinced that he cannot be touched, a despot might more confidently feel free to wage war, to carry out genocide, or simply to engage in blackmailing the world.

This book poses anew the difficult question of the regime defined only by its unpredictability. It cannot provide a definitive policy or solution for the rogue state. It does, however, hope to shatter any remaining complacencies regarding North Korea's intentions. The world cannot stand by and let nothing be done.

ROGUE REGIME

Introduction

[handwritten annotation: Quoting "Bush" (the biggest terrorist in the world) ⟹ This book is aimed as a justification in for America intervening (bombing) the North Korea. Who will be N. Koreans real victims? The impoverished people These poor will have to endure more suffering. How terrible]

Rogue states are clearly the most likely sources of chemical and biological and nuclear weapons for terrorists. Every nation now knows that we cannot accept—and we will not accept—states that harbor, finance, train, or equip the agents of terror. Those nations that violate this principle will be regarded as hostile regimes. They have been warned, they are being watched, and they will be held to account.

—President George W. Bush addressing cadets at The Citadel, Charleston, South Carolina, December 11, 2001

The fictional scenario that follows is based on the notion that one day the United States might launch an attack in order to enforce international law and prevent North Korea from acquiring, selling, and using its weapons of mass destruction. This very nearly happened in 1994, and as President George Bush warned in 2001, this remains a possibility.

Although fiction, the scenario reflects what is known about North Korea's military capabilities as of April 2004. Some of the facts are drawn from U.S. military documents; others are based on reports by North Korean refugees.

Roughly based on events in 1994, the following is not the only plausible scenario that could bring about a crisis. North Korea might yet find an excuse to attack the South. It might simply break apart in a civil war, a succession struggle, or an uprising. One day, sooner or later, the United States might be drawn into a devastating war on the Korean Peninsula. The

1

following suggests what could precipitate that war and what each side would bring to the conflict.

I describe a chain of events that would conceivably be triggered by the decision to launch a pre-emptive strike against the North's nuclear facilities. It is a useful way to describe how the military forces on both sides would most likely be used in a conflict. Most of all, it is intended to bring home the risks that commanders on both sides would need to assess, and the dangers that any miscalculation in Korea would have for the world at large. This fictionalized account is a stark reminder of the possible consequences of failing to rein in a rogue leader who might possess and be willing to use their nuclear capabilities.

Midnight passed and just minutes after Pyongyang failed to respond to the final ultimatum, dozens of USAF F-117 stealth fighter-bombers crossed into North Korea's airspace. Captain Robert Green of the U.S. 7th Air Force Division briefly glanced at the landscape below as the plane banked and noticed how the glittering lights from the prosperous cities and roads of South Korea had disappeared. Below, North Korea lay shrouded in darkness. Nothing gave away the position of its cities, towns, and ports, apart from a faint glow hinting at the capital Pyongyang, not far from the east coast. What was happening down there, he wondered? Was the entire population assembled in bunkers and shelters? Was the million-strong army braced and waiting?

His plane passed the North's capital, and now the nuclear reactor at Yongbyon lay only 60 miles ahead. Within minutes he would release the bombs at the half-finished 200-megawatt reactor at Taechong. This was the moment of no return. Other members on the mission would target the Hysean Chemical Factory on Yanggang-do, the February 8th Vinalon Complex in Hamhung, and the Sakchu Chemical Weapons Factory on the border with China. There were hundreds of targets in the first wave of strikes. The computer screen showed clusters of bright dots representing F-16s and B-1 and B-52 bombers congregating above North Korea. Some were arriving from the USS Kitty Hawk in the Sea of Japan, others from U.S. Air Force bases on Guam or Okinawa. Still others had taken off hours before from Alaska and Pearl Harbor.

Killing
thousands
of innocent
victims

Within the next five hours, the USAF would drop thousands of JDAMs, twin blast munitions designed to penetrate reinforced bunkers and tunnels. The effectiveness of the latest generation of satellite-guided smart ~~stupid~~ bombs would be severely tested against a country that had buried their entire military and civilian infrastructure deep underground. Only the high-intensity, heat-generating bombs, BLU-118Bs, could hope to damage factories hidden in caverns excavated far into the mountains of this rugged peninsula.

Just before the ground was convulsed by the first massive detonations, the submarine USS General Ulysses waited motionless under the Yellow Sea off the east coast of Korea ready to play its role. Inside the thick steel hulks, navigators had finished checking the coordinates for each of the Tomahawk-guided cruise missiles. Within minutes of erupting out of the sea, these missiles would blast the hardened missile silos and bunkers identified as the command and control centers in which Kim Jong Il, the commander in chief of the Korean People's Army (KPA), might be sheltered.

There will be no time for second thoughts once this show starts, Admiral James White thought as he braced himself against a rail of the USS Ulysses. All the distances are so short. Seoul, the capital of South Korea, is just 120 miles from Pyongyang, the capital of the North. His crew was safe here below the sea. They could hear North Korean submarines approaching long before they became a threat. But what if all went nuclear straight away? White had orders to launch the nuclear tipped missiles on board the moment that happened. what hypocrasy. One Nuclear Power telling others not to acquire Atomic

On the stealth bomber, Captain Robert Green's mission was over, and Bombs *any second now, he expected the sky over Korea to burst into light as a blaze of antiaircraft shells and searchlights opened up. The North Koreans had one of the largest air defense systems in the world, and although much of the technology was dated, the North Koreans could put up a much tougher defense than the Serbs or Iraqis had been able to mount against a similar onslaught. But he and the other pilots had been rehearsing such missions since 1989, when Washington first discovered that North Korea was secretly reprocessing spent plutonium rods from an experimental reactor built with Soviet help in the 1980s. The strike had been called off after President Carter had gone to Pyongyang and personally negotiated an agreement. Now there was new evidence that North Korea had flouted its promises and posed a larger threat than ever before. At the U.S. Pacific Fleet's base in Pearl Harbor, naval planners had no doubt that the U.S. 7th Air Force Division could strike the targets, but Green wondered what exactly they would be destroying. Just how good was the CIA's intelligence? How many of these targets were real? How many were dummies, elaborately designed and camouflaged to fool U.S. spy satellites and surveillance planes? And how much war paraphernalia, including weapons of mass destruction, had been hidden in caves and tunnels to escape detection?*

On the bridge of the USS Kitty Hawk, *Admiral Peter Grey watched the F-16 planes taking off and hoped that one them would be lucky enough to catch Kim Jong Il, kill him, and quickly bring the crisis to an end. But this would require more than luck. Divine intervention was needed. Kim was forewarned and forearmed. Washington and Seoul had been warning him for months that if he refused to agree to terms of "complete, verifiable, and irreversible dismantlement of his nuclear programs," he would face "serious" consequences.*

Kim Jong Il had replied with a blast of bombastic defiance. Perhaps he did not have the stomach for a real war, or perhaps he was sure the Americans did not either. He had threatened huge American casualties if attacked. To be sure, it helped him to cultivate an image of irrationality and violence, but the short, pudgy, cognac-swilling Kim Jong Il was no one's idea of a fighting general. Still, Grey mused, the United States had less reliable intelligence about North Korea than any other country. No leader moved in greater secrecy than Kim Jong Il, who feared his own people as much as he feared his enemies abroad.

Kim Jong Il may be vainglorious, Grey reasoned, but his claims to have transformed his country into "an impregnable fortress" were not just hot air. Kim had built 8,000 underground installations—some believed it to be 15,000—and dug over 500 miles of tunnels housing factories, battleships, and planes. Kim could store five or six nuclear bombs, as well as an arsenal of shells and missiles loaded with chemical and biological weapons, and only a handful of people would know where they were. As long as the regime could survive under this aerial bombardment, it would still be able to fire a devastating response at Seoul. Even cutting the Korean People's Army's communications system would not remove the threat. North Korea had been quicker than Saddam Hussein's Iraq to switch from radio communications to fiber optics, which are much harder to intercept or destroy.

Since the 1990s, North Korea had poured a huge share of its scarce resources into developing a family of modern missiles. The North could fire its forward-deployed SA-5 surface-to-air missiles with a range of 250 km, FROG-5/7 ground-to-ground free rockets with ranges of 50–70 km, and anywhere from 400 to 600 Scud missiles that could hit any target in South Korea. It also had 100, or perhaps 300, No Dong missiles capable of striking U.S. bases in Japan. This was the first Third World nation capable of striking parts of the United States with its long-range ballistic missile, the Taepo Dong 2. And with over 1,700 aircraft, and a navy of 990 vessels, North Korea did not have to rely on long-range devices to deliver and explode a nuclear device that could devastate the South, causing huge casualties.

The South's capital, Seoul lay just 35 miles south of the Demilitarized Zone (DMZ). Despite its name, this is the most militarized area in the world. By the early 1990s, Kim Jong Il had moved 700,000 troops, 8,000 artillery systems, and 2,000 tanks—70 percent of his entire force—to within 90 miles of Seoul. Nobody was sure if this was a defensive or an offensive move. For over 50 years, the North has prepared to launch a blitzkrieg invasion of the South, a hammer blow so overwhelming that in three days its tanks would have raced 300 miles to Pusan at the Southern tip of the peninsula. The aim was to reprise the success of the surprise attack that Kim Jong Il's father, Kim Il Sung, had launched in June 1950 during the Korean War. The invasion force had smashed the South's defenses and was about to complete the conquest when the United States intervened. It sent troops from Japan to strengthen the last bastion of resistance around Pusan and then mounted a fierce counterattack. Kim Il Sung had gambled that the Americans would not intervene, and in fact the invasion plan was triggered by the withdrawal of most American troops after 1948.

Making assumptions about what an enemy will or will not do is a dangerous thing, thought Admiral Grey as he watched the red glow of the afterburner of an F-17 fade into the dark sky.

In Seoul, the streets were still choked with traffic even at midnight. On the sidewalks, people stopped to buy grilled squid, the pungent delicacy cooked by vendors on charcoal fires—a final snack before the last subway trains left the center after midnight. Over the years, the majority of Seoul's inhabitants had become inured to the periodic alarms and panic. Some of the metropolis' 12 million inhabitants reasoned that, whatever happened, there would be time enough to run into the air-raid shelters built in the basement of every building. Although tensions had been escalating for months, the South Koreans had become too accustomed to the North's style of brinkmanship to worry unduly about the latest crisis. Only a few older people, with memories of the last war, had moved their families to safety in the south. Through the ups and downs of negotiations with the North, the younger South Koreans tended to discount the threat.

The capture of Seoul would be a great prize for the North. Dubbed the "miracle on the Han River," Seoul was the lyinchpin of South Korea's extraordinary economic success. As much as 40 percent of South Korea's 47 million people lived or worked within 40 miles of the capital and generate half of South Korea's GDP. A war would wreck not just Seoul but shake the global economy and disrupt the vast trade across the Pacific in which South Korea plays a crucial role. When the news of the strike broke, stock markets across the globe would be certain to plummet in a wave of panic selling.

Kim Jong Il had trained a 100,000-strong Special Operations Force (SOF), which was so large that they would only be needed in the event of an invasion. Infiltrating by submarine or through secret tunnels under the DMZ, or even by being dropped from light aircraft, the SOF troops would try to destroy command and communication facilities and assassinate key personnel. Many would be dressed in U.S. or Republic of Korean uniforms to sow maximum confusion and panic. The North Koreans also had disguised MD-500 helicopters to look like U.S. Army helicopters, which could take off from any of the 70 or so airbases throughout the country. There was even an all-female platoon that the Americans dubbed the Mata Hari commandos. Some of these troops could be on the outskirts of Seoul within hours. It would take just one canister of sarin nerve gas to kill tens of thousands, especially if released on the subway. Nothing could then stop panic and chaos, and no civil defense system could cope with that sort of calamity.

The Republic of Korea's 700,000-strong military and the 37,000 U.S. troops were on WATCHCON 4, the highest alert, for the first time since 1994. Troops closest to the DMZ listened attentively to the defiant propaganda booming out from the giant speakers on the North Korean side.

Across the Pacific it was lunchtime and another round in the propaganda war was on. As the first U.S. planes entered North Korean airspace, White House Spokesman Will Garrett took questions in his usual deadpan way: "We expect North Korea to end its defiance of the international community, and to accept its responsibilities under the Non-Proliferation Treaty that it has signed," Garrett told CNN's senior correspondent Jim Schmidt. "We are tired of Kim Jong Il's lies and prevarications. He must cooperate now. He has been told many times that this is his last chance," he said.

Schmidt pressed him, "But North Korea has said very clearly that it will not open its nuclear facilities to International Atomic Energy Association (IAEA) inspectors. Last week it threatened war saying if the UN Security Council announces sanctions, this will be an act of war. Now it has announced its first nuclear test. Does this mean war?"

"We take this very, very seriously. That's all I can say at this moment," Garrett said. Earlier that morning at an off-the-record briefing in the Pentagon, there was no doubt what was afoot. Major General Mark Williams had settled his long face into a mask. "We are confident that a war would last only a couple weeks if the United States were involved. They may figure 'use it or lose it,' but we don't think it will come to that," he said, then paused for dramatic emphasis. "If it does, the combined forces of the U.S. and South Korea would abolish North Korea as a functioning state, end the ~~and its innocent people~~ *rule of its leader, Kim Jong Il, and reorganize the country under South Korean control."*

Then he added slowly and deliberately, "When we're done, they will not be able to mount any military activity of any kind."

Back in Seoul, General Charles Black sat in the Combined Forces Command control center, a bunker buried deep under the city. The row of television screens before him, each showing a different sector of the DMZ, revealed nothing. He looked again at the copy of the latest defiant statement from Pyongyang, and ran his eyes down the confusing and bellicose sentences, trying to interpret any hidden meaning:

"The U.S.-led imperialist forces and international reactionaries are fabricating nuclear, missile, and other issues to strangle the North militarily and economically. We neither want nor will avoid a war. If a war is imposed, we will never miss the opportunity," it said.

Opportunity to do what? thought Black.

He read on, "Marshal Kim Jong Il has strengthened the North Korean People's Army politically and ideologically and innovated the military equipment into modern equipment. North Korea has risen to the position of the strongest power in the world with the testing of a nuclear bomb."

The vanity of the man knows no bounds—he really is crazy enough to do anything, Black thought and continued reading the statement.

"The respected Marshal has created an army-centered politics for the first time in the political history of world and brilliantly materialized it. It is the unshakable faith and character of the Korean people and army to meet a challenge with a thousand-fold annihilating strike and a war of aggression with a liberation war of justice. If the United States misjudges the quality of the Korean people rallied around the great brilliant commander in one mind in the spirit of human bombs and unleashes a war of aggression, the Korean people will not miss the opportunity to rise up as one."

Black let out a sigh as he reached that final threat, saying, "Let's hope the great Marshal is bluffing. All that stuff about human bombs—is he talking about kamikaze suicide bombers or what?" His South Korean counterpart, General Paek, shrugged noncommittally. No point guessing now. If the North did attack, it would be the Americans who would formally assume complete control over both U.S. and South Korean Armed Forces under an arrangement dating back to the 1950s. General Paek was reconciled to this idea after years of conducting annual joint operations, and although he did not like it, his biggest concern was with President Choi. Soon the young president would have to go on air to address the nation, and General Paek was still not sure whether he would rise to the occasion and find the right words at this critical juncture in history.

President Choi had been reluctant to leave the Presidential Blue House and seek safety while the rest of the population slumbered on, ignorant of what was unfolding. Yet, it was better to be at the nerve center of events. Soon, he would ask his officials to inform the leaders in Washington, Tokyo, Moscow, and Beijing what was about to happen. For him it was a bitter pill to swallow. His engagement policy had failed and diplomacy had run its course. President Choi had come to power on a ticket to develop friendly relations with the North and to continue the "Sunshine Policy," which was started by President Kim Dae Jung, the former dissident who had won a Nobel Peace Prize after holding the first-ever summit with a

North Korean leader. The hopes raised then had never been realized. President Choi had come around to agreeing to this "surgical strike" only after Kim Jong Il had broken his promises and carried out the first nuclear test. This was the final abrogation of the North's solemn promises, first made in 1991, never to build a bomb.

Now the South had to rely on the Americans for protection to ward off any nuclear threat. It was also clear to Paek that if Washington felt that a pre-emptive strike was necessary to guarantee its own security interests, it could do so without involving any of its troops stationed in South Korea. Military advances meant that the United States could now act unilaterally if it wished. Despite his proximity to the North, General Paek felt more at ease sitting with his fellow soldier than the president, a human rights lawyer who in his youth had called the military "fascists and imperialist stooges."

For years Paek had rehearsed a war in joint exercises so that both sides knew what to do. The preparations to repel a North Korean attack had been steadily adjusted with each advance in computerized warfare, but the plan's code name, OPLAN 5027, was still the same. Now it would be put to the test.

If North Korea invaded in response to a pre-emptive strike against its nuclear facilities, the combined American and South Korean forces would mount a rapid counterattack. By relying on new strategies and technologies that had proved their worth against Saddam Hussein's forces, many staff officers were confident they could deal as briskly with North Korea's outdated hardware as they had with the Iraqi Republican Guard. Following the Second Gulf War in 2003, U.S. Defense Secretary Donald Rumsfeld and U.S. Deputy Defense Secretary Paul Wolfowitz had pushed through a rapid upgrade of American and South Korean defenses. The U.S.–East Asia command now had a strong technological advantage over the North. Victory would be swift and total.

The new generation of Patriot missiles, the PAC3s, had been installed along the 151-mile-long DMZ and were capable of knocking out any North Korean Scuds fired from buried silos or mounted on mobile missile launchers. Defense Secretary Donald Rumsfeld's missile defense system was also up and running, although not yet tested in wartime conditions. Ground-based midcourse interceptors in Alaska, sea-based midcourse interceptors *on Navy Aegis ships, and an Airborne Laser prototype were ready to shoot down any long-range North Korean missiles.*

Paek's greatest worry wasn't the long-range missiles but the North Korean artillery. North Korea had 10,600 modern artillery pieces that could deliver a terrible punch in the first hour of combat. And it had 200 multiple rocket launchers (MRLs) capable of raining down a barrage of 240-mm shells. Since the mid-1990s, North Korea had doubled the number of long-range artillery tubes within range of Seoul to at least 500. They were deployed in hardened underground shelters ready to fire south at a moment's notice. North Korea too had been busy upgrading its military technology.

During the 1994 crisis, it was estimated that a North Korean artillery attack could instantly kill 40,000 people. A sustained barrage could kill hundreds of thousands even if the KPA did not deploy its chemical and biological weapons. "The tyranny of proximity" had been the telling phrase used by U.S. General John Tilelli, Jr., former commander in chief of the United Nations Command/Combined Forces Command and commander of U.S. Forces Korea, to describe the nature of this military challenge. Technical advances in the last ten years had left Paek sure that this threat had now been neutralized. Seoul was now protected by an extensive shield of air-to-ground guided missiles (HARPY) and counter-artillery radar systems. As soon as a North Korean gun opened up it would be located and destroyed. Computers aided by anti-artillery radar systems could trace shells back to their point of origin and then instantly direct artillery fire or missiles on the enemy guns. The Precision/Rapid Counter and Multiple Rocket Launch systems could instantly target the North's artillery.

The latest version of OPLAN 5027 also incorporated dramatic improvements in the precision, coordination, and mobility learned by the U.S. war machine in two Gulf wars. Advanced digitized computer communications enabled forces in the South to orchestrate ground, air, and sea attacks against the North's targets much more effectively than in the past. The updated OPLAN 5027 had developed a strategy called "defeating the enemy in detail." Every gun and tank emplacement along the DMZ, every ammunition and supply depot, bridge and crossroads, resupply and reinforcement route, air field and naval facility, commando base, headquarters and command post, communications node, munitions factory, electric power grid, and government building in Pyongyang had been accurately mapped and listed. The United States could quickly launch aerial and cruise missile sorties and the North would be helpless.

Once the first wave of aerial and cruise missile sorties had taken out the nuclear and chemical weapons sites, within hours a second wave would be smashing the North's air defense system. Then the North's long-range artillery and bombers would be hit with terrifying accuracy. The entrances of the hardened sites in which the North's artillery were sheltered would be buried beneath a pile of rocks so that the guns would never be pulled out and allowed to fire.

The North's chemical warfare capabilities, however, greatly worried Paek. It would only take a few shells to wreak enormous destruction on the civilian population. One battery of the 240-mm MRLs could deliver roughly a ton of chemical weapons. The North had the ability to produce bulk quantities of nerve, blister, choking, and blood agents, using its sizeable, although aging, chemical industry. North Korea had filled shells with mustard, phosgene, sarin, and V-type chemical agents. Its factories could produce 4,500 tons per year, perhaps 12,000 tons in a war. The aerial sorties aimed to destroy 12 known chemical weapon facilities and the 6 major storage depots, but who knew what else had been hidden?

Paek nervously repeated the American's earlier thought, "Any minute now, they will be making the announcement—then it all starts."

General Black looked again at TV screens to check if the presidential broadcast had started, but CNN was still previewing the day's Wall Street earnings. If it did come to war, and Kim's bluff was called, he wondered how the U.S. troops would perform. When the North Korean infantry surged across the border, they would come in human waves, imbued with a fanatical willingness to die for their Great Leader. Indoctrinated since the cradle to hate Americans, and put through an eight-year military service, they were nothing like his own men, rotated through for less than a year on average. His men did not know the terrain, their host country, or their mission.

On the other hand, the North Koreans were shorter, much shorter. The minimum height requirement had to be lowered to 162 cm after years of half rations, and at an average of 90 pounds, some of them weighed half what his men did. Yet, they had been in a state of almost continuous war readiness. And he also had doubts about the morale of the South Korean troops. He knew they were fit, strong, and well-educated, but this was after all a conscript army, not a professional force, and many younger South Koreans were psychologically unprepared to fight against the North.

His musings were interrupted, as the American president came on air, sitting at his desk in the White House and looking solemn. He revealed that the first wave of planes had accomplished their sorties successfully. "I will not tell you that destroying North Korea's nuclear ambitions will be simple or without risk. North Korea already possesses a large inventory of weapons of mass destruction including chemical, biological, and nuclear weapons. We estimate that the Democratic People's Republic of Korea already has obtained enough weapons-grade plutonium to build six nuclear weapons. If we fail to act now, the security of East Asia, which accounts for 40 percent of the world's trade, cannot be guaranteed. The UN Security Council's edicts have been flaunted for over 15 years. And my fellow Americans, even in the United States we will not be safe from nuclear blackmail by this rogue state."

On the Japanese island of Okinawa 60,000 marines and special forces were going through final checks before embarking for an amphibious landing on the eastern coast of North Korea. Marine Lt. General Samuel Brown was watching the same broadcast. OPLAN 2057 envisaged that in the event of a North Korean attack, ground forces in the South would first be caught up in stopping the initial assault before U.S. forces regrouped for a counterattack. Only then would they mount a full-scale invasion of North Korea, and his men would be ordered to make an amphibious landing and march on Pyongyang.

In a North Korean attack, the KPA forces would move past Kaesong, the nearest town, to the truce village of Panmunjom, through a wide coastal plain and through one of two corridors running through the hills, called the Chorwon and Munsan corridors. The narrow eastern coastal plain was lightly settled and less heavily defended, but the terrain was too mountainous for large forces. The North Koreans knew that they faced well-prepared Republic of Korean (ROK) forces in fortified positions, dug in behind the Korea Barrier System (KBS), an integrated series of obstacles and barriers, including minefields, concertina wire, and dragon's teeth.

The KPA commanders' calculation was that though they could not match the U.S. or South Korean troops in technology, they were fast and could exploit their overwhelming quantities of troops and firepower. The KPA's conventional forces would have to quickly overrun the defending forces along the DMZ, and then encircle Seoul. The brunt of the fighting would be handled by the South's ground troops, while the main U.S. Army fighting force, the 2nd Infantry Division, with 14,000 troops, would back them up.

After 2003, the 2nd Infantry began to relocate away from their static defensive positions, which were spread over 17 camps along the DMZ. Christened the "speed bump," the 2nd Infantry's original role had been to slow the invaders down by acting as a trip wire until reinforcements arrived. They were also there to ensure that the North knew that any attack would automatically bring down the full-armed might of the United States and its allies. In 2003, this was judged a liability; the KPA's artillery knew all of the infantry's exact locations and was trained to concentrate on "annihilating" the U.S. forces in the first attack in the hope that this would weaken the American public's willingness to defend such a distant land. The Second Iraq War had only strengthened Kim Jong Il's conviction that the Americans would not tolerate heavy casualties.

Yet for their plan to work, the North quickly needed to open a second front. While the tanks burst through the DMZ, the SOF troops would conduct raids and disruptive attacks in the rest of the country on such a scale that all of South Korea would become a war zone. With over 100,000 men in 25 brigades, North Korea planned to infiltrate 4,000 of them by air and 15,000 by sea. Others would come in through tunnels, perhaps 20 of them, which had been dug under the DMZ and which the South had never been able to find.

For Lieutenant General Brown, who had grown up on a U.S. army base in Germany, the North Korean forces were modeled on the Spetsnaz forces of the USSR. The Warsaw Pact forces had planned a massive militarized blitzkrieg with tank columns charging across the plains of northern Germany while the Spetsnaz commando forces were parachuted into NATO's rear with orders to disrupt forward defenses through sabotage, assassination, and terror. The KPA's special operations forces had the same mission. They were trained to destroy command and communication facilities, cut off lines of communication, assassinate key personnel, and demolish or cripple major facilities such as airfields.

North Korea had also built about 45 midget submarines designed to infiltrate agents, and there was even an underwater supply vessel (SBS-2) to keep them supplied during their missions. These submarines could operate at will along Korea's craggy coastline. Apart from the mini-subs, the North Koreans had also designed and built 250 special amphibious warfare craft, small semi-submersible infiltration craft, and militarized Kong Bang–class hovercraft like those featured in the James Bond movie Die Another Day. These hovercrafts were capable of sweeping up the peninsula's coastal mudflats and tidal pools at 50 knots. Under a cover of darkness they would be hard to detect. Other amphibious vessels backed up the SOFs, including a high-speed "stealth" patrol boat. All these vessels were heavily armed, even with antiship cruise missiles.

After the Second Iraq War, U.S. and South Korean planners were certain that they could easily halt any North Korean attack using conventional forces. The combined air forces of the United States and the Republic of Korea could quickly establish control of the skies, destroy the North Korean Air Force if it ventured out, and turn any radar-guided air defenses to rubble, if it dared mount a challenge. Ninety percent of North Korean planes were hopelessly outclassed, since they relied on technology dating back to the 1950s and 1960s. Many could not fly at night or in poor weather, and flight training for North Korean pilots had been cut to just 10–13 hours a year.

Although the KPA could throw into battle huge numbers of tanks and armored personnel carriers, these were largely T-55 or T-62 tanks designed 40 years earlier. They would be chewed up by ground-attack aircraft like the A10, and Apache-attack helicopters. Once out in the open, they would be helpless against round-the-clock waves of simultaneous attacks mounted by artillery, tanks, missiles, and drones. Lieutenant General Brown expected that these would demoralize the North Koreans as quickly as they had the Iraqis, and then there would be a swift attack by M1A1 tanks and Bradley Fighting Vehicles.

The new advances in tactics and technology had allowed the U.S. military to halve the speed needed to deploy additional forces. In the early 1990s, U.S. planners assumed that 480,000 troops needed to be on the field to defeat the North. By the mid-1990s, force requirements had been kicked up to 690,000, including 160 Navy ships and 1,600 aircraft. Under OPLAN 5027, drawn up in 2000, such a task force would require 90 days to deploy at full strength and smash an unexpected North Korean attack. Yet in 2003, the success of U.S. troops in Iraq had proved that a much smaller and more mobile force could do the job and assemble within less than three weeks. And besides, Lieutenant General Brown thought, most of the forces and war materiel needed were already in position.

If the North Koreans gambled everything on an invasion, his U.S. Marine Corp expeditionary force could leave Okinawa and land in division strength on the North's western coast. Such landings are the costliest of all military operations. It had worked once for General MacArthur when during the first Korean War (1950-1953) he had ordered UN forces to make an amphibious landing at the port of Inchon, west of Seoul, to cut off the North's troops concentrated in the South of the peninsula. Trying to cut across the narrow waist of the peninsula a second time would be even riskier. Yet while he led his marines ashore, he knew that the 82nd Air Assault Division, along with ROK divisions, would be launching an overland counteroffensive north toward Wonsan from the east coast, or even advancing directly to Pyongyang.

In 1951, UN forces had raced north from Inchon to within hours of the Yalu River bordering China. Then the Chinese invasion had pushed them back, and finally after two years of talks and fighting, the frontline settled again along the 38th Parallel under the armistice. Would China intervene again? Beijing recognized South Korea and might acquiesce to a united Korea, but it would never allow the United States to station troops on its border. Korea had always been in China's sphere of influence, and for hundreds of years, the kings of Korea had obeyed the emperors in Beijing as minor tributary dependencies. If the North Koreans could hold out long enough, the Chinese might intervene again.

North Korea's defenses could enable it to resist even after suffering crushing defeats on the battlefield. The first line of defense was at sea. The North's navy could quickly mine access routes and launch missile attacks against U.S. and ROK vessels. There were 95-km-range ground-to-ship Silkworm missile batteries on both the east and west coasts. The 50-plus Romeo- and Shark-class submarines were fully capable of blocking sea-lanes and attacking the

ROK's surface vessels. Many of the North's other ships were equipped with between two and four Styx antiship missiles with a 46-km range.

Lt. Brown worried it might prove difficult, if not impossible, to destroy North Korean coastal defenses through airpower. The KPA Navy had anchorage and repair facilities blasted out of the mountains and connected to inland lakes by tunnels, some of which housed as many as 10-13 vessels. All along the coast, there were gun emplacements with tunnel entrances protected from direct fire by high concrete and rock sea walls. The artillery tunnels were built near the waterline. And guns would be moved for firing into openings that are three to five meters wide and approximately nine meters high. The openings are secured by double-leaf steel doors with rubber seals to protect against chemical or biological warfare and radiation. The tunnel walls and arched ceilings are lined with steel-reinforced concrete 20-40 cm thick. The firing positions, only a few meters from the tunnel entrance, are constructed of concrete or packed earth and are protected by mounded earth or earth-backed parapets. The troops live inside an underground complex defended by pill boxes and trench works, and many are equipped with ventilation systems.

In addition, most of the North Korean population were well trained and equipped to put up a stiff resistance. Every district had stockpiled enough munitions and food in secret tunnels to wage high-intensity combat for three months to a year. The regime had done everything to ensure that it could survive even a nuclear war. In Pyongyang, the population, which consisted of the core elite of the Workers Party, would quickly descend into the metro on staircases or elevators that took them 70 feet below the surface, far from the reach of any JDAM blast.

Equally worrisome, from across the border, China could deliver a limitless number of men and a vast amount of war material that was beyond the reach of the bombers. Lt. General Brown pushed these thoughts aside as his superior in Fort Bragg came on the line. These might be the orders he had been waiting for.

Back in Seoul, General Paek glanced up at the KBS television news to see if there had been any public reaction to the U.S. president's declaration. He was as worried about how his own country would react as he was about the North. In the days leading up to the strike, violent anti-American *protests had been staged on the streets of Seoul with tens of thousands of students criticizing President Choi for deferring to Washington. Given enough time, Pyongyang could expect political chaos on the streets, especially if SOF commandos did their work well. Kim Jong Il might rightly believe that the longer a war lasted, the more heat there would be on Washington. South Korean society was deeply divided about what to do about the North.*

Public opinion in Japan was hard to gauge, too. Under U.S.-Japan defense guidelines, Japan was obliged to provide logistical support in the event of such a conflict. Fortunately, antiwar sentiment was still low, but it could change if the North could stir up latent anti-American sentiment. After Kim Jong Il had admitted kidnapping hundreds of Japanese civilians and openly boasted about his ability to hit Japan with a rocket capable of carrying a nuclear bomb, he had alienated the majority of the public. Yet, many Japanese also wanted the American bases to close.

General Paek's thoughts turned to China. The Chinese Communist Party's new chief could easily give the green light to anti-American student protests. In 1999, Hu Jintao had done this after U.S. missiles had hit the Chinese Embassy in Belgrade. Who knows how many Chinese diplomats or civilians could be killed in this upcoming air strike and what sort of crowds might pour onto the streets? Mobs might start stoning the American Embassy tomorrow and the Seoul government would find itself caught between siding with the Americans or the Chinese.

It all depended on how resolutely Kim Jong Il would act. Paek knew that however much North Korea hailed him as "the most distinguished of all military geniuses heaven has produced" and the "great general of steel who has won 100 victories in 100 battles," he had no idea how to think on the battlefield. Although American editorial writers might mock him as "Dr. Evil," Paek feared he was more than a comic-book villain. The readiness of men under his command to take part in suicide missions had been shown time and time again. Kim Jong Il had a record of planning daring terrorist attacks and was ready with a loyal core of supporters prepared to die on his orders.

If Kim launched a rocket carrying a nuclear bomb, there would easily be 70,000 dead and 75,000 injured, just as at <u>Hiroshima.</u> *Or if his Special Forces sprayed only a few kilograms of anthrax in Seoul, tens to hundreds*

American Atomic Bomb Killing
hundreds of thousands.

of thousands of people would be infected and many of them would die unless properly treated. Plus, Kim might have sleeper agents in the South or in Japan or the United States ready to launch terrorist operations that no one was anticipating.

An hour had gone by since the stealth planes had delivered the first strikes. So far nothing had happened. The atmosphere in the control room remained subdued. "The entire North Korean war machine seems paralyzed," General Paek observed to himself. Until Kim Jong Il, as the chairman of the National Defense Committee (NDC), issued his orders, no one else would dare act on his own initiative. This committee was the most powerful body in the country and exerted complete control over both the economy and the military. Not even a battalion commander could move his men without first seeking Kim's personal approval. All key information would first be passed to Kim. So compartmentalized and secretive was the North Korean system of government that information about the first wave of attacks could not possibly spread through the system. So, if Kim were in one of his many presidential palaces, drunk or simply asleep, nobody would know what to do. If he was already dead, it would take days before one of his sons or generals would dare assume power.

Yet once rumors did start to fly, Kim Jong Il might not be able to rely on the loyalty of most of his people. They had endured 15 years of starvation and false promises, and Kim was deeply hated. General Paek doubted that Kim could really rally the country behind a prolonged "people's war," especially one that the KPA was clearly losing. How many truly believed in Kim, even in his inner circle, he wondered. And did they really still believe the propaganda that told them that life in the South was a living hell?

As Paek ran through these familiar thoughts, the control suddenly buzzed with excitement and General Black turned and said tersely, "We've spotted a ballistic rocket launch—a Taepo Dong 2—there on the screen—we have just five minutes to shoot it down."

If things turn out for the better and there is no war, it is equally plausible that the United States, because of its historical role in Korean affairs, will be heavily involved in settling the country's fate. North Korea will one day require tens or hundreds of billions of dollars to get back on its feet. Bar-

Does America feel it has a Moral duty and obligation to settle the fate of other countries.

ring the sort of very risky war described above, the government of North Korea seems destined to linger on for some time, a menace to its own people and a threat to the whole world. Even though war was narrowly averted in 1994, avoiding a confrontation has a price. As the next chapter describes, millions of people did perish, not in war but from starvation and disease.

Take for example the following scenario. Brazil tells the American Government; that unless you disarm your nuclear capabilities (the largest in the world) we will bomb your people and invade your country. How ridiculous would this sound?

Fact

America is an imperialist power. They feel they are the international police force. They have taken over from Britain and France, to be the leading Imperialist power in the 21st Century.

"Paper Never Refused Ink"
⤷ Always Question What You Read.

CHAPTER 1

Famine and Flight

The Chinese shopkeeper spotted a ragged figure stumbling about the garbage that cascaded from a nearby hilltop, gave a triumphant yell, and set off in hot pursuit. I plunged after him through the deep snow. He was shouting and grinning when I caught up with him and his prey. As the shopkeeper fished around his pocket for some plastic twine, a dirt-covered face scabrous with pellagra that looked about fifty years old shrunk back into the shadows of a hood made from grey sackcloth, like a medieval leper. The creature whimpered feebly but put up no resistance as the shopkeeper bound her hands. The manhunt was over, and I now found myself bargaining for the life of this woman.

The winter of 1997/98 marked the nadir of North Korea's famine. Millions died in the Democratic People's Republic of Korea (DPRK). People have described how they would wake up each day and immediately check with their neighbours to see who was still alive. At the writing of this book (2004), many are still dying from hunger and disease, others have been left stunted, marked by a lifetime's deprivation. How many remain from a population that officially peaked at over 24 million? No one is quite sure. Some refugees say that official registries record less than 19 million. As factories shut and schools and hospitals ceased to operate, many abandoned their homes in search of food, and some headed toward China.

In 1995, the DPRK applied to the United Nations for emergency food aid after reporting a disastrous summer of flooding. Despite this call for help and famine overtaking the country, the extent and nature of the dark nightmare was poorly understood by the outside world. The refugees who crossed the border carried tales so horrific that many people did not or would not believe them. Ever since the Korean War had ended in 1953, just a hundred or so people have managed to escape this hermit country. Those that did escape often spent weeks in the hands of South Korea or American intelligence agencies, and whatever they said was suspect, tainted by the suspicion that their stories were Cold War propaganda. The war with North Korea has never really ended; there is only an armed cease-fire, an armistice.

In 1997 I came to the Chinese side of the border to search for North Korean refugees and hear their testimony about the most secretive country in the world. The search started before dawn in a thicket of birch trees on the frozen Yalu River. Footprints on the snow crisscrossed the hundred yards between the banks. There was no Iron Curtain of wooden guard towers, minefields, and prowling Alsatian watchdogs, but just as the temptation to go across overcame my caution, a cough and murmur of voices betrayed the presence of soldiers. Pairs were stationed at regular intervals in camouflaged dug outs, not to prevent unauthorized entry but to prevent anyone escaping.

After a fruitless vigil in minus 20 centigrade, I searched the woods nearby. Some 22,000 square miles of dense oak and pine forests contribute to North China's largest natural forest reserve and cover the slopes of Mt. Paektu (Mt. Changbai in Chinese). This is the Mount Olympus of the Koreans, a 13,000- foot massif crowned by a mysterious volcanic crater lake, the abode of a protective deity worshipped in shamanistic rituals. In the 1930s, Kim Il Sung, the Great Leader of North Korea, had led a Robin Hood existence here, leading a band of 200 guerrillas to stage hit-and-run raids on the Japanese. Later, his son told people he was born on its slopes, claiming for himself a mythical and heavenly lineage.

The ancient Kingdom of Korea fell into Japanese hands in 1905, and many Koreans, including Kim Il Sung's own parents, migrated to Manchuria. He went to a Chinese school at one of the rural settlements that had sprung up. Before the advent of the railways, and before China's ruling Manchu dynasty collapsed in 1911, this land remained empty, reserved for the Manchus as their homeland and as imperial hunting or grazing grounds.

The Japanese then marched into Manchuria establishing another colony, and bringing more Koreans with them to build railways, dams, lumber yards, barracks, and schools, which can still be seen. Today the ethnic Korean population of Northeast China in the provinces of Jilin, Liaoning, and Heilongjiang has reached about two million. Many Chinese Koreans have relatives across the border.

A year earlier, in 1996, I stopped at one border village where everyone spoke of the pitiful letters that arrived pleading for aid. A man, who had just returned from the DPRK, pulled from his pocket dozens of tiny pieces of paper rolled up, or folded small enough to be swallowed in an emergency. Strangers on the other side had begged him to deliver them to their relatives. He unrolled one at random: "The children are fine. Grandfather and grandmother are alive but we spend a lot of money on grain. Since February some relatives have died. On March 19, your uncle died. On April 15, cousin Choi died because even retired soldiers do not get anything to eat. In May, we will go to Namyang [a border town] and wait for you. We need 220 pounds of wheat and 440 pounds of corn. We have no choice but to beg for your help."

Unsure if their SOS had reached a saviour, the authors would turn up at one of the handful of official border crossings and wait and hope. "Sometimes no one comes, then they just wait starving," the man told me. Every morning at North Korean border towns, like Hoeryong or Hyesan, the authorities pick up dozens of corpses, hopeful people who died waiting. On the riverbank opposite Hyesan, I observed people walking with the distinctive pinched and urgent gait of those who dare not waste an ounce of energy.

North Koreans travel to Hyesan on the infrequent and overcrowded trains, jumping off at a steep incline when the speed slows to a crawling and then walking the remaining miles to avoid police checkpoints. Those who have no relatives bring scrap metal or something else they hope to barter for food. Some cross over just for a day or two, and then return with what they can safely carry. Others simply trust blind chance that some charitable soul will open the door to them. A day before I set out for my dawn wait at the border, I asked around in the Chinese town of Changbai about the best place to find North Koreans and stopped at a small medical clinic. "Why just this morning, they found the corpse of a girl," the nurse exclaimed. "During the night she had frozen to death on the doorstep of the guesthouse next door. The police have just been here to take the body away." The nurse thought the girl was 20, and said she had no shoes and was wearing nothing but thin rags. "She probably just froze to death, it is common enough," the nurse said. She might have been one of the North Korean women who have nothing to trade but their bodies, and end up as prostitutes or the wives of poor peasants. Groups of children, usually orphans, are also often found. A few days earlier, she said, a boy of around ten had made his own home nearby by digging a burrow out of a pile of saw dust in a construction site and covering it with roofing felt. "He lived there for weeks, scavenging for food, but then he disappeared," the nurse said. "Perhaps he's dead, too."

The boy had come across in the summer, a time when whole families, determined to escape North Korea for good, tried their luck. The river was shallow, and wild forests offered food, mushrooms, berries, wild grasses, acorns, and even wild boar. If they were lucky, they found work and shelter among the ethnic Koreans. Their villages, distinguished by the neat whitewashed cottages of wattle and daub with thatched roofs, are easy to spot. The first thing any escapee must do is beg or steal some Chinese-made cotton garments and get rid of their tell-tale North Korean clothes, often made from a strange synthetic nylon. Walking up through the forest, it was clear some North Koreans had passed by; there were makeshift shelters with charred traces of fire, discarded rags, and broken shoes. At a woodcutter's house, I accidentally roused a Chinese couple from their bed. They hospitably stumbled around to brew up some tea before answering my questions. "You just missed them—there were some here yesterday," the man said, lighting up a cigarette. "A family of five but they have gone already." As one of the Chinese workers brought here in the 1960s to fell the forests, he had interest in the Koreans and said they were dangerous, desperate people. A fortnight ago, local TV reported that some North Koreans had robbed and stabbed a Chinese couple in their home. Even North Korean soldiers came across with their guns to steal what they could. The local authorities had now declared that anyone caught aiding or abetting the refugees, which included giving them a free meal, faced fines of 3,000 to 5,000 Yuan (U.S. $370-600), a year's income in these parts. The woodcutter knew of a man who was handed a three-year prison sentence just for employing a North Korean who commuted across the river every day. The government was now encouraging manhunts by offering a bounty of 5 Yuan for every refugee brought in.

What he said gave me an idea, and I went back into town to find some-one willing to help my search. At a small shop, the man behind the counter offered to go right away. "I hunt them all the time, I know where they like to hide out," he said. We soon set off in his small tractor until we reached an isolated brick kiln with drying huts in which he said they often took refuge. For all the signs that they had been there, it was now deserted. It was then that the shopkeeper pulled out a pair of binoculars, scoured the surrounding countryside, and spotted the solitary woman at the municipal rubbish dump. With her hands tied, the shopkeeper wanted to claim his reward straight away, but I protested and we began to argue. Would 100 Yuan—just U.S. $12—be enough for him to let her go? We settled on 200, the market price for a North Korean life. The shopkeeper spoke some simple Korean and agreed to translate what the unnamed woman said.

She was 28, not 50 as I thought, and a former factory worker from Hamhung, the country's second largest city and a major industrial center on the East Coast. All the city's factories had closed because there was no coal and no electricity; and when her husband disappeared, she was left with a five-year-old. "If you have no work, you get no food. Usually the men have work but the women get nothing," she said. She made her way to the border, after leaving the child in a state nursery, in a last ditch effort to stay alive. Now, she said, she was so tired, she had no heart to run any further. We left her with some money, and I went back into town to find my local Korean guide and more help for her. However, when I arrived back at our hotel, my guide was scared. The police were looking for me, he said, and we had better stay out of trouble. We never went back to find her.

One other evening, I had a chance to carry out a longer interview with another refugee from Hamhung. She was called Kim Ae-sang, and after knock-ing on doors at random in a residential block she had been lucky enough to find a kind Korean family. Now, she crouched on the kitchen floor like a nervous wild animal. Kim was 32 and had left her two children, ages five and seven, with their grandfather in Hamhung. She and her husband once worked at a shoe factory that has since shut down. Since the factory had ceased production, a long time ago, there had been no food rations. The only hand-out was five days' worth of food to mark the Spring festival celebrations a year ago. So, her husband went to the countryside hoping to work for food and never came back. Desperate, Kim Ae-sang set off for the border hoping to sell two kilos of copper stripped from machinery at her defunct factory.

At Hamhung's railway station, she waited along with many others for a train to take them the 300 miles to the border. Every morning the police carted away around 20 people who had died during the night. Those days so many were dying that the authorities no longer bothered to register their names. Many people had traded their identity documents for food. When, finally, a train left the station, it was packed and travelled slowly, held up by frequent power failures. Eight people in her carriage had died by the time the train reached Hyesan. They caught a fever, she thought, and now she had one too; there were sores all over her body. Railway guards had seized her food and beaten her because she had neither a ticket nor a travel permit, but somehow she had managed to keep the copper. Once in Hyesan, she had bedded down in the railway station with other migrants, hoping to sell the metal. Her hope was crushed when border guards caught her and let her go only after confiscating the copper. By then she was left with nothing but her clothes, and she crossed the river hoping to beg for food. She and a younger woman had found someone to guide them across one night. "He wanted to sell me when we got here, but when he heard I was married, he took the other girl, and I ran away," she said. Now she faced a terrible choice: Should she stay in China where she might find work and survive or go back and save her children?

The regime's surveillance system keeps operating despite the economic breakdown. People do anything to get food, even inform on friends. North Koreans who return risk interrogations, torture, and at best a stretch in a labor camp, which many do not survive. Many found guilty of betraying the motherland are shot and their relatives dispatched to the camps. The Party considers any contact with the outside world as betrayal, but it is especially vengeful against those suspected of losing their loyalty to Kim Jong Il by forming strong relationships with outsiders through marriage or contacts with evangelical groups. Women who return pregnant are forced to have abortions and any children born are quickly strangled, sometimes in the presence of the mother.

In the rest of the world many people did not believe anyone was dying of hunger in North Korea. It was the oddest thing about the famine. International aid workers who had travelled in much of the country said they never saw a single famine death. "Oh, you can't believe refugees, they will tell you anything you want to hear," UN officials insisted when asked. Western diplomats in Beijing tended to suspect the refugee stories were a clever South Korean plot to discredit the North. South Korean and Japanese officials thought the North Koreans had cooked up a ruse to extract more aid. Pentagon analysts looked at their satellite photographs and saw none of the signs familiar from African famines, mass graves or hordes of refugees.

In Washington, the State Department's top concern in 1994 was the delicate negotiations to suspend the DPRK's nuclear program. In return Pyongyang had a list of things it wanted, including a million tons of grain. Denied because U.S. laws only authorize such gifts in response to a declared emergency, it looked suspicious when suddenly the following year Pyongyang made its application to the United Nations and reported that massive floods had created just such an emergency.

Member countries chose to give or withhold aid according to their shifting interpretation of their national interests. The United States hesitated. The Republican-dominated Congress opposed the deal and took time to be convinced North Korea really was in desperate need of food aid.

In South Korea meanwhile, then President Kim Young Sam had come to believe that after Kim Il Sung's death in July 1994, the North was on the point of collapse and food aid would only prolong the inevitable end. His last consideration was the suffering of the North Korean people. Moscow, which found North Korea a good customer for its arms and nuclear industries, used the crisis as a way of restoring its status as a great power. China did the same. Its relations with the United States had been damaged badly by China's harsh suppression of pro-democracy protests in 1989, and China offered to mediate. Japan wanted to establish relations with Pyongyang, but first the North Koreans had to return the Japanese citizens it had kidnapped in the 1970s.

Unlike the famines in Ethiopia or Somalia, television crews did not roam around North Korea beaming back images of naked and bony refugees dying by the roadside. There were no pop concerts in aid of North Korean children, and in South Korea, the students reserved their moral indignation for American imperialism and stayed passive about the sufferings of their brothers in the North.

Some disturbing images of emaciated babies had appeared. A year earlier, the UN's World Food Program (WFP) brought in a British journalist, Hilary MacKenzie, to capture the famine on film in order to help drum up donations from governments. After two months, the North Koreans bundled her out of the country, bitterly complaining that photos of dying infants unfairly made the place "look like Africa." After that the UN ensured that it never again embarrassed Pyongyang by contradicting its version of events.

I had taken a photo of Kim Ae-sang in order to make her story more credible, but that same night the Chinese State Security came to my hotel door and took the film away. The Chinese authorities cooperated with the North Koreans, helping to capture refugees, and even allowed North Korean agents to operate freely inside China. There they carried out a campaign of murder, intimidation, and abduction both against North Koreans and those who tried to help them. Christian missionary groups and others had a network of safe houses, orphanages, and escape routes. Some even smuggled people back into North Korea armed with money, food, and Bibles.

Security interrogated me until midnight. At one point the Chinese policeman left the room, and the photos on the desk, so I stole back Kim's photos. I still worried that she might be identified when my story ran on the front page with her photo. Every one who tried to bring attention to the plight of the North Koreans ran this risk that they might actually make things worse, especially for any individual they tried to help.

We thought it wise to leave early the next morning, and half an hour out of town, our car passed a solitary figure walking down the road in broken running shoes and ragged filthy trousers. It was another refugee, who, once in the warmth of the car, told his story with surprising composure. He had eaten nothing for three days and was now planning to walk 100 miles to a city in Liaoning province where he heard a cousin of his father's lived. He was 27, an engineering graduate who had already tramped with two fellow students all the way from Hamhung. At the river crossing, they had studied the border patrols' routine, and at one in the morning, they made a dash across the ice.

"I could hear dogs barking in front of me and shots behind me, I don't know what happened to the other two. Perhaps they were caught. I didn't stop to look around, I just ran for it," he said.

He was one of those North Koreans who had given up all hope of change in the North. Some refugees managed to claim asylum at a South Korean Consulate or Embassy or travel as far as Shandong province, where it was possible to board a ferry to South Korea or at least to find work in a South Korean-invested factory. We wanted to take him with us but the driver refused, saying there were checkpoints everywhere. The driver could end up in prison and the North Korean would be forcibly repatriated, so after giving him clothes and money, we left him by the side of road.

Some groups collected and published summaries of interviews like these that built up a vivid and horrifying picture of the plight of the refugees, who at one time they were thought to number as many as 300,000 in China. The numbers probably fluctuated, and most estimated that around 50,000 to 150,000 stayed for any length of time. The large surveys, made by South Korean Buddhist monk Venerable Pomnyun, the French section of Doctors without Borders, and John Hopkins University, also shed light on the death toll. The Ven. Pomnyun's Korean Buddhist Sharing Movement concluded there were 3.5 million deaths. A North Korean document was obtained that even showed monthly death rates in one mining town. It revealed that 19 percent had starved to death between January 1995 and June 1998, excluding those who died in a cholera epidemic during the summer of 1995 and the 20 percent who had fled the town. The John Hopkins University study, drawing on interviews with 440 refugees from one poor province, North Hamgyong, which borders China in the Northeast, indicated a death rate of 12.9 percent. This province was suspected of being worse off than other places, but if it represented the whole country, this was the most devastating famine in history.[1]

Figures so dramatic met with still greater scepticism. The only North Korean statement admitting the existence of high death rates came in May 1999, when an official, Jon In-chan of the Flood Damage Rehabilitation Committee, told a delegation of aid workers that 220,000 people had died between 1995 and 1998. A statement made by another official who spoke of 2.5 million deaths was later retracted.[2]

As Joseph Stalin said, "A single death is a tragedy, a million deaths is a statistic." When a handful of innocent people are deliberately killed in a terrorist attack, this becomes a top news story. Sometimes civilian massacres like those in Bosnia can stir up such outrage that they can result in military intervention. Those responsible for causing famine deaths tend to escape censure and excuse themselves by blaming natural disasters. Who now blames Mao Zedong for the deaths of 30 million starving peasants?

Besides, hunger deaths evoke the vague feeling that somehow those who died were to blame for not trying harder to save themselves; after all, others managed to survive the same conditions. Even North Korean refugees spoke in these terms. But it is a horrible misperception. In North Korea and in similar calamities, it is small children and the elderly who perish in greatest numbers. And a famine is more terrible than any war, which tends to unite people against a common enemy. Hunger poisons the well of human kindness, sets brother against brother, and tears at the bonds between mother and child, destroying the fiber of any society.

North Koreans described in the interviews how whole families despaired and killed themselves by eating poison. Many people actually brought their children to railway stations or to the border in the hope that some one else might be able to feed them. Other parents attempted to sell their children; in one case I heard they asked 4,000 Yuan for an eight-year-old girl. Many refugees also testified that cannibalism of the worst sort was widespread. "People are going insane with hunger. They even kill and eat their own infants. This kind of thing is happening in many places," a former soldier told me. He said that in a relative's village, a man was caught and shot after they found the head of a corpse in his house. Another man said that in May 1997, a couple in the port city of Wonsan were executed for murdering 50 children and salting and storing their flesh, which they then mixed with pork and sold in the market. A third reported how in August 1997, a woman was accused of doing away with 18 children and was shot in Hamhung. Refugees told American journalist Don Kirk that a family of five was shot to death in Heidong, a district near the Tumen River, for luring small children into their house, drugging them, chopping up their bodies, and mingling them with pork.[3]

Many children were abandoned because their parents died or went on the road in search of food and work. Video footage taken secretly inside North Korea showed beggar children scavenging for food in markets, riffling through refuse, and drinking water from the gutter. The Koreans give a poetic name to these children, calling them *Khot-Jebi* or "flower-swallows."

After Kim Jong Il, North Korea's "Dear Leader," complained about the number of people moving about the country at will, he issued an edict on September 27, 1997. It called on local authorities to arrest all the street children and place them in institutions, called 9.27 camps after the edict's date, in order to "normalize" the country and, perhaps, to keep them out of sight of UN officials. On one border-reporting trip, I went to interview some of these "flower-swallows" who had sneaked across the Tumen River to the town of Yanji in the Yangbian area of the Jilin province. It was shocking to see children so stunted—one 15-year-old who gave his name as Chi Gang was just four feet tall, another 13-year-old was just three feet six inches tall. A bright and lively 16-year-old girl, Kang Minghwa, was so short she looked barely nine years old. Kang said she had escaped from a 9.27 camp because the children were brought in to die out of sight. Every day she was given a bowl of bean powder mixed with what the government called "food substitutes."

"One girl who was fine in the morning ate this at lunchtime and in the evening she suddenly died. Every day another girl died. I couldn't stand the hunger so I came to China," she said. She escaped from the camp's window and then crawled under the railway bridge that crosses the Tumen River. In Yanji, she begged for food on the street and spent the nights in a video hall. Christian groups set up a number of secret orphanages for younger children, including one I came across that housed 34 street children.

The publication of a UN-sponsored survey of 1,700 children released at the end of 1998 proved that girls like Kang were not exceptional. The survey indicated that two-thirds of the country's children were stunted and 16 percent of those under seven were "acutely malnourished." The survey demolished the government's excuse that this was a temporary food shortage due to a succession of unavoidable natural disasters—floods, tidal waves, and droughts. The children were living evidence to the contrary—the food shortages had started well before 1995. An average North Korean is 20 centimeters shorter and weighs half as much as his counterpart in the South; even in the 1970s, the diet was so poor that most girls failed to reach puberty until the age of 18 or 19.[4]

Modern communications and transportation have ensured that famines caused by crop failures rarely occur, and when they do they are short-lived emergencies. Ever since railways have been able to quickly transport food in bulk to any place in need, large-scale famines are man-made. In wars, fighting disrupts normal food distribution or armies seize civilian supplies. In modern times, countries' food production and distribution have also been disrupted by revolutions, especially violent campaigns to outlaw private farming and to force the peasantry into state farms, collectives or communes that enable the state to monopolize grain production. The war for communism that Lenin created in the Soviet Union between 1921–1922 brought death to over five million. Under Stalin, terror and collectivization brought about another great famine in the 1930s, which killed eight million, and similar policies brought huge death tolls in China after 1958 and Cambodia after 1975. Sometimes, as in Mozambique during the 1970s and Ethiopia in the 1980s, collectivization fuels civil war when a peasantry resists the appropriation of their land.

Since the famine in North Korea took place during peace time and the peasantry had been forced into state farms back in the 1940s and 1950s, it was unlike other famines in recent history. This was a state that had long ago assumed full responsibility for food production, food storage, and the allocation of every daily necessity. The most heinous part of the story is that the leadership, especially Kim Jong Il, resisted adopting every policy that could have brought the misery to a quick end. This makes the suffering he inflicted on an entire people an unparalleled and monstrous crime. Kim Jong Il even rejected the solution taken by Lenin in the early 1920s when he staged a retreat from war communism and not only accepted international emergency food aid but introduced New Economic Policies (NEP), reducing the state's seizures of grain, reopening markets, and encouraging small businesses. This allowed the Soviet Union's economy to recover. China's leadership staged a similar retreat after 30 million died following the creation of people's communes in 1958. Although Mao Zedong declined offers of international aid, he tolerated, albeit begrudgingly, a reduction in grain taxes and allowed peasants to grow food on small private plots and sell the surplus.

In both countries, these temporary concessions were enough to revive food production, and they were followed by long-term measures that, given the reality of perennial food shortages under the economic system, prevented further starvation. The Soviet Union with its vast reserves of land encouraged the urban population to spend their weekends working in gardens, sometimes poetically describes as *dachas*, where they could grow vegetables or raise livestock to supplement the state's meagre rations.

Mao was more brutal. He simply emptied the cities when the state failed to gather enough surplus grain. About 80 million Chinese were sent to live in villages and share whatever food the peasants had. As a result, China achieved perhaps the lowest ratios of urban to rural populations in the world. It dropped to a low of 12 percent, compared to an average of 50 percent in developing countries.

In its pursuit of Communist orthodoxy, the Kim dynasty rejected both the solution of authorizing private gardens and that of reducing the urban population. North Korea brought around 70 percent of the population to live in urban areas, and they were strictly forbidden from growing any food in gardens or anywhere else. North Korean peasants were allowed tiny garden plots outside their house but these were smaller than those permitted in Maoist China, and they were forbidden to sell any food in urban areas.[5]

This partly explains why North Koreans had less food and a more precarious rationing system than other Communist countries. It also explains why in North Korea people fled the cities for the countryside—searching for wild foods, a share of the annual harvest, or land to sow their own crops—while other famine people tend to flee from the countryside to the cities for markets and a better chance of finding food. It took only a small deterioration in such a fragile economic system to tip the long-running shortages into mass starvation. Rather than using his power to save lives, Kim Jong Il instead enforced a series of policies that actually made things worse.

In the 1980s, he extended the length of military service from 7 to 13 years, and began to conscript females in order to inflate the military, which became the world's fifth-largest standing army. As there was not enough food available to feed the troops, many began dropping dead from hunger in the early 1990s. In the past, at harvest time, the military would normally take a share of the country's crops, usually the rice crop, and the peasant households were allocated their annual ration, too. Now, to feed the army, Kim Jong Il sent soldiers directly to the farms at harvest time to forcibly grab the harvest. Consequently, by the autumn of 1997, rural households were down to just 220 pounds of grain per person, not enough to last the whole year, as an active person requires at least a pound of grain a day. Now, people began to starve both in the cities *and* the countryside.

Kim Jong Il then did everything to prevent the population from finding alternative ways of feeding themselves, or to use aid worker jargon, from finding "coping mechanisms." "Telling people to solve the food problem on their own only increases the number of farmers' markets and peddlers. In addition, this creates egoism among people, and the base of the party's class may come to collapse. This has been well-illustrated by past incidents in Poland and Czechoslovakia," Kim told party cadres in a speech given in December 1996.[6]

He insisted there would be no retreat into private farming and tried hard to shut down markets that spontaneously sprang up. Everything was done to hinder the private transport of food from surplus to deficit areas. Party officials were told to stamp down hard on any kind of commercial activity, although in practice many ignored their orders. Food, including grain donated by relatives or foreign countries, turned up in black markets. Urban residents began to grow food in patches of land in front of their apartments and raise rabbits on their balconies. They went into the hills to secretly plant food, hunting for wild mushrooms, medicinal herbs, edible wild grasses, and firewood. People searched for anything to sell or barter and even stripped scrap metal or wood from state factories.

Yet local Party officials, and everyone else, knew that all these activities remained unsanctioned and those involved could be arrested or executed in one of the periodic crackdowns. In some counties, the Party secretaries were so cautious they preferred to reject outside aid for fear of being later accused of "treason" in some pending purge.

In the mining town of Musan near the Chinese border, local leaders found themselves caught between the hammer and anvil. When the Musan Party Secretary banned the sale of rice on the black market, the populace threatened to rebel, reportedly saying, "If we don't get rid of this party secretary the people will not survive!" But the authorities said an "antigovernment organization" was behind the outcry and arrested 200 men and women, a dozen of whom were executed in public. Of the town's 130,000 people, refugees said half had died or fled.

All over North Korea officials went to great lengths to hide the markets, especially from foreigners. Police assaulted one diplomat who attempted to photograph a market in Pyongyang. Where there were markets, some officials organized raids to confiscate the goods or profits of traders. North Koreans are normally not allowed to travel without permission, so when they attempted to roam the country there were no buses or trains working, no private cars or bicycles. Even when trade was tolerated, it remained restricted to what people could carry on their backs or, if they were lucky, on a rare ox cart or the odd truck. Foreign visitors passed large numbers of people trudging along the roads or squatting and lying down utterly exhausted.

Kim Jong Il's preferred remedies perpetuated the country's hardships and killed more people than they saved. One example was the promotion of "alternative foods" or "food substitutes," a grotesque innovation of the Chinese dating back to the Great Leap Forward famine. Officials told people to collect roots, bark, seaweed, husks, and cobs to make noodles or "cakes," food with no caloric value. Government scientists assured adults and children, already weak from years of malnutrition, that these foods would help them. Instead, they often died when their digestive tracts failed to process the dense matter that blocked their intestinal and rectal tracts.

The BBC's monitoring service captured a sample of North Korean television broadcasts endorsing the campaign: "Despite the difficult food conditions due to the imperialists manoeuvres to isolate and crush the DPRK, and due to natural calamities for several years running, the Taedonggang Iron Daily Necessities plant is contributing to its employee's diets by producing substitute food using acacia leaves and various other plants."[7]

"Rather than just sitting around complaining, we are dauntlessly producing and supplying substitute foods," says the presenter, dressed in a white coat, in an upbeat tone, showing how the plants are boiled, then dried, ground, and pounded into a paste with a mortar. Then corn or flour is added to the mixture along with two grams of "yeast lactic bacteria," and allowed to ferment for about 12 hours to make it more digestible.

"I think this method of making food can be done easily and everywhere, without effort if one only toils persistently," the announcer confidently continues, adding a warning that "the food situation could grow many times more difficult than it is now" and "food could even run out completely in the future." But this should not matter, she claims, because "our working class is not one that would be shaken or would collapse even if such a situation occurs."

The broadcast showed how workers, relying on the experts' "creative wisdom," made "fried rice cakes, and dumplings" from this matter that provided each employee with a filling lunch. "From now on, by single-heartedly uniting around the respected and beloved general [Kim Jong Il] with a feeling of loyalty and filial piety, we will further cultivate our lives with our hands and become honorary victors on the road of the forced march for final victory."

Another broadcast, about Hamhung's Trauma Orthopaedics Hospital, showed patients happily eating a unique substitute food concocted from "pigweed" and "malt powder," which is kneaded together with goat milk. One frequent visitor to North Korea, the Swiss aid worker Kathi Zellweger, actually saw piles of oak chips at a grain mill that were being made into a powder to stretch out rice and maize. The Party encouraged the starving population, including the children, to wander about gathering the raw material for these food substitutes. In the Party's eyes, individualism was bad and collectivism good; it was determined to find ways to keep people eating in collective canteens at their workplaces and schools, to continue controlling the population.

In a country like Korea, which has suffered from periodic famines, many of its citizens actually knew which wild grasses, tree barks, and leaves are safe to eat. However, this government misinformation confused people with fatal results. In October 1997, *Washington Post* correspondent Keith Richburg visited a hospital in Hamhung where doctors told him most of their 250 patients had rectal, stomach, or liver problems. They also said that without medicines or any working equipment, including electrical lights, they could do nothing for their patients, and the other 750 beds were left empty. The state health system, along with the water and sanitation systems had collapsed, and this meant that many people could officially be described as dying from disease rather than hunger, which to the state somehow sounded better.[8]

The way the refugees described their society reminded me of the situation considered by British civil servants in the 1950s when they drew up contingency plans on how to administer the country after a nuclear attack. They expected that the central government would lose control over everywhere except the capital. Local governments would have to fend for themselves.

Public transport would stop running; schools, hospitals, and factories would close; public utilities like the electricity grid and the water mains would be severely damaged; and the distribution of food would be so dislocated that people would starve because only local food would be available.

In North Korea, much of this actually came to pass, but the regime did not collapse after Kim Il Sung's death in 1994, as many people had confidently predicted. On the contrary, the DPRK continued to successfully complete ambitious technological feats, including the launch of a long-range ballistic missile that flew over Japan in 1998, and two nuclear R&D programs that allowed the bankrupt state to join the world's small circle of nuclear powers (or at least that is what many experts believe). How did this happen?

That Kim Jong Il survived in power after his father's death is owed to several factors: The internal machinery of terror remained intact and he continued to deter external enemies by claiming North Korea possessed weapons of mass destruction and was ready to use them. He obtained enough foreign aid to continue food and goods distribution and maintain the loyalty of core followers in the Workers Party and the North Korean People's Army. Lastly, China made enough border-crossing crackdowns to prevent a mass exodus.

North Korea can best be compared to a large concentration camp in which the guards and their Gestapo officers are able to live as before but the inmates are slowly worked to death. Once a certain part of the population, such as the factory workers, is no longer useful, they are allowed to die. Refugees from big mining centers like Musan and Hoeryong or industrial cities like Chongjin or Hamhung said the less work they did, the less food that the state gave them. When production stopped, so did the food supply, but like the inmates of any camp, they were too feeble and divided to ever stage a successful revolt.[9]

Yet most North Koreans knew that this was no short-term crisis and that they might die, and desperation led to a rise in violent attacks. Refugees reported protests, strikes, local uprisings, the sabotage of official buildings, and the murder of officials and their families. And Kim Jong Il responded with even more terror. He organized waves of purges and a countrywide pattern of summary public trials and executions. In 1995, Kim Jong Il said he wanted to "hear the sound of gunfire again" and ordered the execution of all criminals within three months. The authorities staged more and more gruesome executions. Refugees told of seeing prisoners garrotted or hung or tied to a stake and their relatives forced to light the fire. Doctors Without Borders interviewed one refugee who escaped from a labor camp where he claimed to have personally witnessed over one thousand executions, including some victims who were stoned or bayoneted to death. The man said there were daily executions of "criminals" who had stolen two pounds of maize or a couple of eggs. Since according to the DPRK's ideology all property belonged to the state, anyone found "stealing" corn from a field or killing a cow or chopping down a tree was guilty of a crime against the state.

Just as the food shortages began to be felt by the core elite in 1995, Kim Jong Il started to obtain food aid from the international community, which helped ensure the elites loyalty. The sense of urgency raised through the horrific stories of the refugees was countered by reassuring statements of UN officials. (The role of the United Nation is discussed in more detail in chapter 10.) For instance, UN official Tun Myatt of the World Food Program, who returned from North Korea in 1997, described "a famine in slow motion." Since no official visitors bore witness to any large-scale deaths, there seemed to be time to reach some wider diplomatic settlement with the world. However, the objective of such talks was never to free the North Korean people—who were often reported as beneficiaries of the government's well-organized public food distribution system—but to suspend the regime's nuclear weapons program. This meant that some viewed keeping the regime in place as politically advantageous. Without a government in place there would be "chaos" and failed diplomacy.

China pushed this line of argument hard. It occasionally gave food aid to North Korea, but not in quantities large enough to end the shortages. Its state media reported neither the plight of refugees fleeing for their lives nor starving North Koreans stuck inside. Instead it routinely blamed the United States for creating a diplomatic crisis on the peninsula. Beijing described relations with North Korea as being "as close as lips and teeth," but in practice this only meant they were two sister Communist parties. It wanted to ensure the survival of one of the remaining Communist states and to maintain its influence over the Korean Peninsula.

China feared an exodus of starving people might precipitate the collapse of North Korea, just as when East Germans poured into Western embassies in Hungary claiming asylum and precipitated the downfall not just of East Germany but of the Iron Curtain, which protected the whole Soviet Bloc. So, China hunted down and forcibly repatriated North Korean escapees, especially after 1997, saying they were merely "economic migrants" with no right to claim political asylum. Police in border regions had to fulfil arrest quotas, and those who failed to meet them had their pay docked. Those found harboring or abetting the refugees were punished with high fines. Residents said that when the refugees were handed over, North Korean guards treated them like cattle, pushing iron wire through their noses or even their collarbones, beating and dragging them away. In one incident several prisoners about to be handed over at Tumen tried to resist, grabbing a gun, but they were shot dead on the spot. A handful of refugees managed to escape a second time and report terrifying stories of torture, beatings, and killings at the hands of the North Koreans. And China continued to reassure the world that all those being forcibly repatriated were well-treated.[10]

The United Nations High Commission for Refugees (UNHCR) made a single public protest after Beijing returned one family of refugees applying for asylum and then fell silent. Officials privately said they preferred quiet backroom diplomacy with Beijing. China ignored its obligations under the 1951 Geneva Convention relating to the status of refugees, which obliged it to allow the UNHCR to consider applications for political asylum from anyone with a justifiable fear of persecution in his homeland. Beijing said because they were economic immigrants, they were not covered by the convention. The effort to persuade Beijing to allow the UNHCR to open border refugee camps, like ones it ran in Thailand to process applications from Cambodians fleeing the Khmer Rouge rule, went nowhere.

The Chinese authorities pursued anyone trying to smuggle North Koreans out, even making arrests in obscure places on its border with Mongolia or Laos, and then handed out lengthy prison sentences to those involved. In an effort to turn up the pressure on China and the UNHCR, a group of activists organized a documentary series of publicity stunts, sending refugees to climb walls into the UNHCR building in Beijing, and then into foreign embassies and consulates all over China. Chinese guards were photographed dragging refugees screaming out of the Japanese consulate in

Shenyang. Barbed wire was thrown around all embassy buildings in Beijing in an effort to stop North Koreans from running in. The organizers' most daring effort to attract publicity came in 2003, when a scheme to start an exodus of North Koreans by boat was foiled at the last moment. China shrugged off the adverse publicity, redoubled its efforts to hunt down the refugees, and proudly displayed its support for Kim Jong Il. The rest of the world, even the South Korean government, stayed quiet, fearful of jeopardizing relations with a growing power.

CHAPTER 2

The Kim Dynasty

As his exhausted people struggled to survive another year in their country's "forced march for final victory," North Korea's leader, Kim Jong Il, was busy himself.

The North Korean state news agency (KCNA) reported that his great humanity was on show by his willingness to share their bitter deprivations. One news story described how in January 1998 he arrived on his personal train to inspect a hydropower project and he invited officials to share his modest lunch.

"There on the table for everyone were several pieces of corn bread stuffed with vegetables and a bowl of vegetable Soya soup. With lumps in their throat they could not eat. And looking around Kim said, "We should have corn bread and Soya soup as our meal." The officials were deeply impressed, says the KCNA report, by the noble virtue of a leader who was leading the very simple life of the people. Kim Jong Il was a leader, it declared "who always finds his happiness and joy in the people's happiness and joy" and who refused to eat anything but rice or a few boiled potatoes for his meal.[1] Another report praised the Dear Leader Kim Jong Il for being as frugal as his father and said that even in the best of times, the Kim family preferred to eat boiled maize together with a soup made from dried radish leaves and bean paste.[2]

Other more objective sources paint a quite different picture of the portly Kim's austerity. As millions of his subjects died from hunger and cold,

Kim, possibly the last fat man left in his country, fretted about how to titillate a palate jaded by the dishes served by his permanent staff of Chinese, Japanese, and Korean cooks. As a keen film watcher, he heard about pizzas and in 1997 issued an order. A few months later, the celebrated chef Ermanno Furlanis was in his home in Italy when some mysterious Asians approached him and a colleague, offering them a three-week mission, all expenses paid. "We were handed envelopes with our compensation—all cash and in advance," Furlanis noted in the amusing account he made of his trip.[3]

After stringent medical checkups, the two chefs and their wives departed for North Korea. Upon arrival, they found themselves driving across a desolate landscape to a seaside palace protected by a battery of antiaircraft guns. As they were shown around the three fully equipped kitchens and a library with thousands of recipes, their smiling hosts told them that famous chefs from all over the world had been brought here. They explained to the visitors that their mission was to train three local chefs in the art of Italian cooking; whatever they needed, they were just to ask and it would be brought. The Italians wanted a special pizza oven so sophisticated that the Italian customs almost seized it, fearing it was intended to aid the North's nuclear program.

"Every now and then, a kind of courier would show up from some corner of the world," Furlanis noted. "I saw him twice unloading two enormous boxes containing an assortment of twenty very costly French cheeses, and a box of prized French wines." After which, the visitors insisted only Italian vintages would do and within three days, a shipment of Barolo wines duly arrived.

During their stay they cooked for Kim at his seaside retreat, which was equipped with a water amusement park and a pleasure yacht the size of an ocean liner. Although only ever glimpsing him at a distance, they did hear that Kim Jong Il had complained about one dish—marinated lamb garnished with dried spaghetti—saying it was just a tad too salty. As the World Food Program lobbied hard to raise donations needed to feed almost half the entire North Korean population, life in the palace, even for those downstairs, was so lavish that the Italians and other staff members sat down to meals of fresh lobsters with salad, accompanied by French white wine and Rémy Martin Cognac.

The Italians' story makes Marie-Antoinette sound like a model of social responsibility. In his book *Orient Express*, Russian General Konstantin Pulikovsky, who accompanied Kim on a month-long train journey from Pyongyang to Moscow in the summer of 2001, portrays an epicure absurdly proud of his greed, as if it was a mark of worldly savoir faire.

Offered lunch on a stop in Omsk, Kim rejected a plate of barrel-salted pickles, grumbling that these must be shoddy Bulgarian cucumbers, not authentic Russian ones. When his host then served him tiny pelmeni dumplings, "kopeck-size in a small frying pan baked under cheese and mayonnaise," Kim was even more scornful. "Kim Jong Il picked at them with a fork and said: 'What kind of pelmeni are these? They should be big, boiled and in broth.'" As they traversed Siberia on a luxurious Japanese–built train, eating four-hour meals off a silver service accompanied by carriages containing his drinks, cellar, cooks, and mistresses, Kim's restless brain came up with new whims. His retinue of servants and cooks were enough to provide Kim with Russian, Chinese, Korean, Japanese, and French cuisine at any time, and when he decided he wanted some Bordeaux and Burgundy wines, they were flown in from Paris. Then he demanded fresh lobsters, which were produced and before being cooked were presented live at the table. On the way home, Kim was so impressed by the brown bread he found at a restaurant in Khabarovsk that he ordered an aide to send 20 loaves by air to Pyongyang so that they would be fresh on his arrival.[4]

The train had 21 carriages and was armored and pulled by two locomotives that swept the track for mines. One of the carriages was set up with an electronic satellite navigation screen and a satellite Internet link to allow Kim to follow the progress of his train and to play with his computer and surf the web.[5]

A sushi chef, who first worked for Kim in 1982 and wrote the book *Kim Jong Il's Cook—I Saw His Naked Body*, published in 2003 under the pseudonym Kenji Fujimoto, described the efforts that went into pandering to Kim's stomach. Fujimoto traveled to Iran and Uzbekistan to buy caviar, China for melons and grapes, Thailand and Malaysia for durians and papayas, the Czech Republic for Pilsner beer, and Denmark to fetch bacon. There were also regular trips to Japan to buy tuna, sea urchin, and other fresh fish for sushi. Kim especially liked eel sushi, eating it three times a week, and "toro" sushi—a highly prized fatty marbled tuna. He often raised his forefinger and, speaking a mixture of English and Japanese, said, "Fujimoto, another piece of 'toro.'"[6,7]

His master was fond of Japanese noodles, including the instant kind. "He often made me cook supper late at night. I would be told to come to his place to cook at 2 o'clock in the morning," Fujimoto wrote. Kim would host banquets starting at midnight and ending in the morning. The longest banquet went on for four days and anyone invited dared not fall asleep before Kim Jong Il went to bed. "It was torture for them," Fujimoto recalled.[8] The more expensive and rare the food, the better. He also liked rice cooked with the hard-to-find and costly matsutake mushroom, and shark fin soup, which a Chinese chef cooked for him three times a week.

Fujimoto describes Kim as a confirmed alcoholic given to drinking binges; he disappeared from sight from 1977 to 1978 for treatment. Other sources report that his father once reprimanded Kim at a meeting for turning up drunk. When he turned 50, his doctors advised him to switch to wine. Fujimoto said that he had seen, in the basement of Kim's official residence, a cellar stocked with 10,000 bottles of French wines, as well as famous sake brands, Johnnie Walker whiskey, and Hennessy's XO Cognac.

"I went there many times. After 1994, Kim Jong Il indulged in collecting French wines. Every day, he opened three bottles of these wines to select the day's wine," Fujimoto wrote.[9] The CIA, which investigated these stories, found a jump in French exports of the most expensive brands of cognac and Armagnac, which in 1996 cost U.S. $700,000. There are hints too that the self-indulgent Kim may also have struggled with a drug habit at one time. Soviet diplomats said that in the mid-1980s Kim Jong Il attended several meetings in which he talked such a stream of gibberish that not even a personal translator could follow.

It is no surprise that Kim, growing up as the son and heir of a man worshipped as a living god, would became vain and self-indulgent. It is nevertheless striking that the more wretched the lives of his people, the more extravagant Kim seems to have become. A year after his father's death, Kim spent U.S. $15 million for America's top professional wrestlers to come and entertain him, the most money the American Wrestling Federation ever made on a foreign gig. Kim even invited foreign journalists to Pyongyang to come and write about the event. In 1998, when the United Nations was appealing for U.S. $600 million in emergency aid, Kim splashed out U.S. $20 million on importing 200 new S-500 class Mercedes Benz limousines, adding the latest and most luxurious model to the country's pool of 7,000 Mercedes. What sort of ruler behaves this way and why?

Perhaps, Kim Jong Il imagines himself as another Sun King, the splendors of whose court impressed the world. *"Le'état c'est moi,"* Louis XIV famously said, and he never doubted that his extravagance and the absolutism exercised by all of France's Bourbon kings was sanctioned by God and buttressed by the authority of the Church. Yet, a Marxist-Leninist state like North Korea is the product of a revolutionary ideology whose notions of class struggle date back to the French Revolution.

To understand how this contradiction was reconciled one must go back to study the origins of the DPRK. Instead of relying on church dogma and wily cardinals to legitimize their power, the Kim dynasty employed twentieth-century tools of totalitarian propaganda. No other regime in the former Soviet Bloc based its legitimacy on such a mountain of crude falsehoods as did North Korea. "A lie told often enough becomes the truth" observed Lenin; and Kim Il Sung took this advice to heart. Kim Jong Il grew up with a father that followed Hitler's theory that ordinary people are more susceptible to the "big lie" than the "small lie." From the start of his reign, Kim Il Sung fabricated such "colossal untruths" about his past that even refugees who fled in fear of their lives continued to express a profound reverence for him and his achievements. It would therefore seem natural for his son to believe that through the skillful use of propaganda anything he did could be covered up easily.[10]

History of Kim Il Sung

From the time he first arrived in Korea from the USSR, following the dropping of the first nuclear bomb on Hiroshima and Japan's unconditional surrender, the manipulation of the truth was essential to Kim Il Sung's claim to power. Even his name is false. He was born Kim Song Juh in 1912, and when he arrived in the North, he adopted the name Kim Il Sung from a renowned leader of the resistance against the Japanese occupation that began in 1905. He wanted people to believe he was the real Kim Il Sung, but many Koreans were doubtful the legendary leader was so young.

Kim Il Sung first appears in black-and-white photographs taken in 1945 with Soviet military officers as a stocky handsome figure, already fat at the age of 33. He arrived as a stranger to a country that he had left at the age of seven when his parents, like many others, chose to flee the Japanese occupation. Both parents were Christians, and his father was a Presbyterian elder; they settled in what is now the Jilin province in Northern China, which after the fall of the Qing empire in 1911 was controlled by a Chinese warlord while Russians and Japanese competed for power.

Kim was educated in Chinese at a local school and then spent the next 20 years in the service of either the Chinese or the Soviet Communist Party. So, his loyalty to the cause of Korean nationalism is questionable. By the time he returned to live in Korea, his Korean language skills were so poor that he needed extra coaching to be able to make speeches before Korean audiences. His eldest son, Kim Jong Il, was born on Soviet territory and became the first Korean ruler in history born outside Korea. Once in power, Kim Il Sung later persecuted millions of his subjects for serving foreign masters. He was vociferous in condemning opponents for being "spies," "puppets," and "stooges" of foreign powers, but his own record is no different.

Kim Il Sung returned to Korea to serve as Stalin's handpicked puppet for the occupying Soviet forces. Most of those surrounding Kim during his early years had even more ambiguous loyalties. Following Japan's annexation of Korea, some had sought refuge in the Russian Far East and were assimilated into the new Soviet state. Then in the 1930s, Stalin deported most of them to Central Asia or had them shot as Japanese agents. They would have been terrified of expressing any loyalty to the new Korean state and showing disloyalty to Stalin.

A Chinese warlord, Zhang Zuolin, ruled Manchuria, and there were many Russians living in the big towns, including White Russian émigrés. The Russians controlled the railways, but as the Japanese grew more powerful, they seized control of all Russian interests and then murdered Marshal Zoulin. After annexing Manchuria, they created a colony called Manchukuo, a puppet state ruled by Pu Yi, the last Manchu emperor of the fallen Qing dynasty, to which millions of Japanese were brought to settle.

Resistance to the Japanese was led by Chinese Communists as well as many bandit groups that operated in these lawless times; in many respects their activities were indistinguishable. The barely literate Kim left school at age14 and joined a Communist study group for which he was imprisoned for eight months; in 1932, at age 20, he joined a Chinese Communist Party (CCP) guerilla group. He spent the next ten years with a small group of up to 200 men and women organizing hit-and-run raids against Japanese interests. They financed their guerilla activities by murdering and pillaging wealthy but defenseless Korean villagers. Such groups often gained fresh recruits by kidnapping young men from the villages. Kim eventually served in a minor command in the Northeast Anti-Japanese United Army, which at its peak in the 1930s had some 30,000 partisans.

Kim Il Sung took orders from Chinese political commissars until 1945; his mission was not to gain Korean independence but to win power in China and to annex the resource-rich Manchurian territories. While the Japanese were creating their overseas empire, they scattered over 4 million Koreans, recruited as soldiers, guards, miners, sailors, workers, and "comfort women," around Asia. Many ethnic Koreans joined Mao's armies and some rose to the highest ranks of the Chinese People's Liberation Army. Others stayed in the service of the Soviet Union, which after 1945 seemed set on annexing Manchuria as well. The exact nature of Kim's patriotism at this time is ambiguous. Had the Soviet secret police not selected him for their mission, Kim Jong Il might well have stayed on in China, or the Soviet Union.

Given Korea's long history as a tributary vassal of China, the suspicion that for 20 years Kim was actually working to further China's interests has great emotional resonance. You have only to visit one of Seoul's most historical sites, the Independence Gate next to the imperial pavilion—the "Welcoming Imperial Grace Gate" where Korean officials prostrated themselves before the eunuch envoys who arrived from Beijing each year—to realize the significance.

Since earliest times, Chinese emperors treated Korea as a minor vassal state, appointing its kings, exacting tribute, and monopolizing Korea's relations with foreign states. Right down to the final years of the Qing dynasty, Koreans looked to Beijing to approve any dealings they had with Western powers. The Koreans even had a special word to describe this subservience to China, *sadaeism*, which North Korean propaganda talk calls "flunkeyism." The Korean independence movement that sprang up with the last Korean dynasty and fell into decline in the nineteenth century set out to free Korea of all foreign domination, especially China's. At the turn of the century, leading nationalists, like So Jae-pil, who established an Independence Club to erect the Independence Gate, were determined to cast off China's shackles. Another very symbolic project was to transform the "Hall of Reverence for China," in which Chinese ambassadors were entertained, into an Independence Hall and an Independence Park. In Pyongyang, the vast "Arc de Triomphe" that Kim Il Sung built is also supposed to be the fulfillment of So Jae-pil's dream.

In fact Kim himself actually revived the feudal traditions by traveling each year to Beijing—usually in secret—to pledge his loyalty to the Red Emperor, Chairman Mao, who was ensconced in the gardens of the Forbidden City. Some Chinese even say that when Chinese delegations arrived by train, Kim would always meet them at the border and accompany them into Pyongyang—another demonstration of feudal "flunkeyism."

Korea's opportunity for independence came from the disintegration of the vast Manchu Empire after defeats at the hands of Western powers and many internal rebellions. In the scramble to acquire former tributary states like Mongolia, Tibet, Vietnam, and Korea, Japan was the most aggressive pursuer. It inflicted a crushing naval victory over China and acquired Taiwan and other possessions in 1895, and then went onto Korea. In 1905, 30 Japanese assassins forced their way into the royal palace in Seoul, heading for the private quarters of Queen Min. They stabbed her to death, threw the body on a pile of firewood, drenched it in kerosene, and set it alight. King Kojong, her husband and the last of the Choson dynasty, which had ruled the country for over 500 years, then tried to find safety in the Russian Embassy. By then, Japan and Russia seemed ready to divide Korea between them, but after the newly modernized Japanese navy inflicted two crushing defeats on the Russian navy—first at Port Arthur in 1904, and then at Tsushima a few months later, it was winner take all. Half a century later at Yalta, Stalin was still demanding that Russian rights in Korea, supposedly violated by Japan's treacherous attack in 1904, be restored. By 1910, Japan had formally annexed Korea and renamed it Chosen, bringing in hundreds of thousands of Japanese settlers and administrators. By the 1930s, Japan began a ruthless effort to assimilate the Koreans and extinguish their identity.

Some Koreans looked to the Chinese for help as China had intervened to protect Korea from earlier Japanese aggression. Some joined Mao Zedong in his base at Yanan. Others attached themselves to Chiang Kai-shek's Nationalist Party and set up a government in exile that was based in Shanghai. A few put their trust in the United States and especially Woodrow Wilson's promotion of the rights of smaller nations to self-determination after World War I. Others remembered that the United States had stood aside in 1905, and made an agreement with Japan that recognized Japan's claim to Korea in exchange for Japan's acceptance of the U.S. annexation of the Philippines. Still other Koreans, who embraced Communism and established their Party in 1925, looked toward Moscow and the Comintern for salvation. Stalin, however, became incensed at the stiff-necked independence of these Korean Communists, and in the early 1930s, he expelled them from the Comintern on the grounds that they showed "excessive nationalism."

Kim Il Sung took part in some direct combat against the Japanese in what is now the Yanbian Korean Ethnic Autonomous Prefecture in Jilin province. You can still find the Japanese military governor's headquarters, with its pillboxes and gardens, at the Japanese colonial headquarters in Longjin town, close to Yanji, the current prefectural capital. Japanese police records reveal that Kim's military activities date to early 1935. By 1937, the Japanese military police had hunted down most of these guerilla groups and went on to mount a full-scale invasion of northern China, seizing Beijing. By 1941, all the surviving guerillas had retreated across the border into the Soviet Union. Kim was brought to the Khabarovsk Infantry Officers school and from there to the Vissatsyki camp, where he eventually rose to the rank of captain in a combined unit of 300 Chinese and Koreans under a Chinese commanding officer, Wang Song. This counterintelligence unit was part of the 88th Special Brigade, which was trained to operate reconnaissance missions in Manchuria, not Korea, in preparation for a Soviet attack against the Japanese. As far as we know Kim did not undertake any fighting in those years, and he remained a member of the Chinese Communist Party, not the Korean Communist Party. During this time, his wife, Kim Jong-suk, a fellow partisan, gave birth to his eldest son, Kim Jong Il. He was born in the Soviet military camp in 1941 or 1942. The Russians called her Vera and her son Yura. He who grew up speaking Russian and was educated with Russian children until at least the age of 12.

The official story in North Korea that is drilled into every school child and enforced in films, textbooks, stamps, novels, and paintings is absurd. Koreans are taught that by the age of 14 Kim Il Sung had founded an "anti-imperialism league" and at 19, he had invented the country's *Juche* ideology and was leading a Korean rebel army equipped with tanks. They are told that this force defeated the Japanese and drove them out of Korea, although in fact the Japanese Kwantung Army did not suffer any military defeats in either Manchuria or Korea. In this imagined history, the role of the Americans, the Soviets, the atomic bombs, the Chinese Communist and Nationalist Parties, and virtually every other historical fact vanishes from the record.

After August 1945, the CCP underground in Manchuria took the weapons abandoned by the Japanese and then recruited as many as 20,000 ethnic Koreans to fight in the civil war waged with the KMT (the Chinese Nationalists) for the control of China. The Kim family did not join them. The Soviets entered the Pacific War on August 8, just a week before Japan's surrender. They had been preparing to fight a long war with Japan after Germany's surrender, and Stalin had no clear plans for Korea. The Soviet 25th Army arrived in Korea the following week but did not bother to call on Kim Il Sung or any other Koreans for assistance. The Red Army drove unopposed into Pyongyang on August 15. The Far East Command of the NKVD (the predecessor of the KGB) made the decision to use Kim to front a puppet government at the very last moment. Kim was selected from several candidates presented to NKVD Chief Laventry Beria, who met him several times before Stalin gave his final consent.

Kim seems a curious pick as there were so many older and dedicated Korean Communists who were better qualified. Kim was then just 33, poorly educated, and unknown in Korea. His only merit seems to have been a reputation as a good fighter who disciplined drunken soldiers. Perhaps the Soviets chose him because he had no prior association with the indigenous Korean Communist movement that Stalin disliked so much, and because they could rely on him to show total obedience. It quickly became the priority of the Soviets to prevent any of the famous nationalists leaders like Kim Ku, Syngman Rhee, and Cho Man-sik, all of whom had recently emerged from prison or exile with large reputations and loyal followings, from acquiring power. Their credentials as patriots greatly overshadowed Kim's. Rhee had been a leader of the very important March 1, 1919, nationalist protests and possessed a master's degree in political science from Harvard, plus a doctorate from Princeton, where his supervisor was Woodrow Wilson. Cho had stayed in the country and survived decades in Japanese jails, while Kim Ku had an even longer record of heroic nationalistic resistance. The Soviets ignored these men and seemed intent on enlisting Kim to aid the annexation of part or all of Korea.

After the Soviet Union collapsed, it became clear just how clumsily the Soviets had installed Kim Il Sung. "We created him from zero," boasted NKVD Officer Leonid Vassin. "We did very crudely." Vassin worked in the 7th Department of Special Propaganda of the 25th Army in charge of military propaganda in enemy territory, and says he was in contact everyday with Kim during his first six months.

According to Vassin, Kim arrived in Korea on August 22, 1945, wearing a Soviet army uniform with a Red Army medal pinned to his chest under the orders of Major General Nikolai Lebedev, who was in charge of political affairs. He was by himself although other sources claim that Kim and 66 other former Korean officers assigned to help Soviet occupation authorities returned to Korea through Port Wonsan on September 19, 1945, aboard the Soviet warship *Pugachev*.

"When Kim appeared we noticed he was not fully fluent in Korean," Vassin recalled. On August 23, Vassin says that they received orders to put him in his first civilian suit and gave him three days to learn a speech they had written for him. This was delivered at the first Party Congress organized by the Korean Communist Party veterans who had been freed by the Japanese surrender. As Kim had no credentials or support, the NKVD went on to organize his own political party for him that they called the "The Workers Party." Soon they forced the other parties to merge with it and thus obscured its origin.

"We manipulated the names of the parties to create a smokescreen to hide our intentions," recalled Vassin. "Then we had to destroy real heroes of the national liberation movement." General Anochin of the NKVD had Cho Man-sik framed by spreading accusations that he was a Japanese agent so the Japanese had released him from jail just before their surrender. After this story was broadcast over the radio and put in the newspapers, he had Cho put under house arrest. "This is how the hero became the enemy and how the puppet we pushed forward became a hero," Vassin declared.

As Kim's nom de guerre was widely associated with an older guerilla who had performed legendary feats, many suspected him of being a complete fraud, so the next step was to build up Kim's image. "We elevated him into the status of a hero to bolster his work as a leader of Korea," Vassin said. "We had to prove he was a real person, the tiger of Mt. Paektu. We had to find his relations at the village of Mangyongdae. We also had to discredit the information put out in South Korea that he wasn't the real Kim Il Sung. We had to prove he was an active fighter who had liberated the motherland."

Vassin said that he even suspected an assassination attempt, made at one of the first public meetings he addressed, was staged to burnish Kim's image. In March 1, 1946, Kim was sitting on a podium in Pyongyang when a youth in the crowd threw a grenade at him; it was caught by a Soviet soldier. The handmade grenade blew off part of the soldier's arm, but did not cause further damage. The Soviets blamed Syngman Rhee for the attempt on Kim's life and used the event to illustrate the sacrifices that the Soviet Union was making on behalf of Korea.

At the time, the Soviet occupation force was busy looting the country of its industrial hardware for shipment back to the Soviet Union. It was deeply unpopular with many Koreans, and its troops were accused of committing rape. Anti-Soviet protests spread throughout the country, and in Hamhung, the largest industrial city, more than 1,000 students from junior and senior high schools staged a march, shouting "Red Army Go Home!" The students broke into the provincial office of the Communist Party and smashed office furniture. The Soviets opened fire and the students fled.[11]

For the next ten years, Kim larded every speech and article with slavish expressions of devotion to Stalin and loyalty to the Soviet Union. He urged Koreans to take the Soviet Union as their model and ended his telegrams to Moscow saying "glory to the Soviet Army," to which were added expressions of "deep love and gratitude" to Stalin.

In contrast to Kim's abject expressions of *sadaeism* towards Moscow, the most prominent Korean nationalist leaders, gathered in the capital Seoul, were resolved to resist all foreign intervention. In particular, they resisted the proposal to divide the country under the trusteeship of the Americans and Russians. This was a particularly bitter turn of events for the Koreans who saw the willingness of the great powers to ignore the rights of the Koreans to full sovereignty as an insulting expression of ignorance about existence of the Korean nation. The Koreans has been submerged in the Japanese empire for so long that it was clear many people knew nothing about them.

Their fate was decided in a few words at distant parleys in Cairo, Yalta, and Potsdam. While World War II was in progress, Korea's fate merited little attention. Chiang Kai-shek, who represented China and spoke up for Korea, signed on to the Cairo Declaration of 1943, in which the United States, Britain, and China declared that "the aforesaid three great powers, mindful of the enslavement of the people of Korea, are determined that in due course, Korea shall become free and independent." President Franklin Roosevelt added the words "in due course," thinking the Koreans would need to stay under trusteeship for 20 or 30 years until they were considered fit enough to govern themselves. At the 1945 conference in Yalta, during which Winston Churchill confessed he had "never heard of the bloody place," President Roosevelt went on to propose a U.S.-Soviet-Chinese trusteeship over Korea.[12]

The Americans, who had been preparing for a long war to conquer Japan, had given no serious thought about how exactly this trusteeship would work. So it transpired that on the evening of August 10, 1945, an all-night meeting was convened at the Executive Office Building next to the White House. Around midnight two young officers were sent to an adjoining room to carve out a U.S. occupation zone in Korea. One of them was Lt. Colonel Dean Rusk, and the other Colonel Charles H. Bonesteel, and they were given 30 minutes to find a line to draw across a map. Even finding the right sort of map was a problem. A search turned up an old National Geographic magazine. Using this they picked the 38th Parallel as a convenient way of dividing the peninsula.

The Soviets were just as irresponsible, and to everyone's surprise agreed to an arbitrary demarcation that took no account of history or geography. The North got 50,000 square miles of mountainous territory containing much of the heavy industry left by the Japanese, including the main hydro-electric power stations. The South was smaller but had twice the population and the most productive rice fields. No justification has ever been made as to why Korea had to be divided. Germany was divided as a punishment, but Japan, despite its guilt, was not. As Korea was not an aggressor, but a victim of World War II, Koreans are bitter that through no fault of their own they were again prevented from taking their rightful place in the world. Moreover the division of the country weakened it, once again leaving it at the mercy of the great powers. Many Koreans even regard the division as an American betrayal. Using their land to wage war

Immediately after the decision was made, General John R. Hodge arrived from Japan with troops. The U.S.-backed Republic of Korea was declared on August 15, 1945. The Soviets declared the creation of the Democratic People's Republic of Korea on September 9. Then in December, Moscow hosted a four-power conference during which it was agreed that a four-power trusteeship would continue for five years. In the meantime, a joint U.S.-Soviet Commission would arrange for nationwide elections followed by the withdrawal of all occupying armies. Most of the 700,000 Japanese civilians and troops in Korea started to leave.

Kim accepted the Soviet trusteeship but rejected the UN's decision to hold elections that he would have had little chance of winning. He still depended on the Manchurian Koreans to run his administration, and they formed the backbone of the secret police and military. By 1949, his DPRK was a fully-fledged Stalinist dictatorship with labor camps, purges, arbitrary arrests, public executions, and a personality cult. Kim erected the first statue to himself in 1949 before he was even 40 and began calling himself "The Great Leader," or *Suryong*.

Anyone who might contradict his version of history was either shot or sentenced to decades of imprisonment. According to senior defector Hwang Jang-yop, in 1958, Kim ordered his officials to edit his selected works and destroy all evidence of how he came to power. "Through this project, any records that gave the impression of worshipping the Soviet Union were destroyed, and all records of 'Long live Stalin' were also deleted," said Hwang. The contribution of all other nationalists was erased, indeed even their names disappeared, until it was Kim himself who founded the Korean Communist Party in 1933. The vanity and hubris that marked the next 50 years of Kim's rule were already evident, even before the Korean War erupted in June 1950.

The Korean War

Visitors to Pyongyang are always taken to the grandiose Korean Revolution Museum. In front stands a 70-foot statue of Kim Il Sung, and inside the museum devotes itself to justifying a massive lie about the origins and results of the Korean War. Guides tell all visitors that it was the South that launched a surprise attack on the North on June 25, 1950, but that within three days, Kim's army had responded with a powerful counterattack that reached within a few miles of the southern tip of the peninsula.

There is no mention of Stalin, nor of the 900,000 troops that Mao sent after the U.S.-led forces that threw them back and nearly unified Korea. Even the death of one of Mao's sons in the war is omitted. The museum is exclusively devoted to the aggrandizement of one family's reputation and the maintenance of another huge and crude edifice of lies. North Koreans, and most Chinese, still believe it was the Americans who were responsible for a surprise attack.

The war, which devastated the Korean people, destroying cities and the entire industrial infrastructure to a degree that has few parallels in history, is also unique in other respects. It did not start with an official declaration of war. There were no preliminary negotiations or any official justification— and then it ended without any formal peace. The North Korean army waged total war, simultaneously seeking to wipe out not just their military opponents but those civilians it labeled as class enemies. While there were atrocities on the other side, only the North attempted to massacre civilians in this systematic way. Civilians who belonged to the wrong class or were Christians or adherents of some group that might offer resistance were killed. Altogether, three million civilians lost their lives and another five million became refugees. During the brief occupation of the South, 84,000 were kidnapped and 200,000 pressed into the North's military. 129,000 lost their lives. Many people lost track of family members as they were driven hither and thither by the fortunes of war. Seoul alone changed hands three times. The war created 100,000 orphans, and a million people fled from the North to become refugees in the South. Even as late as 1983, the South Korean Broadcasting System aired a program showing pictures of family members still missing after 30 years. The broadcast led to over 10,000 reunions. Millions of other families remain divided across the DMZ without contact even by phone or letter since the 1953 armistice.

The greatest loser in the war was not the South but the North. A quarter of all those who found themselves under Kim's rule in 1945 fled to the South between 1945 and 1953. Every city and factory of any consequence in the North was flattened. "The war for Kim was a devastating experience," says his American biographer Dae-Sook Suh. "He was branded an aggressor in the war, and he was humiliated by the Chinese. Worst of all he had mobilized Koreans to fight against Koreans but the fate of Korea was once again decided by non-Koreans while the country still remained divided."[13]

His actions had left Korea even more at the mercy of foreign powers than ever before. His own state became completely dependent on foreign aid. Kim was forced to go back to the Soviet Union to plead for reconstruction grants and then to beg the Chinese to cancel all debts. Yet, Kim Il Sung never acknowledged his responsibility for starting the war, nor for losing it. All these truths were submerged in a sea of shrill propaganda. The full extent of his culpability has begun to emerge only recently. It had long been assumed that it was Stalin who pushed Kim into starting the war, but documents recovered from the Soviet archives in Moscow and other East European countries in the 1990s and interviews with key witnesses now suggest a different story. They show Kim taking the initiative in lobbying Stalin vigorously to persuade him to authorize the attack. It seems Kim began planning and preparing for the invasion in 1948 and visited Moscow to seek Stalin's authorization several times. Finally in April 1950, Stalin gave his approval and told Kim to travel to Beijing to obtain Mao's permission. _pressured_

It is true that Kim Il Sung was not alone in calling for a military solution _by the_ to unify Korea. In the South, Syngman Rhee was also calling for a "march _American_ North" to overthrow the communist regime, and stepped up his rhetoric to such a feverish pitch that he alarmed many Americans, who feared he _bullshit_ was provoking the North. The result was that Americans denied Rhee the military potential to threaten the North. Even Kim admitted to the Soviets that Rhee unable to mount an attack.[14]

Washington wanted to use the newly established mechanism of the United Nations to resolve the tensions. Therefore Korea became the first major test case of the new international order that the victors of World War II were trying to put in place. The American government submitted the

Just as the USSR controlled the North, so too did the Americans control the South. Each pushing its own Ideology

Korean issue to the newly created UN General Assembly and called for the establishment of a UN Temporary Commission on Korea to supervise general elections that would lead to the formation of an independent Korean government.

The General Assembly supported the American proposal, but Pyongyang refused to cooperate, denying the UN's authority and refusing the commission any entry to the North. Elections in the South went ahead on May 10, 1948, but not in the North. The elections returned Syngman Rhee to the presidency. The North conducted their own elections for a "people's assembly" with predictable results. In late 1948, the Soviets withdrew their troops, and in June 1949, the Americans followed suit, leaving just 500 instructors behind. The American troop withdrawal led Kim to believe that if his attack were successful, the Americans would not intervene. Stalin thought so too. The misjudgment would prove costly for everyone.

CIA spies

It is important to remember that a war was not inevitable. The Koreans could have opted to stay on the sidelines of the Cold War. Before the Korean War neither of the superpowers considered Korea a vital strategic asset. Had it not been for Kim's invasion, Korean politicians might have been left alone to decide their own fate without much outside interference. Both Soviet and American troops had left. The Japanese were gone, and the Chinese were still busy with domestic civil war. This was exactly the sort of situation that Korean patriots had been dreaming of since the end of the nineteenth century. Instead of involving Stalin in Korea's domestic power struggle, Kim could have devoted his energies to persuading Stalin to leave the Koreans alone.

Kim's attack took place after the United States and the USSR had embarked on that epic struggle that we now call the Cold War. In March 1947, President Truman articulated what became known as the "Truman Doctrine" at a joint session of Congress. He said it must be U.S. policy to support free peoples and oppose totalitarian regimes, which in practice meant challenging Soviet ambitions throughout the world. "We cannot allow changes in the status quo in violation of the Charter of the United Nations by such methods as coercion, or by such subterfuges as political infiltration. In helping free and independent nations to maintain their freedom, the United States will be giving effect to the principles of the Charter of the United Nations," he said.

An ideological struggle between Communism and Capitalism. => What stupidity

America had good reasons to be suspicious of the Soviet Union. New evidence emerged in the 1990s showing how deeply the Kremlin was involved in the preparations for war. One witness, Valentin Pak, who was Kim's aide and translator, says that Stalin's generals drew up the battle plans and plotted all the moves leading up to the invasion.

"The invasion plan was devised by Soviet advisers to the North Korean army," said Pak in an interview on CNN. "The battle plan was handed to us on tracing paper. The Soviet generals and colonels drew it up, then it was translated by Korean officers on their staff."

Up to 20,000 Soviet military personnel were estimated to have taken part in the Korean War—although never on the front lines. Soviet officers trained a 90,000-strong invasion force that was concentrated at the 38th Parallel, and pilots provided air cover. Several weeks after the Chinese offensive began, Stalin sent Soviet MiG-15s with Chinese markings and Soviet pilots, mostly World War II veterans, dressed in Chinese uniforms without documents. They helped prevent U.S. bombers from destroying vital supply bridges across the Yalu River. After making a peaceful reunification proposal, the plan was that the North would attack swiftly, before the Republic of Korea (ROK) and the U.S. could put up an effective resistance. Kim's deputy, Pak Hon-yong, reassured Stalin that the invasion would be supported by hundreds of thousands of partisans in the South. The original plan never envisioned fighting anyone except the weak South Korean forces. Even so, Kim erred in failing to obtain guarantees that if the Americans did return in force, the Soviet Union would back him up.

At first, the Soviet plan for North Korea's invasion succeeded. The North quickly overran all but a small corner of the country in the South, called the Pusan Perimeter, around the port of Pusan. Kim Il Sung himself traveled as far South as Kwangju. At the UN, the Security Council, with the Soviet Union absent, voted unanimously to declare war on North Korea. Truman then hastily sent 10,000 troops from Japan to fight with the ill-prepared South Korean forces. Despite outside help, the combined forces were hardly a match for the 90,000 battle-hardened and strong North Koreans. America's General MacArthur was put in charge of a multinational force under the UN flag that staged a daring amphibious landing at Inchon, cutting the peninsula in two. The forces routed the North Koreans and drove them back beyond the 38th Parallel. Soon the UN forces advanced quickly through the North within a few miles of the border with China.

Only a third of Kim's original invasion force is thought to have made it back across the 38th Parallel. His troops were shattered and disorganized, and Kim retreated to establish a temporary headquarters in the mountains bordering China. No clear picture has emerged of what Kim did during the next three years. Some evidence suggests that Kim tried to persuade the Kremlin to end the war quickly and sue for peace, but Stalin ignored him and decided to use the war to bleed the Americans. Together with his court, Kim remained in a bunker complex in Chagang province, relegated to the sidelines. Kim continued to be consulted, but others always made the decisions, including the negotiation of the armistice. It is also important to note that Kim formally put his troops under the authority of the Chinese and sent his family to China for safety.[15]

On November 25, 1950, the People's Liberation Army of China entered the war. Some 300,000 Chinese "volunteer" troops overwhelmed the overextended UN forces, throwing them into a headlong, southern retreat. From then on the conduct of the war was in the hands of the Chinese General Peng Dehuai, who had little respect for Kim and later blamed him for failing to trap the UN forces as they disembarked from Hamhung during the retreat from the North. The result was that Kim, a member of the Chinese Communist Party from 1935 to 1945, had now ensured that the Koreans once again found themselves placed in their traditional role of a junior vassal tied to the restored Chinese power with ambitions to regain the Qing dynasty's possessions.

China's intervention caught Washington off guard. Mao Zedong had declared victory in the civil war against the KMT in October 1949, when he founded the People's Republic of China. However, his troops were still fighting remnants of Nationalist forces in parts of the country and preparing an invasion of Tibet. The top priority for Mao should have been an invasion of Taiwan, where his chief enemy Generalissimo Chiang Kai-shek had retreated with a strong force. From the Chinese viewpoint, Mao sacrificed his chance to complete the defeat of his chief opponent in order to save Kim, and of course Stalin, from defeat. Mao kept pressing Stalin for military support. Stalin delivered the hardware but feared the appearance of Soviet warplanes and troops in Korea might trigger a world war.

On the American side, General MacArthur lobbied to attack China and even proposed using nuclear weapons. He and many others recognized

America are the only country in the world to use an Atomic Bomb on another country.

that the real prize in East Asia worth fighting over was not Korea, but China. MacArthur was replaced, and the fighting eventually settled into a fixed pattern after the Chinese counterattack was halted on January 24, 1951. The ensuing armistice negotiations stretched out over two years, frequently breaking down over minor issues of face and protocol such as the order of the agenda, seating arrangements, and the size of flags. According to Cold War history researcher Dr. Kathryn Weathersby, Stalin, as the leader of the Communist Bloc, retained the final say. The decision to bring the war to an end on July 27, 1953, was made in Moscow after Stalin's death. It was the first foreign policy decision of the new post-Stalin leadership. Since there was no peace treaty, the war never formally came to an end. The peninsula remained divided more or less as before, although the North did gain the city of Kaesong. Some 33,000 Americans had died along with 3,000 others from UN troops, including Britains, Turks, Frenchmen, Australians, and Canadians. South Korea lost 58,809 men. North Korean combat deaths are put at 215,000, and China lost a staggering 400,000 men. Many prisoners of war were left on both sides. The armistice established the inaptly named Demilitarized Zone, a swathe of land 2.5 miles wide that stretches 148 miles. There is now a 10-foot-tall chain-link barrier and swathes of minefields, hidden bunkers, and tank traps across the mountainous terrain. Since 1953, various skirmishes have cost the lives of 889 North Koreans, 394 South Koreans, and 90 Americans.

The armistice talks have always been held at Panmunjom, the Truce Village, where representatives from the UN command, North Korea, and China meet in a collection of temporary huts. The South Korean side was until recently never represented, and in most of the talks the UN command is generally handled by an American general. North Korea's propaganda has made a great deal of this fact to demonstrate that the North is the only recognized independent Korean state while the South continues to be under the thumb of its American occupiers. Chinese troops left the North in 1958, and Pyongyang refused to treat the South as a legitimate negotiating partner, insisting that the Americans are the only authority with whom it should deal. Pyongyang propaganda also portrayed the armistice as a victory for the North and presented the Americans at Panmunjom as surrendering because they carried white flags. The object of Kim's military and foreign policies became freeing the South from its American occupiers and uniting the country under the only legitimate and sovereign government on the peninsula.

After the war, Kim had to fabricate an entirely bogus history in which he presented the Korean War as another case of how the Koreans had become innocent victims of foreign aggression. Although he was personally responsible for inviting the intervention of foreign powers, Kim now had to persuade the remaining North Korean population to forget what they knew to be true. They had to believe that Kim did not plan and prepare the invasion. The state indoctrinated the population through hate sessions that are called "meetings of revenge." During these sessions, people are repeatedly taught about the "bloody atrocities of the eternal enemies of the Korean people—American imperialism, Japanese colonialism, and their South Korean puppets." Among the major villains are Christian missionaries, who are depicted branding Korean children with hot irons, taking their blood to sell overseas, and spying for their cunning masters in Washington.

The sufferings of ordinary Koreans in a war marked by terrible carpet bombing campaigns were real enough and did not need exaggerating. Yet, it is revealing that Kim's government often based its anti-American propaganda on entirely fictitious claims.

One example is the claim that the United States deliberately spread cholera and other diseases among the civilian population. On February 22, 1952, North Korea told the United Nations that U.S. aircraft had dropped disease-bearing insects in seven raids. Two weeks later, China's Zhou Enlai claimed that the United States had sent 448 aircraft on 68 missions to spread plague, anthrax, cholera, encephalitis, and meningitis. An "International Scientific Commission" led by British biochemist Joseph Needham, an avowed Marxist, issued a 669-page report accepting the Chinese claims on the basis of testimony from witnesses.

The charges spread by the press and the World Peace Council, a Soviet-backed organization with branches in many countries, led to large-scale anti-American demonstrations around the world, especially in Europe. Needham, now dead, repeated the charge in a 1990 ceremony in which he was honored by Beijing on his ninetieth birthday. And the charges were still being repeated in 1989 in a book by British journalists Peter Williams and David Wallace.

To make the charge stick, the Communists took extraordinary measures—like infecting North Koreans awaiting execution with plague and cholera so that their bodies could be shown to outside investigators, and forcing 25 captured American pilots to sign "confessions." Although neither China nor the Russians have ever publicly admitted they lied, new documents from the Presidential Archives in Moscow recovered by historian Kathryn Weathersby and biological warfare specialist Milton Leitenberg of the University of Maryland showed that both knew the allegations were untrue. Conclusive proof came with the discovery of a secret May 2, 1953, resolution of the presidium of the USSR Council of Ministers. With an armistice only a few months away, and Stalin dead, it said: "The Soviet Government and the Central Committee of the CPSU (Communist Party of the Soviet Union) were misled. The spread in the press of information about the use by the Americans of bacteriological weapons in Korea was based on false information. The accusations against the Americans were fictitious."[16]

At the close of the Korean War, Kim still found himself the dictator of North Korea, but kept in power only with the backing of Moscow and Beijing. His legitimacy was now based on two major falsehoods, his claims to have raised an army and defeated and expelled the Japanese, and to have won a second war by defeating an unprovoked American invasion.

The Chinese and Soviets knew both these claims to be absurd and so did most people in Korea. In order to maintain rule, Kim had to go to extreme lengths to make the propaganda credible. He relied on purges both to remove those who might dispute his version of events and to terrify the rest into accepting the lies. Second, he had to isolate the North Koreans even more from the outside world and stir up distrust of his allies. Third, he had to achieve a measure of autonomy from Beijing and Moscow.

Just three days after signing the armistice, Kim held a show trial of a dozen high Party officials who were then shot for aiding and abetting the enemy. They were also accused of plotting to replace Kim with Pak Hon-yong, his second in command, and the man who had confidently promised Stalin that 200,000 partisans would rise up to support the invasion of the South. The former premier was shot two years later after a separate trial. Again, what is striking about the show trials is that even if indeed the victims were plotting against him, Kim never bothered to provide any proof.

It did not seem to matter to Kim Il Sung whether people would voluntarily believe his justifications or not. Some of Kim's closest advisers during the war were condemned for allegedly working for the Americans. Soh describes the charges as "utterly false" and "incredible."

The show trials are similar to the ones that Stalin organized during the Great Terror of the 1930s, when many veteran revolutionaries were made to offer public confessions of the most ludicrous acts of treason. Yet, in general, very few such trials took place in North Korea. In nearly all the cases, the victims simply disappeared and, indeed, sometimes reappeared without any explanation at all. Stalin carried out his purges with some token legal processes. In North Korea it seems any legal framework was dispensed with—no charges, no formal sentencing, no documents, and no appeals. Most of the victims, and their entire families, would vanish into the expanding network of camps without knowing what crimes they had committed or even knowing the lengths of their sentences. Over the next six years, Kim purged anyone with links to the Soviet Union, China, early Communist movements in Korea, or left-wing groups in the South. Reliable figures are hard to come by, but some believe that 80,000 people were caught up in the purges: "some were sent to prison, some to hard labor camps, some placed under observation."

A former North Korean who found exile in Moscow, Lim Un, claims that 90 percent of all those from the "Soviet faction" were executed or exiled to the USSR. Of the 22 members of the first DPRK cabinet, 17 were executed, assassinated, or purged. After the Chinese withdrawal in 1958, all those with links to China, including the leader of the Yanan faction, Kim Tu-bong, who had gone to Mao's wartime capital, met the same fate. From 1958–60, an additional 9,000 people were reportedly purged from the Party and killed, usually for being "anti-party elements, factionalists, poisonous elements and counter-revolutionaries." All those South Koreans who had moved to the North were also condemned as "reactionary and anti-party elements."

The purges also targeted individuals outside the Party. Two hundred thousand North Korean Christians fled to the South, and Kim destroyed 2,000 temples and churches, and 400 Buddhist shrines. All the remaining 109,000 Christians suffered persecution, and by 1962 Kim claimed in a speech to have executed all Protestant and Catholic priests and sent all other religious figures to the camps. The terror spread to all levels of the Party. Kim had 600,000 party members investigated, and 450,000 were punished in some way for violating Party rules. By the late 1960s, two-thirds of the positions for local cadres stood vacant because their occupants had been killed, detained, or demoted. By the end no one was left who was capable of contradicting the bogus history that Kim Il Sung presented as the truth.

CHAPTER 3

The Making of a God King

One afternoon, in February 1997, an elderly man with a shock of white hair, dressed against the winter cold, stepped out of the North Korean Embassy in Beijing, saying he was going shopping. At the Friendship Store, he slipped past his minders, calmly hailed a passing taxi, and demanded to go to the South Korean Consulate. There he told an astonished clerk that he wished to be given political asylum.

Any defection from North Korea was big news in 1997, but for Hwang Jang-yop to walk out was akin, as the *Washington Post* put it, to Goebbels walking out on Hitler.[1] Hwang had started working in Kim Il Sung's private office in 1958, and he moved within the upper ranks of the world's most secretive regime for another 39 years. He was the chief ideologue and creator of the country's *Juche* philosophy, which had turned Kim Il Sung into a living god.

Over the next six weeks, North Korean plainclothes agents in leather jackets waited outside trying to snatch the 74-year-old scholar, whom Pyongyang reported had been kidnapped. Busloads of Chinese police dressed in riot gear surrounded the consulate after shots were fired at the building's rear windows. After lengthy negotiations, Hwang and his companion, Kim Duk-hong, were finally allowed to leave China, and in April arrived in Seoul, calling for the overthrow of Kim Jong Il's regime, which Hwang termed as monstrous as Adolf Hitler's.

Once in South Korea, Hwang began writing books and articles, giving interviews, and occasionally making speeches. Here, for the first time, was a real insider who could tear aside the curtain of conjecture that has hidden the inner life of the North Korean regime. Hwang was able to describe the details of how North Korea mutated from a harsh Stalinist personality cult into something unique, a hereditary and absolute monarchy in which members of the ruling family are worshipped as living gods by a society divided along the lines of a feudal caste system.

Kim recruited Hwang after the death of Stalin, when Pyongyang was caught in the growing rift between Moscow and Beijing. Hwang first joined the Party while working as an economics teacher. After studying Marxism at the Kim Il Sung University, in 1950 he went off to Moscow University, where he was awarded a doctorate, the equivalent of a U.S. Master's degree, in 1953. A year later he was the top lecturer on Marxist philosophy at the Kim Il Sung University. In January 1958, Kim Il Sung summoned him to work in his cabinet and join a team of four secretaries. Three of them were specialists in economics and their job was to polish Kim's crude remarks, described by Hwang as "disorderly and illogical." By this time, Kim was busy purging his party of Chinese, Soviet, and South Korean Communists, having instead surrounded himself with former partisans.

When Kim assumed power in 1945, he introduced the worship of Stalin, and all public and government meetings ended with cheers for Stalin. Then, very quickly, and at a speed that exceeded similar developments in the rest of the Soviet Bloc, he established a dictatorship cult of his own. In 1949, while still in his thirties, he erected the first statue in his honor and had the sole university in the North named after him. Kim ensured too that the Party monopolized political control over youth leagues and access to education. Everyone, even the cleaners, had to be proven loyal Party members before they were allowed access to the Kim Il Sung University.

None of his partisan colleagues had attended school beyond the age of 14, so Kim formed what a Soviet diplomat termed "a brains' trust." As the top adviser on ideology, Hwang was asked to develop a Korean interpretation of Marxism as Kim sought to distance himself from Beijing and Moscow. Hwang discovered in a speech that Kim had delivered to party cadres in December 1955 a useful phrase. Kim had said that "*Juche* means Chosun's revolution." Chosun is the traditional name for Korea and *Juche* philosophy was turned into a brand of xenophobic nationalism that resident diplomats were soon labeling fascistic.

"We decided to expand the term *Juche* and added meaning to it," Hwang wrote. "We then agreed to interpret it as meaning that everything in the North should be decided in conformity with Chosun's reality and in the interests of the Chosun people and their quest for revolution."[2]

By the end of 1959, Hwang was the deputy of the Party's propaganda office, and by 1965, at the age of 40, he was made president of Kim Il Sung University, the high priest of Jucheism. He not only canonized the "theory" but also oversaw a team of scholars who kept fabricating the past to keep up with each twist in its development.

Reports unearthed from Hungarian diplomatic archives show that in May 1963, a Soviet diplomat described Kim Il Sung's advisers as a "political Gestapo." When Pyongyang compelled Koreans to divorce their European spouses and launched a campaign against foreign marriages, which a senior Party official described as "a crime against the Korean race," the East German ambassador termed the speech "Goebbelsian." Admittedly these comments were made when relations with the Soviet Bloc had reached a low point, but they make the point that Pyongyang's *Juche* is not just a brand of Stalinism but a racist ideology. The North Koreans sought to eradicate all traces of foreign influence and then to prevent anything new from the outside world from penetrating.[3]

On Kim's orders Hwang went through his reports and speeches, erasing all the praise of Stalin. Only literature by Kim Il Sung was listed as compulsory reading by party cells, and soon all works by Marx, Engels, Lenin, and Stalin were not only dropped from the study list but became unavailable even to the Party faithful.

Hwang also rewrote the history of Korean Communism, rubbing out, both figuratively and literally, anyone else from the record. Communist pioneers were denounced as anti-Party and sent to the camps. The activities of Kim Il Sung's partisan followers became the only legitimate Korean Communist movement. Their deeds had to be inflated because as Hwang later admitted, they had actually been quite insignificant. Their biggest military success was to hold a small town of 1,400 houses for 24 hours. The history of *Juche* was also reinvented; by the end, it was teenage Kim who coined the term, in 1930.

Jucheism served a useful purpose by establishing a national church of Communism and therefore insulating North Korea from the bitter schism between Moscow and Beijing that split the Communist world. Kim largely sided with Mao during the Sino-Soviet split, and his disgust with Nikita Khrushchev's policies of peaceful coexistence with the West turned to fury when Khrushchev backed down during the Cuban missile crisis. The Koreans then outdid the Chinese in reviling the revisionist Khrushchev, and set about systematically harassing Soviet and East European embassies, tapping their phones and delaying their mail.

At this point the propaganda began to veer into the realms of madness by presenting Kim as the Christ-like savior of Korea. One example of the propaganda, put out in March 1963, describes when the crew of a fishing boat, the *Minchungho*, was threatened by a storm. They gathered in the captain's cabin and began chanting excerpts from Kim's biography, recalling the anti-Japanese armed struggle for 20 minutes. The storm is said to have suddenly and miraculously subsided. It was as if by having fictionalized Kim's early life, his partisan years, his elevation to power, and his "victories" in the Korean war, all inhibitions, all contact with reality, all restraining ties with fraternal parties had been jettisoned.

The deification of Kim may have been ratcheted up to keep pace with the adulation of Mao, which peaked in the late 1960s. The iconography in both countries looks strikingly similar. Hwang points out that when China's Red Guards started making personal attacks against Kim in 1967, it spurred a new stage in the development of *Jucheism*. By then, the Koreans had concluded that they must become more self-reliant. In May 1967, the North Korean Workers Party Central Committee met in secret and approved a project to establish a "monolithic ideological system." At the 5th Party Congress in 1970, *Juche* was formally adopted as the sole guiding principle for all actions. In China, the loudest cheerleader of Mao had been his anointed successor Marshal Lin Biao, who first edited the "Little Red Book" for the army to use as its bible. After losing Mao's trust, Lin Biao died in mysterious circumstances in the early 1970s, apparently trying to flee to the Soviet Union. Mao's wife, Jiang Qing, continued inflating the cult in the hopes of succeeding in power after Mao's death in 1976. In Pyongyang, the succession struggle was between the brother of Kim Il Sung, a remote figure called Kim Yong-ju, and his eldest son, Kim Jong Il. The Dear Leader, as Kim Jong Il liked to be called, was also worried about his other siblings' call on their father's love.

"The two men's rivalry was based on who could put Kim Il Sung on a higher pedestal. Thanks to this competition, the Kim Il Sung personality cult went beyond the Soviet-style dictatorship to become a new concept called "absolutism of the Great Leader,'" Hwang writes.[4] According to Hwang, Kim Jong Il had perfected a toadying routine from an early age. He observed that when he accompanied his father on a trip to Moscow in 1959, Kim Jong Il would even help his father get up and put on his shoes. "Creating the Kim Il Sung personality cult and exaggerating his role in the revolution was the work of Kim Jong Il rather than Kim Il Sung," says Hwang.

Kim Jong Il declined the opportunity to study abroad, preferring to stick close to his father. Instead he studied at the Kim Il Sung University when Hwang was president and still in charge of shaping the *Juche* ideology. Hwang became the younger Kim's personal tutor, a sort of Marxist Socrates to the young Alexander.

Against a backdrop of deepening rivalry within the family, the entire Kim clan began to be venerated as gods. From the early 1960s onward the Korean Workers Party began to institutionalize the very un-Marxist and neo-Confucian concepts of filial piety. Visiting dignitaries had to pay their respects directly to the shrines erected to various members of the Kim family, including his grandfather and great grandfather and his aunts and uncles. Kim Il Sung's father was glorified for allegedly founding the Korean national movement and leading the anti-Japanese movement in Korea after 1919. His great-grandfather was turned into a hero who led an attack in 1860 against an American trading ship, the *General Sherman*.

Kim Jong Il entered the Party in 1964, and within a few years he was in charge of the Party's propaganda machinery. Here he could both indulge a fascination for film and drama and exploit the best opportunities to inflate his father's cult and demonstrate his filial piety to the full. He seems to have taken his cue from what was happening in China. Jiang Qing, the former Shanghai starlet and Mao's wife, used her position to produce a series of Maoist revolutionary-model operas and intensify the worship of her husband as she struggled to become the successor. Kim supervised a team of ghost writers in a unit called 4.15 that also produced a string of revolutionary operas, like "The Sea of Blood" and "The Flower Girl," in the same style and form as Jiang Qing's. They elevated dying for Kim into a cause loftier than the most ardent patriotism. As one slogan puts it, "Glory is theirs, whether they are alive or dead, as long as they have dedicated themselves to the task of carrying out the teachings of the Great Leader."

By 1970, Kim Jong Il was also churning out works like "The Brilliant Master Piece of Our Great Leader Comrade Kim Il Sung who created the Party's unique system of ideology" and "On Correctly Understanding Kim-Il-Sungism's Originality."

Hwang found himself thrust aside. It was now his former pupil Kim Jong Il who was masterminding the development of "Kim Il Sungism," and Hwang has bitterly complained that Kim Jong Il perverted the true universal ideals of his *Juche* ideology to recreate a feudal state. "Filial piety in feudalism demands that children regard their parents as their benefactors and masters because they would not have existed without their parents," Hwang says. "Loyalty to the Great Leader was the most sublime expression of loyalty to the party, working class, and the highest moral good is dedicating your body and mind to the Great Leader."

The logic behind this filial piety was that the Great Leader had created the Communist Party, and without it, there would be no proletariat and indeed no Kim Il Sung nation of North Korea. History was twisted to show that nothing had existed before Kim Il Sung. Therefore, as the "father of the people," they owed him their complete obedience and indeed, as Hwang wrote, "everything in their lives." When the government builds someone a house or buys his produce, such acts are all special considerations granted by the Great Leader. When reprimanding someone, party officials say, "The Great Leader has clothed you, fed you, sent you to school and made you the master of state and society, and in return you forget all about his great benevolence and fail to pledge all your loyalty and filial piety to him, you ungrateful and immoral lout."[5]

Hwang accuses Kim Jong Il, somewhat unconvincingly, of managing to turn Stalinism on its head by making the people serve the leader instead of the other way around. "Stalinism acknowledged the necessity of the dictatorship of the highest leader but maintained that the highest leader had to serve the party, the working class and the people," Hwang writes. However, in *Jucheism* the people serve the highest leader and the working class is indebted to the Great Leader's benevolence.

To celebrate Kim's sixtieth birthday in 1972, Kim Jong Il erected a giant 70-foot-high statue covered in gold leaf costing some U.S. $800 million in the center of Pyongyang. He now towered over the city like a god and the Worker's Party's constitution was amended to declare that it was "guided only by Kim Il Sung's ideology and revolutionary thoughts." Sixty is the age at which a Chinese emperor would customarily choose his successor; in some cases he would keep this a secret and carry the name in a bag around his neck. By the time Kim Jong Il was 30, the competition had reached its peak. In the next year both Kim Jong Il's uncle, Kim Yong-ju, and his younger half-brother, Kim Pyong Il, disappeared from view. Diplomats in Pyongyang heard that Kim Yong-ju was suffering from a long but undefined illness. Some years later, Kim Pyong Il turned up again serving as an ambassador in several East Bloc countries.

Then at a secret meeting of the Worker's Party politburo in April 1974, Kim Jong Il was formally anointed as his father's successor. From then on he came to be referred to as the "Dear Leader." Initially, he kept a low profile. His image did not appear next to his father's in all offices and homes until 1988, and he did everything to avoid appearing to threaten his father's unique status. He began accompanying his father on his official tours but North Koreans did not hear his voice in any public broadcast until 1992, when he formally took charge of the military and the radio carried one brief phrase—"glory to the people's heroic military."

That same year the Party crossed another threshold in the deification of Kim Jong Il by adopting the "Ten Principles for the Establishment of One Ideology." The Ten Principles, elaborated in 65 clauses, are the country's Ten Commandments. Any violation must be punished within 15 days; desecrating any image of either Kim, sitting on their portrait even when in the newspaper, or breaking the frame of their picture constitute crimes. Kim Il Sung's brother had first put the Principles forward in 1967, but it was Kim Jong Il who made them state policy. Hwang claims the Ten Principles constitute Kim Jong Il's personal political platform. They declared Kim to be the leader for all Korean people and the savior for all people engaged in the international Communist movement. This, says Hwang, is when the "Great Leader's absolutism" became institutionalized. All party members had to:

1) Dedicate ourselves to struggle to arouse the whole society in pursuing the revolutionary thought of the great Chairman, Comrade Kim Il Sung.

2) To offer our highest loyalty to the great Chairman, Comrade Kim Il Sung.

3) To make absolute the authority of the great Chairman, Comrade Kim Il Sung.

4) To believe in the revolutionary thought of the great Chairman, Comrade Kim Il Sung and to maintain the uniformity of the teachings of the Chairman.

And so forth. Each member must also observe the following principles:

1) A Party member only recognizes the authority of Comrade Kim Il Sung.

2) A Party member accepts unconditionally the teachings of the Chairman and regards them as a yardstick for making all decisions.

3) When making reports, discussing a topic, giving a lecture, or quoting from documents, one has to refer to the Chairman's teachings and never speak or write about something inconsistent with the Chairman's views.

By requiring slavish obedience to one man, the state and the entire nation were turned into his personal property. It created a hereditary dynasty in which every institution, including the Workers Party, was reduced to insignificance. The move was justified by the adoption of a new political theory, the "Theory of the Immortal Socio-Political Body." The core of this theory holds that "the Suryong (or Leader) is the supreme brain of a living body, the Party is the nerve of that living body, and the masses are only endowed with life when they offer their absolute loyalty."

The Theory states that "without the Suryong, which is the brain, and the Party, which is the nerve, the masses will remain dead bodies because they are no more than arms and legs." And that the "popular masses are the controlling body of history and revolution," but they need a brain, "the top brain," which alone can understand and coordinate the desires of the masses and unite them into one socio-political organism. "For the popular masses to be an independent subject of the revolution, they must be united into one organization with one ideology under the leadership of the party and the leader. Only the masses, who are united organizationally and ideologically, can shape their own destiny independently and creatively." Only those totally loyal to the *Suryong* can become transformed into "self-reliant beings," and only the masses guided by the Party and the *Suryong* are the "masters of history." Indeed, if an individual submerges himself entirely in the being of the *Suryong*, then he will achieve immortality.

An explicit aim of the *Juche* cult, according to Hwang, was to stop people from thinking for themselves. "You must understand that the North Korean system is far more brutal and inhumane than Stalinism. It totally dominates the minds of most normal people. It is hard to believe but people cannot think critically," he said. "This breeding of a personality cult is called 'publicity of the Great Leader's greatness,' and the entire curriculum is under the strict control of the party so that all subjects fit the purpose of emphasizing the greatness of the Great Leader."

The brainwashing starts at two when all children are put in state nurseries and start to be immersed in the Kim thought that they should "think, speak and act as Kim Il Sung and Kim Jong Il." They're taught to emulate the childhood years of Kim Il Sung and Kim Jong Il and then go on to study textbooks in which everything, even science and arithmetic, are larded with quotes from the teachings of Kim Il Sung and Kim Jong Il. "From primary school to university, subjects aimed at strengthening the personality cult account for 33.3 percent of the total curriculum (one-third of all subjects taught). These subjects include history of the revolutionary activities of Kim Il Sung and Kim Jong Il and all their writings about arts and culture. Social Science subjects are naturally all about the Great Leader; even subjects like Physics and Foreign Language & Literature are geared in the same direction," Hwang said.

It is unsettling to witness just how effective this has been. When I visited the country in 1986, our group of journalists was taken to the Ninth of June Senior middle girl's school. There the children literally performed numbers called, "The Song of General Kim Il Sung," "The Song of Our Comrade Beloved Leader," and "We shall live forever in the land of bliss, with his care and happiness in our heart."

One girl, Cho Hong-hee, said that Kim Il Sung gave them their clothes, their toys, their schoolbooks, and that they loved him more than their fathers and mothers. To them he was "the genius of mankind," "a peerless patriot and sun of the nation," "the first great leader in several thousand years," and "the genius of revolution and construction," "who from his earliest days struck people with his exceptional intelligence." The girl declared that she could live without her parents but never without the love of the Kims. Asked what would happen if Kim Il Sung died, she looked horri-fied and then said such a thing could never happen.

It is fascinating to try and piece together how this quasi-religious political cult melds together elements from Korea's own history and borrowings from foreign political and religious movements.

Hwang repeatedly claims that Kim Jong Il has been a keen student of Hitler and his methods. "He worshipped Germany's Hitler from an early date and wanted to become such a dictator as Hitler," wrote Hwang in one article published in the monthly magazine *Chosun*. The *Suryong* doctrine certainly seems to be a replica of the Nazi Party's *Fuehrerprinzip*, which transformed Hitler into the divine executor of Germany's national destiny and hence the source of all laws. The rules of the Worker's Party are almost the same as those listed in the Organization Book of the National Socialist Party of Germany.[6]

Lenin and Stalin also provided models, while Maoism makes an espe-cially revealing contrast. Jiang Qing, who introduced such novelties as the daily "loyalty dance" that the Chinese had to perform before an image of Mao every morning, still failed to secure power at the death of her husband in 1976. The Chinese Communist Party, with a broader membership of revolutionaries, resisted her claims to the succession and she was arrested within months of Mao's death in a coup d'état by veteran revolutionaries who quickly began abandoning many core Maoist policies. None of Mao's children or relatives of Mao have ever risen to senior positions.

The various twentieth-century totalitarian movements may perhaps have put down roots in Korea and in China because of a long tradition of both authoritarian and centralized government. Emperors required absolute obedience and were the source of all laws. In the Ming dynasty (1364–1666), officials had to lecture the masses on the philosophical beliefs of its founding Emperor Zhu Yuanzhang. The state printed and distributed books of his ideas and held morality classes in special pavilions erected in every village. When later in the Ming dynasty eunuchs like Wang Zhen usurped power from emperors too young or too incompetent to rule by themselves, they built temples across the country where people came to make offerings and demonstrate their loyalty.

Kim Jong Il built similar study halls all over the country in which people assembled for two hours a day to worship Kim Il Sung and memorize his speeches. Even at the height of the famine, the state continued building more and more study halls in which the starving population exhausted after a day's work, had to come and praise the benevolence of the Kims.

Most aspects of North Korea's *Juche* kingdom—the caste system, the slavery, the command economy, the officials, the isolationism, and the police state—can all be recognized from the past. In the third century A.D., much of Korea was under the rule of a Silla kingdom with a system of hereditary social stratification, known as a "bone rank system," not too dissimilar from that of North Korea. The rulers were known as "holy bone" families and an individual's hereditary bloodline determined each individual's place in the social ranking. The ruling elite was divided into "hallowed bone" clans of the royal house or the "true bone" clans who had royal blood but were not qualified to become kings.

Sons of the top aristocracy were exempted from military service (as are members of North Korea's ruling elite) and instead were automatically allocated top offices in the bureaucracy. This gilded youth joined the Hwarang or Flower Corps that prepared the most gifted sons of the aristocracy to hold the top administrative posts in a 17-grade bureaucracy. Below the officials came the ordinary people who were graded in bone ranks: one, two, and three.

In the later Koryo State, everyone was equally conscious of rank. There was the *yangban* or official gentry class, and another class of artisans and technicians, known as the *chungin* or middle people. Beneath them were the *yangin*, who were the freeborn common people. At the very bottom were the *chon*, or base class, which included slaves and those doing unclean jobs such as butchers, leather workers, and entertainers.

Hereditary slaves have existed throughout Korea's history, and the institution was only formally abolished in 1894. The names of slaves were kept in a slave registry, and in some periods it is estimated that as much as a third of the population was legally classed as slaves. Thus, the de facto slavery of North Korea's penal colonies may not seem so shocking to any Korean who experienced only a brief interlude between the abolition of feudal slavery and the Japanese occupation. The Japanese treated all Koreans as a subject race, and employed equally large numbers to labor in Japanese factories and mines in slave conditions.

Equally, in the last Choson dynasty (1392–1910), the state ran what amounted to an internal identification system common to all totalitarian states. This was called the "tag law" because every male from age 15 had to wear a rectangular tag around his neck that gave his name, age, and residential district. Differences in status were immediately apparent. Top officials had ivory nametags, and there were five different types of wooden tags for the lower orders. In this system a peasant had such a low status that when addressed by an official, they were expected to kneel in obedience. Those with wooden tags lacked the right to do many things, such as ride a horse.

It is easy to see the similarities with North Korea's system of *songbun*, whereby the entire population is graded into 47, some say 67, ranks according to their class background. This determines everything right down to the monthly food rations. The most trusted classes are families that fought the Japanese, veterans of the Korean War, descendants of pre-revolutionary working people, and especially poor peasant farmers and factory workers. Only such families are allowed to live in Pyongyang and other urban areas where they enjoy privileged access to goods, housing, and hospitals.

At the other end of the scale are the mistrusted people who belonged to the pre-1945 educated elite, who owned lands, who have relatives in the South or abroad, or who were Christians, merchants, lawyers, or workers for the Japanese. The Choson dynasty, like the Kim dynasty, relied on a system of very tight social controls to manage the economy. In the Communist State, farmers had to hand over a large share of the harvest directly to the state, and they could not leave their village without permission.

The feudal state also controlled most industries, ran factories, and had a monopoly over the distribution of commodities like salt. Foreign trade was discouraged and little took place other than exchanges controlled by the state as part of its diplomacy. Internal commerce was tightly controlled, and peasant markets were limited to once every five days—as they are today. The feudal state placed the population under tight surveillance. Peasants were organized into five households whose members were mutually responsible for ensuring that no member absconded or failed to carry out the obligatory corvée duty—the voluntary labor on public works that could last as long as three months. This rigid system of mutual surveillance dates back to the Qin dynasty established by the first emperor of China before 200 B.C. The system sometimes broke down. When there were famines, peasants would run away to escape the taxes that they could not pay. Some became brigands outside the control of the state or escaped into Manchuria, and some uprisings grew into full-scale rebellions.

This kind of society is usually described as Confucian or neo-Confucian, and the Koreans have borrowed heavily from Chinese political philosophers. Although Chinese and Korean officials did worship the Chinese sage, the system borrows more from the totalitarian ideology known as "Legalism," adopted by the Wei state of the first Chinese emperor. He, in fact, buried Confucian scholars alive and burnt all books of philosophy other than legalist tracts. So oppressive was his system of government that after his death, his empire was toppled by a revolt.

The Legalist doctrine with its semi-divine emperor was implemented with particular vigor by China's Ming dynasty (1364–1644), which adopted a later re-interpretation of Confucian teachings. This was diligently copied in Korea by the contemporaneous Choson dynasty. It is noticeable that even after the downfall of the Ming in China in 1644, the Koreans demonstrated their loyalty to the Ming system by wearing Ming dynasty clothing long after it was abandoned in China. Today, South Korea is the last place left where traditional Confucian ceremonies are still performed by priests at temples devoted to the Chinese sage.

South Korea remains heavily colored by Confucian notions of hierarchy and respect for elders; people are submissive to a state in which the officials are considered as the moral guardians of society. It is rare for younger people to correct their elders even when they make mistakes. Even some South Korean airplane crashes have been blamed on the unwillingness of younger pilots to challenge the judgment of a more senior captain.

Confucianism places a particular stress on the importance of filial piety and family ties; so in this respect Kim Jong Il's loyalty to his father falls into a familiar pattern of Korean behavior. Kim Jong Il's propaganda has not shied away from using Confucian phrases such as "mandate of heaven" or "filial piety" to garner legitimacy for his rule.

Korean records show various kings behaving much like the Kims by fabricating noble lineages or insisting on utopian schemes based on neo-Confucian ideas of social harmony. The royal court was often swept by purges that destroyed whole families of any member who came to be suspected of treason. It is also worth recalling the short period in Korea's history when Western political ideas and Christian values came to the fore. The period of liberalization from the close of the nineteenth century to when the Japanese took control of Korea was briefer even than in China. The Japanese set up a very authoritarian fascist police state. They again combined the worship of the emperor and a Confucian society with a centralized state directed by a strong bureaucracy and a controlled economy.

Visitors approach the Kumsusan Memorial Palace through a grove of trees in beautiful parkland. Passing along a monumental avenue, one enters through the giant copper doors and walks along the spotless Italian marble floors (shoes covered in protective cloth) to Kim Il Sung's embalmed body. After half a mile, one crosses a series of vast marble corridors to reach a long chamber with a giant white marble statue of the "Great Leader" illuminated from behind by pink lights to give the effect of the rosy glow of dawn.

The palace opened in 1995 and is dedicated to Kim Il Sung, who is now described as the country's "eternal president." The memorial reputedly cost over U.S. $90 million to build. In front of his crystal sarcophagus, visitors stifle their sobs and bow reverentially before the body clothed in a dark suit and covered by a flag from the chest down. Adjoining rooms contain some of his favorite possessions: a train carriage from Stalin and a bullet-proof Mercedes from Kim Jong Il. The memorial also maintains a selection of some of the 140,000 gifts the "Great Leader" received from around the world.

The Party now openly describes Kim Il Sung as a god—the "Sun of Love"—"superior to Christ in love, superior to Buddha in benevolence, superior to Confucius in virtue and superior to Mohammed in justice."[7] "The sun of the nation. . . . not only protected the political life of the people but also saved their physical life, his love cured the sick and gave them a new life, like the spring rain falling on the sacred territory of Korea," ran the official eulogy.

On the third anniversary of his death, North Korea issued a decree adopting a *Juche* calendar in place of the Gregorian system, with Year Zero marking the birth of Kim Il Sung in 1912 and his April 15 birthday as the "Day of the Sun" and the "greatest festival for the Korean nation." The transfiguration of Kim Il Sung from a foot soldier in Stalin's vast empire to the supreme being was now complete. North Korea therefore became the world's first hereditary Communist state with a leadership sanctioned by divine right. Kim Jong Il managed to pull this off by creating a new syncretic religion that also borrowed from various modern Korean religious movements like Chondoism; feudal Korea was Confucian but not monolithic. The harshness of the Confucian and feudal code was often mitigated by Buddhism, as well as the Korean folk religions and customs. Then from the mid-nineteenth century, Christianity began to exert a major influence on Korean thought. Radical social reform, nationalism, and Protestant ideas of an elect community or nation helped inspire a movement called Chondoism that was originally known as Eastern Learning or Donghak and founded by an obscure scholar, Choe Su-un, born in 1824.

In his autobiography, *With the Century*, Kim Il Sung describes at length his youthful fascination and admiration for the Donghak movement. Kim says he "considered the rebellion of the *Donghak* followers as a great event, which adorned the modern history of our people's struggle against aggression and feudality, and the heroes the war produced were eagles exerting a great influence upon the political and mental life of the Korean nation in modern times."[8] The Donghak movement was different but comparable to the millenarian Taiping movement in China led by Hong Xiuquan, who proclaimed himself the brother of Jesus Christ and almost overthrew the Manchu dynasty to establish a new social order. Like the Taiping rebellion's founder Hong Xiuquan, Choe had both failed his civil service examinations and come under the influence of Catholic missionaries. He then claims to have received divine instructions. In 1862, after meditating in a hut for six years, a strange monk appeared before Choe and gave him a mysterious book called "Pray for Heaven." As he trembled, Choe said he heard the mysterious voice of Hanulnim, the God of Chondogyo, instructing him: "Receive my spiritual symbol (that is the sacred writings) and deliver mankind from sickness. Receive my incantation and teach man for me."

He began to convert followers, baptizing them with holy water, reading to them from his "Great Eastern Scriptures," and asking them to chant hymns. A 21-syllable-long incantation calls on each man to "harmonize his mind with the ultimate energy of Hanulnim." As Chondogyo became an organized religion, it patterned itself on the Christian churches, with Sunday services, hymn singing, holy water baptisms, and annual festivals such as April 5, known as Heavenly Day, to celebrate the founding of the religion. Believers accept a cosmic chronology in which a new era began with the founding of Chondogyo, ushering in a utopia centered on the Korean Peninsula and its people.

The appeal to Korean nationalism is reinforced by contrasting this indigenous "Eastern Learning" with the disloyal adherents to "Western Learning" preached by Catholic and other missionaries. Donghak became a patriotic political force when its members started a rebellion in 1894 in the rural town of Kobu in Jeolla province to protest government corruption. A peasant army sprang up that was suppressed only after the Korean court called in troops from China and Japan. Donghak slogans became increasingly antiforeign, urging the Koreans to "drive out the Japanese dwarfs and Western barbarians." They also demanded basic social reforms including the burning of the slave registries, the end of discrimination against the seven lower castes, and the abolition of the "wooden tag" identification system and the cutting of top knots. The modernizing drive was bolstered by calls for egalitarianism and high standards of public conduct. Donghak troops won public trust by their disciplined observance of military conduct rules.

The rebellion was quashed with the loss of 300,000 lives, and the Donghak leaders were executed. The impact of the uprising was immense. First, the Korean court accepted the need to meet the Donghak demands for social reforms, but the intervention of some two thousand Chinese and seven thousand Japanese soldiers spelled the end of any hopes of Korea freeing itself from being a tributary state of China. Japan fought with the declining Qing dynasty on land and sea and defeated its navy comprehensively by 1895. With the Treaty of Shimonoseki, China effectively recognized Korea as a Japanese protectorate. Ten years later when Russia challenged Japan for control over Korea, the Russian navy was also defeated in several engagements.

Under Japanese rule, the Donghaks registered themselves as a religion called Chondoism and went on to play a leading role in the 1919 March First Independence Movement against the Japanese. The Chondoists then went underground, setting up resistance cells inside Korea and the Koryo Revolutionary Committee, and organizing powerful exile movements in Shanghai and Manchuria, including the Supreme Revolutionary Chondoist

Commission. The Donghaks not only helped to foster a new and powerful sense of national consciousness, they also became a template for similar movements that combined religion and nationalism. One of these was *Jeungsan-gyo*, another was a form of Buddhism called *Daejonggyo*, which in Manchuria helped finance some anti-Japanese guerrillas. In the 1960s, there was Park Tae-sun's Olive Tree Movement. Park is a charismatic faith healer who was expelled by the Presbyterian Church in the 1950s for heresy; he went on to build two towns for his tens of thousands of followers.

Such messiahs promise both personal and national salvation. Leadership in these cults can only be passed from one divine master or teacher to another. Followers are required to show absolute and blind loyalty to the "divine master" and take part in mass demonstrations of devotion and respect that require displays of excessive emotion. They are "brainwashed" by the endless repetition of slogans and catechisms, and are required to hand over all personal possessions for which they are promised a personal transformation and a part in the creation of a new utopia.

Although U.S. State Department human rights reports sometimes describe *Juche* as a religion or a cult, it lacks any overt divine revelations like Chondoism. Yet as a Marxist, Kim Il Sung convinced his followers that he possessed a unique insight into the hidden patterns of history, that he could foretell the future and intervene to change the course of history. He held out the promise of a new glorious era for Korea that would start after he had unified the Korean race under one great leader.

The Unification Church founded by the Reverend Moon Sun-myung with some four million followers around the world is the most successful of these cults. His church—with its holy family and its reputation for brainwashing—bears more than a passing similarity to the *Juche* state. The Rev. Moon also offers the comforting message that the great suffering of the Korean people in the twentieth century is no accident but part of a divine plan for his new chosen people. Moon preaches that the "beginning of the cosmic unification will happen after the Korean Peninsula is united."

In many ways, Rev. Moon's life is a mirror image of Kim Il Sung's. According to official accounts Moon was born in 1920, into a family of farmers in what is now North Korea. As a boy he studied at a Confucian school and around 1930, his parents became fervent Presbyterian Christians, just like the parents of Kim Il Sung. The young Moon became a

Sunday school teacher in a district where many congregations were "spirit-filled" and expecting the imminent arrival of a new messiah who would be born in Korea.[9]

On Easter Sunday in 1935, as he was praying in the mountains, Moon claims that Jesus appeared in a vision and asked him to complete the task of establishing God's kingdom on earth and bringing peace to humankind. "Moon Sun-myung studied the Bible and many other religious teachings in order to unravel these mysteries of life and human history. During this time, he went into ever deeper communion with God and entered the vast battlefield of the spirit and flesh," say Unification Church accounts. Moon then went to study electrical engineering in Japan, and while details of this period are sketchy, he was imprisoned for agitating for Korean independence. After 1945, he organized his beliefs into the Divine Principle and upon his return to Korea began to spread his teachings.

"Subsequently, he was called by God to travel to the communist North. There, he began to teach publicly, despite the dangers of doing so in a country where religion was not welcome," the church says. Then in November 1946, he was jailed, tortured, and almost died in a labor camp: "The police thought him dead and threw his body into the prison yard. Some of his followers found him and carried him away to tend to his broken body. Miraculously, Reverend Moon survived and regained his strength. Undaunted, he began preaching in public again."

Moon was arrested again in April 1948, and sentenced to five years of hard labor in Hungnam prison, which he describes as a death camp where prisoners were worked to death shifting heavy bags of corrosive lime that ate away their skin. Few prisoners lasted more than six months, but Moon survived for nearly three years until 1950. The Communist guards had begun executing the prisoners rather than allowing them to fall into encroaching enemy hands; the day before it was Moon's turn, American forces reached the prison gates. Moon then returned to Pyongyang strengthened by his belief in his divine mission and spent 40 days searching for his surviving followers. When he found two of them, they walked together southward until they reached the port of Busan, where they built the first Unification Church from discarded army ration boxes. On May 1, 1954, Reverend Moon opened the Holy Spirit Association for the Unification of World Christianity in Seoul. The church attracted followers from the famous Christian woman's university, Ewha University, and the university chancellor became alarmed. Newspapers in Seoul suddenly began to print stories about the Unification Church, alleging it was hosting sex orgies. Moon was thrown in jail again and came under suspicion for being a North Korean agent.

Somehow the Church survived these scandals and by 1957, it had spread to 30 Korean cities and towns. After 1958, Moon began sending missionaries abroad, first to Japan and then to America. By 2000, the Unification Church claimed to have 4.5 million full-time members around the world, including 50,000 in the United States. Moon settled first in California in the 1960s, but now the headquarters are in New York. Moon reportedly spends much of his time on a huge plot of land in Brazil acquired by the Church for a sort of religious colony. The Church had moved far beyond accepted Christian beliefs. In his Divine Principle, Moon preaches that the Second Coming will take place in Korea and makes it clear that he is indeed the new Messiah. He claims that Korea is destined to receive the Lord of the Second Advent and that the Korean people will establish the "Third Israel" because they are "God's elect" and "the chosen people."[10]

He preaches that the First Israel suffered the 400-year slavery in Egypt, and the early Christians, the Second Israel, then underwent another 400-year persecution at the hands of the Romans, whom he calls "the Satanic world of that time." He sees the Koreans' 40 years of suffering under the Japanese from 1905–45 as a similar defining event. "Naturally, the Korean people, being the Third Israel, must suffer slavery for a certain length of time corresponding to the number '40' under a nation of the satanic side," claims the Divine Principle.

America's role is vital. It is the "elder son nation" to Korea and the center of the Second Israel. Moon believes he has been called upon to heal a world divided between democracy and Communism, or as he more frequently describes it, between God and Satan. In this way, the 38th parallel of Korea is the frontline in the cosmic clash between good and evil. These beliefs have led Moon to become heavily involved in supporting right-wing anti-Communist leaders and vocally supporting Republican presidents, including Richard Nixon during the Watergate scandal; he has also founded such organizations as the Win Over Communism (WOC) and the Asian People's Anti-Communist League. The latter was allegedly financed from shadowy but powerful figures from Japan's extreme right wing.

Part of Moon's appeal for Koreans is his view that they have a special and manifest destiny. "God has to cut this nationwide sacrifice in two, just as He had Abraham cut his offerings," the Rev. Moon preaches. At other times, he describes the nation as the sacrificial lamb. "The historical course of untold misery, which the Korean people have gone through, was the necessary way for them to walk as the people of God's elect. As a result, the path of affliction has led the Korean people to a great blessedness," he says. Moon promises that when the two Koreas are united, the center of civilization will shift to this "New Eden." Moon credits himself with the power of uniting all religions, and he promises that one day soon all of mankind will speak the same language.

Reading Moon's writings one gets the sense—as with reading those of Kim Il Sung—of the founder's claims becoming wilder and wilder with the passage of time. And there is also the eerily similar "personality cults" centered on the founder's families. Moon's marriage in March 1960 is therefore elevated into something foretold in the Book of Revelations. His wife is Han Hak-ja who with her mother, a devout Christian, fled the South during the Korean War, joined the Unification Church, and married Moon at age 17. They now claim to be the "True Parents" of the world, the first couple to enjoy the complete blessing of God, and credit themselves with the power to bring forth children with no original sin. His followers believe their marriage marks the beginning of the "restoration of humankind back into God's lineage."

The Unification Church preaches that Lucifer seduced Eve and that this sexual union caused the spiritual fall of mankind as well as the fall of Lucifer. They believe that Eve then entered into a sexual relationship with Adam, which resulted in the physical fall of mankind. Therefore the "True Parents" are concerned with blessing couples in order to "graft them onto the true lineage of God" and thus create the ideal families as the "starting point for a peaceful world." As such, the Church likes to host mass weddings in sports stadiums at which marriage partners, whom Moon has often personally selected from photographs and brief biographies, are joined together. So far they have blessed some 40,000 couples.

Life inside Moon's Church is also colored by various Korean folk and shamanistic beliefs, ranging from geomancy to prophesy. It was, however, the "brainwashing" techniques that began to attract public attention in

California in the 1970s when the Church became involved in a number of widely publicized scandals. Some suspect Moon simply copied the "brain-washing" techniques he observed, and participated in, during his years in Kim Il Sung's labor camp. In the 1970s, Moon's tax-exempt status came under scrutiny, and he was imprisoned in 1981 after being found guilty of evading income taxes. After completing 13 months of his sentence, he was freed, more convinced than ever that he was God's instrument for the salvation of the world.

Yet as with the North Korean messiah, the religious claims sometimes seem merely a front for personal aggrandizement. The Unification Church established its own enterprise group in South Korea that supplied the military with everything from rifles to tank cannons. Just how wealthy the Church has become is a matter of speculation, but one indication is that in the wake of the 1997 Asian Financial Crisis the group had debts valued at U.S. $2 billion. Much as North Korea's income from gold exports, arms sales, drug smuggling, and foreign aid is inseparable from the private wealth of the Kim family, the Unification Church's dubious business ventures and assets are treated as the private possessions of the secretive Moon family. Known in Moony circles as the "True Family," there were originally 13 offspring, but several have died and others have tried to escape their father's powerful presence. They describe their upbringing in a string of palatial homes as a stifling existence in the shadow of an all-controlling father. Inevitably there is speculation about which son is going to inherit the empire when Moon dies.

Both Moon and Kim Il Sung convinced their respective followers that each was on a divinely sanctioned mission to unify the Korean Peninsula. While Kim Il Sung sought to manipulate Korean nationalism into a self-serving religion, Moon has tried to adapt Christianity for the cause of nationalism and self-aggrandizement.

CHAPTER 4

Slave State

When Ahn Myong-chol entered the gates of a prison camp No. 11 for the first time, he saw milling around the yard ragged creatures so short and crippled he wondered if they were human. "On average they were about 4 feet 11, walking skeletons of skin and bone," he recalled. Even years after he had arrived in Seoul, he said the scene was so shocking it hit him "like a hammer." "Their faces were covered by cuts and scars where they had been struck. Most had no ears; they had been torn off in beatings. Many had crooked noses, only one eye or one eye turned in its socket. These deformities were the result of beatings and other kinds of mistreatment in the Gulag. About 30 percent of them bore such scars," he said. Many were missing a leg—he later estimated 2,000, or 10 percent—and they hobbled about on crude crutches or just on sticks.

Ahn spent eight years at four prison camps as a guard, often driving around in a truck to make deliveries. He said the lucky inmates would survive 20 or 30 years at most. Those that lived acquired a 90-degree curvature of the spine from carrying 40-pound loads on an A-frame on a starvation diet. Usually they were dead by 50.[1]

Ahn did not work at any of the country's ordinary prisons run by the Ministry of Public Security. Rather, he was employed by some of the country's dozen or more penal settlements called *Kwanliso,* or "special control institutions," reserved for political prisoners and their families. Only a handful of people had ever escaped alive from these camps and little was known about

them until the 1990s. The testimonies of those who did escape, like Lee
Soon-ok who described her six years in a woman's re-education camp in
Eyes of the Tailless Animals, or Kang Chol-hwan, a Korean born in Japan
who was imprisoned at the age of nine along with his entire family and
wrote *Aquariums of Pyongyang: Ten years in the North Korean Gulag*, are
so gruesome that they defy belief.

Yet their accounts are now supported by a growing body of other testimonies and by extremely detailed satellite photographs. These photos show
sprawling encampments, 20 or more miles long by 10 to 20 miles wide,
containing multiple self-contained sections or "villages." These zones are
surrounded by the high walls, watchtowers, and 13-foot-high barbed wire
fences that one expects to find at a high-security prison, and some are also
guarded by batteries of antiaircraft guns and are surrounded by minefields
and man traps to prevent an assault by airborne troops.

As a former guard, Ahn is the only witness to the camps who has gone
public with his inside knowledge of how the camps worked and their history. According to Ahn, the penal system was transformed by Kim Jong Il
after he took over the Party's security apparatus in 1973. As the secret
police and the penal camp system came under his direct control, he reorga-
nized the system, creating the North Korean equivalent of the KGB, called
the *Kukgabowibu*. When Kim took charge of the Department of Organization and Guidance of the Party Secretariat, he set up an institution called
the State Political Safeguard Agency that enabled him to threaten any Party
member.

A South Korean White Paper on Human Rights in North Korea noted
that at that time the number of inmates "swelled phenomenally," and Ahn
says that Kim Jong Il ordered more camps to be built. Ahn thinks the number of inmates immediately jumped by 80 percent, as Kim terrified the
Party elite into submission and removed all those close to his rivals, including his younger brother Kim Pyong-il. When in 1980 Kim Jong Il was
formally recognized as the official heir at the 6th Workers Party, he commissioned four more camps to accommodate at least another 15,000 new
prisoners accused of opposing his succession.

The political prisoner camps became so large that Kim Jong Il turned
them into a vital pillar of the planned economy, an army of slaves who
produced nearly all the food and goods consumed by the Party's elite.

Yodok, the name of the No. 15 *Kwanliso* in South Hamgyong, holds about 50,000 prisoners who work at a gypsum quarry, a gold mine, a textile factory, a corn distillery, and a coppersmith workshop. The inmates also raise rabbits whose fur is used to line soldiers' winter coats, and gather wild ginseng or matsutake fungi on the slopes of mountains to earn foreign currency. Camp No. 25 builds refrigerators and Seagull brand bicycles with which the regime rewards its most loyal followers, and Camps Nos. 14 and 22 supply Pyongyang's elite and its hotels with 100,000 tons of meat a year. In the No. 1 Labor Re-education Camp, Lee Soon-ok relates, the 6,000 prisoners made army uniforms, brass exported to the Soviet Union, doilies for Poland, hand knit sweaters for Japan, and paper flowers for France. The inmates work round the clock, often sleeping under their sewing machines and in fear of beatings or killings for any mistakes.

Not enough is known about the penal system, which has been in existence now for half a century, to make reliable estimates about how many people have died in the camps. It may be at least a million, assuming that 10 percent of a constant prison population of 200,000 to 300,000 perished each year. Yet the prison population probably fluctuates from year to year along with the death rate. Many defectors claim the death rate jumped sharply in the late 1980s as famine tightened its grip over the entire country and the regime took ever more savage measures to maintain order.

The Ministry of State Security, in particular its 7th Bureau, runs the camps for political prisoners, but the Ministry of Public Security runs a separate prison system for common criminals. The Ministry of State Security seems to be the larger organization, and in 1969, Kim Il Sung told the visiting head of the Soviet KGB, Yuri Andropov, that the country had 10,000 common criminals and the majority of prisoners were held for crimes against the state. Hwang Jang-yop estimates that the Ministries of Public and State Security jointly employ 300,000 fulltime officers. However the names of institutions are often changed or given duplicate names, and other bodies beside the two ministries may operate prisons, making it hard to gain a reliable overview.[2]

The first evidence about the penal settlements for political prisoners was found in North Korean Party documents captured by American forces during the Korean War. They revealed that by October 1947, there were

17 special labor camps in North Korea. "The Process and Guidelines for Executing Forced Labor," produced by the Chiefs of Internal Affairs and Judicial Affairs of the North Korean Peoples' Committee, listed six in North Hamgyong province, nine in South Pyongan province, one in North Pyongan province, and one in Hwanghae province.[3,4]

Japanese expert Professor Haruhisa Ogawa of Tokyo University claims the camps were run more leniently in those days. Prisoners were sentenced to a limited term after a formal legal process. They had limited freedoms, such as the right to go on leave and receive visits from family and relatives, and they could even watch movies. Prisoners were paid for their labor and continued to be treated as citizens.

After the Korean War, Kim Il Sung established camps in secluded mountain areas specifically to house political enemies, South Korean collaborators, landlords, and reactionaries. The first such camp was built in 1956 at a coal-mining center in South Pyongyang province. New penal settlements for political prisoners were set up after the 1958 purge when Chinese troops left the country and Kim Il Sung wiped out the pro-Chinese Yenan faction. From 1958 to 1960, some 9,000 Party members were executed and tens of thousand more were sent into permanent exile without trial.[5]

The Party security apparatus was constantly preoccupied with monitoring any sign of deviant thought and with recording what each person said at the daily political classes and weekly self-criticism sessions. The state operated a vast network of informers inside and outside the camps that enlisted as many as one in five people throughout the country who filed reports on their neighbors. Suspects were not arrested but abducted from their homes or offices; they and their families would disappear into the system without even knowing the nature of their crime or the length of their punishments.

Every few years the camps would fill up with waves of prisoners arrested during recurring "loyalty surveys," which coincided with each effort by the Kim dynasty to concentrate its absolute political power. After the Korean War, the authorities organized special "residents registration groups" and conducted eight background checks on all residents. The 1958 purges were then bolstered by a residents re-registration program, under which all "impure elements" were relocated from the capital, major cities, and sensitive border areas. This was followed by another survey from 1966 to 1967 and major efforts between April 1967 through June 1970 that resulted in the entire population being divided into three classes—the Core Class, the Wavering Class, and the Hostile Class—which were subdivided into 51 subclasses.[6]

By this time, the secret police had assembled detailed genealogical files on each individual to identify relatives down to the sixth degree. A top priority was identifying those with connections to the South or who had served under the Japanese colonial administration or who could in some way be regarded as class enemies depending on how much land or how many oxen their family had possessed before 1947. Even so, it appears that some people managed to hide their personal histories, and escapees said they were jailed when the true identity of a parent or relative was discovered years after they had joined the Party.

The Core Class consists of about 30 percent of the population, and above them is an elite of 200,000, or 1 percent of the population, which includes family and relatives of the Kims. At the bottom is the Hostile Class, amounting to about 27 percent of the population, who are always under police surveillance. Members of this class, which is hereditary, are barred from tertiary education, or party or military posts; the children of top officials enter school without examinations and are exempt from military service. A person's political background or *Songbun* also influences the treatment meted out if they are found to be wrongdoers and could determine whether a person is executed or not.

The intensive surveillance, the frequent purges and the accompanying atmosphere of arbitrary terror, the religious adoration exhibited by his subjects: None made Kim Il Sung feel secure. He told Andropov that he could not let up ideological education even for one day without fearing that subversive thoughts might creep into the minds of his subjects.[7]

In 1966, Kim ordered another round of re-registration to accompany his project to create a million-strong worker-peasant army. This round resulted in the execution of 6,000 members of the Hostile Class and exile of 15,000. Adding family members, a total of 70,000 were sent to the camps under this Cabinet Decision Number 149.[8]

The Workers Party's decision in 1967 to create a monolithic ideology around the Kim cult was accompanied by harsher rules inside the camps; and there was a new camp set up for intellectuals and some of the 90,000

Koreans who had volunteered to emigrate from Japan to join Kim Il Sung's utopia who might not accept his rule. It was at this stage that Kim ordered that anyone who opposed him or the Workers Party must be held separately in "absolute control" areas without hope of release. He also brought in heavily armed military units to patrol the camps, and they dealt with the prisoners far more severely than had the previous guards.

According to Ahn the victims of the 1958 purge were put on trains, transported en masse, and then dumped in some desolate area. The boundaries of the settlement were demarcated by simple wooden fences. The settlements were so loosely guarded that inmates frequently escaped and held large-scale riots until the regime tightened security and internal controls.[9]

In 1958, Kim Il Sung issued a directive declaring that the "inmates are class enemies and must be actively exterminated to three generations." He thereby revived a feudal Korean custom of punishing three generations of a family together under the slogan: "Weeds must be eradicated in their season and destroyed to the roots."

After Hwang Jang-yop's defection, rumors trickled out of North Korea that Kim Jong Il had ordered a purge of 2,000 people connected to Hwang, including his family members. His daughter is said to have killed herself by jumping off a bridge as she was being transported to the Korean Gulag.

As a novice guard Ahn had to memorize Kim Il Sung's declaration that "factional elements are stumbling blocks to our revolution and the revolution must single them out for eradication." He was told that "exploitative elements and factional elements in the past got fat by sucking the sweat and blood of our people. We must annihilate these elements without regard for their situation today, and push ahead with no further thought of them."

In the late 1960s, an intensively trained Camp Guard Force was established, and the prisoners were graded and separated into different security zones within the camps. Kim Il Sung issued instructions in 1968 ordering the guards not "to feel the slightest humanity or empathy for class enemies." The beating and killing of prisoners was not only tolerated, it was encouraged and even rewarded.

"They trained me not to treat the prisoners as human beings. If someone is against socialism, if someone tries to escape from prison, then kill him," Ahn said. "If there's a record of killing any escapee then the guard will be entitled to study in the college. Because of that some guards kill innocent people."

Once inside the camps the political prisoners had no contact with the outside world and most would remain there until their death. Sometimes a family would be released at periodic amnesties, such as the one in 1992 or in 2001 on the ninetieth birthday of Kim Il Sung, if the family member who was considered politically dangerous had already died.

Not long after Kim Jong Il came to power, the prisoners at the Yodok camp erupted in open rebellion. Yodok contains a "revolutionizing zone," in which prisoner families lived in work teams and from which it was possible to be released, and an "absolute-control zone" from which there was no chance of redemption. It seems that the family member punished for disloyalty would be sent to the latter, and his relatives would be held in the former, often unaware that their father or mother was close by.

Details of the outbreak are sketchy but it seems that in 1974 some prisoners attacked the largest administration building with sticks and stones, then seized weapons and ammunition with which they began killing the guards and their families. North Korean troops arrived to suppress the uprising and hunt down the prisoners after they fled into the mountains. Ahn reports that afterward Kim Jong Il issued new instructions to the guards: "Bastards who escape must be run to the ground and killed one by one. The Honorable Leader's prestige and foreign influence can be hurt more by an escape than by any other thing. So bastards who escape must be killed without mercy."

Resistance both to his succession and the absolute power claimed by the Kim family seemed so strong that Kim Jong Il stepped up the adulation of his father and created another cult around himself. He gave himself an entirely spurious revolutionary pedigree and sought to portray himself as a shamanistic being. "When he was born at the foot of Mount Paektu on February 16, 1942, a double rainbow appeared and a comet traversed the sky," claims one official account. Another relates, "At the time of his birth there were flashes of lightning and thunder, the ice berg in the pond on Mount Paektu emitted a mysterious sound as it broke, and bright double rainbows rose up."

The propaganda campaign also began to elevate his mother, Kim Jong Suk, so that a holy trinity known as the "Three Generals" appeared. Among the stories circulated about Kim Jong Suk, who bore two sons and a daughter

before dying of tuberculosis at the age of 31 in 1949, was that she sometimes washed the Great Leader's wet socks and dried them in her bosom or
cut her hair to spread in the Great Leader's shoes.[10]

A partisan camp was rebuilt with a simple log cabin where he was supposedly born and other buildings where the resistance fighters lived. In a
touch reminiscent of the medieval craze for holy relics, the state announced
the discovery from the late 1980s of "slogan bearing trees" in the vicinity of
the camps. With the help of ultraviolet lamps and X-ray machines, officials
were said to have found trees carved with statements like, "We inform you
of the birth of the bright star on Mt. Paektu" and "You fellow countrymen,
be happy with the birth of Mt. Paektu bright star, the heir to General Kim."
One is tempted to conclude that the more absurd the propaganda, the
more the fear engendered by the terror apparatus had to be ratcheted up.
As Kim Jong Il was lauded as "the God of the Contemporary World," "The
Saint of All Saints," a deity whose "love and trust in the popular masses are
so absolute as to have no condition whatsoever and so broad as to have no
limit," the worse conditions became in the camps.

In 1979, Amnesty International published a report based on the testimony of Ali Lamada, a Venezuelan Communist Party member and poet
who was recruited to work on translating the collected works of Kim Il
Sung into Spanish in the 1960s. The Koreans tried to force him to confess
to imaginary crimes by keeping him in a tiny solitary confinement cell for a
year during which time he lost 50 pounds. Then he was sent to a camp
called Sariwon where he stayed from 1967 to 1974. From his conversa-
tions with guards and prisoners, he came to believe that by then the country had around 20 camps holding roughly 150,000 prisoners.

As in China, the Ministry of Public Security has its own prisons know as
Kyohwaso, or labor re-education camps, which house ordinary criminals,
and each of the 150 or so counties has its own prison. How many are kept
in these camps is unknown, but conditions in all of them seem the same.
The inmates are often being prosecuted for political crimes.

Lee Soon-ok, for example, was an accountant and loyal Party member
with an impeccable class background who was not arrested for any political crime but became the victim of an internal power struggle. In her book,
she describes in detail the tortures she endured during 14 months at an
interrogation center. Many of her fellow prisoners died from being tor-

tured, but she survived by agreeing to confess. Unlike the political prisoners, she was then sentenced at an open trial and taken to a *Kyohwaso*, where the treatment of prisoners and the death rates seemed as terrible as in those described by Kang Chol-wan and Ahn Myong-chul in their accounts of the various *Kwanliso*.

When she arrived at the camp Lee found the older inmates stunted with deformed spines like hunchbacks, and some were bent nearly double. She was forced to wear stinking and stiff coarse rags taken from those who had already died, and they slept 80-90 in a cell crawling with fleas and lice where many died from frequent paratyphoid epidemics.[11]

She discovered that many of her fellow prisoners were actually jailed for "thought crimes." In one case, a woman was condemned for disturbing the "socialist order" when she was heard singing a South Korean pop song in her home. Another was imprisoned for the crime of "discontent" by complaining that there were no goods in the department store in Pyongyang.

Once a North Korean was arrested for the slightest act of disloyalty, even something as trivial as improperly dusting a portrait of the Kims, he or she ceased to be treated as a human being. The most horrible part of Ahn's story is that his own family disappeared into the very camp where he first glimpsed the stunted inmates. His father had been in charge of a grain depot when in July 1994, he got drunk with some visiting officials and complained about the food shortages. The next day he woke up and, realizing what he had done, killed himself by downing a bottle of rat poison. Ahn's mother and sisters were soon in the camps, but Ahn, who had a tip off, escaped into China, making use of the confusion around the recent death of Kim Il Sung.

Park Chong-il, a 24-year-old North Korean interviewed by Doctors Without Borders, described how he was taken to an underground interrogation chamber in Chongjin, ten minutes from the railway station, after having earlier been caught and forcibly repatriated by the Chinese authorities in 2001. In the chamber, there was a row of cells holding nine to ten prisoners each. They were not allowed to speak, move, or talk, and were only fed a small quantity of hard-boiled corn and a thin salt gruel three times a day. During his first interrogation, Park moved his body slightly and the interrogator shouted "death to a traitor" and kicked his face so hard that he lost two teeth.

Five days later, his main interrogation began in an underground torture chamber the size of a basketball court in which he saw victims beaten with iron chains, rubber belts, wooden sticks, tied up with ropes, hung upside down, and electrocuted. He was ordered to clean the toilet hole in the cell with his tongue for half an hour. One fellow prisoner had to do this for five days as punishment for sleeping on his side instead of his back. Others were punished by having to endlessly repeat gestures, like the clock torture, during which the victim stands on one leg with two hands outstretched to indicate the passing hours and minutes while the other leg swings backward and forward like a pendulum. Park Chong-il was released when he was close to death. He recovered and then tried to commit suicide with rat poison and was taken to the hospital by his relatives. There he tried to hang himself.

Almost all of those who survived describe suffering months of similar gruesome interrogations during which time they were beaten, electrocuted, immersed in cold water, force fed water, and hung upside down. Inside the camps the prisoners were subject to regular beatings and cruel punishments, including being kept for months in isolation cages so small that there was no room to stand or sit. Often they would be forced to kneel without moving; a wooden rod was placed behind the knees to cut off circulation and cause the muscles to atrophy and rot, leading to paralysis or death.

Ahn describes the arbitrary killing of prisoners for even a small infraction. One prisoner was shot on the spot for picking up ripe chestnuts that had fallen at the entrance to a mine. Another was beaten to death for stealing a leather whip and eating the softened leather. Anyone caught trying to escape was publicly executed by a hanging or firing squad, often in a gruesome exhibition designed to degrade both the victims and the prisoners who were assembled to watch. Kang Chol-hwan witnessed 15 executions. One prisoner who tried to escape, Hahn Seung-chul, was killed by being dragged behind a car; the rest of the prisoners were ordered to file past and place their hands on his bloodied corpse. One prisoner who shouted out was immediately shot to death. Lee Soon-ok also described how when her fellow inmates became hysterical at witnessing the executions, they were sent to punishment cells.

The North Koreans were not alone in their harsh punishments. Many features of the penal system seem to have been borrowed from the Japanese occupiers—the underground prison cells for instance, can be see near the center of Seoul at the Sodaemun Museum, built on a spot where many Korean patriots died. Many of the terms, such as *Kwanliso*, are transliterations of Chinese words, or, like *Kukgabowibu*, borrowed from the Russian. Both the Chinese and Russians sent whole families into exile in remote and harsh regions like Siberia, but the North Koreans seem to be particularly cruel. Lee reported seeing a family—grandparents, parents, and children—executed together.

When a whole family was arrested they did not live in barracks but in villages with individual huts within the camp, and the children even attended school. However, the regime was determined to wipe out the family unit. The guards were ordered to prevent single prisoners from having sex, and any women who did so, even if she was raped, was punished. If she gave birth, the child was immediately strangled or drowned, often in front of the mother.

The right to marry, therefore, became the most sought after privilege by life-long prisoners. One South Korean soldier captured in 1950 who was one of 700 prisoners of war sent to labor at a mining camp at Hoeryong on the border with China survived 50 years. He was eventually allowed to marry and live outside the camp. Other prisoners, like a South Korean fisherman, Kim Byung-do, who was abducted, also managed to survive 30 years until he finally escaped.[12]

In 2003, the highly respected human rights researcher David Hawk interviewed escapees for the report "The Hidden Gulag" for the U.S. Committee for Human Rights in North Korea. Hawk's report reveals that North Korean women who were pregnant when they were repatriated from China were also forced to have abortions, or their babies—tainted with foreign blood—were killed after birth.

"All the stories are too similar in too many details to be coincidental," Hawk writes. These eugenics practices reportedly included isolating dwarfs in special remote villages and castrating them to prevent them and anyone else suffering from congenital defects from having children. When in 1988, Human Rights Watch and the Minnesota Lawyers Group published one of the first human rights reports on North Korea, such details provoked scepticism because they seemed too horrific to believe.

Some claims are still in doubt. Lee Soon-ok claims to have twice witnessed prisoners being used to test chemical and biological weapons. In

May 1988 she saw 50 women prisoners who were given pieces of special boiled cabbages to eat. Within half an hour, the women were vomiting, bleeding from their mouths, and moaning on the ground. Half an hour later they were dead, and she saw camp guards loading their dead bodies onto a truck. Lee also claims that in February 1990, she saw prisoners lying on the slope of a hill, bleeding from their mouth and motionless, enveloped by strange fumes and surrounded by scores of guards in gas masks. She says she overheard officials praising Dr. Lee Sung-ki—the inventor of the Vinalon artificial fibres—who is believed to be responsible for the chemical weapons program.[13]

More evidence for the use of prisoners as living guinea pigs came in 2004. Kim Sang Hun, a 70-year-old retired UN official and South Korean human rights activist, obtained documents smuggled out of North Korea by an engineer at the Vinalon factory in Hamhung on February 8. He and other engineers had heard that another plant called "Daily Site No. 2" some four miles away at Hungnam city had a strange reputation. "Many people believed it produced trench mortars but it was in fact a chemical factory. It was difficult even to breath because of the unpleasant chemical smell all around," the engineer said. "Once when I was inspecting the facilities in the power control unit, I saw a prisoner truck that looked like a freezer truck was arriving. I noticed a strange expression on the face of the facility officer at the sight. The steel gate of a tunnel was opened automatically and the truck disappeared into the tunnel."

Once inside the tunnel, he had a brief glimpse of what was going on. "There were large boxes of what looked like aluminum about the size of a large freezer on both sides. Each box had a door in front. There was a large and round window on each door. I witnessed with my own eyes human hands moving inside the box in two of the boxes. I was breathless with shock."

He found out that the Ministry of State Security delivered truckloads of prisoners twice a month. The engineer found an opportunity to go into the office of the manager of the plant and happened to see records lying on a desk. He grabbed four transfer authorizations from a thick pile of similar orders lying on a desk, crumpled them up, and threw them in a waste paper basket so that he could retrieve them in safety later on. Each document gives sparse biographical details of an individual and authorizes his or her transfer from a prison specifically for the purpose of "human experimentation of liquid gas for chemical weapons testing in live experiments." One form gives the name of Nam Chun-hyuk, born July 29, 1975, in Maengsan City in South Pyongan province, whose transfer was authorized in February 2002 and effectuated in July 2002.

The South Korean government has disputed the authenticity of these documents but not the scale of North Korea's chemical and biological weapons programs. Japan tested chemical and biological weapons on live prisoners in Manchuria and left large weapons stockpiles along the border between China and Korea. Hungnam was a base for its nuclear weapons research program. South Korea believes the North has at least 5,000 tons of material to produce nerve gases like VX and sarin, blood agents, and mustard gases. It has large stockpiles of shells filled with poisonous gas, and U.S. Assistant Secretary of State John Bolton calls it "one of the most robust offensive bio-weapons programs on earth."[14]

Prisoners were routinely called on to carry out dangerous tasks, such as cleaning the chimneys of Japanese-era munition plants where there was a high risk of dying from inhaling toxic gases. Ahn says it was common for prisoners, especially young and healthy men, to be transferred out of the camps to work on special military projects. They never returned, and guards believe they were put to work building secret tunnels and then were buried alive.

When the food shortages began to affect the general population in the early 1980s, the prison population was also hit. Prisoners grew their own food and although they were fed only starvation rations—a handful of cornmeal and watery cabbage soup per day—they supplemented this by catching rats, frogs, snakes, insects, and by collecting wild grasses and bark. Kang Chol-hwan reports that about a hundred died of malnutrition and disease every year in his section of Yodok camp, which had 2,000 or 3,000 inmates. Ahn reports a similar attrition rate at Camp No. 23, where 2,000 died every year, mostly children, out of the 50,000 prisoners. In addition, around 10 were executed, usually people caught stealing from the autumn harvest. At Camp No. 22, Ahn reckoned that 5 or 6 inmates died of hunger every day and about 2,000 a year.

However as the famine started in earnest after 1987, Lee Soon-ok reports that in her prison camp the guards began stealing the prisoners' rations. In normal times, each prisoner was given 25 ounces of corn, rice, and beans per day, but this fell to just 11 ounces per day, not enough to keep anyone alive.

By the 1990s, the death toll rose sharply, turning labor camps into death camps. At the coal-mining camp at Hoeryong on the Chinese border, a third of the inmates died between 1991 and 1995, most of them in the first month or two, and very few lasted three years. At Camp No. 77, a gold-mining center in South Hamgyong province, one escapee reported that 2,000 out of 7,000 to 8,000 prisoners died in just two years. The pace of executions stepped up as the ever more desperate survivors were shot for stealing food, even pig slops or the undigested edible grains from animal droppings.

The executions were suspended for about a month after Kim Il Sung's death, but then the word spread that Kim Jong Il wanted to "hear the sound of gunshots again." Doctors Without Borders interviewed one refugee in Bangkok in June 2001, who said that on January 23, 1995, Kim had issued orders demanding executions of all criminals within three months. There were executions every day by stoning or hanging "criminals" who had stolen two pounds of maize or a couple of eggs; on one day alone the refugee said he saw 28 criminals executed. Other refugees said they heard that Kim had in 1996 given instructions that firing squads must aim at the prisoners' heads because their brains were full of "wrong thoughts."[15]

Refugees whom I interviewed said that the authorities emptied the re-education camps run by the Ministry of Public Security because the prisoners could not be fed and would otherwise die. Many escapees also reported that it was common for police stations, interrogation cells, and hard labor camps to release prisoners just before their death in order to avoid having the deaths recorded and blemishing the administrators' performance records.

The deteriorating conditions in the camps may have sparked one of the largest prison camp revolts, in October 1986 or May 1987. This took place at Camp No. 12, which housed around 15,000 political prisoners and was in Onsong close to the border with China. It started when a political prisoner in a coal mine hit back and killed a guard. Others joined him, and after killing their guards, the prisoners massacred hundreds of wives and children at the compound housing the guards' families. Ahn reports that a battalion of troops who encircled the camp and machine-gunned some 5,000 inmates put down the uprising. The surviving prisoners were dispersed to other camps and Camp No. 12 was closed.[16]

As the prisoners died in large numbers, the civilian economy, which depended on their output of food and coal, became badly affected. North and South Hamgyong Provinces relied on the camps to deliver 60 percent of the food that was distributed to the general population. The maize was grown in Camp Nos. 12, 13, and 22, while potatoes came from Camp Nos. 11 and 16. Ahn says that after 1990 three camps were closed, and only Camp Nos. 16 and 22 continued to supply food. Consequently, these two provinces in the Northeast suffered severe shortages earlier than other regions.

With the closure of Camp No. 13 and its coal mine, the Chongjin Thermal Power Plant and the Chongjin and Kimchaek Steel Mill were short by 500,000 tons of high-grade lignite coal per year. Industrial production came to a standstill, and although civilian workers were sent to take over the mining and the farming, they could not be forced to work as hard as the prisoners. The fields were soon overrun with weeds, and the mines now only delivered 100,000 tons of coal a year. The prisoners had also generated a large part of North Korea's hard currency earnings, as they mined gold, coal, iron, and magnesite for export markets and had manufactured export goods and gathered medicinal drugs like ginseng, also for export.

Kim Jong Il closed a total of five camps, including several near Pyongyang, and moved the inmates to other camps apparently because he became alarmed that the outside world might learn about the Gulag. Hwang reports that Kim Jong Il worried that if the United States opened an embassy in Pyongyang, its diplomats would investigate the camps. "Kim's biggest fear in allowing the Americans into North Korea is that his tyrannical rule will be exposed to the world—that when the Americans tell the world, everyone will believe them," Hwang said.[17]

Several of the camps, like Camp No. 12 in which the revolt took place, near the border with China, were closed for fear that the inmates might escape and reveal their secrets of the Gulag. Camp No. 26 at Sungho-ri, which contained political prisoners including Koreans who returned from

Japan, was shut down after it was identified by Amnesty International. The South Korean newspaper *Chosun Ilbo* described how, fearing a possible visit by an Amnesty International delegation, many prison buildings at a camp were demolished and the inmates forced to hide for 20 days in a tunnel. Kim Jong Il must therefore be conscious of how the camps violate every international norm, but not be concerned enough to change them—only to prevent the outside world from learning about them.[18,19]

CHAPTER 5

North Korea's Economic Collapse

The first time Lee Min-bok, a North Korean agricultural expert, saw a man dying of hunger was in 1987 when he was on a research trip to the North East. That was eight years before North Korea appealed to the world for emergency food aid. Many lives would have been saved if only the North's leadership had been willing to admit to the economic crisis. Lee, a dour and austere man in his forties, is bitter for other reasons.

When I met him in 2003, he had been in South Korea since 1995 after a hair-raising escape and an odyssey through China and Russia. Now he was still trying to make his voice heard. In contrast to the countless foreign economists and agricultural experts who glibly parroted Pyongyang's lame excuses for the catastrophe, Lee's six years of research in the countryside concluded that the perennial food shortages had little to do with natural disasters or shortfalls in foreign aid after the Soviet Union's collapse.

"The problem was not outside factors, nor our farming skills, but the whole economic system," he said. Brushing aside friendly advice to toe the line, he spent six years travelling about the country hunting for ideas on how to raise food production. "I was always inspired by Kim Il Sung's slogan that 'Communism means Rice.'"

Agriculture was not a sector that attracted ambitious men but Lee still thought he could make his mark. In 1985, it was clear to him that a breakdown of the food distribution system was undermining the whole economy. That year Lee happened to arrive at a food depot in a small town just as the rations were being handed out. He recalled the scene vividly because to his astonishment a small crowd gathered around the cadre and began muttering mutinously.

"He was fat and people began poking his belly, saying why was he so fat when there was nothing for them to eat," Lee said. "By the standards of most countries, the incident was trivial but in North Korea nobody ever dared act like that towards an official."

The state used to issue food rations twice a month but after 1980, the delays started becoming longer and more frequent. First there was nothing for a whole month, then nothing for two, and then by 1990 the public food distribution system ground to a complete halt. State employees and workers in small cities had the lowest priority and began dying in large numbers.

The country, said Lee, ran short of a million tons of food each year, enough to feed around three million people. The leadership never grasped the extent of the unfolding disaster because no one dared tell Kim Il Sung the truth. The Great Leader had created the state farming system as far back as the 1940s and issued personal instructions on harvests and crops that always had to be obeyed because anything he said was law.

"Everyone knew how to please the Great Leader—all you had to do was lie. So what people did was to cheat by making false reports. Say a party official had to meet a target of 100 tons of grain, and the real harvest was 70 tons, he would report that he had met the quota," Lee said.

"Then, when inspectors from Pyongyang arrived, they would show them 100 tons in a barn by borrowing the missing 30 tons from a neighboring district. When the inspectors arrived at the next district, the favor would be repaid." An abstemious man, Lee was exactly the sort of dedicated follower the Party wanted to breed. Driven by a zealous nationalism, he had an undying faith in Kim Il Sung's wisdom so he went about collecting evidence to show how the problems could be solved. When peasants worked individual plots, instead of collective fields, he discovered that they were producing five times as much food. His conclusions were hardly original. Across the border the Chinese now had plenty to eat by doing just that, but he nonetheless felt the real thrill of making a scientific breakthrough.

"I thought I had found out something fantastic and that if the Great Leader could only see this, then everything would change for the better," he said. He summoned up his courage and explained in writing how the country could become self-sufficient. On May 31, 1990—he remembered the date—he submitted his proposal to the center and then sat back waiting to be congratulated by a grateful state. Instead, the secret police came knocking on his door. He was engaging in "reactionary activities" and they warned that if he knew what was good for him, he should stay quiet.

"I felt betrayed. I now realized that Kim Il Sung's main concern was not the welfare of the people but the security of his regime. And I thought— what is the good of continuing this research?" he said. Lee then began making careful preparations to escape. The first and most important step was to arrange a divorce so that once he was gone, his wife would not be associated with a traitor. Then he went missing and secretly crossed into China from where he made his way to South Korea.

A persistent notion is that North Korea's economy initially outperformed the South's, and it was not until 1980 that South Korea surged ahead of its northern twin. Teasing out the economic history of a country that stopped issuing any statistics after 1984 is hard, but this notion seems unlikely. It is true that statistics in the 1960s and 1970s showed that the North was well ahead of the South in per capita output of steel, coal, and grain, but living standards remained low. North Koreans probably never had as much to eat or wear as those in the South at any time.

Pyongyang boasted that its first five-year economic plan (1957–61) was completed a year ahead of schedule thanks to a *Chollima* campaign in which everyone worked round the clock to achieve impossible targets. A blizzard of dizzying statistics showed how output of steel and other key commodities rose by 700 percent. *Chollima* takes its name from a Korean mythological flying horse. The campaign was modeled on the Soviet Union's first five-year plan started in 1928, also completed a year early, and China's disastrous Great Leap Forward crash industrialization program, which was also launched in 1958 amid reports of equally fantastic increases in the output of everything from grain harvests to literary masterpieces.

The Soviet economic model that Kim Il Sung adopted was designed to accelerate the industrialization of a backward economy by forcing the peasants into giant collective farms. By condensing agricultural operations, the state was able to finance the rapid expansion of heavy industry. In North

Korea, where the peasants had lost their land before the Korean War, this also meant that the state set about requisitioning punitive amounts of grain.

Instead of the state taking a quarter of the harvest, troops arrived to seize half of it. People slaughtered their animals and hid their food rather than having to see it taken away. Lee said there was widespread famine and many people starved to death. Hungarian diplomats stationed in Pyongyang, whose reports have become accessible since the end of the Cold War, confirmed the famine deaths and revealed how the Soviet Union, which was in the midst of a "de-Stalinization" campaign, had strongly advised the North Koreans to avoid the mistakes it had made in 1928. Kim Il Sung, however, ignored this advice. When his exhausted and starving population could be driven no further, Kim Il Sung had to go to Moscow cap in hand and plead for emergency grain deliveries to prevent a complete economic collapse.

Even in the early 1980s, before the famine started, the population was still eking out their lives on the same miserable rations as in 1948. In fact there was hardly a time that most North Koreans were not short on food, housing, clothing, and other basic goods and services.

Kim Il Sung retained a dogged belief in the successes of Soviet agriculture. He followed the Soviet Union by establishing huge cooperative farms and operated them according to the pseudo scientific ideas of a group of Soviet agronomists led by Trofim Lysenko. In the 1930s, Lysenko had convinced Stalin that he could boost harvests if collective farm tractors ploughed deep furrows and sowed seeds close together. This would work because in his opinion, Darwin's theory of the survival of the fittest did not apply to plants of the same species; so, if you planted them close together, they should show class solidarity and not compete against one another. Genetics was another capitalist theory Lysenko rejected in preference for his own theory that plants would change in response to environmental influences. This led the Soviets and the North Koreans to try sowing summer wheat in winter and to try to create better varieties by grafting different tree species or pollinating crops by hand.

In principle, farming, like industry, operated according to a central plan, but in practice, Kim Il Sung continually offered his own personal "on-the-spot" guidance. Chinese emperors had the duty of regulating the agricultural calendar and would start the New Year by symbolically ploughing a field. Kim Il Sung seemed to regard it as his task to tour the country personally deciding when to sow and when to reap. His arbitrary edicts meant that North Koreans did not grow cotton to clothe themselves, nor millet, potatoes, or sweet potatoes to feed themselves. These are the very crops on which tens of millions of Chinese peasants who farm marginal cropland in mountainous areas rely on to survive. No resources were allocated to produce the rich variety of traditional Korean supplementary products that added variety to rural diets. Most of the population lived off a monotonous diet of maize, rice, and cabbage.

Korea's traditional smallholder farming relied on organic livestock and human manure, but North Korea's huge collective farms were conceived of as factories. They depended on unusually large inputs of chemical fertilizers, water pumped in from large-scale irrigation projects, and tractor power. Every ton of rice required an input of two tons of fertilizer, and every 240 acres required six to seven tractors to plough it. These big inputs did produce results at least for a while, and this may have boosted Kim Il Sung's sense of his own infallibility. Food production peaked in the early 1970s when close planting was introduced. Three times the usual number of seeds were planted together, and for the first few years, harvests were up by 130 percent and the country was reaping five to six tons of grain per hectare. Kim then went on to encourage the population to have larger families in the expectation that harvests would keep rising.

Yet the harvest gains were only temporary. By 1990, the country was getting just one ton of grain per hectare. Food production began stagnating after 1978 when Pyongyang stopped publishing details of its harvests. The plan called for a nine-million-ton harvest but probably fell short by two or three million tons. By this time North Korea children were so obviously stunted that in 1979 Kim Il Sung ordered rural households to start planting runner beans in order to create a new source of protein. He specified that the beans should only be planted up against fences so as not to waste fields reserved for grain. The plans promised ever-growing food surpluses but no one dared tell Kim that the system could never deliver this. According to Lee, Kim Il Sung was informed in 1982 that the country had reaped a record harvest of fifteen million tons when the actual harvest was between seven or eight million tons.

We do not know for certain that Kim Il Sung actually believed the glowing reports presented to him, but everyone around him knew better than to challenge his firmly held convictions. As mentioned earlier, North Korea did not grow any cotton under Kim Il Sung, although it was such a staple crop for over 600 years that the white cotton two-piece *Hanbok* outfit was the national dress. In the 1930s, the Japanese had forced the Koreans to grow cotton for them, but Kim Il Sung decided he would dress his people in a stiff synthetic material called *vinalon*. This was not only made from local minerals but was a rare case of a truly homegrown technology—on every level it manifested the efficacy of his *Juche* ideology. Korea's most famous scientist, Lee Sung-ki, supposedly invented it but it seems to have been actually invented by the Japanese. Lee had been sent to study chemical engineering in Japan where he joined a team at Kyoto Imperial University, led by Professor Ichiro Sakurada, that had come up with a way of making a polyvinyl acetate (PVA) solution from calcium carbide. PVA could be spun into a fiber. Japanese production started in 1948, and when Lee defected from South to North Korea in 1950, he brought the technology with him. Even at the height of the Korean War, Lee continued his research on vinalon production, working in a laboratory built inside a mountain cave. A decade later he went on to oversee the construction of the February 8th Vinalon Complex in Hamhung that churned out 20,000 tons per year.

When in the 1970s, another chemical engineering expert, Dr. Oh Kyong Ku expressed doubts about vinalon, pointing out that it is hard to dye, shrinks after washing, and is costly to produce, he was arrested and tortured for "ideological revisionism"; he reportedly committed suicide in 1977. A DPRK defector later described vinalon politics this way: " . . . [Vinalon] was a technology whose economy and efficiency were very suspect. However, given the fact that Kim Il Sung had already praised it and given direct orders [for its production], no one dared bring up the problems it involved."[1]

Of course, heavy industry, not consumer goods, was the top priority in the North, which had a head start over the South. Most of the Japanese investment in heavy industry, including dams designed to generate enough electricity to power the whole peninsula, was in the North, while the South had been directed to produce surplus cotton and rice. The North's economic development plan was skewered toward defense after 1963, following Moscow's climb down during the Cuban missile crisis. Kim launched a program to arm the entire population and convert the whole country into a military fortress. To enable the country to wage a people's war, each province set about making itself self-sufficient in the production of food, munitions, and other basic necessities. The second economic plan (1961–67) had to be extended by three years because "military first" policies made it hard to reach targets for the production of food and other necessities. The following six-year plan (1971–76) also needed one extra year of "readjustment" and after the 1978–84 seven-year plan started, the North stopped issuing regular annual economic statistics.

Part of the population was moved from border or coastal areas into remote mountains in the North to work in defense-related factories. Anything of importance was located deep underground, creating a nation of moles. North Korea built up a "second economy," as it is called, which employs 500,000 workers in 134 underground defense factories like Munitions Factory No. 24 in Chagang province bordering China. A refugee who worked there said that to get in visitors passed through an electric fence, several gates of steel and concrete, and three checkpoints. In a labyrinth of 100 tunnels 300 feet below the surface, hundreds of workers lived year round, eating, sleeping, and having no choice but to marry each other.[2]

China applied the same policies after 1963, but with a small economy like North Korea's the impact was greater. Kim's defense spending probably absorbed a higher share of the economy than any other country in the Communist Bloc. It was certainly more dependent than any other post-war Communist country on foreign aid. The Soviets alone designed and built 60 industrial plants. The East Germans designed and ran the railway system and rebuilt the city of Hamhung. The Czechs built some of the munition factories in Chagang province.

China was also liberal with aid, but dried up ties weakened during the Cultural Revolution and the North turned to its former enemies for help. Japan provided U.S. $80 million to build the Namhung Youth Chemical Fertilizer Complex, the United Kingdom offered $U.S.160 million for a cement factory, and Sweden, West Germany, Italy, and others also provided loans and new technology. This all enabled the Koreans to start manufacturing all sorts of consumer goods, including cotton towels and garments, beer, and various widgets. By 1975 North Korea's buying spree had left debts of U.S. $1.2 billion.

North Korea was marching in step with other East Bloc countries like Yugoslavia, Poland, Hungary, East Germany, and Romania, which all resorted to foreign borrowings to finance imports of industrial machinery; it enabled them to raise living standards and damp domestic unrest. For North Koreans this was a time of relative prosperity, a combination of elevated harvests and diverse production of other goods. All these countries hoped that the loans would be paid off by consumer exports.

None of them managed to do so, and the seeds were thus sown for the huge political upheavals of the 1980s. In Poland the government began to bargain with the striking steelworkers and shipbuilders who set up the Solidarity trade union. When East Germany was faced with economic stagnation, it began to rely more heavily on West German aid. Yugoslavia and Hungary, also heavily indebted, started experimenting with economic reforms. In Romania, then President Nicolaei Ceauşescu launched an unrelenting campaign to squeeze his subjects in an unavailing and punitive effort to pay back the foreign loans.

More than the Europeans, the North Koreans seemed clueless about how to make anything that could be sold in the international marketplace. Stiffened by its *Juche* spirit, it had refused to join the Soviet's COMECON system of planned trading exchanges that Moscow had set up after 1949, so its export goods lacked a guaranteed market. It ran up huge debts with fraternal allies, who complained about erratic deliveries and the shoddy quality of the goods they received in payment. Soviet archives reveal a string of testy complaints about North Korean manufactures with one Soviet diplomat noting that it was unacceptable for North Korea to be shipping these "museum pieces."

The new factories acquired in the West failed to improve the performance of the North Korean economy because they operated outside the planned world economy. Output was constantly dogged by shortages of power and basic necessary raw materials such as cotton.

North Korea at first tried to pay off the debts by forcing the population to hand over gold and silver or to collect wild ginseng and other products that could earn foreign exchange. In 1977, Pyongyang had negotiated a five-year moratorium after it again promised to find buyers for its exports of cement and ferrous and non-ferrous metals. Finally, the North Koreans decided to give up the effort altogether and reneged on all debt obligations.

The solution to North Korea's economic problems are the same now as they were in 1980, namely to build up an export sector that will allow it to import what it lacks. South Korea is not self-sufficient in food either, although South Korean farmers achieve very high yields with high inputs of fertilizer, good seeds, and irrigation. Almost half of the country's grain is imported, much to the fury of South Korean farmers, but the country can afford its high living standard by making and selling high quality cars, ships, computers, and many other goods.

It was Kim Il Sung's choice to neither pay for food imports nor divert resources from the military into the civilian export economy. Instead, with his usual hubristic confidence, he announced ten ambitious economic targets to double the size of the economy by relying on the *Juche* spirit of self-reliance.[3] As he later told East German leader Erich Honecker, he believed he could "solve the food problem completely" with a series of gigantic and daring investment projects.[4]

The centerpiece was the West Sea Barrage project at Nampo, which was intended to add 494,000 acres of reclaimed tidal flats to the country's existing 3.7 million acres of farmland. This sort of project was intended to triple grain output to 20 million tons.

The largest engineering project in DPRK history started in 1981 and cost an estimated U.S. $4 billion. It consists of a five-mile-long barrage closing off the mouth of the Taedong River, which flows through Pyongyang. In addition, a concrete dam creates a 130-square-mile reservoir from which a 40-mile-long canal channels water to irrigate crops in South Hwanghae province, one of the country's rice baskets. The South Koreans had also drained wetlands, especially tidal flats on the West Coast. Chung Ju Yung, Hyundai's founder, was proud of building a barrage by sinking an oil tanker and reclaiming 24,000 acres on which he built a showcase mechanized rice farm. The North wanted to trump these accomplishments.

Next on the list was a scheme to add 741,000 acres of cropland by opening up forested hillsides. Millions were mobilized to fell trees and build terraced fields on slopes as steep as 16 degrees.

Rather than import new technology, North Korea preferred to stick to its *Juche* technology. On the strength of one successful laboratory experiment, the country squandered about U.S. $5 billion, equal to a quarter of the country's annual GNP, to build a new vinalon factory in Sunchon. This plant, the size of a small city, was supposed to exploit a novel oxygen-blast technology and provide a cheaper way of breaking down carbide, anthracite,

and limestone into chemical stocks for chemical fibers, chemical fertilizers, and animal feed. It would deliver 300,000 tons of protein feed that
could be turned into 1.7 million tons of meat and 7,000 million eggs a
year. When it was finished, the population was assured that they would
live better than the Japanese.

A second giant *Juche*-tech project, the U.S. $3.5 billion Sariwon Potas-
sic Fertilizer Complex, was also launched to make aluminum from feldspar
instead of bauxite. All these schemes ended in utter failure. The West Sea
Barrage at Nampo, which I visited just after it was finished in 1986, added
only 100,000 acres, not 3.7 million, because despite repeated attempts
to flush the salt out of the soil, the land could not be cultivated. Even
Hyundai's project when it was finished in 1984 proved to be unprofitable.
After salt-free soil had be dumped on the reclaimed land, the costs soared
to U.S. $760 million; and since it could only produce 54,000 tons of rice a
year, it would take around 200 years for the project to pay for itself.[5,6]

The backbreaking labor that went into felling trees and making the field
terraces was wasted, too. Usually the builders ran out materials to run shore
up the terraces. When the floods came, as they do every summer in Korea,
the terraces, the soil, and the crops were washed away. In the big 1995 floods,
even the barrage was a liability. The water had nowhere to drain and the
sea water backed up. Officials from the World Food Program who toured
the area reported seeing embankments that had burst and flooded fields
after sluice gates had been opened, depositing a crust of sand on the soil.[7,8]

Futhermore, there was no extra fertilizer. The Sunchon plant never went
into operation. When a Russian scientist visited it in 1991, he reported
that soon after it had started up there were dangerous explosions and it
was mothballed. Much the same fate met the Sariwon plant. In short, there
was no increase in the food available and no extra electricity either.[9,10]

Poor designs were to blame for a string of misconceived giant hydropower projects. Of the 4.4 million kilowatts in new capacity planned in the
first half of the 1980s, only 250,000 kilowatts ever came on stream, and at
great cost. The Taechon project required digging a 30-mile water tunnel
underneath rugged mountains to divert streams going north into the River
Taeryong, where they could help irrigate land reclaimed from tidal flats in
North Pyongan province. Yet since the land was too salty for growing crops,
the water was never needed. The huge construction effort therefore resulted

in two power stations with a modest capacity of just 250,000 kilowatts a year. The Mt. Kumgang hydropower project was equally absurd and eventually abandoned. The idea was to redirect three rivers to ensure a steep drop that would generate extra power. Some 50,000 troops were sent to blast two tunnels of 28 miles and 36 miles through granite rocks in high and rugged mountains. They also had to build aqueducts to link up four reservoirs.

Many of these projects actually contributed to the economy's decline. For instance, North Korea has 1,500 reservoirs serving small and large dams, but the terracing projects ensured that flash floods swept down the bare hills washing soil into reservoirs, irrigation canals, and major rivers. As the reservoirs silted up, the twin goals of the dams—flood control and power production—became mutually incompatible. In the dry seasons there was too little water to open the flood gates and turn the turbines, and in the rainy season, there was too much water because of the silt build up. If the water was not released, the dams, shoddily constructed in haste, threatened to collapse, and some, like the Sangwol dam thrown up across the Jaeryong River, did just that. Even the Nampo barrage needed to be continually repaired with mud and boulders because its cement was weak. In fact, most of the dams, tunnels, and waterways fell into disrepair because perennial shortages meant that they were built with only half the required cement.

The heavy investment in water conservancy projects simultaneously created acute shortages of drinking water. With all the rivers controlled by dams and sluices, the pollution discharged by North Korea's factories was not flushed away and quickly accumulated to reach toxic levels. Three-quarters of the North's factories operate without water treatment so most of the water in North Korea is poisonous. Even drinking tap water in Pyongyang can prove fatal because factories like the Hwanghae Steel Works discharged all their waste directly into the Taedong River, and the barrage ensures it is no longer flushed out to sea.[11]

Although experts advised Kim Il Sung that building thermal power plants instead of hydropower projects was a quicker, cheaper way of meeting electricity demand, he always insisted that the priority was to avoid becoming reliant on oil imports. Therefore, some 72 percent of the North's energy comes from coal, and another 18 percent from hydropower. He also ordered the country's railways to be entirely electrified so that even if oil imports were blocked, the transportation system would still function. To be doubly sure that the enemy could not destroy the electricity grid, the transmission lines were buried underground and ran on a low voltage. The leakage rate was high, and the grid eventually disintegrated into fragments.[12]

Not only did the hydropower projects fail to deliver, but coal production started to decline in the mid-1970s. Many mines dated from the Japanese era and relied on dynamite to blast open coal faces. Then the miners, usually political prisoners, moved the coal by hand, working in darkness without lamps or helmets. As each miner could produce just five or six tons a day, North Korea had one of the lowest productivity rates in the world. Annual production remained stubbornly stuck at around 30 million tons, far from the 130 million tons listed in the ten major economic goals.[13]

North Korea had deliberately built very few roads to hinder any invader and relied on trains to carry 90 percent of the freight and 62 percent of all passenger traffic. Kim Il Sung had in the 1960s personally decided to phase out steam engines, hence electric locomotives pulled 80 percent of the trains on the 3,000-mile network.

The whole system wound down like a piece of clockwork. The trains could not shift the coal because there was not enough electricity and vice versa. Without the coal, there was not enough fertilizer or vinalon, and not enough food. The decline had become irreversible even before the Soviet Union's collapse led to a fall in oil imports, spare parts, and raw materials. Without basic necessities like food nobody wanted to work. The most productive part of the economy were the slave labor camps because there the prisoners were forced to work, and they regularly produced five times as much coal and food as outside workers.

It is a curious paradox of all such dictatorships like North Korea's— despite all the terror and the relentless exhortation, people still cannot be compelled to work effectively. They put up a passive resistance, although on the surface the giant projects employing huge numbers of conscripts seem to suggest otherwise. The use of laborers working with primitive tools in a great rush to meet some arbitrary deadline is ineffective. A German diplomat, Peter Schaller, who lived in Pyongyang, gave this colorful description of how a tramline was built to honor the Great Leader's birthday in 1991.[14]

As with most prestige projects, the army took charge of construction, and thousands of so-called "soldier-builders" were brought in. The soldiers broke up the asphalt road surface with large chisels, perhaps 50 cm long. One soldier would hold a chisel while another struck it with a heavy sledge-hammer. The asphalt chunks were lifted to the side by hand and loaded onto waiting trucks. Everything was carried by hand—stones, cement, and of course the rail segments, each of which was lifted by several soldiers on their shoulders. It was bitterly cold in February, the Taedong River was completely frozen, but the soldiers took off their padded jackets and often worked in their undershirts.

The streets were filled with the small, stocky figures in olive uniforms. They toiled single-mindedly, as if possessed. Propaganda companies kept up the soldiers' morale. Martial music and North Korean pop songs droned out of the giant loudspeakers on propaganda wagons, interrupted only by exhortatory slogans. To the left and right of the loudspeakers red flags fluttered on tall poles; banners urging fidelity to party and Leader rounded out this stage-managed display of revolutionary élan and readiness. . . . The closer the magical deadline approached, the more we began to doubt the tramway would be completed on time. The army was under pressure. Night work began, and the soldiers toiled round the clock under spotlights.

After the track bed was complete, it was time for the precision work. One thing, above all, remains in my memory: The rail segments were welded together on the spot, and the rough seams needed to be ground off and polished. This too was performed by hand. For days on end the soldiers crouched, legs apart, over the rails. The men worked on the joints with tiny metal files and—I could hardly believe my eyes—with whetstones. Stoic and machine-like, they completed this senseless and somehow also unnecessary work with completely inappropriate "tools." . . . No one asks any questions, no one expresses doubt about whether the orders make sense. Each order is to be carried out, even in the face of death.

Refugees described how they worked on a twelve-lane motorway from Nampo to Pyongyang, called the Youth Hero Road, and suffered great hardships. Around 50,000 youths were employed to squat on the ground and break small stones by hand or lay hot tarmac with bags of burlap. Squads of men with A-frames on their backs, running at the double, carried all the soil. At times they were allowed just two hours of sleep and to stop only for meals brought to them. There was never enough to eat, and the work site was lit by burning tires so they could work through the night. Many begged to leave or tried to run away but they were usually caught by security agents.[15]

After decades of this backbreaking toil, the population became exhausted and demoralized. A German doctor who worked in North Korean hospitals for 18 months, Norbert Vollertsen, said he found most of the patients suffered from psychosomatic illnesses because they were "worn out by compulsory drills, the innumerable parades, the assemblies from 6:00 in the morning and the droning propaganda. They are tired and at the end of their tether. Clinical depression is rampant."[16]

The losses from the colossal economic gambles made in the early 1980s were compounded by the regime's extravagance as it tried to cover its failures. A year after South Korea celebrated its success by hosting the Summer Olympic Games, North Korea hosted the International Friendship Games. In two years, it spent between U.S. $4-9 billion on building 260 major facilities including two entirely new streets; one was four miles long and graced with residential blocks 24 stories high on either side and four new hotels. Pyongyang also constructed a 150,000-seat Rungnado Stadium that included a table tennis gymnasium, a swimming pool, a handball gymnasium, and a four-lane motorway linking Pyongyang with Kaesong. The sheer folly of these Pharaonic monuments was evident to anyone who traveled down the empty and brand new highway with its blue motorway signs pointing the way to Seoul.

When a country worships an infallible leader whose plans are dogged by obvious failure, the population is compelled to participate in a willing suspension of disbelief. When in November 1986 I went to Pyongyang for the first time, it offered such a feeling of absurd theatricality that it was actually quite enthralling. One felt privileged to observe such a performance. Visitors call Pyongyang Orwellian, Stalinist, Maoist, totalitarian—but these political labels fail to catch its dreamlike quality. Kafkaesque is better. One is dazed by a world where both objects are disproportionate and emotions are oddly distorted. Your car speeds along a motorway, the only vehicle in six empty lanes. Under the metro, the stations have chandeliers bright enough for Cinderella's ball and marble floors polished enough for any Prince Charming to glide along.

One expects a teeming Asian city, busy, chaotic, crowded, and noisy with vendors and touts, but it was orderly, clean, modern, and spookily quiet. The city was evidently designed to serve as a stage set whose props could be moved around at will to convey whatever message seemed appropriate. The inhabitants' chief role is to take part in mass demonstrations of support, and they are constantly in training to perform at some military parade, celebration, or demonstration. They are selected on the grounds of their political loyalty and appearance, so the old, the infirm, or the politically suspect are routinely inspected and, if found wanting, expelled.

You find the same familiar sights as in any big city—department stores, grocery shops, smart hotels, bars, an underground, restaurants, and hospitals—but nothing so mundane as shopping or eating goes on in them. From the outside a grocery store looks normal. The windows and glass counters are clean and hygienic, the vegetables are in the baskets, the tins of meat on wooden shelves, and the condiment bottles are laid neatly in rows. Yet there is nobody there. No one is shopping, and no one ever will. Nothing is actually for sale because when you look closely the vegetables are all made of plastic.

At the department store, people go up and down the elevators. There are racks and racks of new clothing, shoes, and white household goods. Shop girls watch you behind electronic cash machines. No one is buying anything, they are just looking, then you see a crowd. Some socks are being sold at one corner, but the shop assistant is accepting and storing the grubby bills in a cardboard box.

On a tour of the maternity hospital, it is the same. The rooms, full of new, modern medical equipment, are for show too. Not even the plastic wrapping on the electrical plug for the Siemen's heart monitor has been removed.

Soon one succumbs to the irresistible urge to creep around at night for a glimpse behind the scenes, to catch the stagehands at work operating the pulleys. In the grip of an irresistible urge, one sneaks out and goes back to the grocery store, which turns out always to be shut like the department store, or at night creeps inside the apartment buildings, or tries to talk to some one at the railway station. Yet no one looks at you or meets your eye. It is as if you aren't there, a ghost; meanwhile on a guided tour of a school, the children clutch your hand and smile in an exaggerated show of affection.

On the streets, there are traffic wardens, smartly dressed women in skirts and boots with batons who swing around like cheerleaders, marionettes. Yet, there are no cars to direct, and the streets, some with three or four lanes, are deserted. The other women dress like Ukrainian peasants in dumpy uniforms, their heads wrapped in thick woollen shawls, and they queue at the bus stops in subdued Slavic patience. Even when pushing to get on, they stay silent. At the railway station, no one speaks except in low murmurs. At night, strange music awakens one; although near midnight, a brass band is playing for a team of soldiers working at a building site.

The government minders field questions with an amused superior tolerance. Why are people not allowed to enter Pyongyang without permission? Why are there no bicycles? Why is the department store closed every day? Finally one wants to provoke a response just to hear the answers: Are there any prison camps? Does anyone hate Kim? Will he ever die?

Everywhere you feel his great presence, omnipotent, omniscient, and all seeing. Kim watches you from billboards beside every road and major building, from the banknotes, from the lapel pins of every citizen. His image and voice dominate the television and the newspapers, and every place has a plaque on the door recounting that on such and such a date Kim visited to give "on-the-spot" guidance. Books even print his "on-the-spot" words of instruction in darker print.

The guides at the revolutionary martyr's cemetery or at Kim's birthplace, where there is a Bethlehem-like nativity scene, or at the war museum speak a stilted archaic language; they say things like ". . . the U.S. imperialists and their treacherous puppets will pay one hundredfold in blood for this thrice-cursed crime against the Korean people." After a while the visitor feels that he has fallen through a trap door into another world. He starts referring not to Americans but "the American imperialists," and instead of the South Korean government, "the South Korean flunkeys." I even found myself solemnly presenting a gift to Kim Il Sung, a large peacock fan and a bag of Mars bars, that was courteously received as a kowtow. Perhaps they are now numbered among the 20,000 gifts on permanent exhibit in the Friendship Museum.

On another trip in 1989, I caught a glimpse of Kim Il Sung, a silver-haired and dapperly dressed man in a Western suit who looked normal but for a goiter the size of tennis ball that stuck out of the side of his neck. Generally, though, he is portrayed dressed in a Mao suit along with his son, Kim Jong Il, striking the same pose: hands held behind their backs and paunches thrust forward. The young Kim, who never appeared in public, was said to favor a bouffant hairdo and thick heels and platform shoes to make him feel taller.

The most absurd stories gain certain plausibility in this context. One feels prepared to believe anything about this pair, no matter how fantastic. In August 1986, just before my first visit, Seoul reported that along the DMZ, there had been broadcasts lamenting the death of the Great Leader Kim Il Sung. Seoul was confident a vital power struggle was afoot.

According to Pyongyang's diplomats and defectors, Kim Il Sung suddenly fell ill and possibly lapsed into a coma for several weeks during the summer of 1986. Power was up for grabs. Some sources claim that army generals sought to replace Kim Jong Il with his charming and handsome half brother, Kim Pyong-il. These sources date the attempted coup to July 1986 and claim that when the conspirators failed to garner sufficient support they fled to China. It seems that Marshal O Jin-u, number three in the hierarchy, had hurried back to Pyongyang from Moscow to deal with the crisis. He had gone to Moscow for treatment after a mysterious car accident several months earlier. The war hero had reportedly crashed his car into a tree at four in the morning while drunk at the wheel. Car accidents, it seems, had previously been given as the explanation for disappearances of top officials, despite the utter implausibility of such events ever taking place on the country's deserted roads.

One diplomat earnestly speculated that the DMZ broadcasts were ordered by the eldest son, Kim Jong Il, as a ruse designed to lure his opponents into the open so he could destroy them. Another thought that Kim Jong Il secured his right to succession by helping to save his father's life as he lay in a coma and by swearing to uphold his father's legacy. When he recovered Kim Il Sung made Marshal O and the other guerrilla veterans around him swear to stick by his eldest son and ensure a smooth transition of power.

Diplomats also reported sightings of anti-Kim graffiti and posters. Residents in Pyongyang heard that Kim narrowly survived an assassination attempt when his armoured train was ambushed in the provinces in late 1986. Another incident supposedly took place in May 1987, when Kim was returning from a state visit to China and had stopped for three days at Sinuiju station on the border. Several high-ranking army officers had opened fire, and his life was saved by a bodyguard who stopped a bullet. Later five North Korean generals reportedly fled to China and sought asylum.

Whether these stories are true or not, Kim Il Sung's rule had brought the country to the edge of disaster and North Korea's giant neighbour, China, was putting pressure on Pyongyang to reform. Looming over the leadership was the question of whether it could resist these forces in time to achieve its mission and conquer the South. North Koreans were always told that once this was done, attention would turn to fixing the economy and raising living standards. Time was now running out on all fronts.

In the 1960s, Kim Il Sung's strategy to conquer the South had been to provoke an attack from the South, which would start a second civil war. He then hoped the Communist world would rally round and support him again. Moscow and Beijing had both signed mutual defense pacts with Pyongyang in the early 1960s. After starting a new military buildup in 1963, Kim Il Sung believed that he could defeat the South in a second war if they started it. His forces began a pattern of escalating attacks. In 1965, two planes attacked a U.S. reconnaissance plane. Then in January 1968, a 31-member commando disguised as South Korean soldiers infiltrated President Park Chung-hee's office complex in Seoul—the Blue House—intending to kill him, but they were stopped close to the gates. Two days later North Korea seized the U.S. intelligence ship, the USS *Pueblo*, and held the 83-strong crew. In October, 130 North Korean commandos infiltrated the East Coast and a battle ensued in which over a hundred were killed.

The attacks coincided with the Tet offensive in Vietnam. American and South Vietnamese troops defeated an invasion by conventional forces from the North, and an uprising led by the Vietcong in the South. Despite its failures, it proved a turning point for the North as America's domestic resolve faltered. Pyongyang had long sought to create a similar fifth column like the Vietcong in South Korea and had built a strong network of undercover agents and supporters. In 1969, North Korea said it had established an underground revolutionary organization in South Korea called the Party for Unification and Revolution, whose purpose was to overthrow the South Korean puppets and replace them with a "democratic regime." Kim told visiting leaders that he hoped to take advantage of political unrest in the South, order this fifth column to seize power at the right moment, and then invite his troops to intervene.

Since 1960, Moscow and Beijing had been caught up in a bitter rivalry and were almost at war by 1969. During the Cultural Revolution, which had started in 1965, Kim lost the support of Beijing. Mao's Red Guards labeled Kim as the "fat revisionist" who had squandered China's aid during the war while "waltzing the nights away in a snow-white field-marshal's tunic," as one Red Guard poster put it. Kim even massed troops on the border fearing that China would stage an invasion and overthrow him. So, instead Kim turned to Moscow, which began to supply aid including much military hardware. However, since Moscow was pursuing détente, it was not eager to be dragged into another conflict. It would only support Kim if it was clear he was the victim of aggression. Soviet archives reveal that as the Koreans continued their provocations, the Soviet diplomats felt Pyongyang was deceiving them. Meanwhile China, which had sent hundreds of thousands of troops to fight the Americans in Vietnam, began to change. The turning point was President Richard Nixon's visit in 1972. Despite the coldness between Beijing and Pyongyang, this altered everything. When these two colossal powers began to normalize relations and form an alliance against Moscow, pawns like Vietnam, Cambodia, and Taiwan might be traded. The Nixon visit created panic in Pyongyang because Kim feared he might not even be consulted when the two giants decided Korea's fate. The North Korean Embassy in Beijing desperately tried to contact Nixon while he was in Beijing in the hopes of opening its own ties with the United States.

In any event China told the North Koreans to lie low as President Nixon sought to pull out from Vietnam after a decent interval. Kim Il Sung immediately fell into line. The provocative attacks and hijackings stopped abruptly. Kim took the South by surprise with a peace initiative. Talks between the Red Cross officials of both sides began in August 1971 and led to the first family reunions since the Korean War. The director of the South Korean Central Intelligence Agency, Yi Hu-rak, secretly visited Pyongyang, and the younger brother of Kim Il Sung, Kim Yong-ju, went to Seoul. The result was a dramatic joint communiqué with both sides agreeing to seek reunification peacefully, independent of outside forces, and to work toward a "great national unity."

A North-South Coordinating Committee sprang into existence that held three meetings, until the spring of 1973 when the North suddenly lost interest. By July, the Red Cross talks were over and attacks had resumed. The South never quite grasped why the talks started and ended as they did, but Pyongyang said it was because President Park had arrested his rival presidential candidate, Kim Dae Jung. Yet as the 1970s went on, everyone could see that the United States was in retreat across Asia and might even abandon South Korea to its fate. In 1975, South Vietnam fell and the last Americans withdrew in a humiliating scramble. After Saigon, Cambodia and Laos also fell to Communist insurgencies. Washington withdrew a division of its troops from South Korea, and when President Jimmy Carter came to power, he contemplated a gradual but complete withdrawal. He also withdrew recognition of Taiwan, and in 1979 formally recognized Beijing as the only legitimate government.

South Korea certainly looked vulnerable. It was wracked by domestic strife, and there was growing opposition to Park's deepening dictatorship. North Korea set about excavating tunnels under the DMZ to prepare a surprise invasion. One was discovered to be large enough for 30,000 troops plus light artillery to pass through in an hour. North Korean commandos resumed their attacks. In August 1974, a North Korean agent shot and missed President Park but killed his wife. The most notorious incident took place in August 1976 when North Korean soldiers, wielding axes and metal pikes, attacked a group of U.S. and South Korean soldiers trimming a tree in the neutral areas inside the DMZ at Panmunjom. They killed two U.S. army officers and wounded four enlisted men and five South Korean soldiers.

Yet other changes were portents of less favorable trends. After Mao died in 1976, a group of senior generals seized power and threw the ultra-leftists, led by Mao's wife Jiang Qing, into jail. Beijing was no longer committed to the worldwide expansion of the Communist revolution, and the new government was led by Deng Xiaoping, a blunt reformer whom Mao had accused of being the "number two capitalist roader." He had no sympathy for Kim Il Sung's regime. In 1978, Deng led a state visit to Pyongyang and laid flowers at the giant gilded statue of Kim Il Sung on Mansu Hill, making Kim furious.

Deng had slashed China's military budget, cut troop levels, cancelled defense industry projects, and halted the aid for the motley crew of dictators and revolutionaries that Mao had collected. To bring China's client states into line, Deng sent 250,000 troops to the Vietnam border in 1979 and decided to "to teach Vietnam" a lesson in a brief war. Pyongyang took the hint. Kim Il Sung, who spoke Chinese well, visited Beijing each year and knew how to deal with China's elderly leadership, some of whom he had personally known during the Korean War. When Deng talked about democracy, freed millions of political prisoners, opened the economy to outside investment, and planted the seeds of capitalism, North Korea could not ignore him. Furthermore, Beijing secretly started trading with the South and imported some 200,000 black and white television sets, the first step to recognizing the Republic of Korea.

Deng continued supplying North Korea with grain and oil at "friendship prices" in order to prevent Pyongyang from slipping into Moscow's camp. A pipeline from China's Daqing oil fields supplied oil at a very fraternal U.S. $4-5 a barrel, but Deng made it clear that he wanted to move trade into a commercial footing. It was clear that the North should follow China's lead. North Korea at least had to pretend that it was copying China's economic reforms. After Kim Jong Il was sent in 1983 to inspect the "Special Economic Zone," which Deng had created at Shenzhen next to Hong Kong, North Korea talked about attracting foreign investment too. In May 1984, Hu Yaobang, Deng's second in command, visited Pyongyang and insisted on more progress. Kim Il Sung tried to deflect him by arguing that unlike China, which had a huge territory, North Korea was too small to afford the risk of opening up too much. Kim finally conceded: "We will open up but our opening confined to very restricted places."[17]

A lot had to be done to pull the wool over the eyes of the visiting high-level Chinese delegations. Kim quickly introduced a series of measures to placate the Chinese, including a joint venture law modeled on China's. This attracted 69 joint ventures, mostly from loyal Koreans in Japan who made suits and diesel engines or opened restaurants and bars in Pyongyang. One Belgian firm started a diamond-cutting factory and a few Hong Kong companies ran garment factories.

China formally closed its communes in 1984, dividing up the fields between households that contracted to deliver a part of their harvest to the state at a fixed price and were allowed to sell any surplus on the free market. Kim also permitted North Koreans to open farmers' markets and run small businesses such as those that would provide simple foods like tofu or kimchee, the national dish of fermented, peppery cabbage. Kim launched the August Third People's Consumer Goods Production Movement to encourage local-level factories to produce more consumer goods, and the collective farms even started an experiment in dividing up the fields of collective farms. Unlike China's system, North Korean party officials were sent in to ensure that the whole harvest went to the state.

At the same time, the existence of free markets was officially denied. No one was allowed to see or photograph the markets, and in interviews, Korean economists denied there was any need for reforms. "Our superior management system means that we don't need to apply the reform of other countries," one economics professor, Li Ki-song, told me in 1989.

Kim Il Sung knew that there was a fierce struggle over the scope and pace of China's reforms being waged within the Chinese Communist Party. Many conservatives opposed Deng, and after university students in Shanghai and other cities demonstrated democracy in December 1986, conservatives ousted Hu Yaobang, blaming him for encouraging "bourgeois liberalism." As soon as Hu Yaobang fell from power in January 1987, North Korea swiftly halted all reforms. The rural markets were closed, and thousands who had been running stalls ended up in prison camps.

As the country feigned compliance with Deng's wishes, North Korea's internal propaganda reported that he had succumbed to the sugarcoated bullets of Capitalism and betrayed Communism. Indignant North Koreans spat at Chinese students and teachers and even assaulted them. Beijing wanted a peaceful international environment to build up its economy and opposed Kim's warlike ambitions.

While Kim said one thing to the Chinese, he told Moscow something quite different when he visited in 1984 and 1986. The Soviets rewarded him with 60 MiG 23 and MiG 26 fighter jets, SAM-3 surface-to-air missiles, and SCUD missiles. In return, Pyongyang granted Soviet reconnaissance planes the right to fly over North Korea and the Soviet Pacific fleet the right to call at Wonson and Nampo harbors. After December 1985, the Soviet Union started transferring nuclear technology to build an experimental reactor at Yongbyon and promised to build a set of larger Chernobyl-type reactors. China had always declined similar demands, despite Kim Il Sung's requests since China tested its first bomb in 1965.

Pyongyang swung ever closer to Moscow. When North Korea celebrated its Independence Day in 1986, 40 Soviet and just 3 Chinese delegations were present. North Korea's leadership was not interested in reforms that would help revive the collapsing civilian economy; it wanted more weapons to wage war to "liberate" the South.

The tensions that mounted between Beijing and Pyongyang in 1986 lend some credibility to the stories of coup attempts and generals fleeing to China. Yet, as the next chapter explains, it was not until Hwang Jang-yop defected in 1997 that an even more astonishing story emerged about the intrigues in Pyongyang.

CHAPTER 6

Kim Jong Il's Court

In half a century as the god-like ruler of North Korea, Kim Il Sung had built himself many palaces, but his favorite retreat lay in the fresh pine woods of the Myohyang mountains. The Great Leader wanted a special guest, the President of South Korea, Kim Young Sam, to be comfortable. The summer can be hot and humid in Korea, and in the mountains it would be cooler than in Pyongyang, which lies a few hours drive away on the plain.

The Great Leader personally inspected the rooms where Kim Young Sam would stay in a fortnight's time. This visit would be a turning point in the history of the Korean Peninsula, which had been on the brink of a devastating war over the North's nuclear weapons program. Three weeks earlier the Great Leader had entertained Jimmy Carter on his yacht, and they had agreed on a plan to bring the two countries together and end the bitter legacy of the Korean War.

Then, on July 7, 1994, Kim Il Sung had a heart attack. Although he was 82 years old at the time of Carter's visit, President Carter had found Kim in robust health, able to walk up hills without effort. The official media blamed his death on "heavy mental strains," but later let it be known that doctors had been unable to reach the remote villa in time because they were hampered by dirt roads. This was odd. Kim Il Sung travelled everywhere with his entourage of secretaries and bodyguards, plus a team of doctors and nurses who were present at all times. The state provided the best hospital equipment money could buy and an Institute of Longevity was devoted to growing special food and researching diets and treatments, including, some say, transfusions of blood taken from selected virgins to maintain his vigour. Yet he died the following day, July 8, at two in the morning, without being revived or taken to a hospital.

As the country of 22 million plunged into mourning, rumors spread quickly that Kim Jong Il had caused his father's death, determined to both secure the throne and block the détente with the South. Lee Young-guk, a former bodyguard to Kim Jong Il, believes there may be some truth to the rumors. He says that when Kim Il Sung suffered his attack, Kim Jong Il issued instructions that no one, including his doctors, was allowed into his father's room. Later five helicopters were sent from Pyongyang to collect the body, but on the way back, Lee Young-guk claims, the two which were carrying the doctors and the rest of Kim Il Sung's personal entourage crashed, killing all on board. One by one anyone else, including the top officials in charge of Kim's security, either committed suicide or disappeared into the Gulag.

It is impossible to corroborate this story but it fits closely with the account given by Hwang Jang-yop in the first interview he gave while still in the South Korean Consulate in Beijing after he defected in 1997. Hwang said that the senior Kim had his heart attack while in the middle of a furious shouting match with his son. Kim Jong Il was opposing his father's instructions to organize a million cheering people to welcome the South Korean President.

When Kim Jong Il first became the apparent heir in 1974, there was a two-tier structure or a sort of co-kingship—with the father leading. As Kim Jong Il gathered more and more power, he wanted others to treat him as equal in rank to his father, yet he was careful never to let his father see this. "When I overheard him talking on the phone to his father, and he would be as obsequious as one can imagine, using the most honorific terms," recalled bodyguard Lee, "but behind his back he would do what he wanted."

At Seoul's Korea's Institute for Unification, one of the country's top North Korea watchers, Dr. Park Young-ho, confirmed that the father and son had been at odds over a range of issues. "Kim Jong Il had lied to his father about the true state of the economy for years, and when his father found out, they fell out, "Dr. Park said. The two had been at odds for over a year before Kim Il Sung's death.

Kim Jong Il's responsibilities required him to work through the night sorting and drafting replies to hundreds of reports filed by every part of the bureaucracy. Like the chief mandarin of a Chinese emperor, he had to have everything ready for his father by 4 A.M. so that in his morning audience, Kim Il Sung could approve all the documents and rescripts laid before him.

In a meeting with the South Korean media in 2000, Kim Jong Il said that he had developed the habit of sleeping just four hours a day. As the chief secretary of the Workers Party's Organization Department for 20 years, he would receive reports until 3 A.M. Hwang describes how Kim Jong Il gradually introduced a system under which every department had to submit policy recommendations for his personal approval. He would glance through the first three lines of each document to decide what was important. "The documents submitted by each bureau in the central committee every week can amount to a huge pile. The international bureau that I worked in submitted 30-40 papers a week," Hwang has reported. "All this constitutes a huge workload but Kim never passes this work to some one else but handles it personally. . . . No matter how busy he was, Kim Jong Il would personally read all the recommendations submitted and provide his comments or conclusions. For important documents submitted personally by the party secretaries, he would put the approved documents in his special envelope, write the recipient's name in it and seal it before passing to the secretary in charge."

Later on, Kim Jong Il kept his father informed by preparing a taped summary of key issues. Three months before his death Kim Il Sung explained this in an interview given to the *Washington Times*: "Because I have some eye problems, [Jong Il] has arranged for all reports to be recorded to save me from having to spend hours reading them. I am very proud to have such a good son. He is so concerned about my health."[1]

"None of Kim Il Sung's instructions could reach his subordinates without going through Kim Jong Il first," Hwang says. And from 1974 onward not even the most insignificant report could reach Kim without going through Kim Jong Il first. Kim Jong Il maintained his father's trust by continually inflating the personality cult. By the time Kim Il Sung reached his seventieth decade in 1982, his filial son had increased the number of monuments and other images of his father from 12,000 to 30,000. Foremost among the monuments was the gigantic Juche Tower with its eternal red flame and bricks covered with dedications from *Juche* societies around the world.

The junior Kim was the definitive interpreter of his father's beliefs, publishing such works as *Concerning Jucheism* and removing references to Marxism-Leninism. When the Party celebrated its fortieth anniversary in 1985, he also published the ten-volume collection: *The Great Jucheism.* Kim Il Sung certainly acknowledged his son's role in establishing *Juche*, saying that while he had "planted the seed of Jucheism, Kim Jong Il cultivated it into a forest of trees bearing fruits."

The cult was maintained by an unsustainable rate of inflation in the currency of devotion. By the time Kim Il Sung turned 80, the country had 70 bronze statues of him, 40,000 half-length plaster figures, 250 monuments in praise of his achievements, 350 memorial halls, and 3,500 "towers of eternal life." Every citizen wore a Kim Il Sung badge when they went out, and pictures of him and his son hung on the wall of the main room in every house or office.

For his eightieth birthday his son spent over a billion dollars on a three-month "loyalty festival," which included mass gymnastics, dances, and parades, each one bigger than the last. Every citizen was mobilized in "loyalty-pledging" mass rallies, relay races to deliver the people's "loyalty-pledging letters," and the collection of gifts. The Workers Party organized school children and farmers to manufacture a special quilt made of the soft neck feathers of 700,000 sparrows. Elsewhere, North Koreans erected 250-ton granite monuments to immortalize Kim's words of wisdom, including: "Water is Rice, And Rice is Communism" and "Our Socialist Farmers will have Good Harvests Year after Year."[2]

To Hwang's intense disgust, the elderly patriarch had begun sucking up to his son and for his fiftieth birthday had written a "ridiculous ode of praise about a king honouring his royal heir." Kim senior wrote in *For Carrying Forward and Accomplishing the Cause of Socialism* that all credit for the *Juche* is due to his son: "I have not particularly thought about systematizing the philosophical principle of Jucheism. This was taken care of by Comrade Kim Jong Il. Based on his thorough study of the fundamental principles of Jucheism, Comrade Kim Jong Il formulated our Party's guiding idea as an integrated system of ideas, theory and methods."

In this grotesque climate of mutual flattery the true extent of the country's decline was hidden from the Great Leader. Like a king in some Grimm fairytale, Kim Il Sung may have inhabited a world of illusion through a willing suspension of disbelief. He knew that the picture of his past was untrue (or so Hwang says) and perhaps suspected the economy was not quite as good as reported, but he believed a great deal of what he was told because he wanted to believe it.

Just what incident shattered the 80-year-old's illusions and opened his eyes to his son's deception is not clear. There are different versions. One claims that President Carter himself tipped Kim Il Sung off to the true economic situation. Kim went to personally inspect the house of peasants by the roadside and discovered their bare larders.

However, Kim Il Sung must have been aware of the crisis much earlier. In 1991, the government had made an appeal to the World Food Program for food aid, and a team of four experts arrived to assess the situation. After some confusion, they were told the country had no poor people, no malnutrition, and a grain harvest of 10 million tons, so they went home. This suggests that there was already a debate going on inside the Party about how to respond to the food shortages. Another version of events credits Kang Song-san (a cousin of Kim Il Sung by marriage) with alerting the Great Leader around this time.

Kang, premier of the DPRK between 1984–86, had pushed reformist policies like the adoption of the first joint venture law and a partial repayment of Western bank debts. In 1991, he was sent to govern the famine-struck North Hamgyong province and establish the Rajin-Sonbong free trade zone. According to Kang's son-in-law, Kang Myong-do, who defected in 1994, his father-in-law had insisted on briefing the Great Leader in person. This prompted Kim Il Sung to make his own on-the-spot inspections in the province and, noticing people foraging in the countryside, he stopped his car and went to ask what they were doing. The people said: "We are starving and trying to gather these wild foods to eat." Certainly after this event Kim Il Sung brought Kang Song-san back as his premier and dismissed Yon Hyong-muk, a man appointed by Kim Jong Il. Together Kim Il Sung and Kang took stock of the crisis and organized a series of meetings on the economy.[3]

Kim Il Sung had asked his brother Kim Jong-yu to return to power and take over the running of the country from Kim Jong Il. It now looked as if after 20 years as the crown prince, Kim Jong Il would not inherit the throne after all. The elderly Kim Jong-yu had been next in line until 1974, when

Kim Il Sung chose his son to create the first Marxist-Leninist dynasty in history. Kim Jong-yu then disappeared from view. In a further signal of his displeasure, Kim Il Sung also issued new orders that his son should not be appointed general secretary of the Workers Party or given other Party titles, although this should have followed Kim Jong Il's appointment as commander in chief in 1991.

All these stories, while hard to confirm, suggest that Kim Jong Il possessed the motive to remove his father. Although the notion that he might have actually murdered him seems hard to believe, it is still very revealing that many North Koreans hate Kim Jong Il enough to think it possible. For all his crimes and mistakes, even defectors feel the elder Kim merited genuine respect and admiration for his achievements. For his son, however, there is only contempt.

"His father had charisma, was a good talker who could speak without notes and always seemed well informed," said one European diplomat who dealt with both of them. "His son hated to attend meetings and preferred to work behind the scenes." According to Hwang the elder Kim liked to deal directly with people, listen to their views, and then issue verbal "on-the-spot instructions" that left the implementation to the discretion of his subordinates.

His son was more comfortable with paperwork. By the time he had consolidated his grip on the levers of power in 1985, none of the institutions set up by his father functioned in any meaningful way. The Party held fewer central committee meetings and no plenary congresses. The government ministries stopped issuing statistics and drawing up economic plans. The atmosphere in Pyongyang grew tense as Kim stepped up the surveillance and spying on Party officials and searched for new ways to test their loyalty. Every day senior members have to give a list of their activities and are forbidden to meet each other without his permission.

"He actually enjoys harassing party members," Hwang complained, and described him as a "born despot" who praises officials for showing revolutionary zeal when they harshly attack colleagues. After instigating a struggle at one such session at which top officials were goaded into criticizing each other, Kim would then go back to his office in his official residence and watch the proceedings through closed circuit television. Indeed a lot of his time seemed to be spent in his office, which he equipped with television sets so that he could watch a satellite news broadcast and with several computers so that he could surf the net.

The utter concentration of power, and knowledge, in the hands of one person who mistrusted everyone beyond a small group of drinking cronies and a narrow circle of family members, paralyzed the government. Kim Jong Il turned an already tightly controlled and secretive system into his personal fiefdom.

With so much to hide both from the outside world and his own father, it is understandable that his opposition to any reforms and openness could only grow. In China he had seen the Communist Party almost lose power with students demanding democracy in 1986 and again in 1989. Then came the dissolution of the Soviet Union and the outlawing of the Soviet Communist Party, the disappearance of East Germany and the execution of the Ceauşescus of Romania. It is more than plausible that his father would have felt had less to fear from Chinese-style reforms and an engagement policy than his son, as Kim Il Sung enjoyed a measure of genuine respect that lent some legitimacy to his authority. His son's fear that he would be put up against a wall once his extraordinarily lavish lifestyle became known is not unrealistic. Kim junior had everything to lose and nothing to gain from reforms.

Like a Marxist Sun King, he built for his exclusive pleasure at least eight palaces set on sprawling grounds. They contain golf courses, stables for his horses, garages full of motorbikes and luxury cars, shooting ranges, swimming pools, cinemas, funfair parks, water-jet bikes, and hunting grounds stocked with wild deer and duck. The grounds of his palaces are big enough to need cars to drive around and are staffed by his personal entourage of some 2,000 doctors, nurses, cooks, maids, valets, gardeners, masseurs, dancing troupes, and bodyguards. As a security precaution, Kim insists that each villa is always occupied so his enemies are never sure of his location. He travels everywhere accompanied by three different women, aged around 23 or 24, who serve as nurses, secretaries, and escorts and are replaced every six months. He has every rich man's toy from Harley Davidson motorbikes to a cruise yacht. He spends his weekends going duck shooting, exercising his stable of thoroughbreds imported from the Ukraine and Poland, and racing his collection of 100 imported limousines, part of the country's 7,000 Mercedes Benzes.

"In [a] real sense, he is the richest man in the world. There are not limits on what he can do. In South Korea there are rich men but I have never seen any facilities here which can rival what Kim has," his former bodyguard Lee Young-guk said.

"North Korea's economy exists first and foremost to serve the Dear Leader," wrote Hwang. "There is no probably no other country in the world past and present that has [as] many royal villas as North Korea—an army of escorts guards all these places, hostesses are stationed there round the clock in readiness for a royal visit."

Six decades of uninterrupted and absolute power enabled the Kims to create a life of such self-indulgent decadence that it trumps anything Stalinist dictators like Romania's Nicolae and Elena Ceauşescus or Third World despots like Ferdinand and Imelda Marcos of the Philippines ever dreamed of doing.

Much less is known of Kim Il Sung's private life than his son's, but the elder also had a reputation as a womanizer, and after taking power in Pyongyang he enjoyed a droit de seigneur. Anyone who caught his fancy would be brought to him and if necessary kidnapped.

Kim Il Sung seems to have enjoyed a lifestyle comparable to Mao Zedong's as is described by Mao's personal doctor Li Zhisui in *The Private Life of Chairman Mao*. Mao would move secretly around the country on a special armored train accompanied by his cooks and pretty nurses and stay in villas equipped with private swimming pools. He took with him, even on his train, a giant bed on which he slept with teenage girls who were re-cruited by his bodyguards after a careful selection process or chosen from song and dance troupes. In North Korea, I have traveled on a similar train with a large carriage bedroom that our hosts said was once used by Kim Il Sung.

Mao became obsessed with practicing Daoist sexual techniques intended not only for pleasure but to extend his life. He would insist on sleeping with several girls at once, and he even required handsome male guards to massage his groin. Like the Kims, Mao also benefited from a Longevity Institute that kept him supplied with rare and special foods, which accord-ing to the theories of Chinese medicine would extend his life and virility.

Among Communist rulers Kim Jong Il is the only one to have grown up in such a court, surrounded by fawning servants who sought to satisfy his every whim and craving. And growing up in the shadow of a powerful father, so feared that an entire nation worshipped him as a living god, must have had a disturbing impact on his psychological makeup. While Chinese and Soviet leaders have enjoyed the best their countries have to offer, Kim Jong Il has eagerly sampled the best the world has to offer. He sent his children to be educated in the best Swiss private schools and his wives to Geneva for medical treatment. Family members go on shopping expeditions to Finland, Moscow, and Tokyo. One son was detained while traveling on a false Dominican passport to visit Japan's Disneyland in 2001.

In a country that was and still is the most isolated in the world, Kim Jong Il's lust for foreign luxuries seems incredible, even absurd. No one in North Korea outside Kim's court is allowed to listen to foreign broadcasts, and an entire department in the Party is devoted to sending officials to people's homes to check that the dials on their radios are set to fixed frequencies. No written materials, not even packaging or plastic carrier bags, can be brought into the country. The entire population is shut off from the rest of the world so nothing can dilute the absolute reverence shown to the Kims, a complete and total idolatry that even Albania's Enver Hoxha and Romania's Ceausescus failed to achieve. For all the immense privileges enjoyed by these dictators or those who ruled the Soviet Union and China, they did not aspire to live a life completely alien to their countrymen. Stalin might have watched Hollywood films and Brezhnev took imported Western medicines, but they did not show signs of a consuming desire to emulate the tastes of a jet-set billionaire.

After Kim Jong Il won power in the late 1970s, he began to give free rein to his desires. He obsessively craved and was determined to enjoy and acquire foreign goods, books, films, food and drink, expensive brands of clothing, and watches. Kim Jong Il brought in foreign women, prostitutes, strippers, and singers, and all kinds of foreign acts from Turkish belly dancers to Romanian knife throwers, Swedish masseurs, Russian pop singers, and American professional wrestlers. He sought to enjoy every leisure activity that became popular abroad, including golf, karaoke, disco dancing, horseback riding, and duck shooting.

In 1977, North Korea became the first country to declare that it had reached the final stage of socialism and was now a utopia. In keeping with the country's *Juche* notions of self-sufficiency, North Koreans are brought up to believe that all they possess is of a quantity and quality far superior to anything people outside enjoy. The absurd illusion has been so successfully maintained that North Koreans say they are astonished by what they see even in poor parts of rural China.

In order to enjoy his extravagant lifestyle, using the means unwittingly provided by his father, Kim had to hide it by living a double life. Kim Jong Il even managed to pull off hiding the existence of his wife and their children from his father right up to his death. To do this he gathered around him his own court whose members were forbidden any contact with those outside, and he built his own set of palaces at which he could stay as he moved around the country. Even in 1979, the luxury at one of the first palaces he built at Nakwon county in South Hamgyong province was such that Lee marvelled when he started work there and saw Kim's flabby body braving artificial waves in an indoor pool on a motorized body board; the mansion also had a wine cellar, bar, movie theater, and other facilities. Kim Jong Il's rejection of his own country's way of life only makes sense if one considers that as a living god he considers himself beyond good or evil, that is to say not bound by the laws or conventions that apply to ordinary mortals.

Kim Jong Il's first marriage was to Hong Il-chon, the daughter of a revolutionary. They met while she was studying literature at the Kim Il Sung University. He allegedly beat her when she failed to produce any children, and they divorced in 1973 just as he was named as the official heir apparent. That year the elder Kim forced him to marry a girl of his choosing, Kim Young-sook, a typist and the daughter of a top general. She bore him a daughter, and although she is considered his "official" wife, she has never appeared in public with her husband. By the time they married, Kim Jong Il was deeply in love with Sung Hae-rim, a beautiful film star six years his senior. She was the wife of Li Pyong, the brother of one of Kim Jong Il's school friends, and when she became pregnant by Kim, Li Pyong was forced to divorce her.

A great deal is known about their relationship because Sung Hae-rim's elder sister, Sung Hae-rang, has published an autobiography, *The Wisteria House*, in which she describes her elder sister's genuine affection for Kim Jong Il. "If fate had turned out different," she wrote, "they could have made a great couple." Sung writes that Kim Jong Il feared disappointing his father and giving his rivals an opening to attack him. Sung Hae-rim was the daughter of a wealthy landlord so as a member of the "hostile class" she could never be considered a suitable consort. When Sung Hae-rim gave birth to a son, Kim Jong-nam, it had to be kept secret. Each night she was in the maternity hospital, Kim would park his car outside and flick his lights on, and she signalled back to tell him if it was a boy by switching the room lights on and off.

Sung Hae-rim lived in such dread of being discovered by Kim Jong Il's stepmother, Kim Song-ae, that when Kim Jong-nam fell ill and was taken to a hospital, she was terrified that they would be discovered. On one occasion, Kim Song-ae arrived at the hospital on an official visit. Sung Hae-rim took the sick child onto her back, climbed out of the window, and hid in the trees until she had left and it was safe to go back. The strain of this secret life began to cause her to suffer from insomnia and nervous exhaustion. Sung Hae-rim feared Kim Jong Il would throw her into the streets in a fit of rage. So, she went to Moscow, apparently underwent depression and anxiety treatment, and eventually died there in 2002, still in her mid-60s.

As the first-born son, Kim Jong-nam would be next in line to the throne, so it was peculiar that his existence was kept secret. Sung Hae-rang, who was put in charge of looking after him, says he was kept in Kim's private residence like a prisoner. To keep the boy happy Sung Hae-rang brought her own daughter, Lee Nam-ok, who was five years older and his sole playmate from the age of eight. Lee, who now lives in Paris with the son of a French intelligence officer, has been writing her memoirs. In 1998, she gave an interview to a Japanese magazine and described how the two lonely children spent their time in a huge playroom stocked with every possible toy. "Jong-nam was babied so much. I have never seen such a big collection of new latest-fashion toys even after I came to the West," she said. Jong-nam's favorite bedtime reading was *Anne of Green Gables*. Most of the books, television programs, and movies he enjoyed came from South Korea, and when Jong-nam became fond of a famous South Korean comedian he saw on television, his father ordered a countrywide search to find a look-alike who was then trained to deliver the act. "Jong-nam, who was only eight at the time, knew the man was a fake," Lee wrote. "He said, 'I know this isn't real' then stormed off to his room."

When Jong-nam was about ten years old, it was decided they should both study abroad. They first went to Geneva in 1981, and then the next year enrolled at a school for French-speakers in Moscow, but the boy reportedly complained that the toilets were dirty. The two then returned to Geneva where they attended an international school and came home during the holidays. "We sometimes went around Pyongyang in a chauffeur-driven Benz but we were not allowed to get out of the car. Certainly, we could not get out of the car to look around. Attendants always came with us when we went outside," she wrote.

In 1982, Lee's brother, Lee Il-nam, disappeared in Geneva when he was 21, and in 1992, Lee escaped as well; they both lived in hiding for several years. Lee Il-nam resurfaced in Seoul living under a false identity, but in 1996, he published a book on his life in Pyongyang. Their mother, Sung Hae-rang, then escaped from Kim's villa in Geneva and joined them. In 1997, a few months after Hwang's defection, unknown assailants caught up with Lee Il-nam and shot him dead in the hallway of his apartment building in a suburb of Seoul.

Meanwhile, Jong-nam fell into disgrace when at the age of 33 he was deported from Japan for illegal entry in 2001. He was pictured being led, like a prisoner, to a plane at Nariita airport after he and his entourage were found carrying passports issued by the Dominican Republic. He explained that he was on trip to visit Disneyland, but the Japanese press later recounted in salacious detail his visits to massage parlors and the less than flattering comments about his performance by one hostess who had entertained him. The Japanese authorities also revealed that Kim had toured Japan on two previous occasions starting in 1995, always using forged passports.

Kim Jong Il may have fathered at least nine illegitimate children from his various mistresses. He had an affair with Son Nui-rim, the sister of the North Korean ambassador to Russia. They had two daughters, but he discarded her when she became mentally ill in 1991. She moved to Moscow, where her father cares for her. Another long-term lover was Li Sang-jin, who was his classmate at Kim Il Sung University and was married to a Foreign Ministry official. In 1990, Kim seduced the nineteen-year-old daughter of the director of the North Korean Judo Association who became a member of the Mansudae Art Troupe and gave birth to another daughter.

Others have met sad ends like Wu In-hui, an actress born in Japan who was accused of being unfaithful to Kim Jong Il and shot in 1979 before a crowd of 5,000 shouting "kill, kill." According to Lee, she was discovered cheating when she fell unconscious during a tryst with another Korean from Japan. It was a hot summer day and they were in a cold storage truck, a gift her lover brought to North Korea. Another mistress, a singer from the Pyongyang Art Troupe, drowned herself in the Taedong River when Kim tired of her in the late 1970s.

Others did well. Hong Yung-hui, who played a lead role in Kim's evolutionary opera "The Flower Girl," eventually married a man that Kim picked for her. In May 1991, he fell for a new actress, twenty-year-old Chung Hye-sun, because she bore an uncanny likeness to Kim's mother and had the lead role in a television drama series. She was installed in a luxurious villa and given a Mercedes Benz. Kim Jong Il's most important relationship is now with Ko Yong-hee, who caught his eye after she started dancing in the Mansudae Art Troupe that puts on Kim's revolutionary works like "The Flower Girl" and "We Will Follow You Forever."

Ko Yong-hee, the daughter of Koreans who emigrated from Japan in the 1960s lured by fantasies of a socialist paradise, has given birth to two sons and a daughter and is often a hostess at Kim's parties. Her eldest son, Kim Jong-chul, may now be the next in line. He was born in 1981 and studied in Switzerland, where he lived incognito as the son of the driver and cleaner at the North Korean Embassy. He now works in the Party's Department of Agitation and Propaganda. An official campaign has started to glorify his mother as "a respected mother" and "a loyal subject," a sign that one of her sons might now be the crown prince. However in 2003, a Japanese newspaper reported that Kim Yong-hee had been hospitalized after a car accident, which some think means that Kim Jong-nam is trying to prevent Kim Jong-chul from taking over.

In the early 1980s, Kim Jong Il launched "The Project to Guarantee the Longevity of the Great Leader and the Dear Leader," which involved the Workers Party recruiting and training around 2,000 girls for "pleasure groups." At the start of the school year, local Party committees had to find candidates who met the basic criteria, such as a minimum height requirement of 5 feet 3 inches. A list of the top 100 were forwarded to Section Five of the Party's Organization Department and a medical examination narrowed the list down to 50. The Bodyguard Bureau checked their background, and then Kim, after checking their photos, made his final selection. Each group had a "satisfaction team" to perform sexual services, a "happiness team" for massage, and a third for dancing and singing.

One of Kim's former dancers is now in Seoul. O Yong-hui is a petite slender woman with a pale porcelain complexion, and almond eyes beneath finely arched eyebrows. Now 33, she started out living the hard life of a professional gymnast until she was recruited to join one of Kim's four all-girl dance troupes. "I wasn't beautiful enough for anything else, and then I began to get plump," she laughed, exposing a dazzling smile. Two troupes specialized in traditional Korean dances, but she joined the Mok Ran dance group and was one of twelve girls who wore micro-skirts and tank tops to perform disco, tango, waltz, and other modern dance numbers. Like everyone else who joined the court she had to sever all contact with the outside world for five years. Inside this bubble they lived a life of great luxury.

O Yong-hui said she wore handmade Italian shoes and Japanese designer clothes like Yamoto, Kenzo, and Mori. On her wrist was an Omega inscribed with Kim Jong Il's name. Swiss trade statistics show that at the height of the famine in 1998, North Korea imported watches from Switzerland worth $U.S. 2.6 million. At breakfast she enjoyed French croissants, fresh yogurt, and imported fruits because Kim said they must have clear and healthy skin. At lunch there was fresh raw fish Japanese style, and at dinner there were Korean or Western dishes. "We ate off porcelain dishes inlaid with roses and used silver tableware. Everything was imported and nothing I have ever seen in South Korea is as good," she said. A special department organized the catering for Kim and his court, and the food, like everything else in North Korea, had a code name. His food was "number eight item," but central committee members merited only "number nine item" supplies.

O Yong-hui cannot confirm the stories of orgies that some say took place at Kim's regular weekend parties. She says she was never forced to sleep with anyone. However, both the ex-chef Fujimoto and the bodyguard Lee report seeing half-naked girls at the parties. "Many of the girls around Kim are not there for sex. They are like ladies in waiting at a royal court. Kim would lose face if he slept with ordinary girls," she said. On the other hand she thinks that Kim has probably slowed down a lot. "When he was young he mixed with a lot of girls but later he restrained himself." From the 1970s onward he began to kidnap and later to hire prostitutes and entertainers. I can vouch for some of the stories. On a visit to Pyongyang in 1986, our party of journalists was taken to the circus, and in a row of seats in front of us we noticed a dozen outstandingly beautiful blondes. In the interval, we discovered that they came from Sweden and Germany and their leader, a Swede with a gold medallion, said they were on a "cultural exchange." A buxom girl from Bavaria told me they were staying for a week outside the city at an ornate villa with a swimming pool.

Kim usually held a party on Friday or Saturday night, and those who fell out of favor would know it when the invitations stopped. The kidnapped South Korean film director Shin Sang-ok and actress Choi Un-hee first met Kim Jong Il when they were reunited at one of these parties, and Choi recorded Kim's drunken slurred speech. She also describes how when she fell asleep upstairs, she woke to find one of the men groping her.

Choi, who recorded 45 minutes of their meeting on a tape recorder, reveals a man with a streak of self-deprecating wit: "Well Madame Choi, what do you think of my physique? Small as a midget's turd, aren't I?" he said.

"Shall we make Mr. Shin one of our regular guests?" Kim is heard to have asked the crowd drunk on Cognac. One of his generals boasts that he can reach Pusan in a week, and as others come up to salute Kim, a group of dancing girls is on stage screaming "Long live the great leader!" At this moment, Kim shakes Shin's arm and pointing at the display says: "Mr. Shin, all that is bogus. It's just pretence."

He told the South Koreans he wanted them to improve the film industry, which he admitted was profoundly disappointing. "The North's film-makers are just doing perfunctory work. They don't have any new ideas," Kim told the couple. "Their works have the same expressions, redundancies, the same old plots. All our movies are filled with crying and sobbing. I didn't order them to portray that kind of thing."[4]

Kim gave Shin $3 million a year and a staff of 700 to make films, and Kim even insisted on taking part in all the storyboard conferences, saying he wanted to make movies that would inspire both awe and affection for North Korea. Shin made seven movies before he and his wife made a daring escape to Vienna. He describes in his memoir *Kingdom of Kim* how Kim generously sent trucks with pheasants, deer, and wild geese for the crew to feast on after they made the epic *Pulgasari*, based on the legend of a great fourteenth-century Koryo monarch. Many of his palaces have a private cinema, and Shin said he saw Kim's huge underground library of films.

Kim's favorites include Daffy Duck cartoons, James Bond films, *Rambo*, *Friday the 13th,* and Hong Kong action films. In 1996, he wanted to see the Jean-Claude van Damme film *Sudden Death* so badly he ordered diplomats at the United Nations to go out and buy him a copy. Shin says he watches these movies to understand the real world.

Fujimoto, the Japanese chef, describes the same mixture of malicious levity. At a banquet party held in a rural city, Kim suddenly told the dancers on the stage to strip naked and then he ordered his men to dance with them as a prank, saying, "You can dance with them but if you touch them, you will be arrested as thieves." On another occasion, a drunken Kim ordered the dancers to don boxing gloves and fight each other.

Fujimoto was himself given one of the professional singers as a wife and describes their wedding party, held in February 1989, on the second floor of the No. 8 Banquet Hall. Attendees drank bottles of Hennessey XO Cognac, including high-ranking officials. Waking up the next morning, after having downed a bottle and a half, Fujimoto describes how Kim came to see him. "He asked whether I had any pubic hair and I answered 'yes,' but he said to me—'let's go to the bathroom to check it.'" "We went to the bathroom but there was nothing there," he said. While Fujimoto was drunk, Kim had ordered some one to remove it. With a smile, Kim Jong Il told him, "That's how we celebrate weddings."

The drinking parties often started at midnight and went on until dawn; one is said to have lasted for four days. Executive guests were not allowed to sleep until Kim Jong Il went to bed. "It was torture for them," Fujimoto said.

Hwang reports that Kim Jong Il once ordered a political struggle session because Party officials did not clap hard enough during a performance by his "happiness team." "After that incident, Party officials who attend performances by his favorite artists had to make sure they clap long and loud. They have to keep up the applause through several curtain calls and can only leave their seats when the performers no longer respond to their applause," he said.[5]

Kim Jong Il has admitted that he drank a lot before he turned 50, telling South Korean journalists before the 2000 summit that "my doctors won over me, prohibited hard liquors, and recommended that I drink not more than half a bottle of good red wine a day. I prefer Bordeaux or Burgundy, and strictly follow their advice." At one of his sprawling residencies in

Pyongyang is a cellar stocked with 10,000 bottles of wine. Lee says Kim sometimes starts the day by sampling a few bottles.

Fujimoto says Kim had serious drinking problems in his youth and by 1978 was in need of rehab. This may be connected to injuries sustained from a helicopter crash in 1976, which left him with a scar on the top of his hairline. He was also badly hurt in a 1992 horseback riding accident, dislocating his shoulder and losing consciousness, but he refused to take painkillers, saying he did not wish to become a drug addict.

His drinking problems appear to have worsened in the 1980s. Various bodyguards describe someone who drank all the time, often starting at noon and continuing through the night. Kim seems to have had a habit of disappearing on drinking binges for days and sometimes weeks on end. Soviet diplomats reported attending meetings at which Kim Jong Il spoke in such a confused way that it was hard to translate. In one meeting, his father reprimanded him for turning up drunk.

Like a manic-depressive alternating between lows and highs, Kim sometimes surprised his staff with bursts of exuberant generosity. Soviet diplomats have also remarked that Kim often had a good way with people with a reliable memory for their names and their children. Fujimoto said that on one occasion Kim tossed the keys to a Mercedes Benz into his lap and said, "Take it, it's yours." Of course, the car with the plate numbered 2:16 after his birthday still belonged to Kim. When he was in a good mood, Lee confirms, Kim would give his guards deer or ducks that he shot while hunting, or stuff their hands with rare pineapples, bananas, and mandarin oranges.

Those in his court or working on key projects like the nuclear program would get gift packages on his or his father's birthday and at New Year. Kim Jong Il would hand out Japanese color TV sets, Swiss Omega watches, French cognac, as well as imported refrigerators, sewing machines, cassette recorders, clothes, and special foods. Senior generals could expect to be rewarded with a Mercedes Benz 280s and invitations to join him on hunting trips and other junkets. When he took command of the army in 1991, he promoted hundreds of lower-ranking officers to become generals so that by 1992, there were 1,220 general-grade officers giving an absurd ratio of 1 general to every 900 soldiers.

"You can't really describe him as a freak but he speaks very fast and it is frightening, his mood can change just like that," says O Yong-hui. Kim is also known to exhibit a streak of mawkish sentimentality. Sung Hae-rang relates how one day Kim Jong Il arrived home from a hunting trip in great agitation and called a hospital to ask if "mother and baby" were alright. Everyone stared in bewilderment at the distraught Kim until he explained how he had mistakenly shot a pregnant deer. In a fit of conscience, he had rushed doe and unborn fawn to the hospital, where the baby deer was put in an incubator in the maternity ward.

Fujimoto also describes him weeping as he read a letter from Ko Yong-hee when she was in Switzerland being treated for cancer. He also became so depressed after his father's death that his wife, Ko, claimed to have discovered him in a room with a gun, apparently contemplating suicide. Hwang Jang-yop recounts how one winter's day Kim insisted that no one should clear the snow in Pyongyang because he thought everything looked so beautiful."He told everyone that the snow was also good for health and contains all the nutrients a person needs," said the bodyguard Lee, who confirmed the story.

Life in North Korea is shaped by many of Kim's whims, such as a ban on women riding on the back seat of bicycles, on the grounds that it is indecent, and various edicts forbidding women to grow long hair or wear red trousers. A particular obsession is with triplets. The number three is thought to be auspicious in North Korea and triplets are revered. When any one gives birth to triplets, the mother and children must immediately be brought, often by helicopter, to a special hospital ward at the Pyongyang Maternity Hospital. The children are gifted with inlaid silver knives, and the parents given golden rings decorated with rubies. The parents must then abandon their children to the cold care of the state. The official press attributes this treatment to Kim Il Sung, who said, "frequent births of triplets are a sign of the prosperity of the country," but some suspect it stems from an irrational fear, perhaps a fortune-teller's warning that one day triplets would topple his regime. It is believed they are likely to rise to positions of power, which accounts for Kim Jong Il's insistence that they are all raised in state-run orphanages, where their development can be controlled.[6]

Depending on his mood, he could order his staff to get married or send them to their death in a labor camp. It was normal for him to choose the spouses of his subjects, and a small hint was enough for them to consent. "Kim would say, hey, you look pretty, you should marry someone. Then he would suggest the son of some high-ranking official—and a girl can hardly reject such proposals," O Yong-hui said. When she reached 25 and had to retire, she herself was married off to Chou Hyuk, one of Kim's bodyguards. Fujimoto was married off in the same way.

A tantrum by Kim could also ruin the lives of anyone around him. Lee claims he had his barber shot when one day he botched his bouffant hairdo. Another incident he remembers took place in 1984, when Kim sent a 68-year-old servant, No Myung-gun, who had cared for him and his family since his childhood, to the coal mines. One day the old man was smoking a cigarette and took an elevator in one of Kim's palaces reserved for Kim. Kim entered afterwards, detected the stale tobacco smoke, and flew into a rage. He accused the servant of stealing one of the cigarettes kept in a box in the lift for Kim's exclusive use. Once in the labor camp, the other prisoners discovered who the old man was and stoned him to death. On hearing of this, Kim had them all shot.

Sung Hae-rang confirms these stories. "I know of people who died because he abandoned them . . . Losing . . . favor meant the end of one's career and sometimes one's life," she wrote. Once Kim caught his teenage son with an unapproved girlfriend and threatened to send him to the coal mines and cut off food shipments to the house where Jong-nam lived with his mother and aunt. Sung recalls kneeling before Kim, along with the rest of the family, to beg for mercy until he relented. Li Nam-ok said Kim Jong Il was angry at his son's drunken behavior, and he forced the family to forage in the garden for food. He forgot about the incident so completely that two months later, he scolded the family for not ordering their regular food shipments.

The security the Kims have built around themselves is quite remarkable. The key members of the inner court live in ten closely guarded ghettos in the center of Pyongyang, which resembles the Forbidden City area of imperial Peking. A special area is reserved for Kim Jong Il, and like the Forbidden City palace, it is designed according to geomantic principles with a sort of imperial avenue aligning north and south.

The whole city has been designed to enable the regime to survive a nuclear attack. Underground tunnels link each key building or palace within the city to another so that Kim can move from one to another without being seen. Deep under his residence is a nuclear bunker that connects to a series of tunnels sunk below the metro system, which is already 300 feet below the surface. Underneath the vast Kim Il Sung Square is another square with a bunker command post and enough space to marshal 100,000 people. A 30-mile tunnel can take the leader unseen out of the city to a mountain villa in the North at Sunchon where an airport exists for hasty getaways. The design seems identical to networks of tunnels, underground trains, and roads built by Mao Zedong beneath the center of Beijing, which also allow secret access to the military garrison headquarters some 20 miles out in the Western Hills.

Since the 1960s, it has been Kim Jong Il's task to personally oversee the construction of such military facilities, including the Fifth Corps headquarters and the Pyongyang garrison. Hwang describes the garrison as an underground fortress with living quarters for all personnel, movable portals for heavy guns, state of the art lighting, and water and ventilation systems. There are thought to be over 10,000 other underground military facilities in the country, each with a stockpile of food, equipment, and munitions to enable the military and Party to survive a six-month-long war.

The core of the military is highly trained, and the well-equipped professional force of some 100,000 serves as a sort of Praetorian guard like Saddam Hussein's Republican Guard. It is powerful enough to destroy a revolt by any part of the 1.1 million-strong army. Hwang says it also manages numerous enterprises from oil refineries to cooperative farms that supply the elite's needs.

Kim Jong Il is guarded at all times by a unit of around a thousand highly trained men. Lee Young Kook was selected at age 17 for his burly physique out of a lineup of a thousand classmates. He underwent a punishing training in marksmanship, martial arts, and fitness until he could hit a moving target at 700 feet after sprinting in a chemical weapons suit and gas mask. The targets were always mock-ups of American soldiers. Lee joined the group of guards in 1976 and served Kim for 11 years. During his service, he worked his way up to Kim's elite corps of about 280 bodyguards. In his role as a bodyguard, Lee accompanied Kim to public and private engagements and stood guard at his eight residences, one in each province. The guards were only given notice of his movements two hours ahead of departure.

After the Korean War, boys were chosen to act as bodyguards from the many post-war orphanages. It was thought that they could be trusted to show utter loyalty. When the supply of such recruits dried up, the body-guard unit introduced strict background checks and rules to ensure that only one member of any family joined. Once recruited to serve the Great Leader, all traces of their existence were erased and they were forbidden to have any contact with the outside world.

Somehow it was discovered that Lee was serving alongside a younger cousin. Lee had to leave the service and returned home to his parents, whom he had not seen in 11 years. He was shocked, then angry, when he found them barely surviving on a thin gruel. Fujimoto also reports visiting his in-laws with his new wife and finding eight people crammed into two small rooms. When Lee found everyone slowly dying of starvation, some-thing turned inside him. He decided to escape, but was caught in China by North Korean agents who pretended to be South Koreans and brought to a camp for political prisoners where he was brutally interrogated. He lost one eye, and one of his eardrums burst. Blessed with a strong physique and years of harsh training, he survived and managed to escape again.

After the first Gulf War, Kim began to fear a U.S. pre-emptive air strike. The Japanese chef Fujimoto describes how during the military standoff with the United States in 1994, Kim and his entourage moved out after midnight in a convoy of 20 identical Mercedes to escape detection by U.S. spy satellites. Some reports also claim that when the Second Iraq War be-gan, he crossed the border into Russia on his armored train and did not return for six weeks.

During the day Kim's guards are posted 100 yards apart, and at night 50 yards apart, with orders to shoot any intruders on sight. Lee recalls an inci-dent when a fishing boat slipped through the 10-mile cordon in front of one of his beach houses and approached the shore. After warning shots, the guards opened fire, killing two people on board. Another incident ended the same way. A car, apparently lost, drove onto a paved road leading to the house and when Lee arrived, the guards had the driver. The passenger leapt out and was running away when the guards shot him twice in the back.

After the collapse of the Soviet empire, Kim drastically strengthened his secret police and divided it into three separate surveillance organizations, one for the military, one for the party, and another for the general public.

The bodyguard unit was enlarged to 450 men (and, of course, named the 2.16 unit after Kim's birthday). In his training as a bodyguard, Lee had to study the overthrow of the Ceaușescus, the U.S. bombing of Colonel Qaddafi's residence, and the plot to assassinate General de Gaulle. According to Lee, the death of the Ceaușescus made a particularly deep impression on him. The "Genius of the Carpathians" was put up against a wall and shot after a 24-year reign despite the trust the Ceaușescus placed in their dreaded Securitate police force. In the end, even their bodyguards deserted them.

Several refugees I met were convinced that Kim had narrowly survived several assassination attempts. One of his bodyguards reportedly tried to shoot him on March 5, 1998, when residents heard shooting between police and soldiers. A night curfew was imposed on Pyongyang and foreigners and residents were forbidden to leave the city for several weeks as soldiers carried out searches. Rumors circulated about another unsuccessful assassination attempt that took place in 2001 or early 2002 that also involved a bodyguard and allegedly left Kim with such injuries that he was unable to sit or lie down comfortably.

In April 2004, Kim Jong Il may have narrowly escaped another assassination attempt when he returned from a state visit to China. Two parked trains filled respectively with ammonium nitrate and fuel exploded at Ryongchon station, close to the border crossing with China, around the time his train passed in the direction of Pyongyang. The explosion left 170 dead and hundreds wounded. A North Korean report said that Kim's armored train had passed through nine hours before, an effort to dispel rumors that he had been killed in an assassination attempt. Normally the media never reports on his movements. Even if, as North Korea claims, the explosion was an accident sparked by an electrical fault, the event will further fan the paranoia of the Kim clan that internal and external enemies surround them. It illustrates only too well the contradictions of Kim Jong Il's life—a man who enjoys absolute power and the greatest of luxuries but lives in constant fear because of the knowledge that most of those around him wish to see him dead.

CHAPTER 7

Kim Jong Il—The Terrorist Master

When a mysterious vessel was spotted lurking close to Japan's shores in 2001, a naval patrol gave chase. When the intruder refused to stop, there was a brief firefight, and the vessel sank to the bottom of the sea. Later the Japanese navy managed to raise it and put it on public display in 2002. To any casual observer it looked like an ordinary fishing boat, but up close it was possible to see that it was heavily armed with weapons that included a surface-to-air missile launcher. Closer examination revealed that a special door fitted into the hull could open to release a tiny submersible scooter big enough to carry three men for a few miles. It enabled special agents to sneak ashore undetected. A further sinister touch was a switch labeled "self-destruct," which the crew had pressed rather than be captured alive.[1]

The vessel's discovery finally answered a question that had haunted the Japanese for decades: How had North Korea been able to kidnap dozens, perhaps hundreds, of ordinary Japanese peacefully going about their business and smuggle them out of the country and into North Korea? Yet, it left unanswered another mystery: Why would anyone wish to abduct someone like 13-year-old schoolgirl Megumi Yokota? Last spotted by a traffic light carrying her badminton racquet and clutching a schoolbag, she disappeared near her home in Niigata in 1977.

Kim Jong Il apologized for the kidnappings when he hosted Japanese Prime Minister Junichori Koizumi at a summit in 2002. He admitted that agents "carried away by a reckless quest for glory" had abducted 13 Japanese citizens, and eight of them were now dead. North Koreans began abducting Japanese, South Koreans, and other nationalities in the mid-1970s, after Kim Jong Il was formally recognized as his father's successor and took charge of the intelligence services. Of the thousands of South Koreans abducted, sometimes off the streets of European capitals, few have ever escaped. But in 1986, two very famous South Koreans, actress Choi Un-hee and her film-director husband Shin Sang-ok, suddenly resurfaced after six years. They had the evidence, including a tape recording, that Kim Jong Il had personally been behind their abduction from Hong Kong.

Hwang Jang-yop describes his former protégé as a "genius of international terrorism," and these operations reveal his hallmark mixture of zaniness and callous brutality. Yet, the record suggests that far from being a genius, Kim Jong Il has done his own cause more damage than good. Under his leadership, North Korea became a gangster state that has been repeatedly caught smuggling drugs, counterfeiting dollars, harboring terrorists, and trafficking in missiles and nuclear technology. The gains have been small compared to the losses incurred. North Korea has been shunned by its neighbors and by every international institution that could help it.

The case of the 13 abducted Japanese illustrates this vividly. Kim Jong Il offered the apology in the hopes of establishing diplomatic relations, and securing up to U.S. $10 billion in loans and aid that Tokyo was dangling as reparations for the Japanese occupation. However, Kim then balked at allowing the five surviving Japanese hostages to return home, at least not with their families. Furthermore, he refused to meet requests for further information about other missing Japanese who are suspected to have also been kidnapped by North Korea. Consequently, Japan withheld the aid, and the summit, despite his confession, brought Kim no real benefits. As in so many things, Kim Jong Il persisted with a strategy long after it had outlived its usefulness. Why Kim ever thought kidnapping was a worthwhile venture seems inexplicable in the first place. The Japanese captives were forced into performing tasks, such as training North Korean spies, that could easily have been done by others. For example, some of the Chongryon community, the 200,000 ethnic Koreans resident in Japan, might have been recruited. They could have provided any number of false identities, or any amount of language training or translation work. Many of them had migrated to Japan as it industrialized or had been brought there during

World War II, and remained fiercely nationalistic and loyal to Kim Il Sung. About 90,000 of them had voluntarily emigrated back from Japan to take part in the reconstruction of the country after the Korean War.

North Korea projected an image abroad of dynamic self-reliance that won respect even in distant corners of the world. Many leaders in the Socialist and Third World blocs found much to admire in North Korea. The efficiency with which the North implemented its personality cult, autarkic industrial policies, ultra-nationalism, mass mobilization, and militarism drew many admirers, especially among those wishing to distance themselves from the hegemony of the superpowers. In a world full of one-party states run by dictators seeking popular support through strident nationalism, North Korea did not seem so very odd. Some dictators even found much to learn from its hard-line policies.

When Nicholai and Elena Ceauşescus of Romania visited China and North Korea in 1971, they were positively inspired. Romania's Great Conductor loved the huge crowds and the minutely choreographed demonstrations of mass adulation that greeted them in North Korea. When the Ceauşescus returned home, they wanted to start a "mini-cultural revolution" and enjoy a magnificent personality cult of their own. They quickly published the "July theses," bringing an end to the country's period of "relaxation" and instigating a cultural crackdown. It is also interesting to note that both North Korea and Romania's economies, which had earned much praise for their impressive statistics, collapsed at about the same time in the mid-1980s. Even other heavily industrialized states like East Germany, whose performance won high praise from Western scholars in the 1970s, followed the same downward path.

Under Kim Il Sung, North Korea was already involved in operating plenty of "terrorist" attacks, but in the 1960s these were directed against South Korea. As the two were in a state of suspended civil war, these hostile incursions into South Korea did not lose North Korea any foreign friends. During the early 1970s, Pyongyang provided weapons and training to many guerrilla groups, a few of whom won power. In Latin America, it helped radicals in Argentina, Bolivia, Brazil, Chile, Guatemala, Mexico, Nicaragua, Paraguay, Peru, and Venezuela. In Africa, North Korea supported the Polisario guerrillas operating in the Western Sahara against Morocco, as well as the Zimbabwe African National Liberation Front and the Mozambique People's

Liberation Army. In April 1971, Sri Lanka expelled all 18 of the North Korean resident diplomats for giving financial support to the People's Liberation Front, which attempted to overthrow the Sri Lankan government in an armed uprising. All told, the DPRK is accused of running terrorist camps that have trained an estimated 5,000 Third World revolutionaries, including the African National Congress, the Palestine Liberation Organization, and the Popular Front for the Liberation of Palestine.

North Korea became increasingly involved in supporting not just Third World insurgencies but the terrorist acts of radical groups in the developed world. It gave refuge to nine members of the Japanese radical terrorist gang, the Red Army Faction, who in 1970 hijacked a Japanese Boeing 707 airliner to Pyongyang. The gang hoped to establish a base in North Korea and from there foment a worldwide proletarian revolution. Unconfirmed reports also indicate that members of European terrorist groups, such as the Italian Red Brigades and the German Baader-Meinhof gang, received training in North Korea.

In the mid-1970s, North Korea also supplied modest amounts of military equipment and training to countries including Angola, Benin, Burkina Faso, the Congo, Ethiopia, Ghana, Madagascar, Mozambique, Tanzania, Uganda, Zambia, and Zimbabwe. Zimbabwe was North Korea's most ambitious effort, as father and son supported Robert Mugabe even before he took power in 1980 after a civil war. North Korea equipped and trained his Army's 5th Brigade, supplying Mugabe with tanks, armored personnel carriers, trucks, ground- and air-defense artillery, and about U.S. $18 million worth of small arms and ammunition. Training included political indoctrination and Korean-style martial arts. Korean-trained troops have been blamed for the atrocities committed against Zimbabwean political rivals.

North Korea's ambitions to develop a following of Third World allies stemmed from Kim Il Sung's desire to establish himself as a Third World leader, an ambition that Kim Jong Il continued to stoke. The Dear Leader hailed *Juche* as not merely "a banner of victory that leads a nation to infinite prosperity and development" but the foundation of a "world outlook centered on people, a revolutionary ideology for achieving the independence of the masses of the people." Kim Jong Il told propaganda workers in 1976 that Kim-Il-Sungism had a timeless and universal message that Marxism-Leninism lacked. A year later he organized the first international conference on "Korea's gift to the world." The younger Kim started to fund study groups around the world and took out full-page advertisements in Western newspapers. Journalists and scholars were invited to Pyongyang to interview him, and the absurd books compiled by obscure Third World journalists are still sold in the foyers of hotels in Pyongyang.[2]

As Kim Jong Il pandered to his father's vanity, he began to run afoul of both Moscow and Beijing, both of which looked askance at Kim Il Sung's claims. The effort to project Kim as a world statesman who could replace Chairman Mao as the standard bearer of Asian Communism was provocative. The Chinese consider themselves one of the great powers and are extremely conscious of the hierarchy of states. In earlier times Kim would have held the rank of a small king, and in Communist terms he ruled over a territory smaller than most Chinese provinces. By seeking the status symbols of a larger power, such as a nuclear arsenal or the right to host prestigious international gatherings like the Olympics, Kim was going above his station. China repeatedly turned down North Korea's request for nuclear secrets, sending the message that the small state does not require such capabilities.

After Deng Xiaoping came to power in China, he visited Pyongyang on a state visit to celebrate North Korea's thirtieth anniversary in September 1978. As part of the festivities, Deng was brought to pay his respects to a huge statue of Kim Il Sung that was covered in gold from head to toe. Deng, who at the time was doing his utmost to demolish the Mao cult and tear down statues of the former leader, eyed the figure with fury. He later complained to his hosts that they had squandered aid from the hard-pressed Chinese and now had the nerve to demand more. Within a few months the gold, worth U.S. $851 million, was quietly removed and the statue repainted a bronze color. Yet, Pyongyang continued endeavors to enhance Kim's stature in the face of Beijing's opposition but was only led to humiliating rejections. Unsuccessful efforts to corral summit meetings of the Nonaligned Movement into expressing their great admiration for Kim proved embarrassing for all involved.

Just north of Beijing near the Ming tombs lays one of the underground airfields that Mao Zedong built during the height of the Cold War. Planes kept inside a hangar could blast out of a hillside and take off down a runway, safe from attack. After the 1963 Cuban Missile Crisis, when Moscow backed down, China made a vast effort to build nuclear air-raid shelters under all major cities and relocate strategic coastal factories to hidden valleys or caves in the mountains. Aircraft hangars, runways, submarines, and destroyers were all secreted deep inside mountain caves so that after a pre-emptive strike, Chinese forces could sally forth unscathed. China also embarked on an accelerated and successful program to produce its own deterrent force of nuclear missiles, as well as a standing army and an armoury of tanks, ships, and planes that, numerically at least, was second to none.

Kim Il Sung copied these policies completely and from 1963 plunged the country into an effort to create an "impregnable fortress." It is understandable why the North has invested enormous efforts into protecting itself. Even more than the Chinese, Kim had bitter firsthand experience of what a sustained U.S. bombing attack could mean. In the first Korean War, three years of bombing attacks had left almost no modern buildings standing and no more targets to destroy. UN forces, largely American, had flown 720,980 sorties and had dropped 476,000 tons of ordnance. B-29s had flown 20,448 sorties (10,125 by day) and had dropped 168,368 tons of bombs. The war's largest air raid came on August 29, 1952, when Pyongyang was leveled by a 1,403-sortie assault. The bombing had destroyed the entire economy and infrastructure. Cumulatively, the bombs killed nearly 150,000 North Korean and Chinese troops and destroyed 975 aircraft, 800 bridges, 1,100 tanks, 800 locomotives, 9,000 railroad cars, 70,000 motor vehicles, and 80,000 buildings. Airforce attacks shattered three of North Korea's 20 irrigation dams, and the floods wiped out roads, railroad tracks, and thousands of acres of rice fields.

From 1964 onward, Kim Jong Il headed many of North Korea's defense projects. Long after China had realized that technological advances, especially in electronics and communications, had begun to make elements of a Maoist "people's war" obsolete, Kim persisted to invest in a dated military strategy. In the late 1970s, as China began cutting down the size of its armed forces and upgrading its weapons and training, Kim Jong Il expanded the size of North Korea's military and the investment in subterranean defenses. By the 1990s, the North Koreans had built between 8,000 and 15,000 underground installations and dug over 500 miles of tunnels. The state employed around 500,000 people in 150 armaments factories built inside mountains to make them safe from everything save a direct hit by a nuclear bomb. The country had an air force with over 1,700 aircraft, which were also kept under high-security protection. Troops tunneled out mountains, creating hangars big enough to house 50-60 fighter aircraft, their pilots, and the maintenance crews. Entrances to these underground facilities were sealed by large steel-blast doors. The tunnels were so extensive that the aircraft could accelerate on underground runways before coming out into the open.

The Korean People's Army (KPA) had housed a fleet of 900 vessels in anchorage, and blasted out the mountains, linking them to inland lakes by tunnels. Some of these could hold as many as 13 vessels. The coastline is guarded by gun emplacements set into tunnels, the entrances of which are protected from direct fire by high concrete and rock seawalls. The KPA has also hidden tanks and armored cars in tunnel systems estimated to total some 7,500. Some10,600 modern artillery pieces are deployed in hardened underground shelters. And the growing arsenal of missiles is similarly protected in silos and shelters.

When Kim Il Sung adopted what he called the "Four Military Lines policy" in the early 1960s, the whole population had to prepare to wage a people's war and resist invasion in any part of the country. Every district stockpiled enough munitions and food in secret tunnels to keep up a high-intensity combat for at least three months. Project Number 11, issued in 1981, required each area to ensure that all buildings included underground shelters made of reinforced concrete. In addition, every 500 yards antiaircraft guns were installed on top of each apartment, factory, or government office. In fact, the entire country is protected by one of the world's largest antiaircraft systems.

In relation to the size of its economy, North Korea's military expenditure was even vaster than China's. Kim Il Sung and his son did not just want to defend their country, but aimed to conquer the South. To accomplish this, they wanted an army powerful enough to launch a motorized blitzkrieg invasion that would be backed up by a special operations force (SOF). This is similar to the Spenatz commando forces that the Soviet Union planned to use to infiltrate behind Western European enemy lines . Yet, the North Korean force of 100,000 is larger, perhaps the largest such force created by any army anywhere.

The North Korean navy, for instance, could land two navy sniper brigades or 7,000 men and another 8,000 sea commandos at any one time. Forty-five midget submarines, designed to infiltrate agents, are backed up by an underwater vessel to supply them during their missions. The North Koreans have also designed and built 250 special amphibious warfare craft, small semi-submersible infiltration craft, and a militarized hovercraft.

Kim Jong Il became convinced even if the Americans used tactical nuclear weapons, the tunnels and bunkers would enable the regime to survive unaided for six months. In the meantime his special force commandos could strike back. Once infiltrated into South Korea or Japan, they would carry out terrorist-style suicide attacks against U.S. military bases and civilian targets. Others would blow up U.S. military vessels or any American or Japanese civilian ships. Some suspect that Kim has also planted "sleepers" or moles in Japan who would be activated to carry out other terrorist strikes. Many others have been infiltrated into the South, and Hwang estimates there may be as many as 40,000 North Korean agents or collaborators. If the East German STASI, security police, was able to plant an agent who worked in the West German Chancellor's office during the 1970s, then it seems likely, especially given the resources the North has devoted to making such missions possible, that the North has high-placed agents in many key institutions in the South.[3]

If U.S. casualties rose over say 20,000, then Kim might hope that American public opinion would turn against the war and the prospect of a prolonged conflict with a fierce, well dug-in enemy. There exist historical precedents to support such a belief. The Tet offensive that North Vietnam launched in 1968 failed, but it helped persuade the Americans to pull out of South Vietnam. In 1992, determined resistance by a small and badly equipped warlord in Somalia caused enough casualties to persuade the United States to leave the country. Therefore, Kim Jong Il may have wished to demonstrate the damages his special forces are capable of inflicting even though it seemed self-defeating to do so. Thus, in 1996, when the Clinton administration was trying to push ahead with a generous engagement policy, one of Kim's submarines was caught operating along the South Korean coast.

A taxi driver spotted it and raised the alarm when it ran aground near the city of Kangnung. It was one of the mini-subs designed to infiltrate agents into the South. Instead of torpedo tubes, it had a lock enabling a frogman to leave the sub underwater and swim ashore. The incident showed that these submarines could move around undetected by the South's coast defenses and were staffed by men ready to kill and die on Kim Jong Il's command. The 11 members of the submarine crew were found each with a bullet hole in the back of their heads. It seems that the commandos being transported on the mission first murdered the crew, then went ashore undercover when the submarine ran aground. It took the South Korean military two long weeks to hunt down and kill the highly trained commandos, during which time eight South Korean soldiers, two policemen, and four civilians caught in the crossfire lost their lives.

In the later half of the 1960s, North Korea staged hundreds of such provocations against the South designed to provoke a war that Pyongyang believed it could win. Some, including Hwang, suggest Kim persisted with provocative atrocities like the 1976 DMZ axe murders, despite changing circumstances that should have led to major rethink of policies. By the late 1970s, Mao had died and China had changed its domestic and foreign policies to the extent that Pyongyang could no longer automatically count on its support if war broke out. Deng Xiaoping was intent on an open-door policy that required good ties with the West and Japan; and later, when Mikhail Gorbachev came to power in Moscow intent on détente, Pyongyang could not necessarily depend on the USSR's support. Both states were bound by treaties to come to the North's aid if it was attacked, but clearly their national interests increasingly lay in developing stronger ties with Washington and Seoul.

Despite this, the North continued to try and incite the South, and it may well be that the blame for this miscalculation lies more with Kim Jong Il than his father. Certainly, Hwang and other sources claim that Kim Jong Il personally took charge of planning and operating terrorist operations in the mid-1970s, including such events as the DMZ axe murders and several daring assassination attempts.

In 1982, Canadian police say they foiled a plot to assassinate South Korean President Chun Doo Hwan during his visit to Canada. The following year, North Korean agents set off a powerful bomb just minutes before President Chun arrived to lay a wreath at the Martyr's Mausoleum in

Rangoon, Burma. The bomb killed 17 senior South Korean officials and 4 Burmese and injured 14 in the party accompanying the president on a six-nation Asian tour and 32 others. Chun narrowly escaped. He described the Rangoon attack as "a grave provocation not unlike a declaration of war" but he did not respond.

An inquiry by the Burmese authorities found that three terrorist commandos had slipped off a North Korean ship anchored in Rangoon, and then stayed at a North Korean diplomatic residence where they received liquid incendiary bombs, TNT powder, and liquid fuel. The commandos next installed two remote-controlled claymore mines or explosive bombs packed with 700 metal ball bearings in the ceiling of the mausoleum. The three commandos, who were caught after the explosion, then tried to blow themselves up with hand grenades and booby-trapped fountain pens. One managed to kill three Burmese soldiers before being arrested. After the survivors confessed to organizing the plot, Burma broke off diplomatic relations with Pyongyang.

Then in 1986, another bomb blast at Kimpo Airport in Seoul killed 5 and wounded 30, and South Korea blamed the blast on North Korean agents. The most diplomatically damaging incident was the destruction of the Korean Airline Flight 857 in 1987. The plane with 20 crew members and 95 passengers blew up over the Andaman Sea en route from Baghdad to Seoul. Two North Korean agents had planted a bomb and one of them, Kim Hyun-hee, was spotted with a false Japanese passport and arrested in Bahrain. She had tried to commit suicide by swallowing a cyanide capsule but survived. Once apprehended, she was taken to Seoul where she confessed and said Kim Jong Il had personally commanded her mission.

Kim Hyun-hee was sentenced to death in South Korea but was reprieved and went on to become something of a celebrity author, penning the book *Tears of My Soul,* in which she describes her lengthy training at a North Korean spy school. It provided further clues about the fate of the missing Japanese. From July 1981 until March 1983, she lived in a dormitory with a Japanese girl, a language teacher, whom she identified by her Korean name, Yi Un-hye. Later she picked out Yi from a collection of photos of missing Japanese. Her real name was Yayeko Taguchi, a Tokyo nightclub hostess who disappeared in June 1978. Kim described Taguchi in her book as a "stylishly dressed, very beautiful woman [who] was 22 at the time and was working at a bar near the Ikebukuro Station in Tokyo when she was abducted." Yayeko Taguchi was a divorcee whose two small children were at a day care when she disappeared. Kim described how Taguchi often broke down in tears at the thought of her children.

The relatives of Taguchi believed she was simply shot in 1986 once the KAL mission had been launched and she had outlived her usefulness. During the 2002 summit, the Japanese authorities were told she had died in one those mysterious North Korean car accidents and that her remains were washed away by floods. Even less credibly, the North Koreans explained that two other abducted, Arimoto Keiko and Ishioka Toru, had mysteriously died on the same day, November 4, 1988. Had they too been executed?[4]

Arimoto Keiko, a pretty, quiet 23-year-old Japanese girl, was studying in London when she met a friendly Japanese woman who in 1983 lured her to Copenhagen, where she was kidnapped by North Korean agents. Once in North Korea she was forced to marry Ishioka Toru, a Japanese who had been abducted in 1980 while traveling around Spain.[5] The idea was that of Kimihiro Abe, the Red Army Faction Japanese terrorist chief, who employed his wife to kidnap Japanese women abroad in order to marry them off to abductees already in North Korea.

They were not the only ones seized while going about their everyday lives. There was the law student Kaoru Hasuike and his girlfriend Yukiko Okudo who were abducted in 1978 when walking along the beach in their hometown. Just how many Japanese were abducted is still unclear, but there are at least 360 likely missing person cases. It was not just Japanese who disappeared. Thousands of South Koreans, apparently selected at random, also disappeared. These included a South Korean couple who happened to be visiting Belgrade, a man seized while he was teaching in the Netherlands, a student grabbed while studying in Austria, and a South Korean government official working in France. North Korea is also suspected of abducting five Lebanese women as well as women from France, Italy, the Netherlands, Jordan, and Macao, all taken to be employed in the training of agents. Yet, in the baffling nightmarish world of North Korea, anyone who volunteered to help North Korea, like Ali Ramada, a Venezuelan Communist who arrived to work as a translator, ended up in the camps.

This included most of the 90,000 Koreans who had migrated from Japan with all their worldly goods.[6]

The downing of the KAL flight and many other terrorist acts all failed to achieve the intended objectives of destabilizing the South or provoking a war. South Korea was periodically torn by political strife, especially labor unrest, and the North nourished the hope that if it could orchestrate a worker-led uprising, the new leadership would invite Pyongyang to intervene and restore order.

South Korea was not South Vietnam. The prospects of such a scenario unfolding grew dimmer with every passing year. South Korea's economy boomed in the 1980s, and its international standing rose so fast that it was able to win the honor of hosting the 1988 Olympics. By contrast, Pyongyang had reneged on its foreign debts and every fresh terrorist outrage began to undercut its international support.

Sandwiched between the Rangoon and KAL 857 bombing was a brief and curious interlude that took place from 1984–1985. After heavy floods in the South, North Korea unexpectedly offered to send relief supplies for the 200,000 homeless South Koreans. President Chun accepted and hundreds of North Korean trucks delivered rice, cement, textiles, and medical supplies, all of such poor quality as to be almost unusable. This led to meetings on economic cooperation, Red Cross contacts, and family exchanges. Then, after dozens of meetings between high-level emissaries from the two capitals, and just when a presidential summit seemed in the offing, the North lost interest for no clear reason and the initiative withered away.

Pyongyang's olive branch coincided with strong signs that the North was rethinking all its policies. Pyongyang started introducing economic reforms such as instituting farmers' markets, renegotiating the North's foreign debts, and unveiling a joint venture law to attract foreign investment. Kim Il Sung had come under considerable pressure from Beijing to copy China's reforms, and it appears in the mid-1980s that a difference opened up between father and son, and Kim Jong Il did his best to thwart the reforms. If Kim Jong Il was indeed in charge of the agents in the South and preparing intelligence reports on the situation there, he was responsible for a series of policy blunders.

The 1988 Olympic Games in the South provided a prime opportunity to grasp far-reaching change. In the run up to the games it seemed possible that the North would seize the chance to foster trust by taking part in the games or accepting an invitation to co-host them. Instead the North chose to disrupt the games. The KAL bombing seemed intended to deter visitors from attending by showing a dangerous and volatile peninsula. Pyongyang may have hoped that its allies in Beijing and Moscow would decide to stay away but this was a misjudgment. Far from damaging the South, the bombing fatally damaged North Korea's standing in the world.

Shortly thereafter, Washington officially designated North Korea as a terrorist state. From January 1988 onward, Pyongyang became ineligible for any aid, loans, and investment from multilateral organizations such as the World Bank and the International Monetary Fund. The ban, which has still not been lifted, has been very damaging. North Korea was already in dire need of earning foreign exchange, a need that would become more acute in the coming years when Soviet aid dried up after the collapse of the USSR. North Korea has been forced ever more into the role of an outlaw nation, as it tried to find ways to earn hard currency.

However, the currency shortages had started long before in 1972, when in anticipation of the high costs of Kim Il Sung's sixtieth birthday's extravagant celebrations, there was a "foreign currency campaign to express loyalty to the Great Leader." Party members donated gold and silver jewels including wedding rings. Government organizations, including the diplomatic service, were given quotas to fulfil. In 1976, Norway, Sweden, Denmark, and Finland expelled North Korean ambassadors after they were found smuggling cigarettes and alcohol in diplomatic bags to avoid import duties and sell at a profit.

Since the early 1980s, when North Korea started deducting two days of rice from the monthly rations, which was then dubbed "patriotic rice" in order to pay off the country's debts, the currency campaign has grown. The Party set up a separate department called the No.39 Office that allocated quotas to factories and even farms. Each county committee was given the task of proving its loyalty by gathering anything that earned foreign currency, including mushrooms and abalone.

The regime was spared the worst consequences of its foreign exchange shortage by an unexpected piece of luck: Saddam Hussein's decision to attack Iran. Hussein's attack led to an eight-year-long war between the oil-rich neighbors and created an arms bazaar in the Middle East. Both China and North Korea found profitable outlets for their military hardware. Iran became North Korea's chief customer while China mostly supplied Iraq. According to some estimates North Korea earned over U.S. $4 billion from 1981 to 1989. It exported large quantities of munitions, small arms, artillery, multiple rocket launchers, tanks, armored personnel carriers, air defense artillery, SCUD-B short-range ballistic missiles, and some naval craft. It even cooperated so that China could secretly sell weapons to Iran, like the new Silkworm anti-shipping missile. North Korea trained Iranian gunners to operate the Chinese mobile surface-to-air system and instructed the Iranian Revolutionary Guards in unconventional warfare techniques.

The Iran-Iraq War fuelled an arms race in the region and in particular a race to develop longer, larger, and more accurate missiles. This in turn had repercussions for Israel and for Pakistan, caught up in its unequal rivalry with India. Some Middle Eastern countries, especially Libya, Syria, and Egypt, as well as Pakistan, turned to North Korea as a partner and as an intermediary for dealing with China and the Soviet Union.

After 1988, a group of Western banks officially declared North Korea bankrupt and, once Washington labeled it a terrorist state, its few options dwindled. The opportunities for business that opened up in the Middle East ensured North Korea what one might call a diplomatic life of crime and the hard-to-shake-off habits and friends that accompany such a lifestyle. Although international terrorist activities were much reduced after 1988, Kim's personal prestige became more and more vested in the development of his military-industrial complex.

Kim Jong Il took direct control over all key factories and defense industries and began to run them outside the planned economy and beyond the supervision of the Party bureaucracy. Hwang Jang Yop even goes so far as to accuse Kim of cannibalizing the entire military-industrial complex in order to bring all the viable sources of hard currency, such as gold mines or missile exports, under the control of himself and his immediate family. Together with his sister Kim Kyong-hui and her husband, Chang Song-taek, they run the National Defense Commission in secrecy. As other options for North Korea closed off, the goal of becoming a nuclear power armed with ballistic missiles became ever more desirable as a panacea to rescue North Korea from all its problems.

When the economy collapsed in the early 1980s, North Korea cleverly used its military exports to finance its military development. Most of North Korea's military technology was becoming hopelessly outdated, and it had too many weapon systems that had been developed in the 1950s and 1960s. It is prohibitively costly, even for a middle-ranking Western country, to develop a new battle tank or fighter plane, but missiles are comparatively cheap to design and build. North Korea therefore became one of the world's key players in the proliferation of missile technology.[7]

Pyongyang's export-import missile business started in the second half of the 1960s when North Korea acquired Soviet rockets and surface-to-ship missiles. Then in 1971, Pyongyang signed a deal with China to develop ballistic missiles, which were in fact based on Soviet designs borrowed after World War II from the German V2 flying bombs. It also later acquired Scud missiles from Egypt, which the North Koreans could reverse engineer. By 1984, North Korea had developed its own version of the Scud-B, and in 1985, Tehran agreed to finance North Korea's missile program in return for a reliable supply of missiles to fire at Iraq. A deal signed in 1987 committed Iran to buying 90 to 100 Scud-Bs with a range of 200 miles for a price of U.S. $500 million. In 1991, North Korea agreed to deliver about 24 Scud-Cs and 20 mobile launchers to Syria and further Scuds to Iran. This also led to a peculiar incident when the North Koreans contacted the Israelis and started secret negotiations to find out what they would offer in exchange for halting the sales.

The export earnings enabled North Korea to move onto developing its own intermediate-range ballistic missiles, testing a larger Scud in 1990 and developing a rocket called the Nodong with a range of 900 miles. This was finally tested in May 1993 at Musudan-ri in the presence of dozens of Iranian Revolutionary Guards as well as Pakistani officials.

The exports plus the opportunity to hire Russian rocket scientists after the collapse of the Soviet Union enabled the North Koreans to develop a larger rocket called the Taeodong 1. This is a two-stage missile with a Nodong as the first stage and a Scud as the second stage. It was first tested on August 31, 1998, and flew over Japan to place a small satellite in orbit.

However, the final stage, which used solid fuel, failed, and the satellite was never placed. Since then, North Korea has been developing, probably with the help of China, a bigger version called the Taepongdong-2, which has a new frame and could reach parts of the United States. According to one escapee, former diplomat Ko Young-hwan, who testified at a Senate hearing in 1997, the rockets are developed at the January 18 Machinery Factory in South Pyongan province. Over 10,000 people work in the underground factory, and for one missile out of every five, engineers have tried to copy French Exocet air-to-ship missiles, Stinger missiles, and Soviet SS missiles.

Another escapee, Kim Do-sung, who worked for nine years at Plant 38, a huge armaments factory in Huichon, Chagang province, said that most computer chips and electronic components used to build the missile guidance systems were imported from Japan. He recalls unloading one shipment of equipment containing oscilloscopes for analyzing trajectory, special welding machines to make the seamless joints needed in a missile body, computer chips, and picture tubes used in monitors to track missile routes.

Chinese companies have provided special steels as well as gyroscopes and accelerometers (used to measure vibration and g-force), and Russian companies have been fingered for selling high-strength maraging steel used to make missile and centrifuge systems.[8]

The missile projects are designed to enable the North to attack Japan, in particular the U.S. base at Okinawa, and defeat the U.S. Seventh Fleet in case of a war. Other sources estimate that by the end of the 1990s, North Korea had sold roughly 600 Scud missiles, including about 100 No Dong missiles. Ko also said the missile exports enabled the North to earn as much as U.S. $1 billion per year and keep itself supplied with oil.

Many of North Korea's customers, including Syria, Egypt, and Iran, also wanted Pyongyang to help them set up their own domestic manufacturing line in part to escape U.S. intelligence surveillance. As long as North Korea was trading in missiles with other terrorist listed countries such as Iran, Syria, and Libya, it had no chance of escaping designation as a terrorist state. North Korea's ties with Libya date to the 1970s, when it offered to train pilots and some North Korean pilots actually manned Libyan interceptors and bombers. In 2003, the United States also discovered that Saddam Hussein had contracted with the North Koreans to build a missile production facility; he had paid a U.S. $10 million down payment but received nothing in return. In 2003, the Spanish navy stopped a North Korean ship carrying missiles to Yemen.

The end of the Iran-Iraq War in 1988, however, hit North Korea's finances hard. Although it found a few new customers like the Liberation Tigers of Tamil Eelam in Sri Lanka and the United Wa State Army, a drug-trafficking group active in the Burmese sector of the golden triangle, nothing quite filled the gap. Pyongyang sought to make up for the shortfall by exporting opium and counterfeiting dollars, the sort of businesses that guerilla movements in Afghanistan or Latin America, but not recognized governments, rely on. The poppy plantations started in earnest during the late 1980s and by 1997, every collective farm was ordered to devote at least 25 acres to the cultivation of opium, nicknamed the "white bellflower." The crop was grown primarily in the mountainous provinces of North Hamkyong and Yanggang in the North East, neatly processed into heroin, packed for export, and then shipped from docks in Chongjin for destinations like Singapore, Hong Kong, Cambodia, and Macau. North Korea became by some estimates the world's third largest exporter of opium and heroin with some 7,000 hectares under cultivation. In the summer of 2001, Taiwanese authorities seized more than 154 pounds of heroin from a North Korean ship. After a five-day chase, Australian forces captured another ship that was led by a senior North Korean official and was found to be carrying U.S. $48 million worth of heroin.[9]

During the 1990s, North Korea switched to making methamphetamine, partly because of a slump in heroin production but also to earn bigger profits. Street sales in Japan are thought to top U.S. $9 billion a year, and a large part of this is thought to be smuggled into Japan by Kim Jong Il's special operations ships and submarines. Only a small part of the exports have come to light but in April 1997, Japanese investigators discovered U.S. $95 million worth of amphetamines hidden in 12 cans of honey in the cargo of a North Korean freighter docked at Hososhima—the biggest drug seizure ever. Methamphetamine is a pharmaceutical product that is simpler to produce than heroin but relies on expensive raw materials like ephedrine. In 1998, Thai police stopped an Indian shipment of 2.5 tons of ephedrine—also used in allergy drugs—bound for Pyongyang. Thai customs officials became suspicious as to why North Korea needed so much cough medicine.

North Korean diplomats and intelligence agents have also been caught in over 20 countries dealing in cocaine, Rohypnol (a tranquilizer tablet better known as the "date-rape drug"), rhino horn, pirated CDs, and other contraband. In one case, the Russian customs in Moscow stopped two Mexico-based diplomats carrying 77 pounds of cocaine in their luggage. In all, the narcotics trade nets North Korea around U.S. $500 million a year according to one study by U.S. Forces in Korea and South Korea's 21st Century Military Research Institute.[10]

In 1996, the North Korean trade councilor to Romania was expelled for exchanging U.S. $50,000 in forged bills. Also that year, another DPRK official was arrested in Ulan Bator, Mongolia, for dumping U.S. $100,000 worth of counterfeit bills onto the black market. In another case two years later in Vladivostok, Russia, a senior North Korean Workers Party official was caught attempting to exchange U.S. $30,000 in fake currency for rubles. North Korea is thought to print around $15 million in counterfeit U.S. dollars every year, plus an unknown quantity of Yen. North Korea was forced to shut down embassies in many countries that it could no longer finance, despite their importance in these trafficking operations.

The regime possessed a few other sources of income, such as contracting labor to foreign countries. Workers were sent to the Russian Far East to fell trees in the late 1960s as a way to assuage North Korea's debts, which eventually rose to some U.S. $5.5 billion. At one point, there were 30,000 North Koreans in Russia living 20 to a room and earning as little as U.S. $1.90 a day. As the famine gripped North Korea, many of them refused to go back to their homeland and sought to escape the North Korean security guards who accompanied them. Some committed crimes in the hopes of being put in a Soviet jail. When arrested for escaping, one threw himself on a train and another cut open his stomach. Their minders had to resort to shackles, torture, and executions to keep control of the workforce. In the face of public opposition to this practice, Moscow shied away from hiring more laborers.[11]

The remittances from the Chongryon community in Japan declined steeply during the 1990s. At its peak, the pro-Pyongyang community in Japan, which run a great many pinball parlors called *pachinko*, was transferring as much as U.S. $2 billion a year into the coffers of the Kims, as well as providing all kinds of goods and services. The Chongryon community lost much of its savings when the Japanese real estate bubble burst and brought the downfall of the North Korean-affiliated Chogin Osaka Credit Association. It collapsed under the weight of U.S. $2.3 billion of bad loans mostly extended to real estate ventures that went sour. By 1996, Chongryon remittances had fallen, perhaps to as little as U.S. $100 million per year. Many members also lost faith in North Korea after Kim Il Sung's death. Enrollment in Chongryon schools dropped to about 12,000, about a third of what it was in the 1980s.[12]

Despite the shortages of money and the mass starvation, Kim spent heavily on buying new weapons, more than he earned. South Korea's Defense Ministry estimated that from 1997–2002 he bought U.S. $400 million worth of secondhand MiG fighter jets, submarine parts, helicopters, tank and ship engines, and other weapons. Weapons were supplied by Russia, China, Germany, Slovakia, Austria, Belarus, and Japan.[13] Kim Jong Il earned at least U.S. $110 million by exporting Scud-type missiles and missile parts to Iraq, Yemen, Iran, Pakistan, and Syria over the same period. On his trips to Russia, Kim visited Russian armaments factories like that at Komsomolsk-na-Amure, which makes Su-27 fighters, and tried to negotiate deliveries of tanks and air-defense missiles that he could ill-afford.

The income from the missile sales, drugs, remittances, and international aid, between U.S. $1-2 billion a year, was hardly enough to both keep the regime afloat and engage in an arms race against South Korea and its giant ally, the United States. The importance of North Korea's nuclear program therefore continued to grow as it remained the only way of extracting security guarantees from its enemies—Japan, South Korea, and the United States—and the huge sums needed to modernize its economy and its military.

CHAPTER 8

Nuclear Warlord

The plan to bomb North Korea's nuclear facilities seemed simple. President William Clinton sat with his advisers in the West Wing as his Defense Secretary William J. Perry laid out satellite photographs of North Korea's plutonium reprocessing facility. They showed a long narrow two-story factory next to a small experimental reactor at Yongbyon, some 60 miles north of Pyongyang. A wave of cruise missiles and F-117 stealth fighters flying high beyond the reach of the North's air defenses dropping laser guided bombs could easily blast it.

The target list included other sites. The Yongbyon reactor produced just 5 megawatts (MW) of fissile material, and North Korea had also started building another 50 MW reactor and a 200 MW plant capable of providing enough fissile material to make 30 bombs a year. North Korea looked like it was trying to hide a major effort to build the means to manage the entire nuclear fuel cycle on its own, free of outside help or interference. It had thwarted the investigations by the inspectors sent by the International Atomic Energy Agency (IAEA), and the UN Security Council had condemned North Korea for breaking its treaty obligations. If Pyongyang was not stopped now, it would become capable of manufacturing not just enough bombs for its own needs but others too. As it was already exporting its missile technology to Libya, Iran, and Syria, it might go on to supply nuclear weapons and technology that could alter the balance of power in the volatile Middle East. North Korea had the potential to be the world's worst proliferator.

On June 15, 1994, Clinton had to make one of the most difficult decisions any American president had faced since the 1962 Cuban Missile Crisis. He had gone to the DMZ the year before on one of his first foreign trips
since taking office in 1992. At the Bridge of No Return he had bluntly
warned that if the North were ever to use any nuclear weapons it "would
be the end of their country as they know it."

Now he had to ask his circle of advisers if the North Koreans would
respond to the pre-emptive attack with nuclear weapons. In 1992, the CIA
had already concluded that there was "a better than even" chance that North
Korea already possessed one or two nuclear bombs. Although North Korea
had not carried out a nuclear test, it knew how to build a precise shell of high
explosives around a plutonium core and detonate an explosion that would
trigger a nuclear explosion. Satellite photographs taken in 1990 revealed
evidence that the North had tested these explosives in 70 or 80 blasts.

During an inter-Korean ministerial meeting three months earlier in March
1994, the North Korean Chief Delegate Park Yong-su bluntly said: "Seoul
is not far away from here. If a war breaks out, Seoul will be turned into a
sea of fire." Clinton's East Asia Security Adviser Robert Gallucci believed
him and told the president he was certain that the U.S. air strike would
provoke North Korea into launching a war. Even a non-nuclear war would
be lethal. A month earlier, Army General Gary Luck, former chief of U.S.
forces in Korea, had estimated that the consequences of full-scale war on
the peninsula would run to a million casualties and cost the United States
more than $100 billion, plus an extra trillion dollars in economic damages
and lost business. The Pentagon warned that such a war could leave 52,000
Americans dead or wounded in the first 90 days. In an all-out war, there
would be 80,000-100,000 American fatalities.[1] At the White House both
the State Department and Perry recommended that Clinton opt for seeking
tough UN sanctions while moving 10,000 more troops, along with F-117s,
long-range bombers, and an additional carrier battle group to the region.
The United States already had 37,000 troops stationed on the Korean peninsula and some 60,000 stationed in Japan and other bases nearby. Some
of the forces were already busy calibrating a list of targets in North Korea.

"We were within a day of making major additions to our troop deployments to Korea, and we were about to undertake an evacuation of Ameri-

can civilians from Korea," Perry later recalled. In the West, Clinton also heard proposals for mobilizing as many as 50,000 extra troops and bringing them to Korea along with nuclear weapons in order to deter the North from an attack.

Yet Gallucci, an experienced diplomat who had just been in charge of disarming Iraq, disagreed. He was convinced that merely asking the United Nations to punish Pyongyang with sanctions would be enough to trigger a war. "We had been told—I had been personally been told by the North Korean head of the delegation—that a sanctions resolution and actions to implement (the sanctions) could well be taken as an act of war, given that the UN was a belligerent in the Korean War and there was an armistice in place," Gallucci later recounted.[2]

Clinton was even warned that if the United States were to start a troop buildup and evacuate civilians, Pyongyang would jump to the conclusion that an invasion was imminent. The North Koreans might have drawn the lesson from the 1991 Gulf War that giving the United States time to mass its forces was unwise and it was better to strike first.

Meanwhile in South Korea, the authorities prepared for the worst. Seoul started civil defense exercises to prepare the country for an attack. In the North, Kim did the same and evacuated the major cities, placing key personnel in command and control bunkers.[3] As troops on both sides of the DMZ were placed on maximum alert, Perry told Clinton that although all the options were unpalatable, not to pick any would be disastrous. As the critical moment came for President Clinton to make up his mind, the crisis took an unexpected turn with the intervention of President Carter. He appeared on the scene, like a Deus ex Machina, entering from the wings. "My recollection is that before the president got to choose—was asked to choose—the door of the room opened and we were told that there was a telephone call from former President Carter in Pyongyang and that he wished to speak to me," Gallucci recalled.

Jimmy Carter had gone to see Kim Il Sung as a private citizen, and he was now calling to report a breakthrough. Shortly afterward, the White House officials switched on their TV set to hear Carter inform CNN by telephone that the stalled negotiations between the United States and North Korea in Geneva could resume. Carter said that Kim Il Sung had agreed to go back to the negotiating table and "[has] given me assurance that as long as this good-faith effort is going on between the United States and North Korea, that the [IAEA] inspectors will stay on site and the surveillance equipment will not be interrupted." President Clinton, at first disconcerted by being upstaged, then welcomed the opening out of the crisis.

Three years later when Hwang Jang-yop defected to the South, he revealed that Kim Il Sung and his more hawkish son had exchanged heated arguments about how to respond to the crisis. In 1992, Kim Jong Il had formally assumed command of North Korea's armed forces and when he reviewed North Korea' war contingency plans, he became bullish. According to Hwang's recollection, Kim Jong Il felt confident an invasion could succeed and was all in favor of a pre-emptive attack. If indeed the North did have the bomb, however crude it might be, this would have encouraged the younger Kim to be aggressive. The North assumed that it was strong enough to deal with South Korean forces. Certainly, it seemed all too believable that the North still intended to conquer the South. In 1993, the North's media had quoted the words of Vice Marshal Choe Kwang, the chief of general staff who at a state function declared that the military "has the heavy and honorable task of reunifying the fatherland with guns in the nineties without fail."

In the end, it seems Kim Il Sung rebuffed his son's arguments and said the economy was not in good enough shape to start a war. So, the Americans and Koreans went back to the negotiating table in Geneva. The result, the Agreed Framework, is one of the most peculiar international agreements ever devised. North Korea's chief enemy, the United States, now promised to reward Pyongyang's breaches of international nuclear safeguards by giving it more nuclear power stations. Moreover, Washington intended for someone else to foot the large bill for these power stations—two 1, 000 MW light-water reactors priced at U.S. $4.6 billion—and demanded that its allies—South Korea, Japan, and the European Union—open their wallets.

In return for promising to freeze its own nuclear program, North Korea got almost everything it asked for. Until the reactors were up and running in 2000, the United States agreed to provide 500,000 metric tons of heavy fuel oil annually. The reactors were intended to double the country's feeble energy output and solve its energy shortages; their design and the type of plutonium they produce supposedly would make it hard for North Korea to obtain fissile material. Beyond that, the real significance of the deal was that it would pave the way toward an overall peace settlement, formally ending the 1950–1953 Korean War. President Clinton even provided the North with a written assurance that the United States was not contemplating launching an attack nor seeking the destruction of North Korea.

Kim Il Sung died weeks after Carter's June visit when the first-ever summit with South Korea was just two weeks away. Who knows what might have happened had he lived at least long enough to meet President Kim Young Sam as scheduled in July 1994. Perhaps there would have been no more breakthroughs, as the North had already gained much of what it wanted. As it was, the Agreed Framework placed the United States in a role recently vacated by the former Soviet Union. Washington now began to act as North Korea's patron, responsible for supplying it with vital oil and food. It was committed to delivering power stations that Moscow had originally promised Pyongyang in the 1980s. With Clinton's written assurance, Washington was even coming close to accepting the job of guaranteeing North's Korea's security and the continued rule of the Kim family. Instead of trying to remove a failed regime, Washington was on the path to ensuring its survival, and this enraged many people. The deal was savaged in Congress, especially by Republicans like John McCain, who condemned it as "appeasement." Given the extent of congressional opposition, the deal became hard to implement, and the original hopes of using it as a platform for an overall settlement were dashed.

Even within the more limited world of arms-control diplomacy, the Agreed Framework had major and obvious flaws. North Korea agreed to freeze further development of nuclear capabilities, but never committed itself to giving the IAEA inspectors unimpeded access to all seven key nuclear sites. This meant that the IAEA was never able to establish key facts, such as whether the North had in fact diverted plutonium to build a bomb and was therefore in breach of its treaty obligations. Still worse, by failing to determine this, the United States could not, and did not, demand that the North disarm and carry out its early commitment to create a nuclear-free peninsula.

Even odder, the Agreed Framework failed to establish a new climate of mutual confidence that would lead to other security-building gestures. Two months after signing the pact, North Korean forces shot down a U.S. helicopter that had strayed off course during a routine training mission; they killed one soldier and seized the pilot. North Korea accused the helicopter pilot of spying and held him for 13 days until the United States expressed "sincere regret" for the incident. It was only the first of many such unsettling incidents. After Kim Il Sung's death, no one could be sure what Kim Jong Il thought of the Agreed Framework and if North Korea's policies would change. Everyone was hoping for signs from Kim Jong Il that the North had abandoned its intent to conquer the South and was now interested in seeking a new relationship. At the same time, South Korean intelligence became convinced that without Kim Il Sung, the North was on the brink of collapse. Many other Korea watchers thought so too, and enthusiasm for the Agreed Framework dwindled.

The dramatic events that took place in 1994 may not have achieved the results intended by any of the participants, but they did clarify matters that have since had great bearing on future events. The United States once again emerged as the chief arbiter of the Koreans' fate, but simultaneously found itself entangled in a wider effort to promote the powers of the United Nations. The Americans had been here before, some four decades earlier. The 1994 crisis brought together the unfinished business left over from World War II: the hasty division of the peninsula, the Korean War, and the role and authority of the United Nations. Now that the Cold War was over, the United Nations had another chance to assert itself. At the same time America emerged from the Cold War (and victory over Iraq) with enhanced stature, and the other powers looked to see if Washington could bend Pyongyang to its will and what they could do to restore their relative status.

Two of the five permanent members of the UN Security Council, China and Russia, considered the peninsula inside their traditional sphere of influence. China is still bound by a 1961 mutual defense treaty to come to Pyongyang's aid if a war breaks out. Moscow had had a similar treaty that was altered in 1991, making its support less unconditional. However, Russia's role was still significant; after all it was largely the Russians (that is the Soviets) who had built North Korea's nuclear reactors and trained its scientists in the first place. The lessons of history were there for everyone to see as the great powers competed for influence.

In their first history lessons North Koreans learn that the Americans first came to Korea in 1866 intending to bully and exploit a peaceful people. A commonly displayed oil painting shows Korean peasants attacking an American sailing ship, the S.S. *General Sherman*, as it lies stranded and in flames on the River Daedong. Kim Il Sung's own great grandfather is shown, somewhat implausibly, leading the peasants in their heroic resistance to this act of imperialist and colonialist aggression. Even in 1905, a *Daily Mail* correspondent was still being shown the *Sherman*'s anchor chains hanging from the gates of Pyongyang "as a warning to all men of the fate awaiting those who would dare disturb the peace of the Land of the Morning Calm."

What brought the Sherman to Korea was trade, not conquest. The S.S. *General Sherman* was a merchant ship, once a blockade-runner during the Civil War, that was attacked while attempting to reach Pyongyang as Western merchant powers raced each other to open the "Hermit Kingdom" to foreign trade. Japan had just been opened by Commander Perry, and China too was authorizing international trade, albeit reluctantly. A new era of international commerce was beginning in the Far East.

Captain Preston of the *Sherman* at first had little trouble fighting off the Koreans with his cannons, but when the ship was grounded by the tide, a hostile crowd gathered on the shore. The crew, a motley mixture of Americans, British, and Chinese, opened fire. The provincial governor responded by sending burning barges that set the ship on fire. When the crew jumped into the river, they were hacked to death. In 1871, the Americans tried again, sending the American Asiatic Squadron that captured several Korean forts but failed to open the door. Peking, or rather the Manchu imperial court, still controlled Korea's foreign relations.

In the end, it was the Japanese who first shoved their foot in the door. They were able to force the Qing dynasty into allowing them to trade with Korea. However, it was the United States that became the first Western nation to conclude a formal "Treaty of Amity and Commerce" in 1882. A Commodore Shufeldt negotiated this not in Seoul (then called Hansung City), but in Peking. The Americans became popular with the Koreans because unlike other foreign powers, they advocated an "open door" policy instead of seeking exclusive concessions. In the treaty, the United States ambiguously promised to provide the Koreans "offices" in case of an external threat. When the first American diplomat arrived in Seoul, King Sejong is said to have danced with delight. American businessmen obtained franchises to build trolley lines, a city lighting plant, waterworks, a telephone exchange, and a deal to open the Seoul-Inchon railroad.

If the Koreans placed any trust in the Americans, then they were to be disappointed. While the Japanese set about annexing Korea between 1904 and 1909, Secretary of State Howard Taft gave up U.S. interests there in return for assurances that the Japanese would not challenged U.S. interests in the Philippines, where the United States was replacing the Spanish as the colonial power. When the Japanese marched in, the Americans were the first to leave. They soon forgot about the place, but the Koreans did not forget the Americans so easily.

Religion had followed the flag. The high tide of Protestant evangelism coincided with the 30 years between the Treaty of Amity and the Japanese annexation. Missionaries set up churches, schools, and universities in both China and Korea. American Protestants founded the Paejae Boys School in 1886 and the Ewha Girls School, the first educational institution for girls. The generation educated in these missionary schools has wielded an immense influence on Korea's modern history. Christianity became a powerful social force, perhaps more powerful than in any other East Asian nation. One famous graduate of these Protestant missionary schools was So Jaepil, who in 1806 returned as an American citizen with a medical degree. He founded the Independence Club and started the first modern vernacular newspaper in Korea to campaign for democracy.

Kim Il Sung also grew up in a Protestant household, and his father had attended the Sungsil School established by American missionaries in Pyongyang. South Korea's first president, Syngman Rhee, was a Protestant, and recent president Kim Dae Jung is a Catholic.

The Protestant private schools underpinned the modern nationalist movement and were socially progressive. In a Confucian society stifled by notions of hierarchy and where slavery had been common, Christianity won converts because it was "a religion of all classes." Catholicism, which was introduced from 1800 onward, also won many adherents, especially around Pyongyang, even though it was suppressed after Rome outlawed ancestor worship. According to historian Roger Tennant, the Catholic Church was taken up by those searching for both spiritual enlightenment and social justice. Its teachings were welcomed as a kind of "liberation theology," because in Korea it was always the Church that battled against the established order.[4]

"The remarkable appeal of Protestantism was partly due to psychological factors: the feeling of many Koreans that conversion to Christianity was an act of penance for the failings of their traditional society that had led to the loss of Korea's nationhood," note the authors of *Korea Old and New*. Protestant hymns even inspired the birth of a new type of popular song, the so-called *changga*, which became particularly favored by students and independence fighters.[5]

A wave of antiforeign feeling swept through the country after America approved Japan's occupation of Korea, but it did not destroy the faith of the Christian community. On contrary, it engendered a mood of repentance and determination in the Christian community that began with Presbyterians in Pyongyang. (Korea was a stronghold of the Presbyterian movement propagated by Scots, Canadians. and Australians). "Christians publicly confessed all manner of crimes, corruption and sins in a paroxysm of mass emotion," in what is known as the "The Great Revival," reports Mike Breen in *The Koreans*.[6]

Christians went on to play a leading role in the resistance to the Japanese. In 1912, the Japanese authorities charged 105 Christians with attempting to assassinate the governor-general. After Woodrow Wilson's declaration that all peoples had the right to self-determination, many Koreans were inspired to issue demands for independence. In March 1919, they used the funeral of King Kojong to stage nationwide protests. Christians insisted that the protests should be peaceful but demonstrators were shot and bayoneted. In the next six months, 45,000 people were arrested and 7,500 killed. In the 1930s, the Japanese forced the Koreans to worship at Shinto shrines, adopt Japanese names, and use Japanese in schools. The Christians led resistance to this policy of forced cultural assimilation, and at times they offered the only domestic resistance because other political activists had fled to Shanghai, the Chinese Communist Party base Yanan, Moscow, or America.

Despite these historical and religious ties, the Korean aspiration for nationhood did not get much attention in America. Under Japanese colonization the memory of the Koreanism, never very strong, faded. At the 1943 Cairo summit, President Franklin Roosevelt thought they needed to remain under a trusteeship for 20 or 30 years before they would be fit to govern themselves. Later the Americans casually agreed to Korea's division without consulting a Korea expert let alone any Koreans. The Americans had been expecting a long drawn out war with Japan, yet the fact that no one bothered to prepare a plan for Korea's future remains a wound, an injury to Korean pride. The division itself is regarded as a deep and inexplicable betrayal. Why was Korea split when it was not an aggressor like Japan but a victim? And why was Japan not cut in half like Germany as a punishment?

The U.S.-backed Republic of Korea was declared on August 15, 1945, a day after the Japanese agreed to unconditional surrender at the end of World War II, and the Democratic People's Republic of Korea came into formal existence on September 9. By December a four-nation conference in Moscow decided on a four-power trusteeship for the next five years. A joint U.S.-Soviet Commission would arrange nationwide elections to be followed by withdrawal of all occupying armies. Yet, the peninsula was soon dragged into another global conflict. As the Cold War heated up, President Truman articulated the "Truman doctrine." He told a joint session of Congress in March 1947 that the United States must oppose the totalitarian regimes being sponsored by the Soviet Union: "We cannot allow changes in the status quo in violation of the Charter of the United Nations by such methods as coercion, or by such subterfuges as political infiltration. In helping free and independent nations to maintain their freedom, the United States will be giving effect to the principles of the Charter of the United Nations."

In September 1947, the American government submitted the Korean issue to the newly established UN General Assembly and called for a UN Temporary Commission on Korea to supervise general elections leading to an independent Korean government in both halves. The General Assembly gave its support. Pyongyang refused to cooperate, rejected the UN's authority, and denied the commission access. Elections in the South went ahead on May 10, but not in the North. Syngman Rhee, who had a master's degree in political science from Harvard and a doctorate from Princeton, where his supervisor was Woodrow Wilson, became the first president. The North conducted their own unsupervised elections for a "people's assembly," and Kim Il Sung became premier. In late 1948, the Soviets withdrew their troops and in June 1949, the Americans followed suit.

The North's attack in June 1950 would have succeeded had the Americans not unexpectedly decided to fight. The United States drew on the authority of the United Nations after the Security Council voted unanimously to declare war on North Korea. President Truman hastily sent 10,000 troops from Japan to bolster the weak South Korean Army. An American, General MacArthur, was put in charge of a multi-national force under the UN flag.

He crushed the invasion, but later it was the United Nations that signed the armistice, which has lasted longer than anyone could have imagined.

North Korea's destiny was bound up with the United Nation's intent to be more interventionist than its failed predecessor, the League of Nations, which had done nothing to stop Japan from seizing Korea and Manchuria in the 1920s and 1930s. By putting an army under its flag, the United Nations was determined to set an important precedent and show that unlike the impotent League it would uphold international law. The General Assembly vote on Korea slipped in when the Soviet Union was boycotting proceedings. The Korean War became the first proxy war fought between the two blocs; it paralyzed the United Nations, which was never again able to act in such a determined manner.

The war was also bound up with the spread of nuclear weapons. General MacArthur suggested dropping the bomb on China to consolidate his victory in throwing back the invasion. Washington decided against it, General MacArthur was replaced, and Chinese forces thrust the UN forces back down the peninsula. In 1958, the United States deployed nuclear weapons to South Korea, where they stayed until President George Bush withdrew them in 1991. As the Cold War developed, both sides began accumulating ever larger and more accurate nuclear missiles. Mutually assured destruction (MAD) provided a degree of geopolitical stability but proliferation— the spread of nuclear technology to client states like the two Koreas—always threatened to destabilize the whole world.

After the showdown of the Cuban Missile Crisis in 1962, the United States and the USSR (plus Britain and France) began to think seriously about safeguards. The negotiations took place at the United Nations and led to the creation of the International Atomic Energy Agency (IAEA), established in Vienna. Its mandate was ambiguous and contradictory. On the one hand, it was supposed to encourage the spread of nuclear technology— the atoms for peace program—but also prevent proliferation. Nations seeking to acquire nuclear technology had to sign the 1968 Treaty on Nuclear Non-proliferation and subject themselves to inspections. In practice, the IAEA lacked real investigative and coercive policing powers. When the Cold War ended, the superpowers began reducing their arsenals. Their massive threat receded, and the shortcomings of the IAEA's monitoring system became all too visible.

The turning point came with the discovery, in the face of considerable resistance, of just how close Saddam Hussein had come to making a bomb before he invaded Kuwait in 1990. He had pursued an ambitious nuclear R&D program undetected and was only a year or two away from testing a bomb. The special UN weapons inspection program set up after his defeat found out that Saddam Hussein had successfully hidden numerous sites including three parallel uranium enrichment programs from the eyes of the IAEA inspectors. Had he only delayed his invasion of Kuwait until he had tested a bomb, then he might well have gotten away with it. The scale of the deceit so embarrassed the IAEA that the Board of Governors ordered more thorough investigations of what North Korea was up to. And as a result of the uproar, U.S. intelligence began to openly cooperate with IAEA inspectors, and for the first time provided satellite photos of suspected but undeclared North Korean nuclear research sites.

Lee Kie-hyon remembers visiting North Korea's main nuclear research center at Yongbyon just after the Agreed Framework deal supposedly froze the North's nuclear program. She was surprised at the amount of work going on. "The work had actually stepped up. Several new departments, each named after a month, had been set up to do more research and development," she said. Mrs. Lee, a plump middle-aged woman with an air of confidence that comes from membership in North Korea's elite, had worked for years at one research department, first as a laboratory assistant and then dealing with visiting Soviet physicists. Her family had always worked at Yongbyon. Even after she had left the restricted zone to marry a senior military officer, she had gone back on family visits.[7]

She had arrived in South Korea just 18 months before our meeting, and was very cautious about what she could say without endangering her family, which she still hoped to smuggle out. Mrs. Lee had lived in the nuclear complex for 16 years and she quickly sketched out a map. It lies in the county of Yongbyon, about 60 miles north of Pyongyang, in a geographical bowl hidden behind 10-foot-high concrete walls and guarded by rings of police and military checkpoints. The complex is actually called Bungang, and behind the walls live about 10,000 staff, including 120 nuclear scientists plus their families. They are never allowed to leave, and few outsiders are ever allowed in. Even to trusted workers, parts of Bungang are off limits.

"There were many radiation accidents. A lot of children were born deformed and are taken care of in a special hospital," she said. Many in the workforce die in accidents but in return they enjoyed every luxury the country could offer, and even after 1991, when food ran out in many places, their rations were never cut.

The object of the work at Yongbyon was always clear to everyone, she said; it was always to make nuclear weapons and not to generate power. She said Kim Il Sung had started the project in the 1950s to protect himself from the U.S. threat, but it was his son who actually ran the program. "Kim Il Sung only visited a few times but Kim Jong Il came very frequently. He pushed it aggressively. He even built an observation pavilion on Yaksan Mountain to get a panoramic view," she said.

Yaksan is well known because Korean poet Kim So-Wol (1902–1935) once extolled the beauty of its azaleas in a patriotic verse. From there Kim Jong Il could see nearly 400 buildings, including the 2 railway lines, the Kuryong river, the Pakchon airbase, an uranium mine, a fuel-rod fabrication complex, another to reprocess the spent fuel rods and extract plutonium (known as the December enterprise), and the 5MW reactor (February enterprise). Nearby are construction sites where a 50 MW gas-graphite reactor was being built before 1994, and another site for a 200 MW reactor that lies five miles to the north. About 25 miles away lies another large underground complex of tunnels and pipelines at Kumchangri, the purpose of which is not known. U.S. officials inspected it in 1999 and found nothing.

Yongbyon is described as North Korea's Los Alamos, but it actually resembles one of the giant Soviet underground complexes like Krasnoyarsk-26. Stalin ordered 65,000 Gulag prisoners, later replaced by 100,000 troops, to build a small city more than 600 feet below the surface in Siberia. Krasnoyarsk-26 has 3,500 rooms and halls and a system of tunnels as big and extensive as the Moscow metro. Inside, safe from any American nuclear attack, are three plutonium reactors, a radiochemical facility to separate the plutonium from spent fuel rods, storage tanks, and ballistic missile plants. The entrances can be sealed off, and there is a ventilation system with air filters intended to protect the workforce from outside radiation.[8]

Krasnoyarsk-26 is located on the banks of the Yenisey River, which provides water for cooling. When it was still operating, nuclear wastewater was either discharged directly into the river or pumped along a 13-mile-long pipeline to where it was stored or pumped underground into deep wells. As in Yongbyon, the workforce could never leave these closed cities that were unmarked on any map. The Soviet Union had scattered a network of sites across its vast territory, burying some and locating others in remote mountain valleys. Despite the vast intelligence gathering efforts of the United States, the Soviet Union managed to prevent the United States from tracking its production of nuclear warheads. Only with the Soviet Union's fall did it become known that the United States had missed many nuclear production sites, including a second parallel network that was created to ensure that even after a U.S. nuclear strike, the Soviet Union could still produce more bombs. Although the CIA vastly overestimated Soviet military capabilities in some respects, it missed larger parts of the nuclear program, which produced a staggering 54,000 warheads.

Many of North Korea's nuclear sites are also hidden in narrow mountain valleys, or are positioned close to the Chinese border to protect them from aerial attack. Defectors like Mrs. Lee say that a network of factories, laboratories, and mines is buried deep underground. She said that she herself has ventured into a complex of deep tunnels bored into Yaksan Mountain and into the neighboring Sokdeh and Dongdeh Mountains. "The tunneling began in 1965 and most tunnels were wide enough for trucks to drive through. They especially did a lot of work to hide things from the UN and moved a lot of sensitive material into the tunnels," she said.

Anyone trying to assess or monitor the North Korean nuclear program faces a daunting task. They have to shift through the fragmentary clues from "humanint," intelligence gleaned by spies from questioning defectors, and try to match that against the data gathered by reconnaissance planes like the U2, satellite photographs, seismic recordings of any nuclear test, and the like. A particularly useful indicator is the minute quantities of Krypton-85, a radioactive gas that is emitted when spent fuel rods are processed and can be detected in the atmosphere. High-flying reconnaissance planes can help detect the Krypton, but by burying the reprocessing facilities deep underground, the Soviets managed to disguise or minimize Krypton-85 emissions. North Korea might be able to do the same.

Human intelligence can be flawed as well. A defector's testimony can be fragmentary or open to question. Very few people have ever left Yongbyon, and those that have may be technicians like Mrs. Lee who are neither top scientists nor given access to vital secrets. As more North Koreans escaped in the late 1990s, they brought with them tantalizing but unverifiable information that shook the confidence of intelligence analysts in both South Korea and the United States in the reliability of their assumptions. The ability of countries to hide what they are doing has been shown by Iran. In 2003, the IAEA discovered that Iran had managed to hide three sophisticated nuclear programs over 18 years, including a project to use lasers to carry out molecular isotope separation. Although it is clear that the Western intelligence agencies had underestimated the progress made by nuclear programs of Libya and Iran, much about North Korea's program still remains cloaked in mystery.

Naturally, it is in North Korea's interests to bluff its enemies into thinking its resources are bigger than they are if this strengthens its negotiating hand. If Pakistan has been as generous with North Korea as it turns out to have been with Libya and Iran in providing blueprints, centrifuges, uranium hexafluoride, and training, then North Korea might have gone further than had been suspected.

We do know that North Korea opened its first research center with Soviet help as early as 1952. Japan had started its own nuclear program in Korea in 1945, and the Japanese left behind uranium mining and milling equipment that the North Koreans used to export uranium to the Soviet Union and help pay for weapons deliveries and other aid. Around 1956, the North began sending hundreds of scientists to study at the Joint Institute for Nuclear Research at Dubna near Moscow, and three years later Pyongyang signed an agreement on the peaceful use of nuclear energy. Moscow then offered to build a 2 MW reactor and work started at Yongbyon.

China tested its first nuclear bomb in 1964, but when Kim Il Sung approached Mao to ask him to share their know-how, Mao refused. In 1967, the Soviets, then in a state of high tension with China, agreed to Kim Il Sung's requests and supplied the North Koreans with a small experimental reactor and started to transfer plutonium-reprocessing technology.

Mrs. Lee said that at Yongbyon she had worked with Soviet scientists until they left in the 1970s, when the United States and the USSR cosponsored a global Non-Proliferation Treaty, the NPT. For a while the North tried to carry out the research on its own, but in July 1977 North Korea decided to sign a trilateral safeguards agreement with the IAEA. The USSR then resumed supplying the small reactor with fuel. The next stage of close Soviet cooperation began again in 1984, when Kim Il Sung traveled by train to Moscow after a break of 23 years, asked for more help, and got it. The Soviets insisted that North Korea must first formally join the Non-Proliferation Treaty and thus promise not to seek nuclear weapons and to open all its nuclear sites to inspection. North Korea formally signed up in 1985, and then the Soviets agreed to deliver four 440 MW light-water reactors similar to those at Chernobyl for the peaceful purpose of generating electricity.

According to another defector, Kim Dae-ho, who has written a book—*The azaleas of Mt. Yaksan in Yongbyon have not bloomed yet*—about his 10 years working in the North's nuclear program, Kim Jong Il personally took charge of a new and accelerated program to obtain a bomb. "If we fight a war with South Korea we can win but only after a nuclear war," Kim Jong Il reportedly told his troops. Some 30,000 troops were assigned to the project and were given the name of "The Nuclear Development Corps," and a special Fund called N710 was set up to finance the effort. Some were assigned to begin building the reprocessing plant at Yongbyon. Another regiment was sent to build an underground test site at Taechon, and two other regiments were thrown into the effort to start producing bomb material by enriching uranium. They produced and processed the uranium at underground mines in Pyongsan in North Pyongan province. Kim Dae-ho said he worked on such a mine from which "yellow cake" or natural uranium is produced. It takes high quantities of yellow cake to produce tiny amounts of the heavy silvery-white metal, which can be turned into weapons-grade material. The ore is first crushed, then ground up, leached with sulfuric acid, and finally purified to produce the yellow cake. During the next stage, it is turned into uranium hexafluoride by dissolving it in nitric acid. This mixture is then turned into a gas before being inserted into centrifuges that can separate out the right form of uranium. It requires considerable amounts of energy and thousands of centrifuges made from special steels that North Korea has had to secretly import.[9]

For decades North Korea had always considered itself in an arms race with South Korea, but by 1984 the imperative to develop a nuclear arsenal must have been overwhelming as the South was rapidly overtaking the

North economically. Seoul started building its first research reactor in July 1959 and had finished it by 1962. Its first nuclear power plant started commercial operations in 1978. In the early 1980s, South Korea had eight reactors under construction in a bid to become self-reliant on electricity production. By 2015, it will have enough plants running to supply 45 percent of the electricity consumed, and the Korea Electric Power Corporation (KEPCO) is so confident of its abilities to design and construct light-water reactors that it has begun trying to win overseas contracts.[10]

The South could easily have built its own A-bomb and, like Taiwan, was only restrained from doing so by the United States, which then had to put both states under the protection of its own nuclear umbrella. Similarly, in order to stifle an arms race in rockets, Washington also stopped Seoul from developing its own missile technology.

It always made perfect sense for the North to develop its own nuclear weapons and delivery vehicles while persuading the United States to withdraw its tactical missiles from the South. If South Korea could also continue to be dissuaded from developing its own nuclear weapons and missiles by false assurances, then so much the better. At first little attention was paid to the North's nuclear program. The IAEA was supposed to make its first inspection in 1987, about 18 months after North Korea had signed the NPT. When no inspection took place, there was little concern and the IAEA granted Pyongyang an 18-month delay. Then that deadline passed as well and when concern was voiced, Pyongyang demanded "legal assurances" that the United States would never threaten it with nuclear weapons and that the joint U.S.-ROK military exercises known as "Team Spirit" be stopped.

Tensions over the plutonium program at Yongbyon only began in earnest in 1989. CIA satellites caught North Korea secretly unloading enough plutonium-bearing fuel rods from the Yongbyon reactor to process into one or two nuclear bombs. At the reprocessing plant, the five- to ten-foot fuel rods, which contain radioactive plutonium, uranium, and other by-products, are unbundled and chopped into small pieces. The pieces are then placed in a nitric-acid bath to separate out the plutonium, uranium, and by-products from the rod casings. An organic solvent is added to separate uranium and plutonium, and then the liquid uranium is separated from the plutonium and further processed to make a powder, uranium oxide, and plutonium metal. To manufacture a bomb, this plutonium metal is shaped into a sphere, perhaps as small as a grapefruit, and a nuclear explosion is then detonated by using conventional high explosives. Unprocessed fuel rods, clad in a magnesium alloy, are stored in special tanks that resemble swimming pools. If the uranium metal is ever exposed to air, it oxidizes or "rusts" and can ignite spontaneously, releasing deadly radioactive clouds. However, the magnesium alloy casings protect the rods from oxidizing and when intact there is no rush to process the rods.

Satellite photographs also showed that the North Koreans had built themselves a reprocessing plant so huge that it was the second largest in the world. There could only be one explanation for why the North Koreans thought they needed a processing plant big enough to process a hundred tons or two hundred tons of spent fuel a year.

To be sure, the CIA flew flights over North Korea trying to detect the giveaway Krypton emissions. Later, the CIA even persuaded the Russians to install sensors inside their embassy in Pyongyang to help with the detection. To obtain proof that could be made public, however, the IAEA inspectors had to visit Yongbyon and physically count how many fuel rods were left intact in the special tanks.[11]

The crisis escalated in 1990 when South Korean Defense Minister Lee Jong-ku warned that if the North did not sign an additional IAEA safeguards agreement and allow the inspectors in, then the South would attack Yongbyon. Kim Il Sung replied that this ultimatum was a "virtual declaration of war." As the IAEA struggled to persuade North Korea to allow its inspectors in, Pyongyang started negotiations with the South, proposing to make the whole Korean peninsula a nuclear-weapons-free zone, which meant that the United States must remove its tactical nuclear weapons. Then Pyongyang conceded to the additional safeguards inspections under the IAEA and said, otherwise, if its aforesaid conditions were not met, it would leave the NPT altogether.

By this time, with the collapse of the Soviet empire, the nuclear weapons program and the IAEA inspection regime emerged as North Korea's most important interface with the the world. By 1991, North Korea started a routine of using the nuclear issue to extract concessions on every issue. When the last Soviet Foreign Minister Eduard Shevardnadze informed Pyongyang that Moscow was going to recognize the South, Pyongyang reacted by threatening to hold a nuclear test. The gambit failed with Moscow, which went ahead and recognized Seoul, but it succeeded with South Korea. After three days of intense bargaining in October 1991, both Koreas agreed to denuclearize the peninsula. They made a pact not to produce, test, receive, deploy, or possess nuclear fuel or weapons, or the means to make them. Both sides agreed to set up a North-South joint nuclear control commission to organize inspections. They even began discussing whether the South would build the light-water reactors that the Russians were no longer prepared to deliver.

The brinkmanship used during this first crisis also allowed Pyongyang to achieve a number of other objectives, such as entering into direct talks with the United States for the first time. Hitherto, American diplomats had even been forbidden to acknowledge the existence of the North Koreans if they ran across each other at some third-country embassy reception. Now, even though they still did not have diplomatic relations, talks started in earnest. North Korea also opened up ties with its old enemy Japan and received the first offer of war reparations. Lastly, there were clear strategic gains. Washington did remove its nuclear weapons from South Korea and it temporarily suspended the U.S.–South Korean annual "Team Spirit" military exercises. It looked like, as with the Soviet Union, nuclear arms reduction talks could turn into a stage for exploring new relationships.

In a developing atmosphere of trust, North Korea promised in early 1992 to open its entire nuclear program to IAEA inspections. This meant that it was agreeing to do what it had already agreed to do in 1985 when it joined the NPT. On May 4, 1992, North Korea finally gave the IAEA its "initial declaration"—a statement of all its nuclear material subject to safeguards. It told the IAEA that it had seven sites in total and that far from extracting pounds of plutonium to make several bombs, it had merely extracted only 90 grams of plutonium. It said the IAEA could begin inspections to verify the initial disclosure and to assess its completeness. Soon afterward, Hans Blix, the IAEA's director general, visited North Korea for the first time. Among the sites Blix's delegation visited was the reprocessing plant the North Koreans call the "Radiochemical Laboratory." The North Koreans told them it had only been used once, in March 1990, when a few fuel rods had to be removed because their metal casing was damaged. The North Koreans assured the Swede that this was not a sign of any weapons production.

In the summer of 1992, the IAEA made its first proper inspection and collected "samples" that were taken back to the laboratories for analysis. The results showed that the North Koreans were lying. One piece of evidence came from "smear" or "swipe" samples taken from the insides of boxes storing gloves used when handling freshly purified plutonium. By looking for americium 241, a decay product of plutonium 241, it is possible to tell how much time had passed since the plutonium was separated from the fuel rods. Analysis showed that North Korea had in fact separated plutonium in 1989, 1990, and 1991. This supported the claims made by defectors that the North had started reprocessing in 1988 and had shut the reactor down for 71 days in 1989, 30 days in 1990, and 50 days in 1991.

The IAEA also checked to see if the plutonium really did come from the damaged fuel rods the North Koreans had talked about. The ratios of plutonium isotopes in the waste and glove box samples should have had the same proportion of plutonium isotopes 239, 240, and 241 as those from the broken fuel rods, but they did not. So the North must have separated more plutonium than it was admitting. When confronted with the evidence, the North's nuclear scientists simply stuck to their original story. But to find out just how much plutonium—and therefore how many bombs the North might have made—it was necessary for the IAEA to take samples from nuclear waste sites. This they were prevented from doing.

The CIA had provided satellite photos indicating where the waste sites might be—two sites near the Radiochemical Laboratory were big enough to hold large quantities of both liquid and solid nuclear waste. Yet before the next inspection visit, the photos clearly revealed that the North had rushed to cover them up and disguise them by planting trees and fields over them. In early photos, one waste site is visible and looks just like those seen near other Soviet-supplied research reactors in places like Iraq. They all have a distinctive pattern of round and square holes in an aboveground concrete structure. Later photos actually show North Koreans covering up and landscaping the site.

A second suspicious waste site was a building about 50 yards long that looked very much like a reprocessing plant and appeared to be connected to the Radiochemical Laboratory by pipes running under a small hill. Again, the early photos showed a two-story building with two trenches connecting it to the Radiochemical Laboratory, but later photos showed only one story and a truck hauling things away. The lower floor had been buried, probably to conceal the waste tanks. When inspectors did visit this building in the summer of 1992, they could no longer see the lower floor and were not allowed to inspect it. Instead they were taken to a new site nearby that had been barely used. The North Koreans refusal to allow them to go and investigate suspect sites was a breach of their earlier promises that inspectors could go wherever they wanted.

The North Koreans were unlucky to have been caught out. Before the Gulf War, the IAEA inspections were formalities. In addition, the North had taken extraordinary efforts to remove all traces of plutonium from the Radio-chemical Laboratory to the extent of cleaning and grinding down all the metal surfaces of glove boxes. The North could not have imagined that the inspectors would be able to learn so much by wiping innocuous looking cloths along uncleaned surfaces or the nooks and crannies of the glove boxes and adjacent areas. Yet from such samples, the IAEA could indeed detect minute quantities of plutonium at levels far below those anticipated by the North. By their sixth and last inspection, the North Koreans were doing everything to hinder the work of the inspectors, who were reduced to operating at night using flashlights. Still the IAEA was armed with enough evidence in 1993 to declare the North in violation of its obligations.

Pyongyang responded with fury by declaring that it would withdraw from the NPT. The IAEA board recommended sanctions but China and Russia blocked this at the UN Security Council. Instead in the second half of 1993, issue was taken up at four party talks and in bilateral negotiations between the United States and North Korea. By this time the North Koreas still felt confident they had the upper hand and confidently laid out their demands to Robert Gallucci, who led the U.S. negotiating team. The list included U.S. diplomatic recognition, the end of economic sanctions, one million tons in grain, half a million tons of fuel oil per year, the end of the Team Spirit exercises, and the delivery of two light-water reactors worth over U.S. $4.5 billion. The Koreans were quite specific about the sort of reactors they wanted and only these would do.

Although the U.S. hand had strengthened at the end of 1993, the UN General Assembly passed a nine-point resolution with 140 in favor and nine abstentions, urging North Korea to "cooperate immediately with the IAEA in the full implementation of the safeguards agreement." North Korea got nearly everything on its shopping list.

As the bargaining went over the next six months, North Korea kept up the pressure by threatening to escalate the crisis by moving 8,000 stored fuel rods, completing the construction of two other reactors, and preventing any future IAEA supervision. It even haggled over exactly how many rods the IAEA could be permitted to examine. In return, the United States threatened Pyongyang with UN sanctions and a pre-emptive strike, but Pyongyang was not daunted and counter-threatened with a war that would turn Seoul "into a sea of fire."

President Carter's mission in June 1994 allowed both sides to back down, but essentially it was the United States that gave way. Three years earlier South Korea had done the same in return for promises that were never carried out. It is fair to say that in fact neither the United States nor North Korea went on to fulfil their respective obligations under the Agreed Framework. North Korea did not freeze its nuclear program, at least according to the defectors (and later evidence gathered by the CIA), but on the other hand the nuclear plants that the United States promised were never delivered. The U.S. partners in the project did set up an organization called KEDO, but as South Korean companies were charged with carrying out the construction work, progress came in fits and starts. The North Koreans seemed to put unnecessary obstacles in the way. At one stage construction was halted when one South Korean worker was accused of lèse-majesté by sitting on a North Korean newspaper bearing a photograph of Kim Jong Il.

Perhaps as a confidence-building measure, the Agreed Framework might have worked as long as Kim Il Sung had stayed alive. Defectors like Hwang Jang-yop claim that Kim was genuinely interested in détente but his son was not. Set against such assertions, however, is a long history of disappointing negotiations with the North like those in 1972, 1985, and 1992 that show a pattern of agreements entered into, then quickly reinterpreted by Pyongyang and abandoned. And there is a long record of outright lies. When for instance a leading U.S. Congressman, Stephen Solarz, met Kim Il Sung in 1991 for a two and one-half hours of talks, Kim emphatically denied that he had any interest in obtaining nuclear weapons and pounding the table declared, "we have no nuclear reprocessing materials."

Defenders of the deal argue that the North Koreans did stop construction on two new reactors, the 5MW reactor was shut down, and the 8,000 fuel rods remained under IAEA monitoring until 2002. On the other hand,

Kim Jong Il may have continued his search for a nuclear deterrent by building a string of undetected nuclear facilities underground that could produce bomb-grade plutonium and manufacture highly enriched uranium from the country's domestic uranium mines.

It did not look like a genuine freeze was in place. North Korea was certainly caught trying to buy electronic components for bomb triggers and was repeatedly caught red-handed trying to hire East German, Czech, and Russian rocket and nuclear scientists to work in North Korea. There were credible rumors that in the early 1990s North Korea had succeeded in a covert operation to buy 123 pounds of plutonium from the former Soviet Union, enough for ten warheads.

For a long time, much of the information came from defectors like Kim Dae-ho. He was smuggled to the South after he walked into the South Korean Embassy in Beijing. From there he was sneaked out of China on a fishing boat. A quiet, serious man, Kim Dae-ho told the South Koreans that Kim Il Sung announced as early as 1987 that the program to enrich uranium was underway and that by the end of 1989 the Great Leader had declared that North Korea had mastered the necessary centrifuge technology. Other defectors that I met like Mrs. Lee also insisted that the country had an HEU (highly enriched uranium) bomb by 1989. Kim Dae-ho was furious that South Korean intelligence services refused to believe his claims of a successful HEU program and for along time prevented him from going public with his allegations. Clearly, if what he was saying was true then all the negotiations around the Agreed Framework were for nothing. By the time Seoul launched the Sunshine Policy and sought to present an image of Kim Jong Il as a credible partner for peace, this sort of revelation was extremely damaging. If North Korea had never been sincere in its negotiations with either Seoul or Washington then what was the point of further talks?

On the other hand it was hard to double-check the allegations by Kim and others. Doubts surfaced about the depth of Kim Dae-ho's nuclear technology expertise. Further, an HEU program is very hard to detect. There are no telltale emissions of Krypton and any equipment can be easily hidden underground or quickly moved from place to place.

Another North Korean escapee who uses the name of Kenki Aoyama claims that the North had actually gone ahead and tested a bomb. Aoyama, who was born in Japan to Korean parents in 1961, returned to North Korea, where he graduated from Pyongyang's top technology university. He worked at North Korea's National Academy of Sciences and on the missile program and was in touch with colleagues working on the nuclear program.[12]

Aoyama also described how in 1997 when he was working as an industrial spy in Beijing, he met an old friend, a North Korean nuclear scientist. The man looked terrible, thin and wan. His eyebrows had disappeared from accidental radiation and Aoyama asked him: "Are you still working on it?"—"No," came the reply. "It's done. We succeeded."[13]

Aoyoma claims that after 1994 Kim Jong Il had transferred the nuclear weapons program to Kumchangri, some 35 miles north of Yongbyon. When in 1998, Washington demanded to inspect Kumchangri, Kim Jong Il agreed in exchange for 600,000 tons of food. When the two inspections revealed nothing more than empty tunnels, Aoyama said Kim had had plenty of time to move everything to a third location. Even so his credibility (and those of other defectors) was damaged.

In 1998, the suspicion surfaced in the CIA that North Korea might have tested a bomb in Pakistan. The ties with Pakistan started in the 1970s and developed into a strong partnership in the early 1990s when both countries ran out of foreign exchange. Kim Dae-ho confirmed that the HEU program came to a standstill in 1992 because of cash shortages. Consequently the two countries agreed on a barter deal. North Korea would provide Pakistan with the technology to build the medium-range missiles it needed to strike India. In return, Islamabad would provide the centrifuge designs stolen by Abdul Qadeer Khan, the father of Pakistan's bomb, when he worked at the European consortium called Urenco in the 1970s. In 1994, a group of 30 to 40 Pakistani engineers visited North Korea. Then in 1996 or 1997, Pakistan sent a sample gas centrifuge and the blueprints on a special plane to Pyongyang. In May 1998, Pakistan carried out five underground tests in the Baluchistan Desert that used fissile material from its HEU program. However, the Americans picked up the telltale signs of Krypton-85, suggesting that at a second test site in Pakistan a plutonium bomb had been exploded. As if by arrangement, that same year Pakistan displayed its new ballistic Ghauri missile based on North Korean designs and North Korea launched its first Taepodong long-range missile over Japan. The two-stage rocket with a range of up to 2,000 km could carry a one-ton payload and therefore deliver a small nuclear bomb to U.S. bases in Japan and perhaps as far as North America.

The value of the evidence about the nuclear test and the second repro-cessing plant remains disputed, but Americans did begin to accumulate solid evidence of an active HEU program. German intelligence detected a French-registered ship carrying part of the thousands of aluminum pipes that North Korea had ordered in Germany. These are made of a very strong alloy, maraging steel, which is needed in the gas centrifuges. By 2002, the CIA had enough evidence about the HEU program for Assistant Secretary of State James Kelly to take to Pyongyang. In a showdown, North Korea first denied but then admitted that the accusations were true and that it already possessed a powerful nuclear deterrent. This spelled the end of the KEDO project and the collapse of the Agreed Framework. North Korea expelled the IAEA inspectors, withdrew from the NPT, and declared it was going to reprocess the 8,000 spent fuel rods.

It might all still be smoke and mirrors. It is in Kim Jong Il's interests to let his own people believe they are protected by having their own bomb. It also strengthens his hand if the Americans believe this as well. A suspected nuclear bomb is almost as good a deterrent as a real one. It makes it less likely that the U.S. would attack with the same impunity as against Iraq. That might explain why, in 1991 or 1992, the North carried out extensive tests to show that it had mastered the techniques of explosions to com-press a plutonium core. The tests were done in the open, apparently so that they could be photographed by satellites.[14]

Yet, the ten years that have passed since 1994 might also enable Kim Jong Il to move a long way ahead with both a HEU and plutonium-based weapons programs. If either or both exist, then they are now buried under-ground far beyond the reach of any cruise missiles. There would now be little point in bombing the Yongbyon facilities. Besides, North Korea could now perhaps retaliate by launching a Taepodong long-range missile tipped with a nuclear missile.[15]

CHAPTER 9

Kim Jong Il—The Reformer

The first executions in Songrim City took place at nine o'clock one morning in February 1998. A truck carrying five condemned men, all senior executives of the Hwanghae Iron and Steel Works, all blindfolded, bound, and dressed in thick padded cotton clothing, halted before the crowd of steel workers and their families who had been summoned to watch. As the guards pulled the prisoners off the truck the crowd noticed that the men were limping so badly that the guards had to half drag each of them to the execution posts erected on the municipal sports ground. The accused had been tortured to extract a confession of guilt and, when an army colonel declared that the eight had confessed to illegally selling state property and violating party discipline, each of the men made a gesture of assent. The only possible penalty was death. A dozen soldiers lined up and fired three volleys and the condemned slumped to the ground.

In 1998, Kim Jong Il's grip was at its shakiest but against all expectations he managed to hold onto power after his father's death in the face of mass starvation, army mutinies, and economic collapse. Chung Chun-min and Kim Bok-sun, a married couple and former steelworkers, witnessed these events and say they were the start of a terror campaign, one of a number that Kim Jong Il launched to enable him to hang on until South Korea, the United States, and the international community were persuaded to offer him increased amounts of aid. Kim kept up the level of fear by parading troops, imposing martial law on key industrial cities like Songrim, and staging public executions while rewarding his followers with food and gifts.

Chung Chun-min and Kim Bok-sun say that they were awakened before dawn by the tanks thundering through the streets. They ran out of their flat convinced that the long-expected American attack had begun. "The soldiers with fixed bayonets and belts of bullets looked very tense and nervous," recalled Chung Chun-min, a plump, quiet woman.[1]

"All the roads in and out of the city were blocked. Later, when the tanks left after three months, I counted 150 tanks," said her husband Kim Bok-sun, a tall gangly man who now works as a builder in Seoul. At ten that morning trucks went round the town with loudspeakers to summon the population. They announced that the town of 120,000 was under martial law and that those who had stolen anything from the steel mill must return it before a week was up. "We were branded a rebel city," Chung recalled. "They said the steel mill had been ruined because there were South Korean spies among the workers."

The next day, the population was again summoned to witness the first of 20 executions. In the first round, five senior Party officials, including the police chief, the steel mill manager, and the city's party secretary in charge of propaganda, who were accused of selling state property, were shot. The other victims included two fortunetellers and two Koreans who had emigrated from Japan and were condemned for allegedly stealing a tape recorder.

"They wanted to shoot people like that to make everyone afraid and to make it clear to people that they must not expect any change," said Kim Bok-sun as we sat on the floor of their tiny apartment in a distant satellite town of Seoul sipping tea. In all, over 200 people were arrested and sent to the camps. Similar crackdowns took place in other cities like Kimchaek, Nampo, Hysean, and Sinuiju. The pattern was always the same. It was generally a member of Kim's immediate family like his sister, Kim Kyong-hee, or his son, Jong-nam, or brother in law, Chang Song-Taek, who led investigation task forces backed up by troops. They staged public executions to cow the Party officials, and dispatched a few hundred others to the camps to frighten the rest of the population.

Two weeks before the tanks moved in, Kim Kyong-hee arrived quietly in a busload of secret police and quickly established that the mill plant was not working. The Hwanghae Iron and Steel Works had employed 18,000 workers. Production ceased in 1994 after imports of coke from China stopped and domestic supplies of coal ran out. At first the managers kept production going by getting everyone to collect scrap metal but then, by 1996, the furnaces went out.

"When the furnace went out the managers didn't dare tell the central government. They feared that they would be punished and there would be no more food rations. About 200 people in the city had already starved to death," said Chung. The public distribution system formerly supplied them with a pound and a half of grain per day, the highest ration given to anyone in the country other than air force pilots. The Hwanghae plant is one of the country's industrial flagships, and its workforce had enjoyed priority access to food supplies in a region that is considered the country's breadbasket.

Kim Kyong-hee's task force discovered that the management was secretly trading with China, bartering cold-rolled steel for maize, and a cargo ship carrying the grain was seized as soon as it docked at Nampo. The Iron and Steel Works was a conglomerate that included the Chaeryong Iron Ore Mine, the Songrim Maritime Shipping Company, and the Songrim Machine Parts Plant, plus it had its own cargo vessels.[2]

Like so much of North Korea's industrial base, the Iron and Steel Works dated back to the Japanese occupation. The Mitsubishi Corporation founded it as Kyomipo Ironworks in 1918, and in the 1980s it was expanded and modernized by Kim Il Sung in a bid to rival the huge POSCO steelworks that had transformed the South into a major steel power. Two new furnaces and an automatic remote-control rolling production system to make rolled-steel products were imported, followed in 1987 by a stainless-steel plate unit with a 10,000-ton capacity and, in 1989, an ingot factory. The North Koreans expected it to do well by exporting thick and thin steel plates, steep wire, and ropes to the USSR and Eastern Europe. Then after 1990, the plant found willing customers in China, Japan, India, and Hong Kong.

At first, the management tried to maintain production by ordering the workforce to scour the area for scrap metal to melt down, but this could not go on forever. When there was nothing left to scavenge or steal, the factory stopped issuing food and the workers stopped turning up for work. According to an account that Kim Jong Il gave to two visiting Japanese Koreans, the leaders of the pro-DPRK General Association of the Koreans Resident in Japan (Chongryon), Mr. Huh Jong-man and Mr. Suh Man-sul, the management was selling off the machinery:

We found ourselves in dire straits and could not provide enough electric power to the Hwanghae Steel Mill and it stopped operation. Some bad elements in our society in cahoots with the management began to dismantle the factory and sell its machinery as scrap metal to Chinese merchants.

By the time we got wind of what was going on, more than half of the mill had been stripped away. For nearly a year, thieves took over the mill and stole the people's property at will. They bribed Party leaders and security officers, and consequently no one informed us about their thievery. Everybody was on the take at the plant and we had to send in an army to retake the Mill. The army surrounded the plant and arrested the thieves. The army recovered people's property from the thieves. Some of our trading people were involved in this massive fleecing of the plant.[3]

Kim denies reports that an army unit had mutinied and taken over the steel mill. Chung Chun-min and Kim Bok-sum also reject a rumor that the steelworkers were massacred by the troops after they staged a sit-down protest at the mill. "No one would dare to do such a thing," Chung said.

Without hope of any change, Chung and Kim fled, leaving two of their children behind, and reached South Korea in 2001. The couple, like other refugees, found it incredible that anyone in the South could portray Kim Jong Il as a closet reformer. "He wants to keep things as they are rather than attempt reform. He thinks reform will spell the end of the regime. If it started it would mean not just the end of his rule but his life. His only concern is to keep his regime in place," Kim said.

Many Korea watchers in South Korea and the United States believed the contrary, that after his father's death in 1994, Kim Jong Il patiently waited to attempt change. He then had to observe a three-year period of Confucian mourning before being formally installed as the head of the Korean Workers Party at a meeting of the Supreme People's Assembly held in the autumn of 1998. He then prepared to launch economic reforms and agreed to hold a summit with South Korean President Kim Dae Jung, thereby completing what his father was about to do before he died. The next step would be a summit with U.S. President Clinton at which diplomatic relations would be agreed upon, and the North would be taken off the list of terrorist states and receive a large measure of international aid.

When North Korean diplomats held meetings with U.S. State Department officials such as Ken Quinones, they portrayed Kim Jong Il as a closet reformer, struggling to escape the pressures by powerful and archly conservative generals who opposed his efforts to bring about change. American scholar Selig Harrison, who is a frequent visitor to Pyongyang, became convinced that Kim Jong Il was, as he said in his book *Korean Endgame*, presiding over a process of "reform by stealth." Kim, he wrote, was "tacitly encouraging change in the domestic economy without incurring the political costs of confronting the Old Guard in a formal doctrinal debate." Kim was in a deep game of "trying to outflank the old guard and the powerful generals who run the national defense industry" and had managed to pull off "a bloodless military coup."[4]

This view began to filter into American reporting, and Kim began to be described as a "quirky" man searching for a "dose of capitalism." In internal speeches Kim sometimes excused the shortcomings in the economy by saying he didn't know much about running the economy. He told visitors about the need to learn from the capitalist system and, in particular, successful South Korean companies like Samsung. When the daughter of South Korea's former dictator Park Chung-hee came to Pyongyang, Kin admired the way Park had built up the South Korean economy. To Madeleine Albright, he said he did not want the Chinese model of mixing socialism with free markets. What he preferred for North Korea was the Swedish model or possibly the Thai model, with its strong traditional royal system.

The evidence to support the theory that Kim Jong Il would lead a team of younger, better-educated technocrats and change the country was there. There was the joint venture law promulgated in 1984. A few years later, the North Koreans set up the Rajin-Sonbong special economic zone, a fenced-off area in North Hamgyong province that included two ports. This appeared after Kim Jong Il toured China in 1991, and North Korea flattered the Chinese by describing it as a "Hong Kong for the Twenty-First Century."

The United Nations Development Program (UNDP) backed the zone as part of a multinational project to development that corner where China and Russia meet. A senior official in charge of it, Kim Jong-u, claimed to have attracted investments worth over U.S. $700 million, but the real figure was probably closer to U.S. $37 million. Most of it came from a Hong Kong company with a dubious reputation—the Emperor Group, which invested in a hotel and casino. It was a bizarre asset for a province in which 20 percent of the population had starved to death.

North Korea also applied to join the Asian Development Bank and announced its intention to join the World Bank and the International Monetary Fund. It began to send officials abroad on training courses in market economics and international law with the support of the UNDP.

Kim Jong-u, the Chairman of the Committee for the Promotion of External Economic Cooperation and Vice Chairman of the External Economic Affairs Commission, turned up at the World Economic Forum in Davos, Switzerland and similar venues touting for foreign investment. He also went to Washington in April 1996 with a message of reform: "We recognize that the world market has been unified into a single capitalistic market and we are ready to plunge into it. In order to introduce the high technology and foreign capital investment so urgently needed by our national economy, we are introducing across the board business reforms and modes that are taken as universal on the international market," he said.[5] During the summer of 1997, Pyongyang also sent agricultural officials to study agriculture in the United States. The North Koreans toured farms in Minnesota where they spoke about the need for reforms.

At this time, no one knew much about Kim Jong Il, his character, or his intentions. He had only uttered one brief sentence in public and that was in 1992. The South Koreans thought he had a speech defect. He was an enigmatic figure lurking in the shadows, dismissed as a playboy and a drinker with a taste for filmmaking. When U.S. Secretary of State Madeleine Albright travelled to Pyongyang to meet him in 2000, she was told he was reclusive, even delusional, a weak, cautious man hampered by a stammer. Instead, she found a charming, if eccentric, man who seemed reassuringly rational and she later praised him as "a good listener, a good interlocutor. Very decisive and practical."

In his scholarly study *The Guerilla Dynasty*, Australian academic Dr. Adrian Buzo discounts the "consistent speculation on Kim's mental stability," which he blames on "second-hand lurid tales of a dissipated lifestyle." He says, "no convincing evidence has ever emerged of emotional or psychological instability, as opposed to mere eccentricity, on Kim Jong Il's part." Buzo goes on to argue that contrary to such "misleading images," the overwhelming evidence is that Kim is a "pragmatically-oriented" leader.

During this period, Kim met foreign leaders who all rated his abilities highly and praised his knowledge of the outside world. South Korean President Kim Dae Jung praised him as a man of "intellectual ability and discernment," who was "reform-minded and the type of man we can talk with in a commonsense fashion." Chinese President Jiang Zemin described him as a logical and passionate man of great cultural attainments. Other Chinese considered him an intelligent, popular, and kind-hearted man who commands the respect of the world. The widespread confusion and ignorance about Kim Jong Il led to a series of policies, miscalculations one might say, by the United Nations, South Korea, and the United States, which are described in more detail in later chapters.

South Korea, which believed Kim Jong Il had wielded little power while his father was alive, became convinced that he would be overthrown. When this did not happen, they thought he could be flattered or at least cornered into undertaking significant economic and political reforms. This belief became the cornerstone of Kim Dae Jung's "Sunshine Policy," which marked the end of hostile efforts to overthrow the regime.

In order to create a "soft landing" for the North's economy, the South began to try to keep Kim in power by shipping large amounts of grain and fertilizer and by making payments of over half a billion dollars to arrange the 2000 summit. In 1998, when the United Nations was appealing for over U.S. $600 million in emergency aid, Kim was able to spend U.S.$20 million importing 200 of the latest and costliest S-500 class Mercedes, which he distributed as rewards to his followers after the test-firing of a new long-range missile over Japan.

Policymakers in Washington also opted for an engagement policy and by the end of President Clinton's term in office the United States was prepared to make sweeping security guarantees in return for concessions on proliferation. A report written in 1999 by former Defense Secretary William Perry was certain that this was the best option because "there was no evidence at all that pressure would cause that regime to collapse. They have an iron police state in North Korea, and the misery of the people was not likely, in our judgment, to lead to a popular overthrow of the government."[6]

The United Nations stayed silent about the full extent of the famine, which cost over three million lives, perhaps in the belief that it was being instrumental in bringing about change. Perhaps too, it hoped that it might eventually be put in charge of a massive international effort, costing tens of billions of dollars, to rebuild the North Korean economy.

It is impossible to know how close Kim Jong Il came to losing power in the 1990s, but in 1998 at the height of the famine, the situation was very desperate indeed. Kim Jong Il was deeply hated, and although the stories of uprisings, coup d'états, and assassination attempts that refugees tell are hard to verify, he may only have hung on to power by his fingernails. With outside help his enemies might have succeeded in ousting him, but Kim managed to persuade enough people that he was going to serve as an instrument for peaceful change.

The first fragmentary accounts of serious unrest in North Korea surfaced in the early 1980s. In September 1981, armed clashes between soldiers and workers took place in Chongjin, the heavy industrial center on the East Coast, and left 500 dead. Soviet experts working inside North Korea during the 1980s reported similar clashes in Sinuiju on the border with China in 1983. Two years later, there were reports of a massacre of hundreds of civilians at Hamhung when troops opened fire on protestors using the antiaircraft guns commonly installed on the roofs of many public buildings. Diplomats residing in Pyongyang tended to dismiss such stories as the work of South Korean agents, but later as more and more North Koreans arrived in the South and as the food shortages deepened after 1990, the number of such reported incidents began to multiply.

In 1990, a small group of students at the Kim Il Sung University were arrested for organizing protests and tortured into confessing that they had taken part in antistate activities. Around the same time, Lim Young Sun, a young army officer who later defected to the South, claims that he fell in with a group of about 30 or 40 soldiers who formed an underground group determined to overthrow Kim Jong Il. In 1991, they formed "The Supreme Council of National Salvation" and distributed antigovernment leaflets, throwing them out the window of both a train and a truck. "We appeal to the soldier's of the people's army and to the people to join our struggle," the leaflet said and called for the execution of both Kims.[7]

Other sources also speak of a group of army officers who were arrested for opposing the succession of Kim Jong Il, ten of whom were executed. And there are reports that early in December 1992, officers in the general office of the Bureau of Bodyguards attempted to stage a coup d'état. The Tong-a Ilbo newspaper in the South said that in January 1992 the North Korean government uncovered a plot to prevent Kim Jong Il from succeeding to the commander of the army. The authorities executed three senior officers, including a regiment commander, and ten officials from the State Security Department. Then in April of that year the paper reported that the government had found 30 general-grade officers guilty of an unsuccessful assassination attempt. Two of them, the deputy commander of the Seventh Army Corps stationed in Hamhung and Col. General An Jong-ho, deputy chief of staff, were shot, but others fled to Russia.[8]

Many refugees reported that in the early 1990s ordinary soldiers were literally starving to death in their barracks. One refugee, Kim Sum-ming, said that in 1993 he saw 12 fellow soldiers dying of malnourishment. They had so little food that when they were given pork to eat in celebration of Kim Il Sung or Kim Jong Il's birthdays on April 15 or February 15, their digestive systems could not cope. The soldiers had diarrhea and died. Another refugee, Choi Jin-i said that every big unit had a ward for soldiers suffering from edema, or swelling due to starvation. People regarded joining the army as the same as being sent to a death camp because the officers stole the rations of the new conscripts. Half of those admitted to these wards would be expected to die, and desperate parents would try to bring their sons home. Choi met one group of 20 soldiers that was being taken out of a camp; some of the boys were so weak they could not even move their fingers.

Refugees, including military officers, reported that in most units soldiers were put on half rations (which normally average a pound of grain per day) and some soldiers began stealing food from peasant houses, raiding the illegal markets, or directly confiscating food shipments as they arrived on the docks. Armed soldiers would wander around some cities at night and if they saw a light shining, they would force their way in and demand food. In daytime they would prowl the roads like highway thieves, stopping and robbing those travelling on foot who were also looking for food or trying to do some trading.

In 1993, South Korea's head of the Agency for National Security Planning, Kim Tok, said that acute food shortages had led to "rioting, work slowdowns, the beating of food distribution officials."[9] A major incident took place in March of that year at the headquarters of the VII Corps stationed in Hamhung. Thirty high-ranking officials wanted economic reforms and had plotted to stage a rebellion to coincide with inspections by the International Atomic Energy Agency and appeal for international support. Before they could gain an audience with the IAEA, they were arrested.

Another military unit in Sinuiju staged an uprising on April 22, 1993, but they were quickly surrounded and defeated, and those taking part were executed. The uprising coincided with riots by workers protesting the food shortages. Sources also told me that in 1994 some writers were arrested for joining antistate activities. That same year, the secret police arrested ten officers at the Hanggon Military Officers Training School and burned them at the stake on the school grounds after uncovering a plot to assassinate Kim Jong Il. The punishment for militating against the state seems to have been swift, and often deadly.

By 1995, when everyone including Party officials could not find enough to eat, the largest known military plot had been thwarted already. Different versions of this incident have been reported, but it seems that the main leaders were senior officers of the VI Corps based in Chongjin. That corps includes the 24th Infantry Division and a field artillery unit at Kimchaek, home to a steel mill as important as Songrim's. The plotters, whose names are not known, hoped to seize control of the local university, provincial communication centers, the Chongjin port, and various missile-launch installations. Then they planned to call on the VII Corps headquarters down the coast in Hamhung for support before advancing on Pyongyang where their true target lay. However, before the conspiracy began, the state security and members of the bodyguard unit raided Chongjin and arrested all those involved.

One source said senior officers sent to study in Russian military academies during the late 1980s planned to kill Kim Jong Il as he reviewed a military parade on Liberation Day on August 15. A tank was to have fired a live shell at the reviewing stand, but for some reason the attempt never took place. Some months later, when a delegation of Russian military intelligence officers visited North Korea, one of them who knew of the plot asked General Kim Young-chun what had happened. Although the general was not involved, he pretended to know all about it and then informed Kim Jong Il. In October 1995, General Kim Young-chun of the VI Corps was promoted to vice marshal and appointed chief of staff as a reward for the loyalty he had shown.

It seems credible that in 1995 army units stationed in provinces like North and South Hamgyong in the Northeast would be the ones to plan such a revolt. Kim had given orders in 1994 to halt the shipment of surplus food to these provinces, and the civilian economy in Chongjin and Hamhung had broken down earlier than in Songrim. Chongjin is the country's third-largest city with a concentration of medium- and small-sized factories. It is home to what was the country's most prestigious mill—the Kim Chaek Steel Mill—which has now turned to ruins where children scavenge for scrap metal or pieces of coal to hawk. So many of the cables and wiring had been dismantled and sold for scrap that most factories were beyond repair. Electricity came on at best for two or three hours in the afternoon. The water supply had broken down, and people fell sick from drinking river water polluted by an upstream mine. Refugees described the situation in Hamhung, a city with 700,000 people, as worse. They said that 12 percent of the population had died and many had fled.

One authoritative source, former North Korean Colonel Choi Ju-hwal, links these reports of military plots to purges rather than genuine mutinies. He says that the KGB recruited some of the officers sent for training to the Soviet Union. After the collapse of the Soviet Union, a KGB officer sold the North Koreans a list of these spies. During the next three years, the North Koreans interrogated and arrested most of the officers who had studied in the Soviet Union. When Kim Jong Il became commander in chief, he set about purging officers loyal to his opponents such as Marshal O Jin-u and replacing them with officers he trusted.[10]

Other sources discount the notion of rebellions and claim that units like the VII Corps had been caught making money from illegal border trades. Anyone found in possession of foreign currency was liable to be accused of disloyalty and plotting to defect. Perhaps as in Songrim, Kim simply intended to terrorize the army into submission and the truth of the accusations was immaterial.

Anyone who succeeded in launching an uprising could have counted on widespread support. Almost all refugees reported seeing slogans such as "Down with Kim Jong Il" painted on walls, pylons, and railway carriages, and throughout the country there were protests. In December 1996, leaflets that criticized the high cost of embalming Kim Il Sung's body when people were hungry and starving were even found scattered outside the Kumsusan Mausoleum, which held his body. The authors were never found despite a lengthy search. The halls erected for the worship of the Kim family were burnt down, and it was said that mutilated bodies of officials who had been attacked and killed in their homes had been found.

In Sinuiju, two large murals of the Kims at the Nakwon Machinery plant were destroyed in the summer of 1996 and anti-Kim graffiti appeared at the nearby town of Yongchun. In 1997, part of a statue of Kim Il Sung was destroyed one night, and officials hurriedly put a screen around it and spent a month repairing it. The next year someone blew up a statue in Hyesan and across the border people in the town of Changbaishan heard the explosion. Workers in most industrial enterprises in that city had stopped getting their rations as early as 1991 when Kim Il Sung made a speech entitled "Let us eat two meals a day." At the Light Engineering College in Hyesan, on the anniversary of the Korean War, someone painted in bold red paint: "June 25 was the fratricidal war started by Kim Il Sung." The authorities tried to find the author by examining the handwriting of all the students and residents but without success. The authors of such antigovernment pamphlets and slogans had to be careful to disguise their handwriting by using their left hand or they printed materials by carving special letters out of bicycle inner tire tubes to hinder the secret police. All typewriters have slightly different type, which would enable the secret police to identify them.[11]

There were disturbances at food distribution centers at the small provincial town of Pangsan, Yongan province. At another town, Hamgyon near Taechon on the East Coast, the population threw stones at Kim Jong Il's portrait in the railway station. Pamphlets calling for the overthrow of Kim Jong Il and for market reforms were found in street markets in Hamhung, Chongjin, Sunchon, and even in Pyongyang. Reports of protests by students in Pyongyang in 1998 were followed by arrests and executions.

Kim Jong Il ordered Party officials to take drastic measures to terrorize the population into submission. In one major incident in 1998 that was never reported, but diplomats based in Pyongyang had heard about, Kim sent 5,000 troops by helicopters into Orang County on the East Coast, the site of a major airbase, to put down protests over food shortages. Amid reports that up to 500 people died, soldiers sealed off the area and erected roadblocks. Missionaries operating on the Chinese border told me of one gruesome incident when authorities arrested members of an underground Christian cell in Chongjin and beheaded 11 Christians in public as a lesson to others. Their children and wives were then sent to the camps.

In August 1997, the Ministry of Public Security issued a decree that those who were caught trading in food would be shot. The decree "On the Severe punishment of those who steal, sell or waste grain" warned, "Those who engage in trade using grain shall be executed by shooting." Refugees told me how in 1996 they were forced to attend public rallies at which those accused of stealing food or engaging in illegal private trading were garrotted, burned at the stake, or shot. In one incident, refugees described how five men caught stealing grain stored in the railway station were executed in Musan, three by being garrotted.

"Any family suspected of digging up seeds or cutting stalks in the fields disappears during the night. Their houses are sealed and no one dares ask what happened to them," one North Korean villager told me in 1998. Another said that the authorities tried to prevent the peasants from fleeing. "If anyone escapes or leaves their village without permission, their relatives are immediately rounded up and killed," he claimed.

Kim Jong Il tried to divert public anger by organizing the public execution of officials who could be blamed for the food shortages. On September 9, 1998, the Party summoned over 20,000 people to Unification Street Square in Pyongyang to witness the execution of dozens of senior officials, including the agriculture minister, So Kwan-hi. So Kwan-hi had worked in agriculture for 30 years, often accompanying Kim Il Sung on his visits to farms, and was the highest-ranking official ever to be shot in public. He ranked 27th in the hierarchy and was shot for "sabotaging" the country's agriculture and spying for the American imperialists.

For good measure Kim Jong Il also had So Hwan-hi's predecessor, Kim Man-kum, debased even though he had died in 1984. His body had first to be exhumed from the Revolutionary Martyr's Cemetery. As a former deputy premier who had had been in charge of agriculture since 1962, Kim Man-kum was responsible for creating the *Juche* system of agriculture and appointing So Kwan-hi as his successor back in 1973. This was a modern version of the traditional custom in China and Korea of humiliating enemies by disinterring and then decapitating them. Curiously, Kim Jong Il had second thoughts and a year later the twice-dead agriculture minister was reinterred in his spot at the Revolutionary Martyr's Cemetery.[12]

Despite these gestures, Kim Jong Il made it consistently clear in internal speeches that there would be no reforms and the condemnation of these individuals did not signal the start of new agricultural policies. He had voiced his opposition and indeed contempt for Chinese reforms already in the 1980s, calling Deng Xiaoping a "traitor." The dissolution of the Soviet Union and the end of Communism across the former Soviet Bloc in Eastern Europe was to him a clear warning.

Kim Jong Il told his followers that "socialism had been betrayed in Eastern Europe" and North Korea must rely on its own strength from now on. He warned that capitalism would destroy the national culture and paralyze the sense of national independence and revolutionary spirit. "If one retreats one step from the imperialists, one is doomed to retreat two more steps, and one will finally be forced to retreat 100 steps. If one makes a concession on one thing today, one will have to make a concession on everything tomorrow," he said in 1993.[13]

He made an official speech in 1994 declaring:

[T]he crumbling of socialism in various countries does not mean the failure of socialism as science but the bankruptcy of opportunism which has corrupted socialism.

Society based on private ownership and its product, individualism, inevitably splits into hostile classes, produces class antagonism and social inequality, and is accompanied by the exploitation and oppression of the popular masses by a small ruling class.

Today, traitors to socialism are also clamouring for a return to capitalism, harbouring illusions about capitalism and expecting "aid" and "cooperation" from the imperialists. History shows that to expect "good will" or "class cooperation" from the exploiter class is to be make a mess of the revolution.

The speech continues in the same vein for a long time, attacking pro-reformers as "bourgeois reactionaries" and contrasting their greed with North Korea's collectivism and the very high value it places on individual life.[14]

Before Kim Il Sung's death, farmer's markets had flourished and in some places where they were open on an almost daily basis, local officials started to levy taxes on the traders. Kim Jong Il repeatedly ordered them shut and gave instructions that those who persisted in this "individualism" should be severely punished. In a recording of a rambling speech Kim Jong Il made to officials in December 1996, which Hwang took with him when he defected, Kim can be heard threatening to deploy the military to smash any opposition.[15] "Socialism failed in many countries because their parties degenerated and failed to control the army. For the Party to control the army, the Party's leadership over the army should be guaranteed," he said and goes on to voice not only his opposition to free markets but also to foreign aid and international investment. "Telling people to solve the food problem on their own only increases the number of farmers markets and peddlers. In addition, this creates egoism among people, and the basis of the Party's class may come to collapse."

He blamed the cooperative farms for hoarding and hiding grain and criticized the bureaucracy for not distributing food supplies quickly or efficiently. And he shifted responsibility for these economic failures onto his father, saying he had been in charge of other areas such as the military, not the economy.

The message was driven home by sending the military into towns like Songrim and executing officials caught trading. In 1996 and again in 1999, Kim sent his eldest son Kim Jong-nam to lead a special task force to Hyesan, a town to which many Koreans would travel by train and where they would barter for Chinese goods. On the second crackdown against "smuggling," 4,000 people were detained, including government and Party officials. Some 19 people were shot in public, 60 provincial and city-level officials were sent to the camps, 600 others were given prison sentences, and 800 others were sent to work in coal mines. The markets never recovered.[16]

While Kim sent officials abroad to attract foreign investment and aid, the official media warned against interpreting this as a sign of reform. One article in the Party newspaper *Rodong Shinmun* called it "a foolish daydream to try to revive the economy with foreign capital." It went on to insist: "We will set ourselves against all the attempts to induce us to join an 'integrated' world. We have nothing to 'reform' and 'open.'" Another article described imperialist "aid'" as "a noose of plunder and subjugation aimed at robbing ten, and even one hundred, things for one thing that is given."[17]

Kim insisted, "there is nothing more foolish and dangerous than pin-ning one's hopes on the 'imperialist aid,'" which he described as "preda-tory." Editorials called for "pitching a mosquito net to prevent a capitalist yellow wind" from entering the country. They argued that countries build-ing socialism had "collapsed like a wet earthen wall" because they had "neglected the work of checking the imperialist ideological and cultural poisoning." When in 1998 the Supreme People's Assembly adopted a Law on People's Economic Planning, it made it clear that the national economy would not be decentralized.[18]

During regular political study classes on ideology, the population was told of Kim's grim determination to stay in power at all costs. One refugee said they learned how Kim Jong Il had declared that although just 30 per-cent of the population survived the famine, it would be enough to rebuild the country and achieve victory. Propaganda repeatedly called on people to prepare for war and for sacrifice. If need be, a million people should strap dynamite to their bodies, surge across the border, and explode as suicide bombers. Kim told the Koreans that victory was still in sight, reunification imminent, and that there would be plenty to eat. They were told the food crisis would be over by 2000, and soon the country would be rich and powerful. They learned that in China all the state factories had shut and the workers there had been left to starve. "We were told that China is an evil capitalist place," said one refugee, a former teacher. "Kim Jong Il prom-ised us that in three years the economy would surpass that of China." An ever-darker picture of South Korea was presented in television broadcasts showing strikes and protests, but the images were blurred to disguise the fact that in the South people were well dressed and fed and the cities were filled with cars and large buildings.

Kim Jong Il would have been well aware of the death toll, according to Hwang, who in November 1996 asked a senior official in charge of agricul-tural statistics and food how many people had starved to death. He re-plied: "In 1995 about 500,000 people starved to death including 50,000 party cadres. In 1996, about one million people are estimated to have starved to death. . . . In 1997 about two million people will starve to death if no international aid is provided."[19]

Hwang says that in late 1996, Kim asked six senior officials to go to the provinces and collect a separate set of death toll estimates; they returned with estimates that three million people had died. And in response, Kim allegedly said: "Be tough. No uprising will be allowed. I will control military power. Have a strong heart. If the people revolt they will hang us, and if they don't the South Koreans will."

When it was convenient Kim Jong Il allowed foreigners to see the suffering. In August 1996, Congressman Tony Hall returned home stunned by what he was taken to see: hospitals and orphanages with starving children and patients freezing in ill-equipped wards. In a dinner talk with a Chongryon delegation on April 25, 1998, Kim blamed the shortfall of food on "bad seeds" and boasted how he cleverly manipulated the outside world. "To be frank with you, we want to right our economy by educating our people better. Previously, only our foreign service people cried for help but now all people do so. Thus, all of us tell foreigners about this shortage or that shortage, and take them to the worst place for them to see. In the past, foreign visitors were taken to the best show places and people were taught to say that they were living well. But now faced with the economic isolation forced on us by our enemy, we need foreign aid and present sad pictures to foreign visitors," he explained. One of Kim Jong Il's key traits is a habit of stringing people along by telling them exactly what they want to hear. Another facet of his personality is that he often acts on impulse. "He appears to lack the ability to think systematically, treating each issue that comes across his desk in isolation . . . with little or no thought to their impact on each other," said a 1998 assessment by a political analyst in the U.S. Embassy in Seoul. "Told of a particular problem in one factory or city, he issues instructions to give top priority to solving it—then proceeds to give top priority to other problems that demand the same resources. . . . This is reflected in official policy statements over the past four years that give top priority to agriculture, light industry and exports but continue to give the same top priority to mineral extraction and heavy industry. The result is a chaotic situation in which priorities are constantly shifting and no problem receives sustained attention."[20] As Kim grappled with the challenges of rescuing the economy from disaster, he left a trail of officials punished for obeying orders that he later countermanded. The best example of this was Kim Jong-u, who was suddenly dismissed, bringing the foreign investment program to a standstill. Some claim that Kim Jong Il went to inspect the Rajin Sonbong Free Trade & Economic Zone and was

angered by eight commercial billboards that overshadowed ideological slogans praising his father. In addition, he demanded that the name of the
zone have the word "free" deleted from it. Later a report surfaced that Kim
Jong-u's family and two interpreters were imprisoned after U.S. $300,000
in cash at had been found at his home. North Korean officials said Kim
Jong-u was "resting in a sanitarium," but he may have been executed in
December 1987.[21]

A very similar pattern of events occurred with the economic zone that
was started after Kim Jong Il toured China and was shown around Shanghai in 1999. He admired the new skyscrapers, motorways, and bridge; the
brand new General Motors car factory; and the giant Chinese computer
manufacturing company Legend. Afterward a flurry of reports appeared in
China and North Korea suggesting that Kim had been inspired to introduce economic reforms at home.

Soon afterward North Korea unveiled its Sinuiju Special Administrative
Territory, which was declared to be "a new historical miracle." This project
was even grander than the Rajin-Songbon zone. It was to be run by Yang
Bin, a Chinese businessman with Dutch citizenship who was ranked by
Forbes as China's second-richest private entrepreneur with a fortune estimated at U.S. $900 million. His assets included a listed company in Hong
Kong called Euro-Asian Agricultural Holdings, an orchid-growing business,
and a giant real estate project in Liaoning province that resembled a medieval Dutch town complete with canals. The portly Yang Bin turned up for a
ceremony in Pyongyang wearing a gold lame Lacoste golf shirt. Presided
over by the number two in the North Korean government, Kim Yong-nam,
the ceremony was intended to launch the project. Yang explained that a
wall would be built around the border town and its 500,000 residents
would be evicted and replaced by 200,000 model workers. The zone would
be devoted to private enterprise, dedicated to profit, and have its own laws
and regulations that would be enforced by a panel of European judges.
International banks would flock to fund oil refineries and textile mills,
eager to take advantage of low taxes and leases guaranteed for 50 years.
However, within weeks of returning to China, Yang was arrested by the
Chinese authorities and disappeared in jail on charges of corruption and
tax evasion. No more has been heard since of the project.

Under Kim's personal guidance, North Korea has set about creating export industries by investing in ostrich farms and maple and mulberry tree plantations. Schemes to breed bullfrogs, tropical fish, terrapins, edible snails, and catfish have also flourished. *The Economist* magazine visited one 20,000-square-meter ostrich farm outside Pyongyang and found that despite 40 visits by Kim to offer his guidance and an imported computer management system for the meat processing, there were still no exports of ostrich meat after four years. Another pet project was breeding tropical fish for export in towns with hot springs.[22]

"There are several things we must learn from capitalist nations," Kim Jong Il observed in his talk with the Japanese Koreans from the pro-Pyongyang Chongryon delegation. "First of all, we must learn to abide by the law; secondly, we must learn to use the best products ourselves and sell inferior products abroad—we do just the opposite, we sell our best products and keep inferior ones."

The Canadian government was asked to help with planting the maple tree plantation in Hysean because Kim thought the country could simultaneously benefit from maple syrup as well as timber. Kim became fascinated by the benefits of raising goats and sent agricultural experts to Switzerland; North Korea is now supplied with goat milk and cheese. His most useful enthusiasm has been to overturn his father's opposition to potatoes and the seedlings imported from Ireland have substantially raised food supplies.

When Kim has become gripped by similar enthusiasms for such capitalist tools as treasury bond issues or stock exchanges, it is hard to tell what this means. Stopping off in the Russian city of Khaborovsk in 2002, Kim visited its large and impressive Russian Orthodox Cathedral. On the spur of the moment, he decided Pyongyang needed such glorious architecture too and that construction should begin immediately. Four North Korean officials were packed off to a seminary outside Moscow to become priests. Though not necessarily a sign that he will convert to the country to the Russian Orthodox Church, anything is possible.

Malnutrition has stunted the growth of an entire generation of Korean children, some seen here at the Tokchon nursery (AFP).

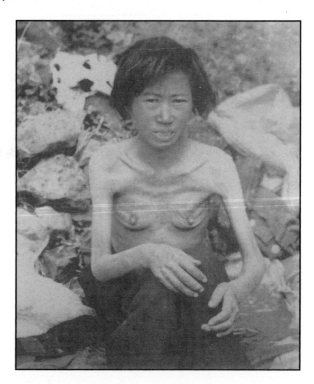

A starving North Korean refugee managed to escapee from Hyesan to Changbai, but died two days after this picture was taken in 2000 (Life Funds for North Korean Refugees).

Hwang Jang-yop, the highest-ranking North Korean official to defect to South Korea, visits Capitol Hill in Washington, DC on October 30, 2003 (AFP/Getty Images).

North Korean women stand in line to collect international food donations, at one of several Public Distribution System (PDS) centres operated by the government of the Democratic People's Republic of Korea (AFP).

North Korean workers sorting micronutrient-enriched biscuits at a UN World Food Programme-supported factory in Chongjin, north Hamgyong province, November 13, 2002 (AFP).

Late North Korean leader Kim Il Sung reviews a military parade (Time Life Pictures/Getty Images).

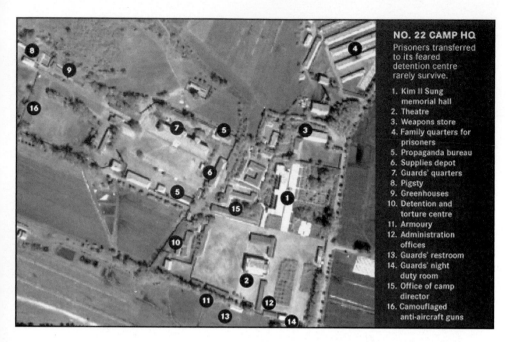

Satellite photo of an unconfirmed military camp on North Korea's northeastern frontier with China that imprisoned about 50,000 people (AFP).

Launch of North Korean multi-stage rocket at Musudan-ri, Hwadae County, in North Hamgyong province. It is disputed whether the launch was a successful satellite vehicle or a Taepo-Dong 1 medium-range ballistic missile (AFP).

Nuclear reactor at Yongbyong
(DigitalGlobe)

North Korean leader Kim Jong Il being briefed by a field commander during a military exercise at an undisclosed location in the North (AFP/Getty Images).

Above: Olive drab-clad former US President Bill Clinton, at sandbagged position, flanked by pair of US soldiers, touring the DMZ during his post-G7 summit trip to S. Korea in 1993 (Time Life Pictures/ Getty Images).

Left: Former US President Jimmy Carter and wife Rosalynn leave North Korea through Panmunjom, the demilitarized zone (DMZ) border village, after Carter's controversial meeting with North Korean President Kim Il-sung on June 18, 1994 (AFP).

South Korea's Hyundai Group founder Chung Ju-Yung waves to well-wishers in Seoul, South Korea after returning from North Korea to discuss business ventures with the nation's leader, Kim Jong-Il, in 1999 (Getty Images).

North Korean soldiers performing at the May Day Stadium in Pyongyang together with some 25,000 card-choreographers presenting an image of military might, in a performance for visiting US Secretary of State Madeleine Albright in October of 2000 (AFP/Getty Images).

South Korean President Kim Dae Jung, left, and North Korean leader Kim Jong Il, right, sing a song entitled "We are Hoping for Reunification" at the 2000 Summit (Getty Images).

Family members of missing Japanese nationals speak to the media having been officially informed of their children's deaths in the wake of the historic meeting between Japanese Prime Minister Junichiro Koizumi and North Korean leader Kim Jong-il in 2002 (Getty Images).

CHAPTER 10

The United Nations and Genocide

"We did not fail. Lives were saved; we are helping turn the situation around. The malnutrition, stunting and maternal mortality rates, while still high, has fallen. Above all, we have established preventive capacity: Another famine cannot happen while we are here and properly supported," wrote Masood Haydar, the United Nations Humanitarian Coordinator of the DPRK, in a *Washington Post* editorial in 2004.[1]

The World Food Program (WFP) began by appealing for 21,000 tons of food for 500,000 people in 1995, and three years later it was feeding 8 million people, nearly half the population. Nine years after it began, the WFP is still struggling to feed over 3 million and lamenting that it cannot do more to help many others..

In North Korea the United Nations undertook one of its largest and longest emergency food aid operations in its history, but it did fail. How big a failure it was remains unclear and we probably will not know unless the regime falls and documentary evidence is published. In the case of Russia and China, it took decades before the full facts were known. At present, basic demographic information is missing and estimates vary.

Some refugees, however, claim that the North Korean government knows. They say that in April 2001, the government announced that the population was less than 19 million, a drop of 3 or 4 million in twelve years. Pyongyang first provided some census data to the United Nations in 1989 when North Korea become a member state and again in 1992 when a new census was taken. In 1989, the given population was 21.02 million and reported to be growing by 1.8 percent annually, then in 1993, the official population count was said to be 22.1 million and growing by just 1.5 percent. Yet this has not clarified much. South Korea declared that in 1998 the DPRK's population was 24 million, but the CIA, using lower-growth rates, calculated it was just 21.38 million. Pyongyang has compounded the confusion by telling one group of visitors in 1998 that it had 23.5 million inhabitants and another, a UNDP delegation, that the population was 22.1 million. Possibly the source of the confusion is that some figures offered by the DPRK exclude the military, which is around 1.2 million.[2]

In their book, *The Population of North Korea*, U.S. demographers Nicholas Eberstadt and Judith Banister also point out that judging from the demographic data that North Korea presented in 1989, their population registration system appears to miss around 15 percent of deaths and over half of infant deaths in normal times. It is also clear that when it suits them, North Korean officials at various levels freely manipulate population data. Some might want to inflate the population size to claim more aid or minimize it to hide a strategic weakness.

Several times the North Koreans were caught doctoring the figures. In one instance, the WFP took the county population figures from the central government and compared them to the census records of county officials. They found that central government figures were much higher. Another NGO public health expert who looked at two counties in the Northwest also found that the population figures were respectively 12 percent and 13 percent lower than those given in the central government census taken in 1992.[3]

If we assume that there were only 21 million in 1995, and subsequently 2 or 3 million died, then the refugee reports that the population had fallen to just 19 million or even 18 million by 1999 sound possible. Given that people began dying of hunger even earlier in 1988, lower estimates seem more likely because the population would have been growing more slowly, if indeed it was growing at all.

The statistics that Hwang Jang-yop obtained before he escaped support a 3 million–plus death toll. Various other North Korean defectors also believe this is likely. The writer Choi Jin-I was told that 300,000 people had died by 1996 in Kangwon province, which borders South Korea. This area is famous for its beautiful Diamond Mountain, but transport is poor, the soil is stony, and she said many of the victims simply died at home when the food ran out. One former prisoner of war, Son Chae-sul, who escaped, also said that more than 3 million starved to death. He heard that on average 30 people a day died.[4]

There is other evidence too. Seoul reported that the North Korean Public Security Ministry conducted a population survey before the July 1999 election of delegates to the Supreme People's Assembly that revealed the population had fallen by between 2.5 million and 3 million. Nicholas Eberstadt has also pointed out that judging by the number of delegates sent to the Assembly, 3 million people are missing. Each delegate is supposed to represent 30,000 people, but the number of delegates remained the same between 1990 and 1998 although the population should have grown by 3 million in those years.

Andrew Natsios concludes at the end of his landmark study of North Korea's famine that 2.45 million people died. Ellsworth Culver of Mercy Corps, whose staff spent considerable time in the DPRK, believes that 2 million people died, while a congressional report by Mark Kirk estimated that between 300,000 and 800,000 people a year were dying from 1995–1999.[5]

Then, as mentioned in chapter one, the data from interviewing refugees in China also points to a death toll running to the millions. The refugees' testimony completes a picture of a North Korean holocaust. Every known indicator of a severe famine—food shortages, hoarding, price inflation of basic foodstuffs, the break up of families, the abandonment of children, cannibalism, mass migration, widespread edema and other signs of malnutrition, long-term stunting, and epidemics of cholera, typhoid, hepatitis, dysentery, and other infectious diseases are described. It is inconceivable that the North Koreans, filled as they are with a strong nationalistic pride, would invent, let alone admit, these things to total strangers if they were not true.

A death toll of 3 million would mean more victims than in Pol Pot's Cambodia, where 1 out of 8 million perished, and more deaths from starvation than in Ethiopia during the 1980s or Somalia, both of which provoked a huge international response. The United States even sent troops to Somalia in 1992 to ensure food aid got through to the needy in a famine that cost around a million lives. If 15 percent of the DPRK's population died, then the death toll, in proportion to the country, surpasses any comparable disaster in the twentieth century. Some 6-8 million people died in the Ukraine's Northern Caucasus and Lower Volga from 1931 to 1933, roughly a quarter of the population of Ukraine, but less than 5percent of the total population of the Soviet Union. Could a calamity of such proportions really stay hidden from outside observers even in secretive North Korea?

UN officials who spent years working and travelling in North Korea doubt it. Yet there are precedents that suggest it is possible. During the Ukrainian famine of the early 1930s, the Soviet authorities hid the evidence from many visitors including the *New York Times* Moscow correspondent Walter Duranty. This allowed some people to cast doubt on what happened. At the time Stalin had ordered the publication of false statistics and the execution of the officials in charge of conducting the survey. Only after the Soviet Union's collapse did the results of a census taken immediately after the famine become available.

The Chinese Communist Party was equally adept at hiding their famine from correspondents and visitors living in China and indeed from many urban Chinese, who were aware of food shortages but not of mass deaths. The distinguished American journalist Edgar Snow spent five months touring China in 1960 and emerged saying nothing resembling a famine he had witnessed in the past could be taking place. The Party also kept all population statistics secret for 20 years, and it has still not fully acknowledged what happened.

When refugees escaped across the border from Pol Pot's Cambodia into Thailand during the late 1970s and described how people were being killed in large numbers, their reports were either ignored or derided as utterly fantastic even by groups like Amnesty International. Despite accurate reporting by U.S. diplomats and journalists, many observers simply found it hard to accept that atrocities could be taking place on such a scale. A similar caution gripped much of the reporting on North Korea; journalists preferred to remain skeptical, worried about being taken in by propaganda.

Yet, North Korea differs in one important respect from these other cases—the United Nations has been present and active in the country during the famine. As such, the views of its representatives, who are considered to be well informed and politically neutral, have carried great weight. UN officials never actually said that there was a real famine in which millions died. Faced with a choice between trying to please their host government on whose cooperation they depended, and speaking out and raising the alarm, the officials took refuge in a confusing ambiguity.[6]

When the famine was at its peak in early 1997, Catherine Bertini, the American head of the WFP, the lead UN agency operating in the DPRK, restricted herself to warnings like "This is a famine in the making" or "the countdown to famine has begun."

Douglas Coutts, the WFP representative in Pyongyang and UN Humanitarian coordinator told one press conference in Beijing, "This is not a famine in the classic sense of the world. It is a very slow gradual building situation."[7] His successor in Pyongyang, David Morton, said in one interview that he hesitated even calling the situation a famine, preferring to describe it as a "shortage of food" because he said famine was such an emotive word.

UNICEF national director Omawali Omawakli also said he believed it would be extreme to use the word "food crisis" and also preferred the term "food shortage," because the real crisis was caused by the diseases spread by poor drinking water and sanitation.

UN documents routinely claimed that the food aid prevented a famine before it took place. The UN Special Bulletin on the Humanitarian Situation of April 1998 claimed, "prompt action by the international community during the past several years . . , has slowed down or perhaps averted a widespread famine." It said the emergency intervention of the United Nations had largely "pre-empted a catastrophe, especially among the most vulnerable segments of the population."

UN officials sounded openly incredulous when testimony from the border refugees contradicted their complacent assessments. "When it comes to cannibalism, I must tell you I have my very grave doubts about these reports[.] And when it comes to massive deaths, there have been some reports of deaths of close to two million people, once again I find it very hard to believe that 10 percent of the population would have disappeared," said WFP assistant executive director Jean-Jacques Graisse in Tokyo in June 1998.[8] Other UN officials asked for their views on high death tolls consistently refused to say anything or simply quoted the North Korean government's low figures.

UN officials rarely contradict their host governments, and usually then only in retrospect. The United Nations also genuinely underestimated both the length and breadth of the crisis. The notion that the famine started many years earlier and covered the whole country, and that its victims included those valued by the regime, such as industrial workers and soldiers, was rejected. It simply did not fit in with the way famines had played out in other countries.

The United Nations became convinced that the food shortages started because the richer rice-growing provinces in the west had been hard hit by a succession of floods, droughts, tidal waves, and typhoons. A June 1999 WFP/FAO (Food and Agriculture Organization of the United Nations) food assessment typically blamed "severe drought and successive national disasters" for the lack of food. The claim was endlessly repeated in all news agency reports until it became an established fact.

The United Nations accepted the North's explanation that the food shortages were recent phenomena and the hardship was limited to certain areas. Hard hit grain surplus areas had stopped distributing their surplus to the grain deficient provinces in the Northeast. When WFP official Tun Myatt was denied access to the Northeast, he became convinced that there was a "blackhole" or a localized famine going on. A decision by Pyongyang to cut the East Coast off from both internal shipments and foreign aid in 1995 and 1996 and to direct relief food to the West Coast was blamed for the crisis.

American famine relief expert Andrew Natsios who spoke to refugees from North and South Hamgyong provinces developed a more elaborate version of this "triage" theory. He believed the central government responded to the crisis by actively concentrating the state's resources, including the shipments of aid, on the geographical and social groups essential to ensuring the regime's survival, leaving the rest to die. While some speculated that food was being distributed according to a family's *Songbun* ranking, Andrew Natsios argues that the government probably allocated food depending on whether an individual was useful to the regime.[9]

Later, the United Nations became worried that the DPRK might be hiding famine deaths in 50 counties that held 20 percent of the population and to which it was given no access. The DPRK said the entry would compromise national security, and when the WFP finally did gain access to one of them, Sakju county in North Pyongan province, in October 2001, it did not shed much light on the question. The inhabitants were certainly starving, especially the 150,000 urban dwellers, but why this or other counties came on or off the list never became clear.

At the same time, some UN officials also became convinced that border provinces might be better off because the inhabitants were busy begging relatives in China for food or doing barter deals to obtain extra grain. Even so, the first WFP representatives in Pyongyang, Englishman Trevor Page, followed by Canadian Douglas Coutts, and another Englishman, David Morton, deserve credit. They had to fight very hard to convince a skeptical outside world that any emergency aid was needed and that it should be given without being tied to concessions in other areas. As the United Nations had initially underestimated the scale of the humanitarian disaster, the food did not start arriving in large quantities until 1998 when it was already too late. This often happens in famine relief operations, but the United Nations appears to have made other avoidable mistakes. After they started work in 1995, one of the first tasks was to assess the country's needs and take stock of its agriculture, especially the flood damage. Consultants appointed by the FAO toured the country for a week or two, looked at the crops in the field, and then forecast the harvest. They then divided the harvest by the size of the population and calculated how much food needed to be imported to avert a famine.

North Korea treats harvest and food reserve information as military secrets, but UN officials touring the country had to rely, at least in part, on what local North Koreans told them. Korean officials regularly reported upward, whatever harvest targets had been set by the leadership in the plan. If they wanted to be promoted, they inflated the figures and promised to send surplus grain to the center.

The UN experts caught some officials cheating by exaggerating the impact of the natural disasters and then assumed that there was more food than they said. An FAO/WFP crop assessment estimated that only 15 percent of the deficit could be attributed to natural disasters and that Pyongyang had exaggerated the number of hectares damaged and the decline in the harvest. It also said that the DPRK exaggerated the number of workers who needed food subsidies under the food-for-work program, which provides food for North Koreans that work to repair and restore dykes, irrigation systems, and paddy fields.[10]

At the end the FAO made its calculations, but so did various experts in South Korea and different agencies in the United States where experts could use remote-sensing satellite images. U.S. experts usually came up with bigger harvest forecasts because seen from above, the crops in the fields looked much healthier than they actually were. On the Chinese side of the border, Koreans grew maize taller than a man, with a full cob, but in the fields in North Korea the plants grew half as tall, stripped of leaves, and with only a few seeds on a stunted cob.

Crop assessments are subject to other pitfalls. North Koreans calculate the harvest on what it weighs before threshing rather than after and exclude crops like potatoes from the grain harvest. Further, after harvesting, the grain is taken from the farms and stored in closely guarded granaries. In the process as much as 30 percent of the harvest is lost through pilfering and disease.

In general everyone has worked on the assumption that the country needed a bare minimum of 6 million tons of food a year, but forecasts for the domestic harvest varied between under 3 million and over 4 million tons. For instance, an FAO/WFP report said that the 1997 harvest had reached a low of just 2.66 million tons—1.1 million tons of maize and 1.5 million tons of rice in the November to October marketing year. It therefore concluded that the country needed to import at least 2 million tons, but assumed that half of this would come from China and the rest from the United Nations and other donors.

UN officials became convinced that China was delivering as much as one million tons during this critical period, and this seems the source of their biggest miscalculation. Chinese deliveries of food as well as fertilizer, coal, cotton, and oil are believed to have played a key role in staving off North Korea's total collapse in 1997 and 1998.

My own research uncovered no trace of such big Chinese food shipments. The Chinese Foreign Ministry and the China National Cereals Oils and Foodstuffs Import and Export Corporation both denied shipping large amounts of grain to the DPRK in 1996, 1997, and 1998. In July 1996, China did announce 100,000 tons of food aid to mark the 35th Anniversary of Peace and Cooperation. The next year it sent 150,000 tons of grain, and in 1998 China said it actually cut deliveries by 30 percent to 100,000 tons of food and 20,000 tons of fertilizer.[11]

Perhaps more food arrived secretly by rail or truck through Sinuiju, the main transport hub, or by ship to Nampo, the largest port near Pyongyang. However, shipping a million tons would have put such a strain on China's infrastructure that it would surely have influenced UN operations and have been widely noticed. The Nampo port was so poorly equipped that it was unable to handle bulk shipments until the United Nations itself had to install machinery to unload its grain ships. By 1998, the border trade had shrunk so much that three out of the five border posts along that section of the border closed. Chinese flights to North Korea had been suspended, and there was little rail traffic because the North Koreans did not return the railcars.

Moreover, relations with China had been poor since Beijing recognized Seoul in 1992. The following year, China began demanding payment from North Korea in hard currency for oil deliveries. Indeed, rather than rushing to prevent its collapse, Chinese officials and academics said that China was withholding aid to pressure Pyongyang into introducing market reform. In 1993, China slashed the amount of subsidized grain it sent to its ally from 800,000 tons to 300,000 tons for domestic reasons. Beijing introduced a blanket ban on all grain exports in response to a domestic grain shortage that drove up inflation to dangerous levels. This hit Pyongyang hard.

Yet, China could easily have afforded to ship large quantities of maize after 1996, when Beijing stimulated production by raising its state-purchasing price and began to accumulate such large surpluses that grana-ries ran short of space to store the grain. This was particularly the case in Jilin province bordering North Korea, but Jilin officials in the border pre-fecture of Yanbian denied any of it was going to North Korea. On the con-trary Yanji trade officials said that in 1996 they had suspended border trade because the North Koreans failed to honor earlier contracts. Yanbian prefectural authorities even decided to limit the amount any individual could carry over the border to 20 kilos.

The only profitable trade going on in the Northeast consisted of smug-gling second-hand Japanese cars through Rajin port that were then driven into China or Russia and sold at a big markup. This also stopped in 1997 when China wanted to protect its own growing motor industry. Chinese businessmen involved in this trade said the profits that North Korean offi-cials made were not used to import grain but luxuries for themselves and their families.

In short, it is quite possible that both the imports were lower than the UN thought and the harvests were smaller. In fact as WFP representative

Douglas Coutts once admitted to me in a moment of candour, the United Nations had to operate in a fog of ignorance. "We have no idea what is going on, We are completely in the dark. We don't even know how many people live in the country," he said in 1997.[12]

The United Nations had greatly handicapped itself by making a fateful decision to ask the government to handle the distribution of all aid once it arrived at the docks. They could have insisted that as a precondition for working in the country it must be allowed to operate its own system of distribution. In many emergencies the United Nations uses its own trucks to transport the food so it can ensure it reaches the neediest. A key task in famines is to prevent small groups from hoarding grain either out of greed or to punish their enemies. When local warlords in Somalia prevented proper distribution, UN agencies demanded and obtained military protection from an international peacekeeping force. In difficult circumstances another option is to offer the food to local merchants and use existing commercial channels to distribute the food. Although not ideal, this drives down the price of food in local markets until it becomes generally affordable.

North Korea had no commercial distribution system and the United Nations decided that the only institution with fuel and trucks was the military. As soon as the food arrived, military trucks took charge of it and the United Nations lost all control. "The trucks deliver most of the food, without them nothing would work. The only fuel is in the army bases, and they are the only force that can get anything done," Coutts explained.

When this provoked criticism, especially in the U.S. Congress, the United Nations consulted several experts. In 1997, USAID sent expert Dr. Sue Lautze to assess the situation. She returned warning that the regime would use the state rationing system, known as the public distribution system (PDS), to channel food toward the elite and sustain their ambitions to concentrate resources on the military buildup. The United Nations disregarded her warnings and instead heeded the assessment of an expert from the United Kingdom's Save the Children Fund, Lola Nathanail, who praised the PDS as an efficient instrument committed to ensuring an egalitarian share of scarce resources.[13]

Army trucks delivered the grain to where it was said to be needed, then the local officials allocated the rations. However, the United Nations then became hostage to the goodwill of Pyongyang to deliver the food and to monitor its distribution. In order to maintain its credibility in the eyes of donors, the United Nations had to hide its own doubts, praise the PDS, and defend the integrity of the Korean Workers Party, which operated it. FAO officials especially described it as a "well functioning public administration" and an "elaborate food distribution network" that "greatly facilitated the distribution and accounting of food assistance."[14]

The country had 3,600 public distribution centers supplying 15.4 million people, and when the WFP was feeding over 8 million of them, there were 57 staff members, including 34 expatriates, to supervise the distribution. None of them could travel without applying for permission, usually a week in advance, and once outside Pyongyang, they could not leave their hotel unless accompanied. Pyongyang did not issue visas to Korean-speaking aid workers. The WFP staff had no contact with the population if North Korean officials were not present and translating. Even doctors were not allowed to handle patients or see operations.

The government gave them a list with the number of institutions per county and the number of beneficiaries per county, but withheld the names of those receiving the aid and even the names of the institutions. The WFP's expatriate staff would visit on average 40 nurseries per month out of a total of 22,000 nurseries receiving food aid. So, when the WFP would ask to visit a nursery in a certain county, the government would decide which one to show them. The aid monitors were supposed to carry out random checks, but in practice they informed the Koreans beforehand what they wanted to see, and usually when they arrived this is exactly what they found. The authorities slowly increased the number of places the monitors could travel to, but in any county they were only allowed access to the county town and nowhere else.

In other emergencies an aid agency's first task was to carry out a random health and nutrition survey of the target groups, but throughout the first three years North Korea refused to allow this. Finally, the DPRK government consented to the examination of a small and unrepresentative number of children. The authorities selected 3,780 children from 0-7 years attending 40 nurseries and kindergartens in four of the nine provinces. No household food surveys were authorized. The survey found 17 percent of the children surveyed to be seriously malnourished, but the sample was neither random nor large enough to give it any credibility. It took another five years of hard bargaining for Pyongyang to allow another sample, this time 6,000 households in seven provinces, that allegedly showed the proportion of underweight children had fallen from 60 percent to 20 percent. It too had little scientific credibility.

Although the first survey provided useful publicity for attracting donations, and the second was used to show an improvement in health, they did not provide the answers to key questions about the famine. Some of those working in North Korea became convinced that the aid was not reaching the most vulnerable groups and that the North Koreans themselves were deliberately diverting the aid.

Along with the alphabet of UN agencies came a flock of NGOs, some of which rely on government funding and others that are national or international charities. One of the most active in the DPRK was the Roman Catholic relief agency Caritas, represented by a large and ever-cheerful Swiss lady, Kathi Zellweger. In over 30 visits, she managed to channel some U.S. $27 million into the country, but chose never to confront the authorities publicly. Other NGOs, like the French group Action Contre la Faim, began to harbor strong doubts about what they saw and decided not to keep silent.

Action Contre la Faim began to doubt the government's claim that it had 22,000 nurseries and 1.47 million children under four. In North Hamgyong province, where they were working, they only ever saw 200 nurseries, although officials told them there were 1,442. During their visits to the province's nurseries and kindergartens in 1997 and 1998, the expatriate staff noticed that only half the number of children supposed to be there were actually present. When challenged, the provincial officials said they would "update" the list of beneficiaries, and suddenly, without further explanation, 47,870 children were removed from the list of those supposedly attending. And among the children that Action Contre La Faim did examine in the nurseries, less than 1 percent were suffering from malnutrition, a finding that contradicted that of the UN survey.

There were other puzzling incidents, such as when a nutritionist from Action Contre la Faim visited the provincial orphanage in Chongjin in July 1999 and found it full of dirty, neglected, and severely malnourished children living off goat milk mixed with water and sugar. No one at the orphanage could explain what had happened to the two tons of High Energy Milk UNICEF had reportedly delivered to there in May.[15]

Humanitarian organizations operating in other provinces noted the same sort of discrepancies. Some refugees arriving in China claimed the aid workers were the victims of elaborate deceptions. Many reported that the authorities would clear the streets of corpses or vagrants before foreigners arrived. Sometimes residents were carefully coached on what they should say when the inspectors arrived and were handed out bags of grain that would be taken back once the inspectors had gone. Philippe Pons of the French newspaper *Le Monde* reported several such testimonies: "All refugees know that their country receives foreign aid. But few among them claim having received any . . . [A] wood carrier heard on South Korean radio (which is forbidden) that tons of rice had arrived from South Korea and the US. 'I never saw any of it, and I wonder if the South didn't lie about that,' he says."

In Chongjin, a youth heard that when a ship carrying aid is unloaded under UN watch, the military dresses as civilians and maneuvers to take everything. Another refugee from Onsong says that several times he carried aid bags in 1997 and 1998 from a hangar where the food was stocked "in case of war" to a kindergarten, in anticipation of a UN inspection.[16,17]

In North Korea, any unauthorized contact with a foreigner constitutes a severe crime, so the inspectors never obtained information that contradicted the official line, nor could they visit the black markets where refugees alleged maize and rice were on sale still in their original packaging. Many became convinced that instead of helping the most vulnerable members, like the street children in the 9.27 camps, they were merely helping the children of Party officials and that the Party officials were selling off the rest on the market. Refugees even claimed that the 9.27 camps were established to ensure that the foreigners would not see the street children.[18]

WFP officer Thomas Hoerz described how, on an arduous two-week trip around the East Coast in March 1999, he saw unploughed fields and hundreds walking and trying to hitch lifts. In a pediatric ward he encountered "eight children with thin brownish hair barely covering the scaly skin on their heads. Their bodies appear to be those of children half their age, yet their faces look old and wizened." At the same time he often saw perfectly plump and healthy children playing on the road and skating on the ice. Just why this should be, he struggled to explain.[19]

An expatriate Korean who stocked a children's home with toys, clothes, and imported food in the Rajin Sonbong zone eventually realized that only the children of local Party cadres were allowed there. He could see other children, their bodies swollen by edema, on the roadside.

The feeling that DPRK officials were constantly lying to them and that they were not able to reach out to the poorest provoked a deep crisis of conscience for many NGOs. Should they stay and try to work things out, or should they speak out and leave? By the end of September 1998, many of them, including Doctors Without Borders, Action Contre la Faim, Oxfam, Medecins du Monde, and Help Age International withdrew, and some, like Save the Children, partially withdrew.

Many found coping with the moral strains of the situation intolerable. Jean Francois, a leading authority on the famine, with the French Doctors without Borders, committed suicide while under the stress of this moral conflict. Those that decided to stay then had to justify the decision by defending the integrity of the DPRK and the fairness of the PDS.

The bitterness this created can be illustrated from my own experiences. In the winter of 1999, I went to the border to interview more refugees together with the *Times* correspondent James Pringle, a very distinguished foreign correspondent. After we listened to the dreadful descriptions of life inside the country, he wrote a front-page story describing the horror un-folding across the Tumen River. This so incensed a British academic who had been monitoring the distribution of aid on the other side of the river that she lodged her grievance with the Press Complaints Authority, accus-ing Pringle of recklessly distorting reality. The academic also turned against a German doctor, Norbert Vollertsen, and in a paper on the refugee crisis attacked him for, amongst other things, describing himself as "a public relations manager for Jesus Christ."

Vollertsen volunteered to work in North Korea for a charity, Cap Anamur. Initially impressed by the DPRK's commitment to egalitarianism, equality of the sexes, daycare for all children, free schooling, and full public welfare, he became convinced that something terrible was going on. He was ex-pelled on December 20, 2000, after trying to show journalists accompany-ing U.S. Secretary of State Madeleine Albright the dark side of the country. Since then he has been devoting himself to exposing the regime and help-ing the refugees, especially in their efforts to claim political asylum. As he says, he feels that if he stayed silent it would be tantamount to tolerating the Nazi holocaust.[20]

Everyone faced a terrible moral dilemma for which there was no obvious right or wrong. Once aid workers left, there was little they could do to help those they were abandoning. Those that decided to stay on tried and sometimes succeeded in making progress in the face of great obstacles. They distributed a huge range of supplies, including water treatment kits, soap, shampoo, detergents, winter clothes, medicines, measuring scales, vitamin C, palm oil, meat, winter shoes, boots, coal, blankets, and iodized salt. Relief workers built greenhouses, windmills, solar kitchen units, wooden stoves, and micro-chlorination units. The North Koreans learned how to grow soybeans, sweet potatoes, and potatoes, and breed rabbits (even in orphanages), goats, and trout. The Swiss showed them how to make yoghurt and cheese, the Americans planted apple trees, the Canadians contributed maple trees, and the Irish introduced blight-free potato farming.

It would have been unusual if the North Koreans had not tried to divert as much food as possible to its own soldiers when they were starving to death and the country was on a war footing. Chairman Mao had done the same at the height of the famine during the Great Leap Forward, diverting the grain seized from the peasants and keeping it in underground granaries as a reserve for the war with the United States.

Oliver Mohr, another German doctor with Cap Anamur, paints a picture in his book *Behind the 38th Parallel* of ineptitude rather than deceit. He describes a PDS system that far from being efficient did not seem to work at all. In one section, he describes a search for the High Energy Milk UNICEF was supposed to have delivered to three hospitals in the city of Haeju. Finally, a North Korean lorry driver told him all supplies were always brought to a central storehouse. When they arrived, tons of the milk were indeed there and still unpacked, as well as boxes of badly needed antibiotics from an Italian relief agency and other vital supplies that hospitals had been waiting to receive for months. The storekeeper told him the supplies had stayed there so long because they were waiting for a lorry that had been allocated some diesel. Mohr then spent a day transporting the milk to the hospitals by himself.

For Catherine Bertini, the head of the World Food Program, the moral dilemma was also acute. Unlike the NGOs, it was not so easy for the United Nations to stage a protest walkout. However, she did have the authority to speak out and sound the alarm. Instead, she kept quiet about any death toll and avoided condemning the behavior of the North Korean government. This undermined the credibility of those that accused Kim Jong Il of allowing millions to die and made the United Nations a silent partner in the North Korean holocaust.

On the other hand, Bertini did stage a confrontation with the DPRK in 1998 and issued an ultimatum, a move that required considerable resolve. She said that unless the North Koreans accepted the normal UN conditions associated with emergency aid, including unrestricted access to the 50 closed off counties before May 18, she would scale back deliveries. Bertini may have felt that since the WFP was then appealing for over U.S. $600 million worth of aid on behalf of the DPRK, this ought to give the WFP some clout. "We owe it to our donors to ensure that we are able to monitor the food they provide through the WFP," she declared, mindful of the U.S. Congress, where there were deep misgivings about sending the food in the first place. The same doubts extended to the IAEA and its ability to monitor North Korea's compliance with the Agreed Framework.

Kim Jong Il, who was always too busy to meet Bertini, called her bluff and ignored the ultimatum. Bertini responded by lowering the appeal by 8 percent and withholding food for 765,000 people, equal to those in the inaccessible counties.

The WFP had a low status in the eyes of the North Koreans, who dealt with it through an obscure and low-ranking organization inside the Foreign Ministry called the Flood Relief and Rehabilitation Committee. North Koreans treated the food aid not as charity but as payment for agreeing to take part in negotiations or opening suspected nuclear sites for inspection. When in 1998 North Korea launched a new long-range missile that flew over Japan, ostensibly to put a satellite into orbit, it did not matter that it endangered relief work.

The European Union, a major donor, issued an angry statement saying: "We are deeply concerned that a country which for several years has required and received from the international community extensive humanitarian assistance chooses to put its own scarce resources into developing an offensive weapons system."[21] Japan too halted aid shipments as public indignation reached a new pitch at this recent military offense. The WFP reacted to this setback by speaking out even more forcefully on behalf of the DPRK. Although the DPRK had made no significant concessions other than agreeing to the nutrition survey, WFP deputy executive director Namanaga Ngongi said in October 1998, "the amount of flexibility [by the DPRK government] has increased phenomenally."

"This has given us increased confidence that the resources are being and have been used correctly," he told a press conference in Beijing. "I cannot guarantee every grain of food sent by the WFP goes to the neediest person. But I can guarantee that [the] vast majority of resources channelled through the WFP is put to proper use in North Korea." After all, he continued somewhat absurdly, it was unlikely that food was being diverted because "the authorities are very aware if they are seen diverting food, they will not get it."[22]

The deputy head of the International Fund for Agricultural Development, Klemens van der Sand, returned from a visit in 1998 so impressed that he said "food production and food security had visibly improved in households he had randomly visited" and that he had certainly not come across any signs of famine or deaths from hunger.[23]

As in all other areas, neither confrontation nor cooperation brought rewards. Despite delivering food worth U.S. $1.6 billion, the WFP had to admit in 2002 that almost nothing had changed. "We simply don't have the same opportunities for access, for accountability, for transparency that we have elsewhere," James Morris, the WFP regional director, said in November 2002, seven years after WFP first arrived.[24]

The UN stance would be more defensible if there was a strong case for showing that the extended UN presence had helped steer the country toward agricultural reforms. Another UN agency, the United Nation's Development Program (UNDP), tried and failed using a different tactic. It brought together 50 governmental and non-governmental donors with a North Korean delegation in Geneva to discuss a U.S. $2 billion plan to restore North Korea's rural economy.

A proposal put together by a wily Belgian, Christian Lemaire, avoided any ultimatums but tried appealing to higher authority. Lemaire's staff combed through the ten-volume collected works of Kim Il Sung for quotations to support the cause of reform and show that the Great Leader endorsed farmers markets and material incentives from the grave. He also used deliberately woolly language, saying, for instance, that the DPRK should modernize the productive capacity of agriculture by embracing the "diversification of farm activities" or by "strengthening rural institutions, like individual households."

In other words, North Korea like China should dissolve its collective farms and redistribute the fields to make individual peasant holdings. Supported by loans and new and better seeds, farmers would be encouraged to sell their crops at the market price, and thus the UNDP promised that within three to five years, North Korea would double its harvest to six million tons of grain a year. The conference, despite being hailed by its organizers as "an historic event," was a failure. The European Union, the biggest food donor in 1997, bluntly warned that without such public commitments to reform, it would halt further aid—and the North Koreans said no.[25]

The UNDP found itself entangled by its own frequent public endorsement of the government's excuses for the famine. The North Korean representative at the Geneva meeting, deputy foreign minister Choi Su-hon, brushed aside the calls for change. Although he admitted that agricultural production had dropped by 75 percent, Choi said all that was needed was U.S. $230 million to prop up the existing agricultural system, to get the tractors running, restore power plants and pumps, and above all to restore the chemical fertilizer plants. In short, he only wanted the aid donors to help in restoring the system of state and collective farms.

Disappointed by this response, the European Union subsequently refused to contribute anything other than small amounts of emergency aid. The UNDP package fell through, a third roundtable meeting was cancelled, and no similar plan has since been mooted. Indeed, instead of helping to change North Korea, the United Nations could be accused of sustaining the old system. The United Nations continued to push food through the PDS system, even when the government stopped using it, and thereby helped the Workers Party to maintain, if not tighten, its control over the population.

In order to benefit from aid, people had to send their children to the state kindergartens, schools, and other public institutions and demonstrate their continuing obedience and loyalty to the leadership. At these public institutions, the populace attended daily indoctrination classes that often specifically aimed at fostering hatred of the outside world, especially the Chinese, South Koreans, Japanese, and Americans who were providing the bulk of the emergency aid. People were even warned not to eat Chinese food because it was poisonous, or to smoke Chinese cigarettes because they would explode.

In fairness to the United Nations, the system was never designed to respond to a situation where a government is prepared to let its own people die in huge numbers rather than adjust its policies or agree to minor conditions. After its negotiating setbacks in 1998, the United Nations did try harder to target the most vulnerable groups, such as pregnant and nursing mothers, the elderly, and children in the state kindergartens, with products that would not be used by soldiers. The United Nations set up its own factories to make noodles, a corn-soya blend only suitable for small children, and daytime snacks like enriched biscuits for older children.

Some refugees described trying to eat this corn-soya blend and feeling sick afterward. His account, like others, also showed the flaw in the scheme. Although the United Nations was feeding small children, their parents were being allowed to starve to death. When their factories stopped production, neither the state nor the United Nations provided the parents with any food. As a result they either died of hunger, creating orphans, or they left home in search of food or work and abandoned their children.

North Korean food production improved slowly from 1995. On the advice of foreign experts the North improved its crop mix with double cropping, crop rotation, and more potato and sweet potato fields, but grain harvest rose only modestly. The situation eased enough for the United Nations to say that by 1999 the worst was over, but famine-related deaths continued. In a famine the weakest and most vulnerable are quick to die and later the death rate slows and stabilizes. In North Korea's case, where perhaps 15 percent perished, demand and supply might simply have reached a new equilibrium. There was more food to go around because there were fewer mouths to feed.

In private, UN officials argue that all in all it was always better to increase the amount of food available to the country no matter who had first pick. Even if the Party and army took the best as the refugees alleged, then at least there was more left over for the rest. What would have happened if the United Nations and others had not delivered the relief food that they did—some 3.5 million tons valued at over U.S. $1.5 billion by the end of 2002—beggars the imagination.

CHAPTER 11

Kim Dae Jung and the South Korean Way

Five hundred and one mooing cows dressed in garlands were shepherded across Panmunjom in 1998 by an elderly and bespectacled man dressed despite the June heat in a raincoat and hat. When Chung Ju-yung fled to the South over 50 years ago to seek his fortune, he had stolen a cow from his home village of Asan, 30 miles north of the DMZ on the East Coast. Now he wanted to return the favor with interest. The son of poor farmers, Chung had founded Hyundai, the giant conglomerate or *chaebol*, whose name literally means modern. Chung, a contemporary of Kim Dae Jung, belonged to that remarkable generation of patriarchal figures that had helped modernize the backward country, turning its once starving people into manufacturers of world-class cars, ships, computers, microprocessors, and mobile phones.

Now, at the age of 82, he dreamed of creating another economic miracle in the North and bringing peace to the peninsula. He had been nurturing the idea since 1988 when his first secret contacts with the North were made. Now he had the full backing of President Kim Dae Jung, who had won the elections a few months earlier and was fully committed to engagement with Kim Jong Il in the North. Kim Dae Jung would realize his dream of holding a summit with Kim Jong Il. It would be the first such meeting in history and Kim Dae Jung would go on to win a Nobel Peace Prize. Chung's journey would end in tragedy with the suicide of his fifth son Chung Mong-hun in 2003, huge economic losses for Hyundai, and deep misgivings about all dealings with Pyongyang.

The three were the most unlikely partners one can imagine, and perhaps it was no surprise that initiatives started in 1998 brought results far short of the high hopes placed on them. To understand why, we need to go back and look at developments since 1961 and the beginning of South Korea's economic boom. For 17 years Chung had been a close partner and confidante of President Park Chung Hee, the South Korean military dictator and archenemy of Kim Dae Jung. Thanks to Park's patronage, Chung had become the richest man in South Korea, while Kim Dae Jung narrowly escaped death at the hands of Park's thugs.

Kim Dae Jung was hounded under Park's rule as a dangerous Leftie and Communist, even though watching from Pyongyang Kim Jong Il could hardly have regarded him as such. A self-educated man and a Roman Catholic who believed he was acting out God's plan, the charismatic Kim Dae Jung was known to be a man with strong beliefs and had repeatedly risked his life in defense of democracy. Kim Dae Jung had survived to see a democratically elected government try to sentence to death one former military dictator, Chun Doo Hwan, who had voluntarily given up power while his successor Roh Tae Woo earned a 17-year jail term, all for crimes that would count as nothing when set beside those of Kim Jong Il.

Kim Dae Jung had spent most of his life dealing with, or rather surviving, military dictators and perhaps understood as well as anyone the challenges and opportunities before him. North Korea has often been seen as a modern Sparta confronting the Athens of the South. For many years, however, the South under Park Chung Hee was the mirror image of the North. The former major general, who seized power in a military coup in 1961 when he was just 43, created a police state. He then channeled huge investments into heavy industry and over-ambitious projects in a dash to build up the country's strength.

While Kim Il Sung drew upon his experiences in Stalin's Soviet Union to plan his country's development, Park looked at how Japan had managed to modernize and become powerful. After leaving school, Park was trained by the Japanese in a military academy and after emerging at the top of his class in 1943, he was brought to the Tokyo Military Academy for two more years of training. After 1945, he was arrested for being a leading member of a Communist cell and sentenced to death for his part in an abortive uprising. During the Korean War, he fought for the South and continued his military career until frustrated by the inefficiency and confusion of the post-war years.

The Japanese way is best described as fascism. As in Benito Mussolini's Italy, a powerful state directed the economy through big corporations, a model that the Japanese call *Zaibatsu*. When the Japanese military developed new colonies in Korea, Manchuria, Taiwan, and elsewhere, companies like Mitsubishi were given a leading role. Park fostered the growth of big South Korean conglomerates like Hyundai to manage the economy and created the Korean Central Intelligence Agency (KCIA) to instill discipline and establish a military-style order. He tried to recreate the tough social controls and self-sacrificing patriotism of 1930s Japan and suspended the constitution and most civil liberties. At first, he ruled through a sort of junta called the Supreme Council for National Reconstruction with a membership of 32 military officers, but increasingly relied on the KCIA. It recruited many people who had belonged to families that had collaborated with the Japanese and fled South. Their chief task was to carry out surveillance of domestic enemies and not North Korean agents. The KCIA became a sort of state within the state with octopus-like tentacles that reached everywhere through a network of informers. The KCIA maintained extensive files on nearly everyone, and its agents did not hesitate to arrest, torture, and assassinate Park's enemies, even those who fled abroad. South Korea became a society permeated by fear. Neither criticism of the president nor of the government was permitted. Park built up his own personality cult, and it became mandatory for his picture to hang in all offices. Many of his domestic policies seemed to his critics drawn straight out of the Communist book.

Each household had to attend monthly neighborhood meetings to receive government directives, and in 1971 he inaugurated the Saemul Undong—the New Village Movement. This rural development program organized rural Koreans into collectives and drew the particular admiration of the North. It was an effort to raise living standards in the countryside where 70 percent of the population lived. Although it had achievements—the building of roads and the provision of electricity to all villages—it was essentially coercive and had all the hallmarks of a North Korean political campaign. Every morning villagers were treated to broadcasts from omnipresent loudspeakers of the Saemul pledge and the Saemul song. The collectives were also given the sort of presidential commands familiar in the North such as Park's order that all the straw roofs of their houses should be replaced by corrugated metal roofs and tiles because that was more modern.

Like Kim Il Sung, President Park liked to tour the country giving "on-the-spot inspections" of his favorite economic projects, giving out advice, and rewarding or punishing his followers depending on the degree of personal loyalty that they exhibited. He also returned from foreign tours inspired to commission new projects. Visiting West Germany in 1964, he was so impressed by its autobahns that against all expert advice, he decreed that South Korea needed its own motorways.

He exhorted the country to strive to fulfill five-year economic plans that were so ambitious they tested the limits of the endurance of both people and machines—and also used the same sort of slogans as the North. 1966 was declared the Year of Hard Work, which was followed by the Year of Progress in 1967, and the "Fight while Working, Work while Fighting" political campaign of 1968.

Like other fascist leaders, President Park also believed in the power of the human will. As he drove the population to catch up and overtake Japan and other advanced nations of the world, he wanted, like his counterpart in the North, a militarized workforce where everyone worked long hours in sweatshops. On a forced march toward industrialization, he commissioned bigger and bigger industrial and infrastructure projects. In this scheme of things, heavy industry, especially steel, was king.

In those days South Korea was a grim sort of place, under a quasi martial law, tough censorship, and a midnight curfew. The state discouraged private consumption, prevented people from buying imported goods, encouraged the accumulation of hard currency reserves, and directed domestic savings into nation-building and state-mandated projects. Under President Park's leadership South Korea looked like it was becoming another Third World one-party state that was strong on exhortation and obsessed with building capital-intensive mega-projects. Just as in the North, Park's goal was complete self-sufficiency; so why did he succeed where North Korea failed?

A key factor is that, unlike Kim, Park delegated the implementation of his ideas to men like Chung Ju-yung, Hyundai's founder, who were good and innovative businessmen. When President Park first seized power, his instinct was to have all the leading businessmen arrested. He forced them to donate all their money to the government and sought to bring the private sector under state control by such actions as banning illegal curbside lending. However, he soon changed his mind, and gave up trying to micromanage a command economy. Instead, Park began to work with leading businessmen, and about 40 *chaebols* sprang up, of which only the best survived. The Reverend Moon's Unification Church set up 16 companies known as the Tong Il (unification) Group. Colonel Pak Bo-hi, the KCIA liaison man in Washington, became Moon's right-hand man, and the group won contracts to supply small arms and other goods to the military before expanding into other areas. Samsung, Daewoo, Kia, Lucky Gold-Star, and the others also flourished under government patronage.

Park's motto "Enrich the Nation and Strengthen the Army" sounded similar to that of the North, which had made defense a top priority from 1963. In actuality, however, the South's priorities were different. The South did not plan a military buildup with the intention of subjugating its rival. Instead it concentrated on building up the nation's industrial base. Instead of autarky, Seoul imported as much Western technology as it could and paid for it by making export goods. Park set export quotas and even created an Export Day on November 30.

The South Koreans therefore had to manufacture products good enough to find buyers in international markets. When Park seized power in 1961, this was a dubious proposition. South Korea had a per capita GNP of $80 a year, on the level of Ghana and Sudan, and relied heavily on aid. The World Bank singled out the Philippines and Burma as the two most promising regional economies and expressed grave doubts that Korea could realize its hopes of becoming an exporter. The prevalent view of a group of U.S. State Department experts was that "Korea was an economic basket case that would always depend on American handouts for its existence." Half the government budget came from aid, especially U.S. government aid, and each year before the barley harvest was gathered many people went hungry.

Just how President Park turned this around is best described through the personal story of Chung. Against his father's wishes, Chung left his family's small holding to seek his fortune in the city. First he found a job in the docks, then as an errand boy for a rice mill, before buying an auto repair shop in 1940. After World War II, his younger brother who spoke English helped him win construction contracts from the U.S. military. A famous story showing his ingenuity as a contractor concerns a visit by U.S. President Dwight Eisenhower to the UN cemetery in Pusan where he wanted to honor the soldiers who had recently died in the war effort. As Eisenhower arrived in the dead of winter, the fields were brown and desolate. Chung decided he could change that by finding some green barley shoots and transplanting them in the cemetery. He managed it by bringing in 30 truckloads of shoots. "From then on, all construction projects for the 8th Army were mine," he would later recall. He went on to build the 8th Army-UN Command headquarters in Seoul and then won a U.S. Army contract for Incheon harbor.

Chung also tried to win the goodwill of the government by making the lowest bids even if it meant swallowing losses. Chung finished the country's big bridge project, the Koryung Bridge over the Nakdong River near Taegu, in 1955 despite incurring a big loss, but a year later his perseverance was rewarded when he won contracts to build five bridges across the Han River in Seoul. By 1960, Hyundai was the largest construction company in the country and when President Park and his Junta seized power, Chung eventually gained his confidence and later became one of his closest associates. He did this by bidding a token one *won* for a contract to rebuild the original Han River Bridge in Seoul, and then finished the job ahead of schedule. On another key project, the dam across Soyang River, the Korean government leaned toward inviting the Japanese to construct a conventional concrete gravity dam, but Hyundai, the face of conventional wisdom, proposed an fill dam with earth and gravel that would be a third cheaper. President Park accepted Chung's bid, and again Hyundai finished the job as promised.

The government then began to help Hyundai and other favored businessmen expand into new products and new markets. As Korea had to import the cement for these construction projects from Japan, Park used a loan from the U.S. Agency for International Development to build a cement plant and gave the project to Hyundai. With government support, Hyundai also won construction contracts abroad. In 1966, Hyundai workers went to Thailand to build a highway for the U.S. military and undertook dredging work in Vietnam. On the Thai project Hyundai again lost money, but the experience enabled Hyundai to become a big contractor during the post-1972 oil hike construction boom in the Middle East. In the interval, the Vietnam War provided a big boost to the South Korean economy as it sent 23, 000 workers to Vietnam, a job that accounted for 20 percent of the country's foreign exchange earnings. Later Hyundai became the largest contractor in the Middle East.

Other "Asian Tigers"—Taiwan, Hong Kong, and Singapore—also profited from the Vietnam War and began exporting light industrial goods to the United States. For a while, South Korea's chief exports were much the same—plywood, wigs, and textiles—but under President Park's direction, South Korea's economy took a different course. President Park pushed his countrymen to think big and delegated the job of building motorways, industrial parks, shipyards, steel works, cement factories, fertilizer plants, and car factories to his favorite businessmen. Park ordered a special industrial zone at Ulsan on the coast, and this is where Hyundai built its huge shipyard and first car plants. These policies forced the country to run up huge debts, but by the 1980s, when South Korea emerged as a fully fledged industrial power, they began to bear fruit.

Japan provided U.S. $500 million in loans and grants when the two countries normalized relations in 1965, and Seoul sought to pay its foreign debts by giving its businessmen preferential loans and rebates to exporters. Yet, in financing South Korea's development, President Park often brushed aside the advice of patrons like the World Bank. After its experts had spent months studying Park's dream of building the country's first motorway linking Seoul with Pusan, the second largest city and its biggest port, the World Bank said that there was not enough traffic to justify it. Park went ahead anyway and summoned Chung to the presidential mansion, the Blue House, where they had their first face-to-face meeting. Park gave Chung the lion's share of contracts, and they found they shared the same philosophy: "[T]o my way of thinking, there may be miracles in religion but not in politics or economics. . . . In fact we succeeded because our people devoted their enterprising spirits. They use the force of their minds. Conviction creates indomitable efforts. This is the key to miracles. . . . Man's potential is limitless," Chung Ju-yung wrote in his autobiography, *Ordeals, but No Failures*. Later, Chung became a frequent visitor at informal banquets at which the two sat around drinking *makkoli*, a milky fermented rice drink.

Chung's estimate for the motorway was, of course, well below other bidders. He then drove his workers to labor round the clock in multiple shifts to fulfill his commitment. Many died in landslides and cave-ins, machinery and equipment broke down constantly, and eventually Chung faced a revolt and had to double wages to prevent them from leaving.

Once the highway opened Park wanted to see it filled with Korean-built cars, and in 1967 Hyundai opened its first car plant assembling Ford kits. When production started in 1975, the plant had an annual production capacity ten times larger than South Korea's entire domestic car market. By the time shipments to the United States began in 1986, the project had run up huge losses but the company went on to become one of the world's largest car manufacturers.

President Park also allowed Hyundai to build the Ulsan shipyards. Although no one in Korea had ever built a vessel bigger than 10,000 tons, Chung managed to win a contract from a Greek shipowner for two 260,000-ton crude oil carriers, to find financial backers in Britain, and to start building the ships as the shipyards were being constructed around the vessels. That deal never made money either, but South Korea went on to become the world's largest shipbuilder.

In the 1970s, Park kept spurring investment into heavy industry. In 1973, he inaugurated the Heavy and Chemical Industries program, setting goals that seemed absurdly ambitious such as reaching U.S. $10 billion in annual exports and per capita GDP of U.S. $1,000 by 1980.

In the 1970s, as the United States began the retreat from Vietnam and pulling troops out of South Korea, President Park held elections and faced strong opposition from Kim Dae Jung. Kim found supporters in the working class from agricultural regions like Jeolla who did not benefit from the industrial boom and were underpaid and overworked. He was also supported by the intelligentsia and the churches, who objected to the dictatorship and wanted the restoration of their civil liberties.

The thuggish KCIA stopped at nothing to destroy the opposition. In 1971, Kim narrowly survived an assassination attempt when a truck smashed into his car, leaving him with a permanent limp. After Park won the election by the narrowest of margins, he promptly started a big political clampdown in 1972. He declared martial law and pushed through what he called the new Yushin or revitalizing constitution that effectively prohibited any sort of criticism.

As the government's chief critic, Kim Dae Jung posed the biggest threat. In 1973, KCIA agents kidnapped him in a Tokyo hotel room, tied him up, and took him blindfolded to a beach. There he was brought onto a motorboat, and his captors fastened weights to his arms and legs. He spent the next two days manacled and blindfolded at the bottom of a boat praying for his life to be spared. By extreme good fortune, or in Kim's mind by divine intervention, the American and Japanese government intervened and persuaded Park to keep him alive. Finally, he was brought back to Seoul and dumped outside his house.

Others were not so lucky. In the 1970s, the KCIA kidnapped antigovernment students and activists abroad and sometimes assassinated them. At home, critics were ruthlessly detained and tortured and workers who tried to organize unions were jailed or blacklisted. The economy ran into growing problems, worker unrest grew, and the losses from most of these projects mounted, but Park justified the repression by harping on the military threat from the North. His critics saw instead a corrupt government in which bribery was all too common. South Korean officials were even caught trying to bribe American officials in an attempt to head off criticism of the country's human rights record.

The big *chaebols* like Hyundai not only had an unhealthy symbiotic relationship with President Park and his cronies, they were themselves run as nepotistic family businesses. Chung had five brothers and a sister, and eight sons and a daughter, most of who ended up holding top positions in the company. One younger brother, Chung Se-yung, was president of the Hyundai Motor Company and another brother, Chung In-yu, ran the Hyundai INC.

The pent-up tensions came to a head in 1979. In a still mysterious and melodramatic incident, President Park was shot dead by his own KCIA chief, Kim Jae-gyu, while the men were drinking whiskey in the basement of the safe house not far from Blue House. Some accounts say that when Park accused him of failing to bring labor protests under control, Kim fell into a rage, pulled out his gun, and shot Park dead.

Park's funeral attracted two million mourners, and there were scenes of near hysteria on the streets. For a few months, his passing led to a democratic spring, marked by workers demanding pay rises and huge student protests, until another general made a grab for power and imposed martial law. To carry out this second coup, Major General Chun Doo Hwan, and his deputy, Major General Roh Tae Woo, pulled troops from the DMZ. Later they also used frontline troops to put down with considerable bloodshed an uprising at Kwangju city in South Jeolla province, the home province of Kim Dae Jung. Such a misuse of troops, nominally under the control of the U.S. military, provoked considerable anti-American feelings. Previously, the Americans had enjoyed broad popularity, but now a younger generation believed the Americans had somehow authorized or at least condoned this illegal power grab.

Chun and Roh belonged to the first post-war class of military academy graduates. Chun himself was sent to the United States to study psychological warfare and undergo ranger and airborne training. This new officer corps used the excuses that President Park had used to justify domestic repression—the need to "restore order" and "deter an invasion by the North." Chun set up a Special Committee for National Security Measures and orchestrated a sweeping purge, described as a "purification movement" with special measures to eliminate "social evils." This targeted over 38,000 who ended up in "re-education camps" where the treatment was so brutal that 50 people died in detention. Kim Dae Jung was again arrested, stripped and tortured in jail, put on trial, and then allowed to leave for exile in America. Chun offered to trade Kim Dae Jung's life in exchange for becoming the first head of state to go to Washington after Ronald Reagan became president. The offer was accepted, but Kim Dae Jung was cast as a Leftwing, dangerous man whose sympathies lay with the North.

As the country was then in a recession, and President Chun knew nothing about running an economy, he soon found himself in difficulties. He began to meddle directly in the affairs of the *chaebols,* and his new government soon earned itself a reputation for corruption. Yet the investment of the 1970s finally began to yield dividends and exports surged, especially after 1986. The South Korean economy was unexpectedly boosted by the 1985 Plaza Accord, the international accord that raised the value of the yen and the deutsche mark against the dollar. This allowed the Korean exporters to grab market share from the Japanese and Germans and soon, South Korea had overtaken Mexico and Brazil as the largest exporters to the United

States. The economy began racing ahead at a rate of 12 percent a year, and the boom lifted South Korea's international standing.

With Chung's help, Seoul had beaten off Japan to win the right to host the 1988 Summer Olympics. For the first time the Koreans were playing a role on the world stage. As a leading member of the Olympic Bidding Committee, Chung also took charge of planning a series of construction projects costing some U.S. $6 billion. Part of Seoul was redeveloped with the construction of a new Olympic Village on the south bank of the Han River and a splendid Olympic stadium. Across the DMZ North Korea tried and failed to match this by constructing its own giant stadium and Olympic village.

Less visible was the unrest simmering among the members of the workforce in the South who were made to work long hours for low wages. In Pyongyang, the leadership was told that the growing labor unrest showed growing support for its cause. In the universities, some students did form neo-Marxist study groups and tried to exploit the anger at the military dictatorship. South Korea was rocked by waves of mass protests led by students in Seoul and by workers all over the country. Striking Hyundai workers rioted and took hostages until Chung agreed to deal with independent union leaders who over the next five years fought bitterly to raise wages and reduce working hours. The resulting scenes, in which protestors faced off against massed ranks of riot police dressed in black gear with helmets like Darth Vader as clouds of tear gas swirled around the center of the capital, created an impression of political chaos.

Despite appearances, most South Koreans did not want to exchange one dictatorship for another. They were caught up in a wave of popular democracy movements that swept Burma, the Philippines, Taiwan, Thailand, and eventually China as well. By June 1987, President Chun surrendered and agreed to step down. His anointed successor, Roh Tae Woo, agreed to direct presidential elections, to release many political prisoners, and to rescind the ban on opposition politicians including Kim Dae Jung. Despite these successes, the opposition did not triumph at the polls. The two leading presidential candidates, Kim Dae Jung and Kim Young Sam, split the opposition vote and allowed Roh to win the presidential elections. President Roh found support among the older generation by playing up the threat from the North. Just to rub home the message, on the eve of polling, the state-run television broadcast *The Killing Fields*, the film about the Khmer Rouge takeover of Cambodia.

Despite victory at the ballot box, President Roh's government had to make more and more changes and these loosened the tight bonds linking government and big business, and government and military. The de facto state of emergency was lifted, enabling citizens to enjoy basic democratic rights. They could form political parties, read and write what they wanted, and organize independent trade unions to fight for higher wages and better working conditions. The process was not very pretty to watch. In the early 1990s, tens of thousands of Hyundai workers at Ulsan went on a rampage throwing rocks and firebombs and demanding hefty pay rises. The workers stopped at nothing and some even committed suicide. So fierce was the struggle that in one case the government sent troops to surround the factories and demanded under gunpoint that the two sides reach an agreement within 48 hours.

The protests by the elite advance guard of the Korean labor force shattered Chung Ju-yung's carefully fostered illusion that he had indoctrinated workers so well that they would perform as loyally and obediently as soldiers. Working at Hyundai was like joining a closed cult, complete with songs and books venerating Chung's leadership. Members of the workforce were required to give him their complete loyalty and accept his paternalistic guidance in many areas of their life. As a Hyundai orientation manual says: "An indomitable driving force, a religious belief in attaining a goal, and a commitment to personal diligence tempered with frugality have materialized as a major part in the development of heavy industry in Korea."

These very public rebellions against the paternalistic leadership cults of such business leaders lent immense credibility to Kim Dae Jung's long-held views about the nature of the Koreans and their attitude to authority. Kim rejected Singapore leader Lee Kuan Yew's view that the history and culture of East Asians led them instinctively to prefer authoritarian government and reject democracy and human rights as implanted "Western concepts."

President Lee Kuan Yew who used neo-Confucian ideas to legitimize his own semi-totalitarian rule, manage the economy, and intervene directly in all aspects of the lives of his citizens, argued that this was only what his subjects wanted. Kim disagreed. "The question is whether democracy is a system so alien to Asian cultures that it will not work. . . . A thorough analysis makes it clear that Asia has a rich heritage of democracy-oriented philosophies and traditions," Kim Dae Jung wrote in an article published in the influential American journal *Foreign Affairs*.[1]

To accept Lee Kuan Yew's views amounted to accepting that South Koreans had President Park's repression to thank for their prosperity. By extension, this implied that Kim Jong Il's only mistake was the mismanagement of the North Korean economy. If Kim Jong Il were to embrace the market and generate some economic success, then North Koreans would be content living in a military-run totalitarian state.

In South Korea, the military's economic achievements came under scrutiny after Kim Young Sam won the 1992 presidential elections. The extent of the corruption came out and finally both Roh Tae Woo and Chun Doo Hwan were put on trial. Chun, who had already apologized for his misdeeds and spent two years in a Buddhist monastery to show his repentance, was sentenced to death. Roh was given a 17-year prison sentence. Dozens of others were also convicted, including the younger brother of Chun Doo Hwan, Chun Kyung-hwan, who was found guilty of illegally diverting huge amounts of money from the Saemul Foundation, President Park's favorite rural development program.

Hyundai and its founder, Chung, also came under investigation and he was charged with corruption, as were other *chaebol* leaders. By this time, Chung had formally retired, but at the age of 77 he was still humiliated by being tried and given a three-year suspended jail sentence.

The cozy and secretive relationship between big business and the Park-era government had been so disrupted that Chung himself decided to run for president. Although he founded his own political party, the effort failed. It took the 1997 Asian Financial Crisis to completely discredit President Park's economic model. The country, along with the top *chaebol*, was declared officially bankrupt and had to be rescued by the International Monetary Fund (IMF) with a U.S. $58 billion package. The country had run up huge debts because the state had always encouraged the state-run banks to lend money to the *chaebols* without restraint. That is how they could expand so quickly, despite poor or negligible returns.

The headstrong recklessness of the South Koreans parallels that of the Koreans in the North. Both economies, after being driven so hard, had now crashed. The Korean won lost half its value, there were massive layoffs, and

South Korea had to accept some bitter and humiliating medicine. Assets of some of the biggest *chaebols* had to be sold off to foreign companies—GM for instance bought Daewoo Motors Co.—and the country was obliged to open up closed sectors of the economy. The IMF and other creditors demanded structural changes, especially banking reforms that ended the old command economy, which had driven the *chaebols'* helter-skelter expansion. The new economy became increasingly driven by consumer rather than state-directed spending. The crisis further weakened the ties between the military, government, and industry and helped transform the South into a more open and democratic country. Now the problem was how to do the same in the North.

When Kim Dae Jung finally triumphed at his fourth attempt and won the presidential elections in 1997, he had the chance to put his long-held convictions to the test. He had always said it was better to engage the North than to confront it. Ever since the collapse of the Soviet Union, the South had confidently expected that it was only a matter of time before the North collapsed. By the beginning of 1998, when Kim Dae Jung formally took office, Kim Jong Il was still in power and Kim Dae Jung had an opportunity to try another tack.

When he looked at the North, he was confronted by an extreme version of South Korea under his old antagonist, President Park: a military, government, and economy that were entirely fused into one entity under the sole control of Kim Jong Il and his family. The history of the South also showed that as the threat from the North weakened, it became harder for the South's military dictators to justify a state of war-time emergency and therefore to resist the restoration of normal civil rights. If Kim Dae Jung could persuade the North of the South's peaceful intentions, then Kim Jong Il might also be willing to relax his war-time emergency posture, which would pave the way for reforms.

Kim Dae Jung, who is as well read in Western and Eastern literature, borrowed the name of his Sunshine Policy from Aesop's fable about the Wind and the Sun. In the tale, the Wind and the Sun have an argument about which of them can persuade a man to take off his coat. The Wind tries and fails to tug it off. The Sun, however, succeeds by warming the man with his rays. For the engagement part of his policy, Kim Dae Jung turned to the big business tycoons like Chung who knew best how to get results while working under military dictators. Kim Dae Jung's hope was that they could prize open up North Korea's sealed economy by offering to create an export-oriented industrial base—a transitional stage on the way to deeper social and political change. The unspoken risk was that Kim Dae Jung would simply transplant the worst aspects of the old system to the North—that Seoul would tell South Korean banks to finance the *chaebols* at the bidding of the North's dictator, which would turn out to be more white elephants.

To work, the Sunshine Policy also required a willing suspension of disbelief. From his inaugural address in early 1998, Kim Dae Jung insisted, and went on to insist at every opportunity, that he had no intention of undermining or absorbing North Korea. In the same breath however, he also made it clear that the end objective was a unified state based on South Korea's economic and political system. He argued that gradual change, a soft landing, was better for everyone. He put forward a three-stage plan that started off with a South-North economic community. Before the two governments became closely engaged, Kim Dae Jung wanted nongovernmental organizations and especially the big *chaebols* to build economic bridges between the two sides. In the next stage, he foresaw a gradual preparation for unification with the formation of a confederation in which both sides retained their sovereignty for ten years. There would be two republics in one federation. Then, in the third stage, left to some remote hazy future, there would be a new and unified Korea devoted to democracy and an open-market economy.

Kim Dae Jung did his best to change the climate of distrust in many ways. At home he ended support for any activities that might seem hostile, including, of course, covert military and intelligence operations against the North. Abroad, he persuaded President Clinton to support the Sunshine Policy, and other U.S. allies followed suit. As such a long-standing "dissident," he had a track record that could easily inspire confidence. Kim had spoken out in favor of détente with the North 30 years earlier, and in 1972, the North had used the abduction of Kim Dae Jung as an excuse for breaking off the first round of North-South talks.

Kim Dae Jung vehemently insisted he was against any "German-style absorption of the North" and he was quite different from his successors.

Yet this was not true. The object was clearly the absorption of the North, and it was never clear why Kim Jong Il should believe otherwise. He might go along with the pretense for some short-term gain, but the whole Sunshine Policy rested on a shaky assumption that secretly Kim Jong Il was willing to abandon his *Juche* philosophy and his life-long ambition to unify the peninsula under his family's rule. Some thought Kim might acquiesce out of dire need, but clearly once the North stopped offering a clear political or economic alternative, its *raison d'être* was lost.

To demonstrate the sincerity of his abjuring even such a hope, Kim Dae Jung's officials repeatedly told all who would listen that it would be disastrous for the South if the North did collapse, on the grounds that it would simply cost too much. It had cost West Germany U.S. $130 billion to absorb East Germany, especially after all its inhabitants were allowed to swap their East German marks for West German deutsche marks for a 1:1 ratio instead of the usual 4:1 exchange. On top came the tens of billions West Germany was investing in the East in a fruitless effort to salvage the East German economy.

"Look at what happened to the strong West German economy after it absorbed East Germany," Kim Dae Jung told legislators in 1998. "How are we going to deal with the disaster if the North collapses? We should do everything possible to start a dialogue and avoid a war." Kim Dae Jung seemed to think that Kim Jong Il would be willing to rely on the South Korean *chaebols* in the same way that President Park had. That way Chung Ju-yung and the other tycoons could introduce the North Koreans to the market and thereby diminish the iron grip of the military command economy. South Korea would benefit too, as the North could be treated as a sort of colony. It offered cheap non-unionized labor and a protected market. The possibilities excited everyone. The Korea Development Institute, a leading think tank, predicted that North and South Korea could form a powerful single economic bloc by 2020, if Pyongyang was willing to embrace the market. And if the South became the North's largest trading partner, then war would be unthinkable. The peace dividend would make everyone richer.

Hyundai wanted to be the first in and found itself bidding against other *chaebols* to win exclusive concessions, like the right to run package tours to Mount Diamond (known as Mount Geumgang in Korea) near Chung Ju-yung's home village just over the DMZ. The fairytale landscape of craggy limestone peaks, pines, waterfalls, and Buddhist pagodas had won the praise of generations of travelers, poets, and hermits.

This project had first been mooted in the late 1980s when Kim Il Sung was still alive. Tourism was chosen as the first sector to benefit from South Korean investment because it was safe to assume this would help the North's military in the way that, say, building power station or roads might. Chung had received an invitation to visit the North three months after the Seoul Olympics and arrived in January 1989 for a ten-day visit. Next in 1991, the Reverend Moon was in Pyongyang holding hands with Kim Il Sung and discussing the Mount Diamond tourist proposition and other projects. Moon spent eight days in the country and visited his home village and his parent's grave. The next year Daewoo's chairman, Kim Woo-joong, came with proposals to fund light-industry factories at the newly opened Rajin-Songbon economic development zone. The North Koreans even invited 120 experts to look around, but they returned shocked to find port facilities dating from the 1930s and an industrial zone the Soviets had built in the 1950s—all in a state of advanced decrepitude.

All these early negotiations went nowhere, but in the summer of 1998 Chung tried again when he drove his cattle over the border. He did it again that autumn, herding 500 cows and trucking across 50,000 tons of grain grown on reclaimed tidal land at his Seosan Farm. By the end of the year, he had reached a deal to develop the Diamond Mountain project that had expanded to include plans for ski and beach resorts complete with golf courses and luxury hotels. The first tourists came by sea on a cruise ship. After they landed, every effort was made to prevent any contact with the North Koreans. The number of tourists peaked at 250,000 in the year 2000, when Kim Dae Jung finally travelled to the North to hold his historic summit with Kim Jong Il. Three days of meetings produced a South-North Joint Declaration, which asserted that the Korean people should solve all Korean problems by themselves. In addition to such vague principles, the declaration detailed some joint economic projects.

These projects included reconnecting the Seoul-Sinuiju railroad, opening an overland route to the Diamond Mountains, and developing a new industrial zone at Kaesong, a town just over the border from Panmunjom. The railway project had great potential because it would enable South Korea to ship goods directly to China, Russia, and Europe. In addition, both sides were committed to studying another huge project—a pipeline to take gas from Siberia to South Korea and Japan.

Kim Dae Jung was heartened by Kim Jong Il's willingness to reach out to the rest of the world. The North Korean made state visits to China and Russia and received a string of high-level diplomatic delegations, including U.S. Secretary of State Madeleine Albright. North Korea came close to normalizing ties with the United States. If that happened and it was taken off the list of terrorist states, the North would qualify for all sorts of international loans and credits. Normalizing relations with Japan, which depended on resolving the issue of the abducted Japanese, would also be rewarded with a generous settlement. Tokyo has offered compensation for its colonization worth at least U.S. $5 billion, although some reports say as much as U.S. $15 billion.

For every negotiation and for every visit, Kim Jong Il garnered gifts of grain, oil, fertilizer, and other credits, and he now stood on the threshold of obtaining a huge aid package that would transform North Korea's fortunes. Economists competed to calculate how much it would cost to rebuild the economy. The more that was learned about the North Korean economy, the higher the price tag. Restoring the North's railway system was first projected to cost U.S. $500 million, but it then became clear that it was in such poor shape that it would really cost over U.S. $3 billion to enable to it to transport goods in any quantity.

Hyundai invested U.S. $600 million in the Mount Diamond venture, and by 2003 it had run up operating losses of U.S. $300 million. Altogether the company poured U.S. $1.5 billion into the North, but in keeping with Hyundai's business philosophy this sort of loss did not matter. It had won the most valuable concession of all, the right to undertake all major infrastructure projects for the next 30 years. This would have been Chung Ju-yung's biggest deal—first chance at all the lucrative contracts to build the new roads, harbors, airports, power stations, and residential housing complexes that the North would need. Just how much North Korea would need is anyone's guess—U.S. $50 billion, U.S. $100 billion—perhaps much more if the railways provided a fair sample.

By the time the dizzy optimism of the 2000 summit had subsided, Chung had died, leaving behind a poisoned legacy. After Kim Dae Jung stepped down at the end of his term, Hyundai's deal making came under tight scrutiny from the opposition in South Korea. A criminal investigation revealed that Hyundai had paid the North U.S. $500 million just before the summit, including U.S. $100 million-worth of unauthorized payments. State prosecutors went to question Chung's fifth son, Chung Mong-Hun, who was in charge of business with the North. Late one night in August 2003, he threw himself out of the window of his offices on the twelfth floor of the Hyundai headquarters in downtown Seoul. In the end, 18 men, including two Hyundai executives, linked to the deal were given suspended prison sentences.

The case was a watershed. The *chaebols* were not going to transplant the corrupt business practices, outlawed in the South, to the North. It seemed Hyundai had first beat off the competition by making the largest bribes, then the government had stepped in to make a state-run bank provide a loan. This sort of backroom sweetheart deal was exactly what Kim Dae Jung had always sworn to root out. Even worse, a large chunk of the money, U.S. $50 million, was spent on a gymnasium in Pyongyang, called the Chung Ju-yung Memorial Gymnasium, one more vanity edifice for the starving country.

Chung Mong-Hun's suicide was assumed to be a protest against the injustice of being hounded after he had merely been acting on the instructions of President Kim Dae Jung. The half billion was transferred just before the summit, and it now looked to all the world that Kim Dae Jung had merely bought the summit and the Nobel Prize to boot.

Yet, some would argue this was not enough to discredit Kim Dae Jung's strategy of engagement. Kim Jong Il had accepted a large bribe from the South and that showed he was corruptible, which was a lesson everyone, including his followers, learned. In return, however, he did take measures that showed tensions were easing. For instance, Hyundai started direct bus tours to Mount Diamond and South Koreans started travelling by road and air directly to Pyongyang.

However, the notion that South Korean business could subvert the North's system by setting up shop in the North took a severe knock. All but a dozen of the 500 South Korean companies who had rushed to sign up for factories in the Kaesong industrial zone withdrew, fearing that there was no longer government backing for their projects.

It is also true that confidence was undermined by the skeptical attitude of the incoming Bush administration toward the Sunshine Policy, especially after President George W. Bush listed North Korea in his "axis-of-evil speech" in early 2002. Yet most investors, like the Reverend Moon, found that North Korea simply was not ready, and perhaps never would be under the Kim dynasty. Most investment merely added to the extensive list of industrial white elephants, like the eight-lane motorway to Nampo whose construction, described in chapter five, cost so much sweat and blood.

After the Unification Church failed to win the bid for the Mount Diamond project, it was invited to start North Korea's auto industry. At Nampo, it built an auto plant with the capacity to build 100,000 sedans a year, and by February 2000, it began assembling kits shipped by Fiat. Under the original deal, the North Koreans promised to buy the first cars, and later the struggling Italian automaker hoped to use the cheap labor to build an export base to penetrate East Asian markets. There were two models—the Cuckoo or *Ppeokuyi* at U.S. $14,500, and the Whistler or *Hwiparam* priced at U.S. $12,500. The Unification Church even put up advertising billboards and built a petrol station in Pyongyang.

The whole venture seemed to imitate what South Korea had once successfully done—build a motorway, then start making the private cars. Yet in North Korea, the Unification Church found to its horror that their host simply took the delivery of the first batch of 7,000 cars and never paid for them. After that production had to stop. There was no real market for cars in North Korea—no one had any money—and there were not even public vehicles using the huge autobahn to Nampo. All public transport had ceased to function. Nor were there any takers abroad. The workforce turned out not to be cheap or productive. The state took their wages and left the workers a pittance, and the officials who controlled the workers did not understand concepts like profits, marketing, and quality control.

The Unification Church whose own *chaebol*, Tong Il Industries, had sunk in the Asian Financial Crisis with debts of over U.S. $2 billion also had other goals in mind than mere profits. The Reverend Moon had won from Kim a 99-year lease, with extraterritorial rights, on a nine-square-kilometer parcel of land around his home village in Jongju. There he imagined he would create his very own Bethlehem, a Moonies Holy Land theme park with hotels and rides for his four million followers. Beyond paving the road to his family's village, this project too went nowhere. The Moonies found, as many others did, that once the North Koreans had pocketed the money, they lost interest. As the next chapter describes, the same fate befell the Americans who tried to negotiate a grand bargain over the disposal of the North's nuclear weapons' program. In this case, the risk was a thousand times bigger.

CHAPTER 12

Grappling with a Rogue State

U.S. Secretary of State Madeleine Albright was in Pyongyang in the last months of the second Clinton Administration holding talks with Kim Jong Il when he announced he had prepared a special surprise for her. That evening they arrived at the May Day Stadium for a performance by 100,000 citizens, which Kim confided would help the Americans understand North Korea. A huge crowd gave forth a volcano of rapturous sounds as they arrived. "It began with a giant image of a hammer for workers, a brush for intellectuals, and a sickle for farmers. Then suddenly, everywhere, there were children, dancing gymnasts cartwheeling, sequined costumes swirling and people flying about on little rockets. There were youngsters dressed up as flowers, soldiers thrusting their bayonets, fireworks and people shot from canons into a net. There was a human card section rapidly and precisely flashing tens of thousands of placards showing detailed murals and illustrated slogans accompanied by thunderous patriotic chants," Albright recalled in her memoirs *Madam Secretary.* In the midst of all this the card section showed a Taepodong missile being launched into the sky and before the applause faded, Kim turned to her and said, "That was our first missile launch—and our last."

One of the central mysteries of North Korea is what Kim Jong Il has really been trying to achieve in the ten years since his father's death. No coherent long-term domestic or foreign policies have emerged, and in the absence of a convincing plot line, conflicting theories have been put forward with great passion.

After the collapse of the Soviet Union, most observers predicted North Korea would either collapse or reform like China. If Kim Jong Il hung on in power, it seemed inevitable he would give up his weapons, normalize relations with the United States, and enter the international community if offered enough guarantees and financial rewards. An opportunity to do exactly this arrived following the summit with Kim Dae Jung in June 2000, but he fumbled it just when success seemed within his grasp. The summit inspired the Clinton Administration to make a major push to finalize a deal with North Korea.

It took months for Kim Jong Il to send top-ranking emissary Vice Marshal Cho Myong-rok to Washington, and when he arrived at the White House on October 9, there were talks about organizing a summit in Pyongyang and finding ways to remove North Korea from the list of terrorist states. A joint communiqué issued on October 12 declared that "neither government would have any hostile intent toward the other."

When Albright led a delegation to Pyongyang for two days of banquets and talks, it seemed certain that Clinton would go to Pyongyang and the two countries would start a new relationship. In her memoirs, Albright said that Clinton was "more than willing to make the trip," but he was torn between going or staying home to focus on an Israel-Palestinian peace accord, which seemed promising but eventually failed. In a final effort to do both, Clinton invited Kim to Washington. However, since Kim's invitation to Clinton was already public and given the lateness of the U.S. invitation and the importance of "face" in Asian diplomacy, the North declined.

Key details of the agreement package had not been fixed in the rush of October diplomacy, including a deal under which Washington offered to pay hundreds of millions of dollars if the North ended its missile program. Kim seems to have missed his best chance to win a favorable deal, due in part to odd conventions of North Korean diplomacy. A North Korea head of state could visit his allies, China and Russia, but the leaders of hostile countries had to come to him as if they were to pay tribute and finally acknowledge his authority. It was essential that leaders of South Korea, the European Union, Japan, and the United States first come to Pyongyang. However, Kim Jong Il has never reciprocated a visit and has even broken his promises to visit Seoul.

One day before leaving office, Clinton and Albright spoke by telephone. "Fuming about all the time we had invested in [Palestinian leader Yasser] Arafat, he said he wished he had taken the chance of going to North Korea instead of staying in Washington to make a final push on the Middle East," Albright recalled. Perhaps, as some say is the case with Arafat, Kim miscalculated by holding out for more or simply was not capable of accepting a deal that fell short of his dreams.

In America, the defenders of engagement blamed the Republicans for squandering a great opportunity. "I do think if the Bush administration had picked up the hand of cards on the table that we had left them, we might be in better shape now," Albright has argued. "While I make no apologies for Kim Jong Il, who is a horrible dictator and has starved his people, I don't blame him for being a bit confused."[1] Albright said her successor, Colin Powell, had led her to believe the new administration "would pick up roughly where we left off" but instead, the incoming Bush administration undertook a year-long policy review. Before this was finished, the September 11 terrorist attacks redefined the priorities of U.S. foreign policy and made the war on terror and the eradication of weapons of mass destruction the top priority. At the start of the Bush administration, his leading advisors were deeply divided on how to deal with North Korea. Much of the debate centered on the merits of the 1994 Agreed Framework.

Influential voices, including Leon Sigal, director of the Northeast Asia Cooperative Security Project at the Social Science Research Council in New York; Selig Harrison, senior scholar of the Woodrow Wilson International Center for Scholars; and professor Bruce Cumings of the University of Chicago, blame Washington's errors for the failures of the Agreed Framework.[2]

Just weeks after the deal was signed, the Republicans triumphed in Congressional elections, and President Clinton had great difficulties overcoming the skepticism among leading Republicans merely to go ahead with the terms of the agreement. The Clinton administration also faced opposition from Seoul, where President Kim Young Sam hoped for the collapse of the North. Kim Young Sam, who might have become the first South Korean leader to hold a summit with the North, if Kim Il Sung had not died suddenly after the Carter visit, subsequently refused to attend Kim Il Sung's funeral, thereby insulting Kim Jong Il. Both Kim Young Sam and the Republicans wanted to step up the pressure in the hopes of speeding the inevitable collapse of the North.

President Clinton also knew that Congress would not ratify a treaty with Pyongyang, nor would it pay for the nuclear power stations. The delays both in starting the reactor project and supplying the heavy fuel oil undermined the Clinton administration's efforts to create a climate of trust after the face-off in 1994. The United States dragged its feet on relaxing economic sanctions imposed under the Trading with the Enemy Act, which dates back to the Korean War. The advocates of engagement argued that as the larger more threatening power, the onus was on Washington to take the first steps and overcome North Korean doubts, and some even made this a moral obligation. Others, like Bruce Cumings, pointed out that the United States was to blame for dividing the peninsula and for launching a devastating bombing campaign in the Korean War, which had helped create the North's fearful and defensive-aggressive mentality.

Wendy Sherman, a special adviser on North Korea to President Clinton who accompanied Albright, later said, however, that the Clinton administration itself was never enthusiastic about implementing the Agreed Framework after Kim Il Sung's death. "Everyone was so overwhelmed that a million or two million people were dying of starvation, the economy had clearly collapsed, the dynamics were changing. . . . We just thought all that would bring about the collapse of the North Korean government within two or three years. I think that was the conventional wisdom and we were totally wrong."[3]

When Kim Dae Jung became president in 1998, it galvanized President Clinton and he again set about persuading a skeptical Congress to allow him to open diplomatic ties and negotiate a broad treaty ending the state of war that had existed since the armistice. He enlisted retired Defense Secretary William Perry to carry out a sweeping review of the options on Korea and forge a bipartisan consensus. Perry traveled widely and consulted everyone, including the North Koreans.

In his 1999 report, Perry concluded that there was no evidence the regime was about to collapse, and besides even that result was not good enough. As he later said in a television interview, "Even if that strategy were successful, the most optimistic [projections were that] it would take several years. In the meantime, the North Koreans would get their nuclear program. They would get their nuclear bombs, and we would be facing that danger. So we rejected that."[4]

Perry also believes a great opportunity was missed:

> I thought it was quite likely that what the North Koreans were saying
> then was right—which is they were prepared to close the deal at that stage,
> which was to accept the proposal that I had made to them: Offer to give up
> their missiles, offer to give up their nuclear weapons, offer for reasonable
> verification of all of that in return for moving forward on this upward path.
>
> They would want to negotiate what some of the terms would be, and
> they would hope that the visit of President Clinton would allow them to do
> that. But the purpose, what their proposal was for his visit was to close the
> deal. The president was intrigued, and probably would have done that, had
> the offer come sooner.[5]

When George W. Bush narrowly won the election, the most influential
voices in the incoming administration remained divided on what to do
next. Some, like General Colin Powell, the new secretary of state, favored
continuing the Clinton-era negotiations. Others argued for "hawk engagement," that is a renewal of the "coercive diplomacy" of 1994 when the
threat of U.S. military action forced a freeze of the plutonium program at
Yongbyon. Some thought the avowed goal should be "regime change." As
Bush's National Security Adviser Condoleezza Rice argued, "truly evil regimes will never be reformed and . . . such regimes must be confronted,
not coddled."[6]

Richard Perle, chairman of the Defense Policy Board, an influential civilian group advising the Pentagon shared this belief. In the Reagan administration, he served as assistant secretary of defense for international security
policy from 1981 to 1987. He lambasted the Agreed Framework as appeasement. "The basic structure of the relationship implied in the Framework Agreement is a relationship between a blackmailer and one who pays
a blackmailer," he said.[7]

Several incidents were evidence of this. After U.S. intelligence reports in
August 1998 raised fears that North Korea was building a large underground facility at Kumchangri that might house a reactor or a reprocessing
plant and be a breach of the 1994 Agreed Framework, the United States
demanded the right to inspect it. North Korea only agreed after Washington promised over 600,000 tons of food aid, although in public it denied
the food aid was tied to the inspection. When the team arrived in May

1999, it found nothing, perhaps because the North Koreans used the time to remove the equipment.

The same trick seemed to be going on with the missiles. The Clinton administration offered to pay the North Koreans for suspending their missile program after Pyongyang launched the Taepodong missile over Japan in 1998. The detail was never finalized in Pyongyang, although Albright was prepared to offer hundreds of millions if verification problems could be solved.

After Bush was installed in the White House, Kim Dae Jung was quick to meet him in Washington, but left disappointed with his Sunshine Policy badly holed. It emerged that Bush's strong personal feelings determined the policy towards Pyongyang, and Kim Dae Jung could not deflect him. *Washington Post* journalist Bob Woodward quotes Bush: "'I loathe Kim Jong Il! Bush shouted, waving his finger in the air. 'I've got a visceral reaction to this guy, because he is starving his children. . . . Maybe it's my religion, maybe it's my . . . but I feel passionate about this. . . . They tell me, we don't need to move too fast, because financial burdens on people will be so immense if we try to, if they were to topple. Who would take care of . . . I just don't buy that. Either you believe in freedom, and want to . . . and worry about the human condition, or you don't.'" On another occasion, he told a group of senators that Kim Jong Il is a "pygmy" who "acts like a spoiled child at a dinner table" and who is "starving his own people" in a "gulag the size of Houston."[8] The same views came through strongly when President Bush visited Seoul in February 2002 and declared:

> I am troubled by a regime that tolerates starvation.
>
> I will not change my opinion on the man, on Kim Jong Il, until he frees his people and accepts genuine proposals from countries like South Korea or the United States, until he proves to the world that he's got a good heart, that he cares about people that live in his country.
>
> North Korean children should never starve while a massive army is fed. No nation should be a prison for its own people.

President Bush made it clear that now it was Kim Jong Il who had to make the first move.

> I am concerned about a country that is not transparent, that allows for starvation, that develops weapons of mass destruction. . . . I think the burden

of proof is on the North Korean leader, to prove that he does truly care about people and that he is not going to threaten our neighbor.[9]

Bush's disgust at Kim Jong Il's behavior may explain why North Korea was included among the three countries named in the "axis-of-evil speech." The Clinton-era deals were now off the table, and as the United States mobilized an invasion force on the borders of Iraq, North Korea felt it could be next.

"I think that one of the things that is important to understand in North Korea is that the past policy of trying to engage bilaterally didn't work," Bush said at a July 30, 2003, news conference. "In other words, the North Koreans were ready to engage but they didn't keep their word on their engagement. And that ought to be a clear signal to policymakers of what to expect with North Korea."

Evidence that the North Koreans had been insincere was clear. In October 2002, Assistant Secretary of States James Kelly traveled to Pyongyang with evidence of a second and hidden nuclear weapons program using uranium enrichment technology. His North Korean counterpart, Kim Yongsam, the man who had negotiated the Agreed Framework was at first startled. He returned from meetings armed with instructions from a furious Kim Jong Il to express defiance. The North Koreans admitted the accusations were true and then boasted that they possessed still more terrible weapons of mass destruction. For critics of the engagement policies, the truth was now plain to see.

This was a serious tactical mistake by Kim Jong Il, who instead of denying it had made things easy for the Bush administration. He could have first demanded the Americans prove their allegations. Kim compounded the mistake by raising the stakes in the belief that if he threatened to start mass producing bombs, Washington would give in. He expelled the IAEA monitors, withdrew from the Non-Proliferation Treaty, and declared that the 8,000 nuclear fuel rods at Yongbyon would be reprocessed.

The KEDO consortium, which was supposed to be building the nuclear reactors in North Korea, withdrew. Food aid deliveries were cut off. The United States mounted an effort—the Proliferation Security Initiative—to tighten the screw by stopping ships at sea and reducing North Korea's revenues from drug smuggling and missile exports. Defense Secretary Donald

Rumsfeld announced a new program to modernize the South's defenses, costing U.S. $11 billion over four years to introduce new weapons and strategies, 150 improvements in all, which had proved effective in Iraq. He also announced plans to move the U.S. military headquarters out of central Seoul and the 2nd Infantry Division from the frontline and cut the 37,000 U.S. troops stationed in the South by 12,000. The troops were no longer so vulnerable to a North Korean attack.

The deal struck with the Clinton administration, once hailed as a textbook case of how to deal peacefully with even the most hostile regime, had now completely fallen apart. The engagement camp was horrified. William Perry warned that the United States was heading for war. It was said that now that the North Koreans could manufacture a dozen or more bombs a year, they would begin selling their technology or their bombs to anyone, just like they had done with the missiles.

"I think we are losing control," Perry said. "The nuclear program now underway in North Korea poses an imminent danger of nuclear weapons being detonated in American cities." He warned that the policy of isolation and containment would never work, "We can hardly isolate North Korea more than they are already isolated."[10]

Yet in the wake of Saddam Hussein's rapid defeat in the second Gulf War, and his later arrest and humiliation, Pyongyang was in a much weaker position. The United States now raised its demands, instead of freezing its nuclear program North Korea was now asked to dismantle all its weapons of mass destruction, verifiably and irrevocably. "For the North, it's not time for face-saving or brinkmanship diplomacy," Kim Dae Jung said. "We saw the Hussein regime disappearing in Iraq. North Korea should learn a lesson from that."[11]

Even Jimmy Carter now endorsed these demands. China's position changed too when the war in Iraq started. North Korea suddenly became a top foreign policy issue in early 2002, when U.S. Assistant Secretary of State James Kelly came to Beijing and threatened a pre-emptive strike. According one Western diplomat in Beijing, China's President Hu Jintao asked the People's Liberation Army (PLA) to consider invading the North and overthrowing Kim. The PLA concluded that it lacked the mobility to successfully carry out a lightening attack. Beijing briefly cut off oil supplies to North Korea and found other ways to turn up the pressure on Kim to agree to take part in talks. In August, troops were sent to man the border with North Korea.

Kim Jong Il also fumbled an attempted to divide his enemies by reaching out to Japan. Japanese Prime Minister Junichiro Koizumi decided to take the bold step that was urged on both Presidents Clinton and Bush. He travelled to Pyongyang in the autumn of 2003, hoping to establish diplomatic relations. At first it seemed to go well, then Kim Jong Il confessed to the abduction of 13 Japanese and offered an apology. He hoped to be rewarded with a package of aid and loans worth U.S. $12 billion, a huge advance on the U.S. $300 million package that the Japanese had offered in the early 1990s during indirect talks, led by Kanemaru Shin, the former leader of the ruling LDP Party, about the normalization of relations. Pyongyang let five of the kidnapped Japanese go home, but only temporarily. When after two weeks they chose to stay, Pyongyang refused to allow their families to join them and accused Japan of abducting the people whom it had abducted in the first place. When the Japanese authorities, in response to public opinion, also wanted to know about other Japanese suspected of being abducted and for more details about the deaths of the other seven, the deal collapsed.

Kim Jong Il was fortunate on the other hand that after Kim Dae Jung stepped down, his successor was President Roh Myung-hoon. He narrowly won the 2002 elections on a groundswell of anti-U.S. sentiment among younger voters following an incident in June 2002 when a 60-ton U.S. armored vehicle drove down a narrow two-lane road through some small villages north of Seoul. The driver failed to see two 13-year-old school girls walking on the road to a friend's birthday party and they were crushed to death. The subsequent row on whether Korean courts had the right to try the servicemen for manslaughter, and who should pay for the relocation of the U.S. base in Seoul, brought to the fore a strong South Korean wish to be allowed to deal with North Korea on its own terms and to be treated as an equal. Public opinion polls showed that South Koreans feared the United States might launch a pre-emptive strike and this was the greatest threat to their security. If the United States did launch an attack, Seoul could be destroyed by a North Korean artillery barrage. President Roh's Foreign Minister Yoon Young-kwan reportedly told Bush administration officials that it would be better for Kim Jong Il's regime to build more bombs than for it to collapse.

Under pressure from China, North Korea agreed very reluctantly to Washington's demands to take part in six-nation talks in Beijing. The first round was held in Beijing in August 2003 and ended inconclusively. A second round took place nearly six months later and diplomats from the six countries, including Russia, Japan, and South Korea, seemed set on a very slow and laborious process. North Korea had raised its demands and was no longer just seeking the "negative security assurance" that it had obtained from the Clinton Administration. Now, it wanted a positive security guarantee that Kim Jong Il would be safely kept in power and richly rewarded with aid.

The more Kim Jong Il tried to play for time the worse his position seemed to become. Although it helped him that the United States and its allies failed to find any weapons of mass destruction in Iraq, raising questions over the intelligence information about North Korea, it did not help him as much as it could since he repeatedly flaunted his breach of the NPT and his intention to process the plutonium rods.

Then there followed a series of stunning admissions by Libya, admitting to an extensive and hidden nuclear program. It quickly set about a complete and irreversible WMD disarmament in exchange for the lifting of sanctions and new relations with the United States and its allies. Further evidence emerged of Pakistan's pivotal role in helping Iran, Libya, and North Korea with their covert programs, and of North Korea's role in transferring missile technology to Libya, Iraq, Iran, and Pakistan. All the worst suspicions about the role of North Korea and its double-dealing now seemed either proven or very credible.

Iran confessed that it had managed to hide another extensive effort to enrich uranium and separate plutonium for 18 years from IAEA inspectors. The *New York Times* reported the findings, quoting U.S. intelligence and IAEA reports:

> Tehran acknowledged building two centrifuge plants and finishing a third site, the Kalaye Electric Company, which made centrifuge parts and did extensive centrifuge testing and experimental purification of uranium. Inspectors were blocked from entering the electric company's facilities earlier this year; they now know that behind a false wall of boxes were scores of centrifuges, in what appeared to be a pilot program to produce weapon-grade uranium. That is exactly the kind of program that North Korea is also

believed to be involved in as an alternative to the country's main nuclear weapons development program. The project was discovered a few years ago by South Korean intelligence officials, though its exact location is still a mystery.[12]

North Korea now looks as if it had never taken part in any previous negotiations in good faith. It had actively pursued its nuclear weapons program from 1989–1992 while proposing a wide-ranging treaty—the North-South Joint Declaration on the Denuclearization of the Korean Peninsula—that prohibited both Koreas from constructing uranium-enrichment facilities and committed them to ridding the peninsula of all nuclear weapons. Even after signing another pact with the United States in 1994, it had plunged ahead with a second uranium-enrichment facility. This made it more than likely that it also had a second plutonium program, although this had yet to be proven.

Given this history, even those countries like Russia that opposed many areas of U.S. foreign policy could do little to help North Korea. The events taking place in the Middle East led to a public declaration by IAEA's Director General Mohamed El Baradei that the existing arms control needed to be completely overhauled since there were such glaring past failures. He criticized North Korea in harsh terms:

> After a decade of noncompliance, North Korea has simply walked away from the NPT, and now, it is obvious, believes that its alleged weapons capability can be used as a bargaining chip—for security guarantees, for humanitarian aid, and possibly for raising its stature as a regional power. But at this bargaining table, the stakes are high. In seeking to defuse a volatile situation, the international community must not inadvertently legitimize the possession of nuclear weapons as a currency of power for would-be proliferators—a precedent that could jeopardize the future of the nuclear-arms-control regime.
>
> It is vital—not simply for North Korea, but for other countries watching closely as the scenario unfolds—that "nuclear blackmail" does not become a legitimized bargaining chip. We must not send the message that the threat of acquisition of nuclear weapons is a recognized means of achieving political or security objectives, or that it affords special status or preferential treatment.[13]

U.S. Undersecretary of State for Arms Control and International Security John Bolton repeated the same thought in a speech in Seoul on July 31. "To give in to [Kim Jong Il's] extortionist demands," Mr. Bolton noted, "would only encourage him, and perhaps more ominously, other would-be tyrants around the world. The days of DPRK blackmail are over. Kim Jong Il has already squandered the first decade of his rule," Bolton told the East Asia Institute.

Richard Perle suggested only military action would sway Kim. In a book co-written with David Frum, *An End to Evil: How to Win the War on Terror*, Perle said that an IAEA inspection team should be based in North Korea and allowed to go anywhere at any time. It must be allowed to remove North Korean nuclear scientists and their families to neutral territory and interview them there. If the North demurred, then the United States should take decisive military action.

"But we hope—and this hope is, we think, well-founded—that a credible buildup to an American strike will persuade the Chinese finally to do what they have so often promised to do: bring the North Koreans to heel. In return, the Chinese get peace on their frontiers and a North Korean government friendly to them. It may be that the only way out of the decade-long crisis on the Korean Peninsula is the toppling of Kim Jong Il and his replacement by a North Korean communist who is more subservient to China. If so, we should accept that outcome," Perle writes.

China is bound by a 1961 treaty to come to the North's defense if it is attacked, and the PLA would wish to prevent seeing U.S. troops again on the Yalu River and a thriving democracy across the border. There would also be South Korean opposition and a problem of justifying an attack that might lead to war. The U.S. government would have to show that North Korea poses an immediate danger, but as long as North Korea keeps repeating that it wants to negotiate, this is hard to do. Kim Jong Il's active support of international terrorism diminished in the 1990s and what remains, the drug smuggling, the counterfeiting, the infiltration of agents into the South, and so on does not seem so threatening to the American public. Kim has no signs of planning an international campaign of terror, like Al Qaeda did from its base in Afghanistan and other radical Islamic groups have done. It could be argued that he might be tempted to sell a bomb to other dangerous terrorists, but this is a stretch. He would surely only do so if the price was in the billions, which is more money than he would get from cultivating friendly ties with Japan, South Korea, and the United States.

A U.S. surgical strike would be hard to carry out for other reasons. With over 10,000 underground military sites and hundreds of miles of tunnels and multiple programs, North Korea can hide whatever it wants out of reach of most bombs. The United States now has the BLU-118/B made by Lockheed Martin which chews through six feet of concrete before detonating a high-intensity thermobarbic heat blast that billows through underground passageways and around corners. It is not clear, though, whether this could destroy the North's bunkers.

Then there is the risk that Kim would respond to an attack by "turning Seoul into a sea of fire," which the North threatened to do in 1994. The North has so much artillery close to the DMZ that it could fire up to 500,000 rounds per hour without stopping or moving anything.

On the other hand, Seoul is now protected by an extensive shield of ground-to-air guided missiles and counter-artillery radar systems. Computers aided by antiartillery radar systems can trace shells back to their point of origin and then instantly direct artillery fire or missiles on the enemy guns with pinpoint accuracy. If the North did open a barrage, it would be silenced within minutes by this new military technology. The latest version of OPLAN 5027, the battle plan to respond to a North Korean attack, also incorporates dramatic improvements in the precision, coordination, and mobility learned by the U.S. war machine in two Gulf wars. Since 1994, U.S. forces have also acquired defenses against the missiles the North Koreans have hidden in caves, silos, and on mobile launchers.

The new generation of Patriot missiles, the PAC3s, are probably capable of knocking out most North Korean Scuds. Ground-based midcourse interceptors in Alaska, sea-based midcourse interceptors on Navy Aegis ships, and an Airborne Laser prototype are also ready to shoot down any longer-range North Korean missiles. Still, North Korea has so many rockets that intercepting them all would be hard if not impossible. Just one of them loaded with chemical or even biological weapons could do immense damage. And with so many tunnels in which to hide its weapons, locating all weapons of mass destruction in time would be difficult.

The North has at least 12 known chemical weapons factories that produce 4,500 tons per year of mustard gas, phosgene, sarin, and V-type chemical agents. These weapons could be delivered by rockets, artillery, or even foot soldiers. Kim Jong Il's force of 100,000 Special Operations Forces (SOF) is ready to sneak into the South by submarine, light aircraft, or hovercraft. They could be hard to stop. It would take just a few men carrying one canister of sarin nerve gas to get on the Seoul metro and kill tens of thousands of civilians. Nothing could then stop panic and chaos, and no civil defense system could cope with this sort of calamity.

North Korea's chances once it starts such attacks are very limited. Although the NKPA has amassed huge quantities of tanks and armored personnel carriers, it is now clear from the Second Iraq War that as soon as these are out in the open, they would be defenseless against ground-attack aircraft like the A10 or Apache attack helicopters. The troops that are underfed, poorly trained, and rarely have a chance to practice with live ammunition might easily crumble under a sustained attack. New U.S. military tactics and technology have also allowed the military to halve the time it takes to deploy extra forces. In the early 1990s, U.S. planners wanted 480,000 troops on the field, and by the mid-1990s this figure had risen to 690,000 including 160 navy ships and 1,600 aircraft. Under Donald Rumsfeld's leadership, the Pentagon now thinks a much smaller and more mobile force could do the job and be assembled within less than three weeks. In the event of a North Korean attack, OPLAN 2057 envisages a marine expeditionary force to make an amphibious landing at Wonsan and then march quickly on Pyongyang.

If Kim were faced with defeat like this, then he might, as he once told Hwang, decide to "take the world with him" and use one of the nuclear weapons he is believed to possess. He might even have nuclear weapons small enough to be fitted on ballistic missiles and fire one that could reach an American city.

Many remain absolutely convinced that Kim Jong Il is now committed to negotiations and to reforms because he has no other way out. They counsel patience and slow confidence-building measures. "North Korea wants to escape from its status as a rogue state," Mr. Roh told the American press on January 16, 2003. "I believe once those things are guaranteed, North Korea will abandon its nuclear ambitions. . . . If you treat someone with mistrust he will come back to you with more mistrust and skepticism."[14]

Donald Greg, former ambassador to South Korea and chairman of the Korea Society, thinks Kim has been unfairly demonized when in fact he is a highly intelligent and flexible thinker held back by hardliners. "I believe it is counter productive to treat Kim in a decisive or disdainful manner. For all his defects he demonstrates a willingness to learn from neighbouring countries' economic policies and to differentiate his rule from that of his father." In an article in *Newsweek* from February 3, 2003, "Kim Jong Il: The Truth Behind the Caricature," Donald Greg expresses his belief that Kim actually wants to be another Park Chung Hee, the dictator who boldly transformed the South Korean economy.[15]

A lengthy portrait in the *New York Times Magazine* describes him as an intelligent man who can be courteous and charming, who has never been known to have raised a hand against anyone, who is neither a hard drinker nor a playboy and really resembles "Jimmy Carter on an authoritarian tear." In fact, the article describes him as running a sort of Singaporean dictatorship that mixes high technology with Confucian traditions, a harmless sort of "cyberfeudalism."[16]

The authors of *Crisis on the Korean Peninsula: How to Deal With a Nuclear North Korea*, Michael O'Hanlon and Mike Mochizuki, argue that the "core cause" of the crisis is simply the economy. They avoid the issue of whether it is necessary to remove Kim Jong Il from power to repair the economy by saying they are "agnostic" about this point.

Defectors like Hwang Jang-yop who have known Kim intimately for 40 years believe this is the only point that matters. Hwang believes he has never given up his father's ambition to conquer the South and is now merely playing for time and the right opportunity. "It's like . . . asking whether a venomous snake will bite or not," Hwang said in one interview. "Kim Jong Il has sacrificed a lot—the economy, the people. . . . And all the sacrifices were for the expansion of his military. I don't believe he was (just) trying to display them and brag about the fact that he has these things. He really intends to start a war."[17]

Other defectors say the United States must destroy him. "Many North Koreans believe that the United States is their savior and the only nation that can liberate North Korea," Park said. Furthermore, "U.S. strikes against North Korean targets would force Kim Jong Il to seek asylum in China. Kim Jong Il is a coward. If attacked, he will flee the North. The North Korean army would not fight after the regime collapsed," said Park Gap-dong, former chief of the North's European Section for Propaganda. "Kim Jong Il made the decision that the development of nuclear weapons would be the only guarantee of the safety and security for the North Korean regime. They will not give up these weapons but will instead hide them from inspectors," he believes.[18]

Such men fear that at worst Kim Jong Il has calculated, correctly, that he can use the threat of nuclear war to keep him and his family in power. And if Kim can continue to drive a wedge between Washington and Seoul, he can use his weapons of mass destruction to intimidate the South and force it to do what he wants.

Some geopolitical changes are working in his favor, including the growing influence of China over South Korea. In 2003, South Korea's trade with China at U.S. $58 billion equaled its trade with the United States for the first time. As South Korean companies had invested U.S. $11 billion in China by 2002, the bilateral ties look destined to grow in strength. South Korea might one day soon find itself back in the role of Beijing's vassal state. The anxiety both to win China's backing and avoid antagonizing Pyongyang has meant that Seoul often stays silent when China mistreats North Korean refugees and punishes any South Koreans who help them by giving them long prison sentences. In addition to the protection they ought to receive under international laws, South Korean laws recognize the refugees' right to citizenship. Yet, Seoul has even allowed China to station guards inside the South Korean Consulate to hinder refugees from entering to beg for sanctuary. Mr. Roh has gone so far as to speak out against those "manipulating" the situation to encourage more North Koreans to flee.

Underlying this stance is the comforting assumption that sooner or later North Korea will inevitably have to follow China in slashing the military, privatizing the economy, and building an export industry to finance the food and energy it lacks. South Korean experts say that in July 2003 North Korea introduced one package of economic reforms and more will follow. The reforms legitimized the farmer's markets and increased the monthly average pay of officials from 110 Korean won to 2,000, and some workers such as miners were to be paid 6,000 won. The central government also raised the purchasing and sale price of grain and other commodities to match those on the black market in order to encourage peasants to sell food directly to the state. The centrally planned economy seems no longer to function, and visitors to Pyongyang report more vehicles on the streets, more goods on sale, and other signs of an improving economy.

The slow pace of change and many other false sightings of economic reforms in North Korea in the past make one instinctively cautious. Much of what has happened since Kim Il Sung's death also supports the view that Kim only makes minimum concessions that could be retracted at any moment. There has been no change of heart. His still-growing arsenal of weapons and rockets has allowed him to continue extracting "protection money" and supporting his lavish lifestyle. The North's willingness to take part in any activity—meetings, small NGOs, Taekwondo competitions, the search for MIA remains—is only bought with protracted negotiations on the size of the payoff.

Therefore, the more weapons he acquires, the bigger the rewards. Even so, it is hard to imagine that he would ever get a payoff large enough to make it worthwhile giving up his weapons of mass destruction. Various delegations, including one led by Congressmen Curt Weldon, favor a "grand diplomatic bargain" and propose offering U.S. $3-4 billion a year in exchange for complete verification. Unlike the fictional villains of James Bond movies who acquire a bomb only to blackmail the world, Kim simply cannot put the gold in a Swiss bank account and disappear to enjoy a life of luxury on a tropical island. And why abandon the ultimate deterrent in exchange for paper promises of security?

Afterword

When the North Korean crisis is defined as being just about proliferation or restoring the economy, Kim Jong Il has already won. The issue is no longer a moral one about bringing an evil tyrant to justice and holding him accountable for crimes against humanity, it is reduced to a merely technical problem.

Foremost, North Korea poses a moral question. Between them, Kim Il Sung and his son are responsible for the deaths of over seven million Koreans—three million civilians in the Korean War, and, by some estimates, three million in the famine and at least a million deaths of political prisoners during the last 50 years. After a succession of statesman—Jiang Zemin, Vladimir Putin, Kim Dae Jung, Sweden's Goran Petersen, Madeleine Albright—have returned home to tell us how rational, well informed, witty, charming, and deeply popular Kim Jong Il is. President Bush's judgment that Kim is loathsome seems the only honest and truthful one.

The moral case against the North Korean regime was already strong in 1994, but has been strengthened immeasurably with the famine. After Kim Jong Il deliberately allowed three million of his own people to die in the famine, should he be allowed to stay in power? Genocide is normally interpreted to mean the mass killings of another race—the Turks murdering the Armenians, the Germans against the Jews, the Serbs against the Bosnian Muslims and the Kosovo Albanians, the Tutsi against the Hutu in Rwanda—but this too is a form of genocide.

Rarely, however, has the world community acted against a state because it was murdering its own people. In March 2004, British Prime Minister Tony Blair called for a change in international law to legitimize pre-emptive military action against rogue states "whose leadership cared for no one but themselves; were often cruel and tyrannical towards their own people; and who saw WMD as a means of defending themselves against any attempt external or internal to remove them."[1]

Ever since the Treaty of Westphalia in 1648, a country's internal affairs have not provided grounds for outside interference, but according to Blair, "we surely have a responsibility to act when a nation's people are subjected to a regime such as Saddam Hussein's." Blair defended the notion of intervening on humanitarian grounds, which had been used by NATO to attack Serbia over Kosovo and to intervene in other cases like Sierra Leone. He argued that there needs to be a change in the way the United Nations operates in order to legitimize forceful action against rogue states like North Korea.

In the wake of the invasion of Iraq, the issue of how to deal with rogue states has polarized opinion in Britain, the United States, and the rest of the world. The issue evokes strong passions because it touches on everyone's core beliefs about how to respond to evil and how to defeat it. This is not merely a geopolitical issue; it is a philosophical attitude that determines how people instinctively act in private and public affairs.

Years ago people were equally divided about the best way to deal with the Soviet Empire. Some now credit the tougher and confrontational approach of Ronald Reagan and Margaret Thatcher for its downfall. Others praise the role played by Willy Brandt and his Ostpolitik in the 1970s and other forms of engagement such as the lengthy arms reduction negotiations or the Helsinki accords that recognized the importance of human rights.

We still do not know what brought about the collapse of the Soviet Union, whether external or internal pressures were more important, or whether impersonal economic forces or individuals made a difference. If Mikhail Gorbachev had not entered the Kremlin when he did, would history be different? Certainly the choices he made had consequences that no one, least of all Gorbachev himself, could have predicted.

It is hard to draw practical lessons from the Cold War and apply them to North Korea. It is in most ways unique. Unlike other East Bloc countries, in North Korea there are no nongovernment organizations like the Catholic Church in Poland or the Solidarity trade unions to provide a nucleus of a legitimate alternative authority. North Koreans do not sit down each evening and watch South Korean TV as East Germans watched West German TV. The North Koreans remain hopelessly ignorant of the world around them. Even if they do become better informed, it may not make a difference. East Germany ultimately collapsed because its leader Erich Honecker's authority ultimately derived from Moscow, and when Gorbachev refused to back him, his authority collapsed. Kim is not vulnerable in this way like Honecker. And one must remember too that when trying to borrow from recent history, Kim has also had plenty of time to draw his own lessons from the mistakes of Honecker, Gorbachev, and Ceauçescu.

Another favorite comparison is between China and North Korea. President Roh has urged Bush to follow the example of President Richard Nixon, who in 1972 undertook a visit to Mao Zedong seven years before formal diplomatic relations were established. Roh says that Nixon's daring gesture led to major improvements in China's human rights.[2]

This is a little misleading. Thirty years later China remains as undemocratic as before and the economic changes, profound though they are, are only distantly related to Nixon's visit and any policy of engagement. Within months of Mao's death in 1976, Deng Xiaoping organized a conspiracy with other military leaders, staged a coup d'état, arresting Mao's wife and other loyalists, and formed a new regime. Deng then ushered in a deliberate program of economic reforms drawing on the lessons he learned in 1961 during the Great Leap Forward famine.

Those who urge engagement, and cite precedents like Nixon and Mao, Brandt and Honecker, Reagan and the "evil empire," are not necessarily offering a guide to future events. Rather, they are saying that even if a Western leader considers his counterpart to be "evil," to have committed crimes odious enough to put him beyond the pale of civilized society, it may still be necessary and advantageous to deal directly with him.

Another line of thinking holds that it is misleading to describe North Korea as a rogue state because Kim Jong Il and his father have always acted quite rationally, consistently, and indeed predictably. Perhaps one will even see them as sane if one regards them as trying to preserve North Korea's "unique way of life." Other states like Israel, South Africa, South Korea, and Taiwan have also in the past felt it necessary to try to develop nuclear weapons that would secure their survival, so why not North Korea?

If Kim Jong Il, and his father before him, have a legitimate right to keep their dynasty going, then it could be argued that they have acted with shrewd calculation, successfully outmaneuvering opponents at home and abroad. Kim Jong Il could thus be termed "rational" for rejecting any political or market reforms. Look at how other Communist leaders in the Soviet Union and its allies were swept aside once they opened up their economy. Having seen what happened to Saddam Hussein, who failed to acquire a nuclear bomb in time and could not keep the Americans at bay, it was logical for Pyongyang to acquire more WMD as a deterrent.

By the same logic, we can say that Kim Jong Il was right to reject a policy of following China's example and embracing economic reforms. Once the Democratic People's Republic of Korea starts to imitate the Republic of Korea, then it has no further reason to exist because it would no longer offer the Korean nation a credible alternative. That was the fate of the German Democratic Republic. Moreover, Kim Jong Il has correctly judged that once the full extent of his cruel record and his greed are revealed, his bogus claims to divinity will evaporate and with them his hold over the minds of the North Koreans.

Whether Kim is deemed rational and a cunning preserver of the North Korean state or simply a madman or rogue, there is something abhorent about the thought that engagement could leave Kim Jong Il and his family in power and handing out construction contracts worth tens of billions of dollars. It does not seem just that South Korea's government should be bending over backward to avoid offending Kim Jong Il and stiffing his critics like Hwang.

Anyone proposing to offer Kim Jong Il cast-iron security guarantees and unconditional aid thus has to engage in a kind of "double think." They must ignore their better instincts in order to justify engaging him and simultaneously believe that, given his track record, he is capable of unleashing nuclear weapons. Chinese diplomats routinely claim that there would be tremendous civil disorder if he fell from power. Kim therefore becomes the pillar of regional stability. South Korean officials claim the burden of restoring the North Korean economy is too huge even to think about. Instead of being seen as the chief obstacle who needs to be removed in order to make progress, Kim Jong Il is elevated into becoming the vital conduit for change.

From there it is but a short step to argue, as some do, that it is wise to keep him in power and achieve a "soft landing for North Korea" and that anyone trying to escape from North Korea should indeed be arrested and sent back for fear of encouraging a destabilizing refugee exodus. Equally, they argue, it would be wrong to encourage an alternative government in exile. How damaging it would be for everyone if his victims were allowed to air criticisms of his regime; this would only encourage his paranoia and deter him from embarking on reforms.

There is also a line of complacent thinking that draws heavily on a version of the "historical inevitability" theory of Hegel and Marx, only in this case it is not Communism that is inevitable but democracy, or at least market economics. As North Korea has proved to be such a resounding economic failure—and South Korea such a success—it is inevitable that sooner or later North Korea and its problems will be taken care of. All one has to do is sit back and wait for the tide of history to sweep North Korea into making all the right changes.

Perhaps this last is true, but so far it is not turning out that way. After 1989, North Korea found itself destitute, friendless, and destined to disappear from the map along with the Soviet Union, East Germany, Yugoslavia, and other unloved creations held together by fear. Fifteen years later, Kim Jong Il now finds himself supported, and indeed praised, by new friends, all seemingly anxious to advise him on how best to prolong his rule. This is presented as an honorable path in a stream of articles being published urging Western leaders to overlook his faults.[3] Those who decided to collaborate with Kim have been rewarded. Kim Dae Jung won the Nobel Peace Prize. The United Nations too won that prize in 2001, and the World Food Progam and the United Nations High Commission for Refugees escaped censure, let alone any critical scrutiny in their dealings with North Korea. China too has escaped condemnation for forcibly returning the escapees and punishing the Good Samaritans who tried to help them. In fact it has been repeatedly praised for its constructive help in solving the crisis.

The Agreed Framework, held up as a model of modern peacemaking and the high point of engagement with Kim, failed in many ways. It did not freeze Kim's nuclear weapons program and did nothing to remove the threat of weapons of mass destruction from the world. It not only did not prevent the North from enlarging its stock of WMD, but it also gave the DPRK more time to devote to research and development of missiles and nuclear technology. It did avert war, however it did not save lives. Millions died in North Korea and one wonders whether without the aid that flowed in from 1998 on, the regime would have collapsed because it could no longer have fed even its core members.

Kim Dae Jung helped stabilize Kim Jong Il's rule when it was at its weakest, but there has been no reward. No political or economic reforms of any importance followed. Those who tried to engage Kim over the past decade, including the United Nations, the South Korean government, the chaebols, and others, have little to show for it. There have been some small and very incremental changes in Kim's rule, a corrosive corruption that is weakening the Juche faith but this is not enough to justify consigning the North Koreans to his tender care for further decades.

Children are still dying of malnutrition. The United Nations and many other parties who tried to help the North Koreans have had to pay the price of for repeating his lies and excusing his personal responsibility for the famine. In order to stay in the country, they too claimed that he was a victim of outside forces, and the collapse of the economy was blamed on the weather or the loss of foreign aid. His dominant role in running the country from the 1970s onward was not recognized, and his record of blocking economic reforms and of squandering the country's small resources on his palaces was covered up or not investigated. In the three years from 1998 Kim used the extra aid merely to indulge himself. The number of U.S. $1,000 Omega watches that he imported from Switzerland tripled to total $10 million in 2001.

It is also profoundly wrong that no one can recall the name of a single one of his victims. There are no prisoners of conscience in North Korea. No pictures of graves or executions. No equivalent of Nelson Mandela, no Aung San Suu Kyi. No voice other than that of the ruling party's escapes from behind its impenetrable walls. Even the mere idea of internal opposition to Kim's rule is ridiculed as preposterous. No one would dare finance an underground opposition party. The very few who have tried to help the refugees have been fined, threatened, imprisoned, and sometimes killed.

Instead of seeing the North Wind and the Sun at work with persuasion and peace conquering force, we have seen another of Aesop's fables enacted.

Kim has gone on to terrify his subjects into submission, and now, with his arsenal of WMD, he is terrifying his neighbors with what he might do to them. The powers of the world are like the mice in another of Aesop's tales: They agree that the best way to deal with the cat is to hang a bell around his neck to give them warning of his approach —only none of the mice is brave enough to be the one that bells the cat. The past 15 years show that real change can come only when Kim Jong Il and his family are recognized as evil tyrants, removed from power, and put on trial. Otherwise Kim Jong Il will hand power to one of his sons and perpetuate this dynasty. Is there nothing that can be done to stop him, or other Rogue States?

The question is not new. The ancient world's Pax Romana was often disrupted by the challenges of wicked kings or rebellious tribes, which hindered Roman efforts to establish common standards and rules to peacefully regulate the affairs of the world. Dictators like Kim Jong Il thrive on wars and deliberately seek to whip up fears and keep tensions on the boil. A dictator is in fact a Roman term for a leader who has been granted emergency powers to govern the state during a national crisis, in particular, a war. The leader of a rogue state is one who inverts this process by artificially fostering a state of war in order to prolong or justify his dictatorship.

What can we do to prevent such dictators from continually stirring the pot? We have abolished other age-old evils like slavery and piracy and we could do the same to limit the spread of nuclear weapons and curtail the threat of rogue regimes. In the 19th century, it took a century of international cooperation to wipe out these practices which for millennia had seemed part of the natural order of things. Without these achievements, the modern world would not exist. Further steps could be taken in the coming century to ensure basic human rights.

The story of North Korea shows that the world needs new mechanisms to deal with the threat of rogue states. These new processes must include two elements: a new framework in international law as Tony Blair is proposing and a method to enforce these laws through the legitimate use of military force.

The current system clearly does not work and the United Nations has became discredited by its repeated failures in Iraq, Rwanda, Kosovo, Bosnia, Somalia, Sudan and, of course, in North Korea. The flaws in the UN machinery include the fact that major states often block effective responses to unfolding genocide or delay imposing sanctions. In the case of North Korea, it is folly, as this book has shown, for the UN to continue treating North Korea as a normal and legitimate member state at the expense of helping the millions of its citizens who died of hunger. Any country that requires nine years of emergency food aid is clearly not normal and needs special consideration.

It is also patently quite absurd that one arm of the UN should be acting as North Korea's quartermaster and feeding a third of the population while North Korea refuses to cooperate with another arm, the International Atomic Energy Agency inspectors. It is all too similar to what happened in Iraq where the UN had a dual role of delivering food and medicine through the oil-for-food program while investigating the hidden WMD programs. It is clearly in the interests of the international community to do something to improve the system to prevent a repetition of the events in Iraq. There must be new mechanisms to ensure that the United States, the world's most powerful country, retains trust in the effectiveness of the UN system to regulate relations between states.

After the 9/11 attacks, the United States doubted the effectiveness of the UN to police countries deemed to pose a threat to its security and acted unilaterally in Afghanistan and Iraq. This has created both a crisis in international relations but also an opportunity to think about changing the UN to make it work better. Dealing with rogue states should be easier than dealing with international terrorism for the obvious reason that the UN is all about the conduct of states rather than amorphous terrorist groups like Al-Qaeda.

Of course, many people will raise questions about who has the right to judge what is a rogue state, or to say when it should be outlawed, and who should be permitted to use force against its rulers. For much of the 19th century the powerful Royal Navy patrolled the high seas stopping and inspecting ships of any nationality which it suspected of transporting slaves. It did so even though in some countries like Brazil (and Korea) the trade was not declared illegal until the 1890s. Those countries which took a leading role on eradicating slavery, piracy and opium trading (despite earlier being prime beneficiaries in these lucrative but immoral activities) have retained a tradition of undertaking such crusades and willingness to deploy their armies in such causes.

It is also obvious that many nations are loath to authorize the United States and its Anglo-Saxon allies like Britain to act as the world sheriff.

When the UN allowed Saddam Hussein to abuse the UN oil-for-food program and to siphon off money for bribes and palaces while simultaneously refusing to cooperate with the weapons inspectors, the UN became so discredited that Washington invaded Iraq in a pre-emptive move. No one would wish a repetition of these events on the Korean Peninsula. As events in Iraq have unfolded, this aversion has only become stronger and the need for new international rules has increased.

It is surely not only realistic but also imperative to establish accepted benchmarks for identifying a rogue state's behavior just as there is a definition of the crime of genocide. Once rogue behavior is identified as such, the world could agree on a set of tough measures such as targeting the assets of the leadership, penalties for countries deemed to help rogue states with weapons or nuclear technology, and tightly enforced conditions on aid.

No such parameters would be perfect, of course, but defining offenders and meting out prescribed punishments would be an improvement on the tools currently available. For instance, it should be made difficult for China to continue supporting North Korea, feteing Kim Jong Il, and repatriating escaping North Koreans. The latter especially is tantamount to supporting a modern version of slavery. Kim Jong Il's behavior in contravention of basic standards needs to be officially recognized as such in China and elsewhere, and he should be liable to be held personally accountable for his deeds at an international tribunal or the Court of International Justice. Finally, there needs to be strictly defined limits on the length of time a state can breach or abuse the Non-Proliferation Treaty without provoking war or military reprisals.

Some may suspect that it is wishful thinking that one could eradicate the threat of nuclear weapons for good in the same way that the world has cooperated in wiping out diseases like polio. Once a technology has been invented it is hard to uninvent it or to stop this knowledge from spreading. It certainly may require a long term policing effort. But this is not the same problem as dealing resolutely with North Korea or similar states. With the right political will, the world could quickly agree on remedies to disarm a criminal state clearly unable to feed its own population and which tries to holds its own people as hostages and to take its neighbours hostage with nuclear weapons. North Korea and Kim Jong Il, a rogue state and its rogue leader, could and should be held to account.

Notes

Preface

1. "Rogue States cannot hope to blackmail America or her allies," *The Times*, March 1, 2000.

Chapter 1

1. Korean Buddhist Sharing Movement (KBSN), *The Food Crisis of North Korea Witnessed by Food Refugees*, Reported in five issues: February 23,1998; March 23, 1998; May 23, 1998; and November 23, 1998; also Medecins Sans Frontieres (MSF), "North Koreas: Testimonies of Famine, Refugee Interviews from the Sino-Korean Border," New York: Doctors Without Borders/Medecins Sans Frontieres, August 1998 (Posted to their website: http://www.doctors withoutborder.org/publications/reports/before10999/korea_1998.shtm on October 2,1998); Korean Buddhist Sharing Movement, *Daily Life and Human Rights of North Korean Food Refugees in China: Based on Field Survey in 2,479 Villages in Three Northeast States in China*, Seoul, June 1999; and Courtland Robinson, Myung Ken Lee, Kenneth Hill, and Gilbert M. Burnham, "Mortality in North Korean Migrant Households: A Retrospective Study," *Lancet*, Vol. 354, No. 9175, July 1999.
2. Associated Press, "North Korea Says 220,000 Dead in Famine," May 10, 1999.
3. Don Kirk, "North Korean Desperation—Reports of Executions to Halt Hunger Crimes," *International Herald Tribune*, March 24, 1999.
4. Nutritional Survey of the Democratic People's Republic of Korea: Report by the EU, UNICEF and WFP of a Study Undertaken in Partnership with the Government of DPRK, Rome, United Nations World Food Program, 1998.
5. It was only around 2002, a decade after the start of severe food shortages, that the state started to reduce the population of Pyongyang, where 13 percent of the country lives.
6. "Kim Jong Il Berates Cadres for Food Anarchy" (in Korean), *Wolgan Chosun* (Chosun Monthly), Seoul, March 20, 1997, pp. 306–31; translation as "Kim Jong Il, Speech at Kim Il Sung University, December 1996!" British Broadcasting Corporation, March 21, 1997.

7. Korean Central Television, "Plant Makes 'Substitute Food' to Serve to Employees," Pyongyang, July 10,1998, BBC Summary of World Broadcasts, July 13, 1998; Korean Central Television, "Hospital Makes 'Substitute Food Powder' to Supplement Diet," Pyongyang, July 20,1998, BBC Summary of World Broadcasts July 22, 1998.
8. Keith Richburg, "North Korea on Brink of New Crisis," *Washington Post*, October 20, 1997. Also see "Beyond a Wall of Secrecy, Devastation" and "Seeing a Different Face of Famine."
9. Peter Hennessy, *The Secret State—Whitehall and the Cold War*, London, Penguin Books, 2002.
10. Jasper Becker, "A Bridge to Their Deaths," *South China Morning Post*, May 17, 2000.

Chapter 2

1. KCNA, "NK's Leader Simple Diet Gives Rise to People's Loyalty," August 22, 1999.
2. KCNA, "Both the leader and the people; sharing sweet and bitter together," June 9, 1999.
3. Ermanno Furlanis, *Asia Times*, August 4, 2001; *Heartland Magazine* 1-2001.
4. Konstantin Pulikovsky, "Bow When You Hear that Name," *Christian Science Monitor*, March 14, 2003; James Brooke, "A Telling North Korean Journey," *New York Times*, May 12, 2002.
5. RIA Novosti, Russian News Agency.
6. Interview with German Cold War historian Bernd Schaefer, August 2003.
7. Richard M. Steers, *Made in Korea—Chung Ju Yung and the Rise of Hyundai*, New York, Routledge, 2001.
8. Kenji Fujimoto, *Kim Jong Il's Cook – I Saw His Naked Body*, Seoul, Chosun Ilbo, September 22, 2003. Translated from original and published by Fuso Publishing House in Tokyo.
9. Shigemi Sato, "*Tell-all sushi chef in hiding*," Agence France Press, Tokyo, July 24, 2003. I was unable to fully confirm his consumption of cognac and wine, but French trade statistics for 2003 show that North Korea directly imported 225 liters of cognac from France. *Shukan Post*, June 25, 2003.
10. In *Mein Kampf*, Hitler wrote "All this was inspired by the principle—which is quite true in itself—that in the big lie there is always a certain force of credibility; because the broad masses of a nation are always more easily corrupted in the deeper strata of their emotional nature than consciously or voluntarily; and thus in the primitive simplicity of their minds they more readily fall victims to the big lie than the small lie, since they themselves often tell small lies in little matters but would be ashamed to resort to large-scale falsehoods. It would never come into their heads to fabricate colossal untruths, and they would not believe that others could have the impudence to distort the truth so infamously. Even though the facts which prove this to be so may be brought clearly to their minds, they will still doubt and waver and will continue to think that there may be some other explanation. For the grossly impudent lie always leaves traces behind it, even after it has been nailed down, a fact which is known to all expert liars in this world and to all who conspire together in the art of lying. These people know only too well how to use falsehood for the basest purposes."

In an attempt to stem the southward flow of nationalists, the Soviet Red Army organized a Soviet-style mass celebration of the March First Movemment on March 1, 1946 at the Pyongyang Rail Station Plaza. This was the second Soviet-style mass gathering in North Korea—the first being the welcome home mass meeting for Kim Il Sung on October 14, 1945.

11. Lee Wha Rang, "The March 1, 1946 Plot," Joonahn Ilbo Archives; Lee Wha Rang, "Who was Kim Gu?" March 30, 2000; Lee Wha Rang, "What Is Jucheism?"

12. Roger Tennant, *A History of Korea*, New York, Kegan Paul International, 1996, p. 255.

13. Suh, p. 138.

14. See Weathersby, Cold War History Project: Document VI: Ciphered Telegram from Shtykov to Vyshinsky, January 19, 1950.

15. Bruce Kennedy,"The Moscow Connection," CNN Interactive, New documents reveal Kremlin's undercover participation in the Korean War Cold War Series

16. Mike Feinsilber, "Proof Soviets Lied," Associated Press, November 16, 1998.

Chapter 3

1. *Washington Post*, February 13, 1997.

2. Hwang Jang-yop.

3. Interview with Hungarian scholar Balazs Szalontai, August 2003.

4. "He worshipped Germany's Hitler from an early date and wanted to become such a dictator as Hitler," wrote Hwang in a treatise provided to *Monthly Chosun* reporter Kim Yong Sam.

5. The problem of human rights in North Korea

6. In Nazi Germany, complete and total authority was vested in the Fuehrer, who directly controlled all institutions. Many of the following statements from the Organization Book of the National Socialist Party of Germany seem to have been duplicated in Juche textbooks, the rules of Korean Workers Party, and the whole Suryong theory.

> As Organization Book of the Nazi Party states: "The will of the Fuehrer is the Party's law." (1814-PS)
> The first commandment for Party members is that "The Fuehrer is always right." (1814-PS)
> "He (the Fuehrer) is responsible only to his conscience and the German people." (1814-PS)
> "The Fuehrer's power descends to subleaders in a hierarchical order."
> "The Fuehrer unites in himself all the sovereign authority of the Reich; all public authority in the state as well as in the movement is derived from the authority of the Fuehrer. We must speak not of the states authority but of the Fuehrers authority if we wish to designate the character of the political authority within the Reich correctly. The state does not hold political authority as an impersonal unit but receives it from the Fuehrer as the executor of the national will. The authority of the Fuehrer is complete and all-embracing; it unites in itself all the means of political direction; it extends into all fields of national life; it embraces the entire people, which is bound to the Fuehrer in loyalty and obedience. The authority of the Fuehrer is not limited by checks and controls, by special autonomous bodies or individual rights, but it is free and independent, all-inclusive and unlimited."
> "The Fuehrer-Reich of the (German) people is founded on the recognition that the true will of the people cannot be disclosed through parliamentary votes and

plebiscites but that the will of the people in its pure and uncorrupted form can only be expressed through the Fuehrer." (2771-PS)

"Thus at the head of the Reich, stands a single Fuehrer, who in his personality embodies the idea which sustains all and whose spirit and will therefore animate the entire community." (2780-PS)

7. Lee Hy-Sang, *North Korea—A Strange Socialist Fortress*, Westport, Conn., Praeger, 2001, p. 10.
8. Sources on Chondoism: Kim Il Sung, "The Chongdyo People's Movement, National Movement and Cultural Movement. With the Century 15.5" and Kim Young-gan, "The Confucian Christian Context in Korean Christianity," Thesis at Sungkyul University.
9. Sources on Unification Church: Reverend Sun Myung Moon, "God's Will and the World," Sermon; Also Rev. Moon, "Victory or Defeat and the Present Time," Sermon given in Seoul, December 5, 1971; *The Healing of The World—An Introduction to the Life and Teachings of Sun Myung Moon Divine Principle*, Black Book, 1973; *God's Day* ' Midnight Address, Jan 1., 1992; Reverend Michael Jenkins, "The Elder Son Nation—America," Sermon, March 31, 2003; "Teaching of Rev. Moon Address Upon Arrival at East Garden," Sermon, April 6, 2000; Richard Johnson, "The Dark Side of the Moon Family," *New York Post*, July 10, 1998; Harry V. Martin & David Caul, *The Moonies*, Napa Sentinel, 1995.
10. Reverend Sun Myung Moon, Black Book, 1973, p. 520.

Chapter 4

1. "Testimony of Ahn Myong-chol" *Wolgan Chosun* (Chosun Monthly), March 1995, p. 175, and "Testimony of Ahn Myong-chol" *Wolgan Chosun*, July 31, 2003.
2. Telephone interview with Hungarian scholar Balaczs Szalontai, August 2003.
3. Prof. Haruhisa Ogawa, "Correlation between Juche Ideology and Political Prison Camps in North Korea," Paper presented at The 1st International Conference on North Korean Human Rights and Refugees, Seoul, 1999.
4. There were 17 in total at Kungshim, Hakpo, Hamyon, Kokonwon, Aoji, Obong, Kobang, Dokchon, Sungheung, Shinchang, Doksan, Heungnyong, Sokpoom, Anju, Kaechon, Yoduk, and Sariwon.
5. Richard Kagan, Matthew Oh, & David Weissbrodt, "Human Rights in the DPRK," Report prepared for the Minnesota Lawyers International Human Rights Committee and Asia Watch, Minnesota, December 1988.
6. *White Paper on Human Rights in North Korea*, Korea Institute for National Unification, Annual Report, Seoul, 2002.
7. Telephone interview with Hungarian scholar Balaczs Szalontai, August 2003.
8. *White Paper on Human Rights in North Korea*, Korea Institute for National Unification, Annual Report, Seoul, 2002.
9. "Testimony of Ahn Myong-chol," *Wolgan Chosun*(Chosun Monthly), March 1995, p. 175, and "Are they Telling Us the Truth ?" International Group of Human Rights Volunteers, Tokyo, Japan, March 2002.

    However his father's memoir *With the Century* makes it clear that the family was in the Russian Far East at the time his son was born in 1941. North Koreans were therefore obliged to accept two completely contradictory stories. Kim Jong Il insisted that they accept his birth as a year later inside Korean territory at a secret guerrilla camp on Mt. Paektu.

10. See various KCNA Reports in 1997: "Slogan-bearing trees discovered Pyongyang," February 6; "New revolutionary stories Pyongyang," February 6; "Pyongyang," August 27; "Pyongyang," September 12; and "Slogan-bearing trees praising Kim Jong Suk—Pyongyang," December 24.

These tree-carving sightings multiplied as the state sought to convince the population that the son's succession was pre-ordained at his birth. The Korean News Agency reported: "More than 200 slogan-bearing trees have been found so far throughout the country. Among the slogans discovered in north and south Hamgyong provinces and other areas are 'Korea, let the world know of the birth of the bright star above Mt. Paektu' and 'Let us the 20 million Koreans boast of the sun which rose above Mt. Paektu.'" More and more began to be found even in places implausibly distant from the secret camp that acclaimed "the birth on Mt. Paektu of the bright star heir to President Kim Il Sung" and the "Star of new general who will succeed to President Kim Il Sung has risen above Mt. Paektu brightening Korea."

"The slogans, valuable treasure of the nation, encourage the Korean people in the forced march for the final victory," the news agency said, adding that they "reflect the Korean people's unshakable will to hold General Kim Jong Il in high esteem and their best wishes for longevity and high glory to him." Those convinced by these signs and wonders were also supposed to believe the absurd slogan that "Kim Il Sung is Kim Jong Il and Kim Jong Il is Kim Il Sung."

11. Lee Soon Ok, *Eyes of the Tailless Animals—Prison Memoirs of a North Korean Woman*, Bartlesville, Okla., Living Sacrifice Book Company, 1999.

12. Choe Sang-Hun, "South Korean POW finds his way home after 50 years," Associated Press, July 20, 2003, and Yonhap, "Couple Reunites after 30 years," July 23, 2003.

13. "Are they Telling Us the Truth ?" International Group of Human Rights Volunteers, Tokyo, Japan, March 2002.

14. John Bolton, Speech to East Asia Institute in Seoul, July 2003.

15. Don Kirk, "North Korean Desperation—Reports of Executions to Halt Hunger Crimes," *International Herald Tribune*, March 24, 1999.

16. The White Paper gives one date, but Ahn gives the latter. He also refers to another possible uprising in Camp 13 that took place in 1989.

17. Interview with Hwang Jang-yop, "A Rare Portrait of North Korea," *Time Magazine*, September 7, 1998. "North Korea has been negotiating with the U.S. about establishing a US liason officer. But when I was in North Korea, Kim Jong Il was adamant about not allowing the Americans to set one up in Pyongyang. He thought he could keep other embassies under his control and cut off all contacts between those diplomats and North Koreans. But Kim thought keeping the Americans under control would be difficult because they are not an obedient people. Kim's biggest fear in allowing the Americans into North Korea is that his tyrannical rule will be exposed to the world—that when the Americans tell the world, everyone will believe them."

18. The *Rodong Shinmun* published an editorial in 1993 that said, "There is no organization and no place in North Korea whatever which violates human rights."

19. "What happened at 'Yoduk?'" *Chosun Ilbo*, November 10, 2001.

Chapter 5

1. Eric Croddy, Senior Research Associate, Non-Proliferation Program, "Vinalon, the DPRK, and Chemical Weapons Precursors," Center for Non-Proliferation Studies, February 4, 2003.

2. *Choson Ilbo,* November 11, 2002.
3. The goals were to raise annual electricity output to 10 megawatts, coal output to 120 million tons, steel output to 15 million tons, and grain production to 15 million tons.
4. Interview with German Cold War researcher Bernd Schaefer, August 2003.
5. Richard M. Steers, *Made in Korea—Chung Ju Yung and the Rise of Hyundai,* New York, Routledge, 2001, p. 105.
6. Lee, p. 137
7. WFP Special Alert No. 270, September 6, 1996.
8. Interview with Dr. Kim Young-hoon at the Korea Rural Economic Institute, a think tank for the agriculture ministry, and Koh Il-Dong, a researcher at the state-run Korea Development Institute, Seoul, July 2003.
9. Lee, p. 141.
10. The country had one plant at Hungnam built by the Japanese in the 1930s, which relied on an outdated coal-gasification technology and produced half of the two million tons of fertilizer that the economy needed every year. By 1998, this and the other 12 plants had stopped production altogether.
11. Roger Dean Du Mars, "Pyongyang 'Poisoning the Country,'"AFP, April 24, 2001.
12. Prof. Chong-Sik Lee, "Political Leadership and Economy of North Korea," Conference Speech, University of Pennsylvania, March 1995.
13. Lee, p. 105.
14. *Nordkorea: Ein Land im Banne der Kims,* Böbligen, Anita Tykve Verlag, 1994.
15. Network for North Korean Democracy and Human Rights, Vol. II, Winter 2003.
16. Norbert Vollertsen Testimony, United States Senate, Committee on Judiciary, June 21, 2002.
17. Lee, p. 157.

Chapter 6

1. *Washington Times,* April 19, 1994.
2. *Japanese Monthly Shukan Bunshun,* April 16, 1992; also *North Korea: After Collapse of Socialist Camp,* Naewoe Press, May 1993; Fiammetta Rocco, "Why I Had to Flee My Country," *Daily Telegraph,* September 30, 1997.
3. Andrew Natsios, *The Great North Korean Famine—Famine, Politics, and Foreign Policy,* Washington, D.C., United States Institute Peace Press, 2001, p. 1987.
4. John Gavenfeld, "The _____from Hell," *The Guardian,* April 4, 2003.
5. Translation of Hwang Jang-yop's writings, *The Problem of Human Rights in North Korea 1 & 2,* Network for North Korea Rights and Democracy.
6. KCNA, antidote about King Jong Il, February 23, 2001; KCNA, "Ornamental Silver Knives and Gold Rings," November 6, 1996; KCNA, "300th Birth of Triplets at Pyongyang Hospital," December 11, 1996; "Korea's Lucky Triplets Seized," *Daily Telegraph,* February 31, 2003.

Chapter 7

1. I rely chiefly on the articles and books by Joseph Bermudez for the information on the North Korean military.

2. Pyongyang, *On Some Issues of Conforming Our Society to Kim-Il-Sungism*, February 19, 1976.

3. Interview with Hwang, *Die Welt*, May 10, 1998. "Kim must personally approve sending every single agent—especially on major operations," Hwang said.

4. Fred Hiatt, "Japan Kidnappings May Lead to North Korean Spy Case," *Washington Post*, January 20, 1988; Erid Talmadge, "Details Emerge of Lives of Abducted Japanese Most Died Young, Reports Reveal," Associated Press, September 20, 2002; "Abductee May Have Been Executed After Tutoring Plane Bomber," *Japan Times*, September 21, 2002.

5. Unmesh Kher, "Accounted for, at Last," *Time*, September 20, 2002.

6. Richard Kagan, Matthew Oh, & David Weissbrodt, "Human Rights in the DPRK," Report prepared for the Minnesota Lawyers International Human Rights Committee and Asia Watch, December 1988.

7. For information on North Korea's missile program I relied on: "North Korea: Nuclear Missile Chronology," *The Risk Report*, Vol. 6, No. 6, December 2000; The Wisconsin Project on Nuclear Arms; Bertil Lintner & Steve Stecklow, "Paper Trail Exposes Missile Merchants," *FAR Eastern Economic Review*, February 13, 2003; Papers prepared by the Center for Non-Proliferation Studies at the Monterey Institute of International Studies; Statement of Ko Young-Hwan in his appearance before the Subcommittee of International Security, Proliferation, and Federal Services of the Committee on Governmental Affairs, U.S. Senate, October 2, 1997.

8. Alain Pilon, "Arsenal of the Axis," *Time Asia Magazine*, July 14, 2003.

9. James Dao, "North Korea Is Said to Export Drugs to Get Foreign Currency," *New York Times*, May 21, 2003; and Jay Solomon & Jason Dean, "Heroin Bust Point to Source of Funds for North Koreans," *Wall Street Journal*, April 23, 2003. This article quotes a defector, Kim Dok Hong, who says Kim personally gave instructions to grow opium.

10. Kim Ah-Young, "Targeting Pyongyang's Drug Trade Addiction," *Asia Times*, June 18, 2003.

11. Giles Whittell, "Kim Sells Workers to Gulags in Debt Deal," *The Times*, August 6, 2001.

12. Mary Jordan & Kevin Sullivan, "Pinball Wizards Fuel North Korea," *Washington Post*, June 7, 1996.

13. "N. Korea buys weapons despite poor economy," Associated Press Wire, October 22, 2003.

Chapter 8

1. AFP, "South Korea Stopped U.S. Strike on North Korea's Former President," May 24, 2000.

2. Interview with Robert Gallucci by CNN's Jamie McIntyre, October 4, 1999.

3. PBS Frontline TV Documentary Program, "Kim's Nuclear Gamble," Transcripts of Interview with William Perry Broadcast in 1999. Also Interviews with Richard Perle.

4. Roger Tennant, *A History of Korea*, New York, Kegan Paul International, 1996.

5. Carter J. Eckert, Lee Ki-baik, Young Ick Lew, Robinson Michael, & Wagner Edward, *Korea Old and New*, Korea Institute, Harvard University, Ilchokak Publishers, Seoul, 1990, p. 250.

6. Michael Breen, *The Koreans—Who Are They, What They Want, Where Their Future Lies,* London, St. Martin's Press, 1998.

7. Interview with Author, Seoul, January 2004.

8. *Zheleznogorosk Reprocessing plants in Siberia Working paper,* Working Paper 4, Nuclear Russia on Bellona Web (www.bellona.no), April 1995; *Krasnoyarsk-26/ Zheleznogorsk* (Global Security.org); North Korea in fact was caught trying to employ unemployed scientists from Zheleznogorosk in 1992.

9. Interview with Author, Seoul, January 2004.

10. Chang Sun-Sup, "The KEDO Light Water Reactor Project: Its Implications for Peace and Inter-Korean Relations LNCV," Korean Peninsula: Enhancing Stability and International Dialogue, Rome, June 1–2, 2000.

11. James Risen, "Russia Helped U.S. on Nuclear Spying Inside North Korea," *New York Times,* January 20, 2003.

12. "Former Pyongyang agent speaks to DPJ—Ex-engineer warns of nuclear program, makes plea on behalf of defectors," November 21, 2002; Doug Struck, "A Cold Shoulder for the Spy Who Came in from the Cold," *Washington Post,* November 28, 2002; Maril Yamaguchi, "Mysterious Spy Intrigues Japan with Stories of N. Korean A bomb," Associated Press, February 7, 2003.

13. Associated Press, "North Korea defector creates stir, Japanese government cancels testimony on nuclear claims," June 18, 2003; James T. Hackett, "North Korea Ripe for Change," *Washington Times,* December 2, 2002.

14. Yossef Bodansky & Vaughn S. Forrest, "Pyongyang and the U.S. Nuclear gambit," Task Force On Terrorism & Unconventional Warfare, House Republican Research Committee, U.S. House of Representatives, August 11, 1994.

    Kang Myong-to, the son-in-law of Kang Song-san, the DPRK prime minister who defected in May 1994, also reported that the DPRK "already possess[ed] five nuclear warheads" in October 1993, and would have about ten warheads by the end of 1994.

15. Douglas Frantz, "US Claims on North Korea Doubted," *Los Angeles Times,* September 12, 2003; David E. Sanger, "New C.I.A. Concerns on North Korean Weapons," *New York Times,* November 9, 2003; David E. Sanger & William J. Broad, "Surprise Word on Nuclear Gains by Iran and North Korea," *New York Times,* November 12, 2003.

Chapter 9

1. Interview with Author, Seoul, January 2004.

2. The adjacent South Hwanghae province grows a quarter of the country's rice.

3. "Kim Jong Il's candid conversation caught on tape," Transcript from a conversation that took place on the evening of April 25, 1998 at Kim Jong Il's villa was provided by Japanese intelligence and published in the South Korean monthly magazine *Chosun Wolgan.*

4. Korean Endgame, p. 27.

5. His name is also sometimes spelled Kim Cong U.

6. PBS Frontline, "Kim's Nuclear Gamble," February 26, 2003.

7. Donald Macintyre, "Northern Exposure," *Time Magazine,* November 4, 2002.

8. "Tonga Ilbo reports on military coup attempts against Kim Jong Il in nineties," BBC Summary of Worldwide Broadcasts, 1995.

9. BBC Monitoring, November 15, 1993.

10. Choi Ju-hwal, "An Inside Perspective: North Korea's Unalterable Stance," *Institute of East Asian Studies*, Vol. 11, No. 4, Winter 1999.

11. KBS Television, "Big Explosion Reported," Seoul, July 14, 1998; BBC Summary of Worldwide Broadcasts, July 16, 1998.

12. Kim Kwang-in, "NK Exhumes and Decapitates Body of 'Traitor,'" *Choson Ilbo*, October 5, 2002; "North Korea executes 3 alleged spies," *Kyodo*, March 18, 1998.

13. Nodong Sinmun, "Socialism is our people's faith and life," Pyongyang, March 15

14. Kim Jong Il, *Socialism is Science*, DPRK, November 1994.

15. "Kim Jong Il berates cadres for food anarchy" (in Korean), *Wolgan Chosun* (Chosun Monthly), Seoul, March 20, 1997, pp. 306–17, translated from Kim Jong Il Speech at Kim Il Sung University in December 1996; BBC Summary of Shortwave Broadcasts, March 21, 1997.

16. BBC Summary of Worldwide Broadcasts, September 2, 1998; KCNA, "Paper Warns Against Capitalist Ideological Poisoning," Pyongyang, August 24, 1999; BBC Summary of Worldwide Broadcasts, August 26, 1999; "North Korea Leader Shuts Down Free Markets," *Kyodo*, September 1, 1999.

17. Kim Jong Il, "On Preserving the Juche Character and National Character of the Revolution and Construction," Speech, Pyongyang, June 19, 1997.

18. The text of law says in Article 3, "It is the consistent policy of the DPRK to manage and operate the people's economy under centralized and unified guidance"; Article 36 states, "no items that are not included in the people's economic plan can be produced"; *Rodong Sunmun* reported, "Our Party will not tolerate any so-called decentralization or liberalization," April 9, 1999.

19. Hwang Jang-yop (in Korean), *North Korea: Truth or Lies?* Institute for Reunification Policy Studies, 1998.

20. Larry Robinson, "Through a Glass Darkly: Reflections on North Korea," end of tour essay by chief North Korea watcher in the U.S. Embassy in Seoul, 1998 cable posted on the web, see www.washtimes.com/investga/.

21. "Free Trade Zone Chief 'Secretly Shot,'" *Kyodo*, September 23,1998.

22. "Free Market Stirrings in North Korea. Special Report: Stitch by Stitch to a Different World," *The Economist*, July 25, 2002.

Chapter 10

1. Masood Haydar, "In North Korea: First Save Lives," *Washington Post*, January 4, 2004.

2. "North Korea: North Korean Population at 22 million, Less Than Half of South Korea," *The Korea Times*, August 27, 1999; Reuters, Seoul, "South Korea—270,000 North Korean Famine Deaths in 1995–1998," August 27, 1999; and Yonhap News Agency, "North Korea, South Korea, CIA differ in North Korean Population Figures"; BBC Summary of World Broadcasts, October 2, 1999.

3. Andrew Natsios, *The Great North Korean Famine—Famine, Politics, and Foreign Policy*, Washington, D.C., United States Institute of Peace Press, 2001. Natsios interviewed the NGO expert Milton Amayun in September 1997.

4. "Over Three Million Reportedly Died of Hunger," *Chungang Ilbo*, May 25, 1999.

5. Ellsworth Culver of Mercy Corps, "Keeping an open mind in dealing with NK," American Council for Voluntary International Action (ia@international.org), November 18, 2002.

6. Many have also been cautious because the governments of South Korea, the United States, China, and Japan have not come out and claimed a high death toll. Washington did not use the word famine in any statement before July 1997.
7. Rone Tempest, "Starving a Nation with the Politics of Illusion," *Los Angeles Times*, January 23, 1997.
8. Reuters, Tokyo, "WFP Rejects Report of Cannibalism in North Korea," June 22, 1998.
9. Natsios, *The Great North Korean Famine*.
10. Natsios, *The Great North Korean Famine*.
11. Reuter, Beijing, "Grain, Coal Aid for North Korea," June 5, 1999; and Reuters, Tokyo, "Japan: North Korea Food Imports Fall Despite Food Shortages—JETRO," August 16, 1999. JETRO said the North's imports of agricultural products and food dropped 46.4 percent in 1998.
12. Telephone Interview May 1997, see Jasper Becker, "Help Us, But On Our Own Terms," *South Morning China Post*, April 11, 1998.
13. Sue Lautze, "The Famine in North Korea—Humanitarian Responses in North Korea," Cambridge, Mass., Feinstein International Famine Center, Tufts University, June 1997; and Sue Lautze, "06 June 1996 North Korea Food Aid Assessment," Tufts University, 1996.
14. Conor O'Cleary, "North Korea May Be Deluding the World about Disastrous Famine," *Irish Times*, March 21, 1998.
15. Jean-Fabrice Pietri, "The Inadequacies of Food Aid In North Korea," Action Contra La Faim, Speech at 4th International Conference of North Korean Human Rights and Refugess, Prague, March 2–4, 2003.
16. Philippe Pons, "Escapees from North Korean Hell," *Le Monde*, May 14, 2001.
17. Sophie Delaunay, Regional Coordinator for North Korea MSF (Doctors Without Frontiers), in a statement delivered to the House Committee on International Relations Subcommittee on East Asia and the Pacific in Washington, D.C., May 2, 2002, provided other similar testimony.

   Man, 23, from Musan county, North Hamkyong Province. Interview conducted in July 2001: "I have seen some foreign guys from the UN traveling around. I don't know what they are doing but when they are traveling, just around this time, government suddenly becomes very busy, you know, try to find those undernourished boys and children. . . . They keep them away, you know, those undernourished children, at some place. . . . Perhaps they were expecting that these UN guys visit welfare facilities inspection, so they want to be prepared for it."

   Man, 19, from Hamhung city, South Hamkyong Province. Interview conducted in February 2001: "Last year I saw UN guys coming to Musan to assess flood damage. The government dug up the river and the streets to make it look more damaged, in order to get more rice. The UN investigators came back to Musan a number of times."
18. Interview with street child conducted by Marine Boussioniere & Sophie Marine of MSF France in June 2001.
19. Thomas Hoerz, *Irish Times*, March 19, 1999.
20. Hazel Smith, "North Koreans in China—Defining the Problems and Offering Some Solutions," Warwick University, July 2002.
21. Declaration by the presidency on behalf of the European Union on missile test undertaken by the DPRK, Brussels, and Vienna on September 3, 1998.
22. Reuters, Beijing, "U.N. Food Official Says North Korea Cooperating," October 5, 1998.

23. Reuters, Geneva, "UN Official Says N. Korea Food Situation Improving," October 10, 1998.
24. Transcript of Press Conference with James Morris, Beijing, November 16, 2002; and Mark Kirk, "Trip Report of the House of International Relations Committee," August 13–30, 1997.
25. This was officially called the UNDP Thematic Roundtable on Agricultural Recovery and Environmental Protection.

Chapter 11

1. Kim Dae Jung, "Is Culture Destiny? The Myth of Asia's Anti-Democratic Values," *Foreign Affairs*, November/December 1994.

Chapter 12

1. Madeline Albright Interview with Reuters, Washington, September 16, 2003.
2. Leon V. Sigal, "N. Korea: Fibs vs. Facts," *Baltimore Sun*, August 5, 2003; see also his book *Disarming Strangers—Nuclear Diplomacy with North Korea*, Princeton University Press, 1998; Damjan de Krnjevic-Miskovic, "North Korea and Non-Proliferation: A Conversation with Selig Harrison," *The National Interest* (www.thenationalinterest.com), Vol. 2, No. 4, May 3, 2003; and Bruce Cumings, "Wrong Again," *London Review of Books*, December 4, 2003.
3. Philip Gourevitch, "Alone in the Dark," *New Yorker*, November 5, 2003.
4. PBS Frontline, "Kim's Nuclear Gamble," February 26, 2003.
5. PBS Frontline, "Kim's Nuclear Gamble," February 26, 2003
6. Interview on Voice of America, Washington, April 24, 2002.
7. Interview with Richard Perle, PBS Frontline, March 27, 2003.
8. Bob Woodward, *Bush at War*, New York, Simon & Schuster, 2002, p. 340.
9. White House Press Releases.
10. Thomas E. Ricks & Glenn Kessler, "Former Defense Secretary Says Standoff Increases Risk of Terrorists Obtaining Nuclear Device," *Washington Post*, July 15, 2003.
11. Interview with Kim Dae Jung by Seoul's national KBS-TV in 2003 on the anniversary of the summit.
12. David E. Sanger & William J. Broad, "Surprise Word on Nuclear Gains by North Korea and Iran," *New York Times*, November 12, 2003.
13. Mohamed El Baradei, "No Nuclear Blackmail," *Wall Street Journal*, May 22, 2003.
14. Howard W. French, "South Korea's President-Elect Rejects Use of Force Against North Korea," *New York Times*, January 17, 2003.
15. Don Greg, "Kim Jong Il: The Truth Behind the Caricature," *Newsweek*, February 3, 2003.
16. Peter Maas, "The Last Emperor," *New York Times Sunday Magazine*, October, 19, 2003.
17. Associated Press Interview in Washington, "Hwang Jang Yop: N. Korea's Kim Is World Problem," November 1, 2003.
18. Charles R. Smith, "Attack North Korea Before It's Too Late, Key Defector Warns," *Wall Street Journal*, July 10, 2003.

Afterword

1. George Jones, "Blair's Blueprint to Strike at Terror," *Daily Telegraph*, March 6, 2004.
2. Howard W. French, "South Korea's President-Elect Rejects Use of Force Against North Korea," *New York Times*, January 17, 2003.
3. Michael Parks and Gregory F. Treverton, "Keep North Korea on Life Support," *Los Angeles Times*, March 27, 2003.

Bibliography

Ahn Myong-chul, "Political Prisoners' Camps in North Korea," *Monthly Chosun*, Seoul, January 2002.

Tsuneo Akah, ed., *The Future of North Korea*, New York, Routledge, 2002

David Albright, "How Much Plutonium Does North Korea Have?" *Bulletin of Atomic Scientists*, 2000.

Madeleine Albright, *Madam Secretary*, New York, Miramax Books, 2003.

Amnesty International, *Pursuit, Intimidation, and Abuse of North Korean Refugees and Workers*, Report—ASA 24/06/96, London, 1996.

Amnesty International, *Persecuting the Starving—The Plight of North Koreans Fleeing to China* SA 24/003/2000, London, December 15, 2000

Tai Sung An, *North Korea in Transition; From Dictatorship to Dynasty*, Wesport, Conn., Greenwood Press, 1983

"Are they Telling Us the Truth?" International Group of Human Rights Volunteers, Tokyo, Japan, March 2002.

Judith Banister & Nicholas Eberstadt, *The Population of North Korea*, Institute of East Asian Studies, Berkeley, University of California, 1992.

Thomas J. Belke, *Juche: A Christian Study of North Korea's State Religion*, Bartlesville, Okla., Living Sacrifice Book Company, 1999

Joseph Bermudez, Jr., *The Armed Forces of North Korea*, New York, I.B.Tauris, 2001.

Yossef Bodansky & Vaughn S. Forrest, *Pyongyang and the U.S. Nuclear Gambit*, Task Force on Terrorism & Unconventional Warfare, House Republican Research Committee, U.S. House of Representatives, August 11, 1994.

John R. Bolton, Under Secretary for Arms Control and International Security, *Nuclear Weapons and Rogue States: Challenge and Response*, Remarks to the Conference of the Institute for Foreign Policy Analysis and the Fletcher School's International Security Studies Program, Washington D.C., December 2, 2003.

Michael Breen, *The Koreans—Who Are They, What They Want, Where Their Future Lies*, London, St. Martin's Press, 1998.

Adrian Buzo, *The Guerilla Dynasty Politics and Leadership in North Korea*, Boulder, Westview Press, 1999.

Chang Sun-Sup, *The KEDO Light Water Reactor Project: Its Implications for Peace and Inter-Korean Relations* LNCV, Paper for Korean Peninsula: Enhancing Stability and International Dialogue, June 1–2, 2000, Rome.

Choi Ju-hwal, *An Inside Perspective: North Korea's Unalterable Stance*, Institute of East Asian Studies, Seoul, Vol. 11, No. 4, Winter 1999.

Mark L. Clifford, *Troubled Tiger—The Unauthorised Biography of Korea, Inc.*, Singapore, Butterworth-Heinemann Asia, 1994.

Erik Cornell, *North Korea Under Communism—Report of an Envoy to Paradise*, translated by Rodney Bradbury, New York, Routledge Curzon, 2002.

Eric Croddy, Senior Research Associate, CBW Nonproliferation Program, *Vinalon, the DPRK, and Chemical Weapons Precursors*, Center for Nonproliferation Studies, February 4, 2003.

Bruce Cumings, *Korea's Place in the Sun—A Modern History*, New York, W.W. Norton, 1997.

———, "Wrong Again," *London Review of Books*, December 4, 2003.

Barbara Demick, "Nuclear Hub is Pride of Nation," *Los Angeles Times* , January 13, 2003.

Martina Deuchler, *Confucian Gentlemen and Barbarian Envoys—The opening of Korea 1875–1885*, Seattle, University of Washington Press, 1977.

Chuck Downs, *Over the Line—North Korea's Negotiating Strategy*, Washington, D.C., The American Enterprise Institute Press, 1999.

Nicholas Eberstadt, *The End of North Korea*, Washington, D.C., The American Enterprise Institute Press, 1999

Nicholas Eberstadt & Richard J.Ellings, eds., *Korea's Future and the Great Powers*, Seattle, University of Washington Press, 2001.

Carter J. Eckert, Lee Ki-baik, Young Ick Lew, Michael Robinson & Edward W. Wagner, *Korea Old and New*, Seoul, Korea Institute, Harvard University, Ilchokak Publishers, 1990.

Food and Agriculture Organization of the United Nations, *Special Report FAO/WFP Crop and Food Supply Assessment Mission to the Democratic People's Republic of Korea*, Rome, October 30, 2003.

Kenji Fujimoto, *Kim Jong Il's Cook—I Saw His Naked Body*, Seoul, Chosun Ilbo, September 22 2003, translated from Japanese original published by Fuso Publishing House in Tokyo.

Philippe Grangereau, *Au Pays du Grand Mensonge*, Paris, Le Serpent du Mer, Paris, 2001.

Hahn Ho-Suk , President of Center for Korean Affairs Inc., *The Real Hwang Jang Yop*, Paper.

Selig S. Harrison, *Korea Endgame: A Strategy for Reunification and U.S. Disengagement*, Princeton University Press, 2002

———, "North Korea and Non-Proliferation: A Conversation with Selig Harrison," conducted by Damjan de Krnjevic-Miskovic, *The National Interest*, May 3, 2003.

Haruhisa Ogawa, *Correlation between Juche Ideology and Political Prison Camps in North Korea*, Paper presented at The 1st International Conference in North Korean Human Rights and Refugees, Seoul, 1999.

David Hawk, *The Hidden GULAG Exposing North Korea's Prison Camps—Prisoners' Testimonies and Satellite Photographs*, U.S. Committee for Human Rights in North Korea, October 2003.

Peter Hennessy, *The Secret State—Whitehall and the Cold War*, London, Penguin Books, 2002.

Thomas H. Henriksen, "The Rise and Decline of Rogue States," *Journal of International Affairs*, Vol. 54, No. 2, Spring 2001.

Michael Hickey, *The Korean War—The West Confronts Communism 1950–1953*, London, John Murray. London, 1999.

Helen-Louise Hunter, *Kim Il-Song's North Korea*, Westport, Conn., Praeger, 1999.

Human Rights Watch, *The Invisible Exodus: North Koreans in the People's Republic of China*, New York, Vol. 4, No. 8, November 2002.

Hwang Jang-yop, *The Truth and Falsehood of North Korea*, Seoul, Institute for Reunification Policy Studies, 1998.

———, *I Saw the Truth of History*, Seoul, Hanwul, 1999.

———, *Life of the Nation More Valuable Than Life of Individuals*, Seoul, Sidaejungsin, 1999.

———, *Hwang Jang Yop's Grand Strategy: A way to Win Without Waging War with Kim Jong Il*, Seoul, Wolgan Chosun, 2003.

———, *Problems of Human Rights in North Korea 1 & 2*, translation of Hwang's writings, Network for North Korean Rights and Democracy.

IAEA, *Fact Sheet on DPRK Nuclear Safeguards*, January 8, 2003.

IEER Report, *Plutonium End Game*, Arjun Makhijani, January 2001.

Institute for South-North Korea Studies, *The Human Rights Situation in North Korea*, Seoul, 1992.

Amos A. Jordan and Jae H. Ku, "Coping with North Korea," *The Washington Quarterly*, Vol. 21, No. 1, Winter 1998, p. 33

Richard Kagan, Matthew Oh, & David Weissbrodt, *Human Rights in the DPRK*, Report prepared for the Minnesota Lawyers International Human Rights Committee and Asia Watch, December 1988.

Kang Chol Hwan, *Aquariums of Pyongyang: Ten Years in the North Korean Gulag*, New York, Basic Books, 2001.

Tipani Keskinen, *Kim Jong Il—The Genuine People's Leader*, Pyongyang Foreign Languages Publishing House, 1987.

Kim Dae Jung, *Prison Writings*, translated by Choi Sung-il, Berkeley, University of California Press, 1987

———, "Is Culture Destiny? The Myth of Asia's Anti-Democratic Values," *Foreign Affairs Magazine*, November/December 1994.

Kim Il Sung, *For the Independent Peaceful Reunification of Korea*, New York, Guardian Associates, 1976.

———, *With the Century*, Pyongyang, Foreign Languages Publishing House, 1992.

———, *Kim Il Sung: Selected Works*, Pyongyang, Foreign Languages Publishing House, 1996.

Kim Jong Il, "Our Socialism for the People Will Not Perish," Talk given to senior officials of the Central Committee in May 5, 1991, published in *Nodong Sinmun*, May 27, 1991.

———, "Historical Lesson in Building Socialism and the General Line of Our Party," Talk given to senior officials of the Central Committee on January 3, 1992, published in *Nodong Sinmun*, February 4, 1992.

———, "Socialism is a Science," *Nodong Shinmun*, November 1, 1994. KCNA translation, November 7, 1994.

———, "*Kim Jong Il Berates Cadres for Food Anarchy*" (in Korean) *Wolgan Chosun* (Chosun Monthly), March 20, 1997, pp. 306–317, translated from "Kim Jong Il, Speech at Kim Il Sung University, December 1996!" British Broadcasting Corporation, March 21, 1997.

———, "On Preserving the Juche Character and National Character of the Revolution and Construction," Speech given in Pyongyang, June 19, 1997.

Kim S. Samuel, *North Korean Foreign Relations in the Post-Cold War Era*, Hong Kong, Oxford University Press, 1998.

Kim Young-gan, "The Confucian Christian Context in Korean Christianity," Thesis at Sungkyul University.

KBSM, *Report on Daily Life and Human Rights of North Korean Food Refugees in China: Based on Field Survey in 2,479 Villages in Three Northeast States in China*, Seoul, June 1999.

———, *The Food Crisis of North Korea Witnessed by Food Refugees*, reported in five issues: February 23,1998; March 23, 1998; May 23, 1998; and November 23, 1998.

Korean Overseas Culture and Information Service, *The New Administration's North Korea Policy*, Seoul, February 1998.

Andrei Lankov, *The Repressive System and Political Control in North Korea*, An enlarged and re-worked English version of a chapter from *Severnaia Koreia: vchera i segodnia* (North Korea: Yesterday and Today), published in Russian, Moscow, Vostochnaia literatura, 1995

Sue Lautze, "North Korea Food Aid Assessment," Conducted for the U.S. OFDA, USAID, June 6, 1996.

———, *The Famine in North Korea: Humanitarian Responses in Communist Nations.* Cambridge, Mass., Feinstein International Famine Center, Tufts University, June 1997

Lee Hy-Sang, *North Korea—A Strange Socialist Fortress*, Wesport, Conn., Praeger, 2001.

Lee Soon Ok, *Eyes of the Tailless Animals—Prison Memoirs of a North Korean Woman*, Bartlesville, Okla., Living Sacrifice Book Company, 1999.

Li Zhisui, *The Private Life of Chairman Mao*, translated by Professor Tai Hung-chao, London, Chatto Windus, 1994.

Hans Maretzki, *Kim-ismus in Nordkorea—Analyse des letzen DDR-Botschafters in Pjongjang*, Germany, Anita Tykve Verlag, 1991.

Alexandre Y. Mansourov, "The Origins, Evolution, and Current Politics of the North Korean Nuclear Program," *The Nonproliferation Review*, Spring/Summer 1995.

Medecins Sans Frontieres (MSF), *North Koreas: Testimonies of Famine, Refugee Interviews from the Sino-Korean Border*, New York, Doctors Without Borders/Medecins Sans Frontieres, August 1998. Posted to their website: http://www.doctorswithoutborder.org/publications/reports/before10999/korea_1998.shtm on October 2,1998.

Ministry of Unification, *The Policy for Peace and Prosperity*, Seoul, Republic of Korea, 2003.

Oliver Mohr, *Hinter dem 38. Breitengrad—Mit CAP ANAMUR in Nordkorea*, Germany, Lamuv, 2000.

Reverend Sun Myung Moon, *Divine Principle*, 1973.

Moon Ching-in & David I. Steinberg, eds., *Kim Dae-jung Government and Sunshine Policy*, Seoul, Yonsei University Press, 1999.

Network for North Korean Democracy and Human Rights, trans., *The Ten Principles for the Establishment of the One-Ideology System.*

Lola Nathanail, *Food and Nutritional Assessment, Democratic People's Republic of Korea 16 March–24 April 1996*, Rome, UN World Food Program, 1996.

Andrew Natsios, *The Great North Korean Famine—Famine, Politics, and Foreign Policy*, Washington, D.C., United States Institute of Peace Press, 2001.

Larry A. Niksch, *North Korea's Nuclear Weapons Program*, Congressional Research Service, Issue Brief for Congress, April 5, 2002.

Marcus Noland, *Avoiding the Apocalypse—The Future of the Two Koreas*, Washington, D.C., Institute for International Economics, 2000.

———, *Working Paper on Famine and Reform in North Korea*, Washington D.C.., Institute for International Economics, July 2003.

North Korea: After Collapse of Socialist Camp, Seoul, Naewoe Press, May 1993.

Nuclear Russia on Bellona Web (www.bellona.no), "Zheleznogorosk Reprocessing Plants in Siberia Working Paper," Working Paper 4, April 1995.

Don Oberdorfer, *The Two Koreas—A Contemporary History Reading*, Addison-Wesley, 1997.

Oh Kongdan, *Leadership Change in North Korean Politics*, Rand Publication Series, October 1988.

Oh Kongdan & Ralph Hassig, *North Korea Through the Looking Glass,* Washington, D.C., Brookings Institution Press, 2000.

Michael O'Hanlon & Mike Mochizuki, *Crisis on the Korean Peninsula*, New York, Brookings Institution Book McGraw Hill. 2003.

Meghan L. O'Sullivan, "The Dilemmas of U.S. Policy Toward 'Rogue' States," Politique Etrangere, Review of the French Institute of International Relations, Paris, Spring 2000.

William J. Perry, Special Advisor to the President and the Secretary of State, "Review of United States Policy Toward North Korea: Findings and Recommendations," October 12, 1999, available at http://usinfo.state.gov/regional/ea/easec/nkreview.htm.

Daniel A. Pinkston, *When did WMD Deals between Pyongyang and Islamabad Begin?* North Korea Nuclear Program Overview: History and Status IAEA-North Korea: Nuclear Safeguards and Inspections Chronology Center for Nonproliferation Studies, Monterey Institute of International Studies.

Daniel B. Poneman, *The History of the 1994 Agreed Framework*, The Forum for International Policy, March 7, 2003.

Pyongyang, *Sea of Blood*, Foreign Languages Publishing House, 1987.

C. Kenneth Quinones & Joseph Tragert, *Understanding North Korea—The Complete Idiot's Guide*, New York, Alpha Books, 2003.

Pierre Rigoulot, *Nordkorea—Steinzeitkommunismus und Atomwaffen—Anatomie einer Krise,* translated from French by Martin Breitfekd, Germany, Kiepenheuer & Witsch, 2003.

W. Courtland Robinson, Myung Ken Lee, Kenneth Hill, & Gilbert M. Burnham, "Mortality in North Korean Migrant Households: A Retrospective Study," *Lancet,* Vol. 354, No. 9175, July 1999.

David E. Sanger & William J. Broad, "Pakistan May Have Aided North Korea A-Test," *New York Times*, February 27, 2004.

Peter Schaller, *Nordkorea—Ein Land im Banne der Kims*, Germany, Anita Tykve Verlag, 1994.

Rinn S. Shinn, *North Korea: Chronology of Provocations, 1995–2000*, Congressional Research Service, U.S. Library of Congress, March 15, 200.

Leon V. Sigal, *Disarming Strangers—Nuclear Diplomacy with North Korea*, Princeton University Press, 1998.

Hazel Smith, "North Koreans in China—Defining the Problems and Offering Some Solutions," Research Paper for the Center for East Asian Studies, co-hosted with the United Nations University, International Conference on Globalization, Migration, and Human

Security: Challenges in Northeast Asia. Center for East Asian Studies, Monterey Institute of International Studies, October 2002.

Scott Snyder, *Negotiating on the Edge—North Korean Negotiating Behaviour*, Washington, D.C., United States Institute of Peace, 1999

Russel Spurr, *Enter the Dragon—China at War in Korea*, London, Sidgwick and Jackson, 1989.

Richard Steers, *Made in Korea—Chung Ju Yung And the Rise of Hyundai*, New York, Routledge, 2001.

Dae-Sook Suh, *Kim Il Sung The North Korean Leader*, New York, Columbia University Press, 1988.

Dae-Sook Suh & Edward J. Shultz, *"Koreans in China" Papers of the Center for Korean Studies*, Hawaii, University of Hawaii, 1990.

Balázs Szalontai, *You Have No Political Line of Your Own—Kim Il Sung and the Soviets, 1953–1964*, unpublished paper based on Hungarian national diplomatic archives, 2003.

———, *The Dynamic of Repression: The Global Impact of the Stalinist Model, 1944–1953*, unpublished essay, 2003.

Roger Tennant, *A History of Korea*, New York, Kegan Paul International, 1996.

Adam Tolnay, *Ceauşcus' Journey to the East*, Georgetown University Thesis, 2002.

Unification Church, *The Healing of The World—An Introduction to the Life and Teachings of Sun Myung Moon*

United Nations Consolidated Inter-Agency Appeal for Democratic People's Republic of Korea, United Nations, November 1998.

———, November 1999.

———, November 2003.

United Nations World Food Program, *Nutritional Survey of the Democratic People's Republic of Korea: Report by the EU, UNICEF and WFP of a study Undertaken in Partnership with the Government of DPRK*, Rome, 1998.

Joby Warrick, "N. Korea Shops for Nuclear Arms Gear," *Washington Post*, August 15, 2003.

George Wehrfritz & Richard Wolffe, "How North Korea Got the Bomb," *Newsweek*, October 19, 2003.

White Paper on Human Rights in North Korea, Seoul, Korea Institute for National Unification Annual Report, 2002.

James A. Winnfeld, *Worst-Case Planning for a Nuclear-Capable North Korea: Implications for U.S. Force Deployments*, RAND, 1993.

Wisconsin Project, "North Korea: Nuclear/Missile Chronology," *The Risk Report*, Vol. 6, No. 6, November–December 2000.

Bob Woodward, *Bush at War*, New York, Simon & Schuster, 2002.

World Food Program, Fact Sheet, UN World Food Program Operations in North Korea, August 1999.

World Food Program, DPR Korea, Review of Operations, 2001.

———, 2002.

Acknowledgments

The North Korean challenge caught my imagination on my first visit in 1986. It seemed then, and it still does, the strangest and most haunting place I could ever have imagined. Any attempt to research it is hard, and the risk of failure is high, the journalistic equivalent of trying to climb the north face of the Eiger. The handholds are few and often slippery, so one is particularly grateful for the ropes and pitons left behind by others who have gone before.

In addition to the authors listed in the bibliography, I am particularly grateful for help from Paul Shin and his wife, who arranged many interviews, organized translations, and guided me through the baffling complexities of spelling Korean names in English.

Editor Dedi Felman of Oxford University Press conceived of the project and pushed it through even though it changed shape several times.

In America, thanks go to Andrew Natsios, administrator of the U.S. Agency for International Development, Ellsworth Culver of Mercy Corps International, Scott Snyder of the Asia Foundation, Debra Liang-Fenton, executive director of the U.S. Committee for Human Rights in North Korea, Dennis Halpin of the House International Relations Committee, Congressman Mark Kirk, and Tim Peters of Helping Hands Korea.

In South Korea, I must mention Kwak Daekung of the Network for North Korean Democracy and Human Rights, Haksoon Paik of the Sejong Institute, Professor Chung Min Lee of Yonsei University, Chun Ki Won of the Durihana Mission, human rights activist Sang Hun Kim, Venerable Pomnyun, and Jenny Park.

Among the scholars who helped are Nicholas Eberstadt of the American Enterprise Institute, Dr. Kathryn Weathersby of the Woodrow Wilson Center's Cold War International History Project, Hungarian scholar Balazcs Szalontai, and German scholar Bernd Schaefer.

Although I did not speak to them directly, I benefited a great deal from reading the articles, interviews, and books by top Korean watchers including: Joseph S. Bermudez Jr., the leading expert on the North Korean military; historian Bruce Cumings; Chuck Downs; Don Oberdorfer; Aidan Foster-Carter of Leeds University; Professor Victor D. Cha; Selig Harrison; and economist Marcus Noland.

Many people who worked in Pyongyang have been generous with their advice, including Christian C. Lemaire of the United Nations Development Program, Kathi Zellweger of

Caritas, and from the World Food Program (WFP) Gerald Bourke, Douglas Broderick, Douglas Casson Coutts, and David Morton.

In addition, I must also acknowledge a debt to the late Aleksander V. Platkovski, former Pyongyang correspondent of *Komsomoskaya Pravda*, a good friend who is much missed.

The unremitting efforts of two dedicated activists, Marine Buissonniere and Sophie Delaunay, and their colleagues at Medecins sans Frontieres to uncover the truth made a great difference.

Many Chinese who helped me would prefer not to be named, but I should mention two from Yanji, Kim Chin-Kying of the Yanbian University of Science & Technology and Professor Piao Changyu.

Quite a few eminent diplomats, Germans, Swedes, Canadians, Chinese, French, and British, also helped considerably, but in keeping with their profession, they may prefer to remain in the shadows.

Last, but not least, I thank fellow writers on North Korea: Bertil Lintner, Mike Breen, and John Pomfret of the *Washington Post*, James Pringle formerly of the *Times*, Robert Gifford of National Public Radio, and Hilary MacKenzie.

Index